THE
BOOK LOVERS'
ANTHOLOGY:

A Compendium of Writing about Books, Readers and Libraries

EDITED BY

R. M. LEONARD

'Here I have but gathered a nosegay of strange floures, and
have put nothing of mine into it but the thred to binde them.'

MONTAIGNE (Florio's translation)

Printed on acid free ANSI archival quality paper.

ISBN: 978-1-78139-448-9

PREFACE

One of the most delightful of the *Last Essays of Elia* is entitled 'Detached Thoughts on Books and Reading', a title which would serve very well to indicate the contents of this anthology. In bringing together into one volume the tributes and opinions of a galaxy of writers, my object has been the glorification of books as books, a book being regarded as a real and separate entity, and often as an end in itself. There is a wide circle to whom this collection should appeal, in addition to bibliomaniacs or mere collectors of first or rare editions to whom the contents are often anathema, for the love of books is not confined to scholars or great readers. This love is incommunicable: it comes, but happily seldom goes, as the wind which bloweth where it listeth; it is perfectly sincere, and knows nothing of conventions and sham admirations.

No greater lover of books has ever lived than that Englishman who was born at Bury St. Edmunds seven hundred and thirty years ago--Richard de Bury, Bishop of Durham, author of *Philobiblon*, and, as Lord Campbell said, undoubtedly the founder of the order of book-lovers in England. Centuries passed, and then the more modern worship of books was promoted by one of even higher station than this lord chancellor and lord high treasurer of England--by King James, whom sycophants and cynics called the British Solomon. The sixteenth century saw also the births of Bacon, Burton, and Florio, the inspired translator of Montaigne, and Ben Jonson, who all deserved well of the order. Milton, with prose and poetry, handed down the sacred fire in the seventeenth century, and his

soul was like a Star, and dwelt apart.

Dr. Johnson, nearly a hundred years later, filled a niche of his own, irreverent though he was to books except for their message. The latter half of the eighteenth century is especially memorable, for it synchronized with the early years of Southey, Lamb, and Leigh Hunt, the very temples of the spirit which I have sought to enshrine in these pages, and of Hazlitt, and of two who should be dear to librarians, Crabbe and John Foster. I should like to claim an honoured place in the nineteenth century for Bulwer Lytton, who, although he understood 'the merits of a spotless shirt', understood books also and appreciated them thoroughly; and for the Brownings, especially the author of *Aurora Leigh*. Emerson is conspicuous, not only as a book-lover, but also as a professor of books, and as a missionary in the sense that Carlyle and Ruskin preached the gospel of books. Many others deserve honourable mention, but I must pass on to some of those who adorn the present day. It would have been very pleasant to have seen Lord Morley, Mr. Frederic Harrison, Mr. Austin Dobson, Mr. Edmund Gosse, Mr. Andrew Lang, and Mr. Augustine Birrell appearing in this cloud of witness, but happily they are alive to testify to the faith that is in them, and for that reason are beyond the scope of an anthology confined to authors who are dead.

It may be pointed out that there has been an increasing tendency to write not so much about books as about the authors of books; but to have included literary criticism, except incidentally, would have increased this volume to prodigious size. While I have been obliged for the same reason to ignore, as a rule, individual volumes, an exception has been made of the Bible, which is itself a library, and this is justified by the fact that many pages are devoted to libraries. Scores of poems have been prefixed to volumes or addressed in apology to possible readers, but these, and colophons, interesting though they may be, do not fit in with my scheme. However tempting it seemed to give versions of Catullus, Horace, or Martial, translations from ancient classic writers have been excluded; but room has been found for classic writers of comparatively modern times, for it would have been ridiculous to have passed over, for example, Montaigne, whose immortal essays have been handed down in the splendid English dress of John Florio's design. For the rest, the contents of this volume, in which more than 200 authors bear their varying testimony, must speak for themselves.

The passages will be found grouped more or less according to subjects, though the dividing lines are fine, and chronological order within the limits of the groups has been a secondary consideration. After forewords by Lamb, the anthology deals with books as companions, the love of and delight in books, the immortality of books and the immortality which they convey, the multiplicity of books and the distraction of choice; ancient and modern books and their respective claims; books that are or may be thought injurious; novels and romances; bookmaking of various kinds--plagiarism, books about books, anthologies, abridgements, dedications, presentation copies, bibliographies, translations, and quotations; books and preachers, and books as 'the true university of these days'; critics and criticism; rules for reading, commonplace-books, abstracts, epitomes, and marginalia; casual and superficial reading, talking from books, brains turned by books, over-reading; books and life; books as an enemy to health and as pharmaceutical preparations for mental indisposition; reading in bed, at meal-times, and out-of-doors, and the call of the book of nature; the horn-book and other books for children; advice on youthful reading, and the early preferences of some notable book-lovers; love and literature, and the conflict between matrimony and the library; women and books and libraries; the human species of book-worms, bibliomaniacs, and pedants; the proper handling of books; bindings, book illustrations, &c.; book pests--worms and moths; 'finds' at second-hand bookshops and what Leigh Hunt calls 'bookstall urbanity'; booksellers and publishers; mammon and books; book borrowers and book borrowing; bookish similes; books for magic; the Bible; literary geography; libraries--as studies and keys to character, private libraries real and imaginary, public libraries--from the provincial reference library to the British Museum, reflections in libraries, Crabbe's masterpiece, the libraries of Oxford and Cambridge with fitting tributes to Bodley; and, finally, a memorable tribute to books and the priceless treasury that a library affords. The source of the quotations is generally given; and the index of authors quoted or referred to, together with a full list of contents, and, it is hoped, the notes, should serve the convenience of the reader.

Many years ago Mr. Alexander Ireland gave me a copy of *The Book-Lover's Enchiridion*, and my debt to that 'treasury of thoughts on the Solace and Companionship of Books' is great. Mr. Ireland's object was 'to present, in chronological order, a selection of the best thoughts of the greatest and wisest minds on the subject of Books--their solace and companionship--their efficacy as silent teachers and guides--and the comfort, as of a living presence, which they afford amidst the changes of fortune and the accidents of life.' In this volume I have taken the subject and myself less seriously than would have been possible to Mr. Ireland. The 'thoughts' which I have collected are more 'detached', and they cover a wider field. I am under much obligation also to the *Ballads of Books*, which Mr. Brander Matthews compiled nearly a quarter of a century ago and Mr. Andrew Lang recast, and to Mr. W. Roberts's *Book-Verse*. Mainly, however, I have relied upon my own personal reading--'blessing,' as Lamb said, 'my stars for a taste so catholic, so unexcluding'--and upon research, in which I have had invaluable assistance from friends and colleagues. I am fortunately able to include many copyright pieces, and I have to thank the following for the necessary permission:--

Messrs. G. Bell & Sons, Ltd., for B. W. Procter's autobiographical fragment, 'My Books'; Messrs. Chapman & Hall, for what I have taken from a contribution to the *Fortnightly Review* by Mark Pattison, and for the passage from Carlyle's *Historical Sketches*; Messrs. Chatto & Windus, for the poems by Laman Blanchard, also for the passage from R. Jefferies' *Life of the Fields*; and Messrs. Macmillan & Co., for the excerpt from the same author's *The Dewy Morn*; Messrs. Constable & Co., and the executors of the late George Gissing, for the passages from *The Private Papers of Henry Ryecroft*; Mr. A. C. Fifield, for Samuel Butler's whimsical irreverence quoted from *Quis Desiderio*; Mr. Edward Garnett, for Richard Garnett's poem; the Houghton Mifflin Co., for Whittier's 'The Library'; Messrs. Longmans, Green & Co., for R. L. Stevenson's 'Picture Books in Winter' (and Messrs. Charles Scribner's Sons in respect of copyright in America); Mr. Elkin Mathews, for Lionel Johnson's poem; Messrs. G. Routledge & Sons, Ltd., for Longfellow's 'My Books', and 'Bayard Taylor' (and the Houghton Mifflin Co. in respect of copyright in America); Messrs. Smith, Elder & Co., for J. A. Symonds's poem from *Lyrics of Life*; and Dr. A. Stoddart Walker, for permission to quote from J. S. Blackie's *Self-Culture*.

In *Guesses at Truth* the brothers Hare wrote: 'They who cannot weave a uniform net, may at least produce a piece of patchwork, which may be useful, and not without a charm of its own.' It is my modest ambition that book-lovers shall find this volume useful and not without charm.

R. M. LEONARD.

CONTENTS
By Author

THE BOOK LOVERS' ANTHOLOGY

GRACE BEFORE BOOKS

I own that I am disposed to say grace upon twenty other occasions in the course of the day besides my dinner. I want a form for setting out upon a pleasant walk, for a moonlight ramble, for a friendly meeting, or a solved problem. Why have we none for books, those spiritual repasts--a grace before Milton--a grace before Shakespeare--a devotional exercise proper to be said before reading the *Fairy Queen*?--but, the received ritual having prescribed these forms to the solitary ceremony of manducation, I shall confine my observations to the experience which I have had of the grace, properly so called; commending my new scheme for extension to a niche in the grand philosophical, poetical, and perchance in part heretical liturgy, now compiling by my friend Homo Humanus, for the use of a certain snug congregation of Utopian Rabelaesian Christians, no matter where assembled.--C. LAMB. *Grace before Meat.*

THE DELIGHTFUL SOCIETY OF BOOKS

These friends of mine regard the pleasures of the world as the supreme good; they do not comprehend that it is possible to renounce these pleasures. They are ignorant of my resources. I have friends whose society is delightful to me; they are persons of all countries and of all ages; distinguished in war, in council, and in letters; easy to live with, always at my command. They come at my call, and return when I desire them: they are never out of humour, and they answer all my questions with readiness. Some present in review before me the events of past ages; others reveal to me the secrets of Nature: these teach me how to live, and those how to die: these dispel my melancholy by their mirth, and amuse me by their sallies of wit: and some there are who prepare my soul to suffer everything, to desire nothing, and to become thoroughly acquainted with itself. In a word, they open a door to all the arts and sciences. As a reward for such great services, they require only a corner of my little house, where they may be safely sheltered from the depredations of their enemies. In fine, I carry them with me into the fields, the silence of which suits them better than the business and tumults of cities.--PETRARCH. *Life* by S.

Dodson.

THE CONTENTMENT I HAVE IN MY BOOKS

Here is the best solitary company in the world: and in this particular chiefly excelling any other, that in my study I am sure to converse with none but wise men; but abroad it is impossible for me to avoid the society of fools. What an advantage have I by this good fellowship that, besides the help which I receive from hence, in reference to my life after this life, I can enjoy the life of so many ages before I lived!--that I can be acquainted with the passages of three or four thousand years ago, as if they were the weekly occurrences! Here, without travelling so far as Endor, I can call up the ablest spirits of those times; the learnedest philosophers, the wisest counsellors, the greatest generals, and make them serviceable to me. I can make bold with the best jewels they have in their treasury, with the same freedom that the Israelites borrowed of the Egyptians, and, without suspicion of felony, make use of them as mine own. I can here, without trespassing, go into their vineyards, and not only eat my fill of their grapes for my pleasure, but put up as much as I will in my vessel, and store it up for my profit and advantage.

How doth this prospect at once set off the goodness of God to me, and discover mine own weakness? His goodness in providing these helps for the improvement of mine understanding; and my weakness in needing them. What a pitiful, simple creature am I, that cannot live to any purpose, without the help of so many other men's brains! Lord, let this be the first lesson that I learn from these silent counsellors, to know my own ignorance: other knowledge puffeth up, this edifieth.--SIR W. WALLER. *Divine Meditations.*

HE THAT LOVETH A BOOK WILL NEVER WANT

The calling of a scholar ... fitteth a man for all conditions and fortunes; so that he can enjoy prosperity with moderation, and sustain adversity with comfort: he that loveth a book will never want a faithful friend, a wholesome counsellor, a cheerful companion, an effectual comforter.... The reading of books, what is it but conversing with the wisest men of all ages and all countries, who thereby communicate to us their most deliberate thoughts, choicest notions, and best inventions, couched in good expression, and digested in exact method? The perusal of history, how pleasant illumination of mind, how useful direction of life, how spritely incentives to virtue doth it afford! How doth it supply the room of experience, and furnish us with prudence at the expense of others, informing us about the ways of action, and the consequences thereof by examples, without our own danger or trouble!--I. BARROW. *Of Industry in our Particular Calling as Scholars.*

THE COMPANY OF MUTES

I often derive a peculiar satisfaction in conversing with the ancient and modern dead,-- who yet live and speak excellently in their works.--My neighbours think me *often alone,--* and yet at such times I am in company with more than five hundred mutes--each of whom, at my pleasure, communicates his ideas to me by dumb signs--quite as intelligibly as any person living can do by uttering of words.--They always keep the distance from me which I direct,--and, with a motion of my hand, I can bring them as near to me as I please.--I lay hands on fifty of them sometimes in an evening, and handle them as I like;--they never complain of ill-usage,--and, when dismissed from my presence--though ever so abruptly--take no offence. Such convenience is not to be enjoyed--nor such liberty to be taken--with the living.--L. STERNE. *Letters.*

A CONSOLATION FOR THE DEAF

I read with more pleasure than ever; perhaps, because it is the only pleasure I have left. For, since I am struck out of living company by my deafness, I have recourse to the dead, whom alone I can hear; and I have assigned them their stated hours of audience. Solid *folios* are the people of business, with whom I converse in the morning. *Quartos* are the easier mixed company, with whom I sit after dinner; and I pass my evenings in the light, and often frivolous, *chit-chat* of small *octavos* and *duodecimos.*--LORD CHESTERFIELD.

SWEET UNREPROACHING COMPANIONS

I armed her [Olivia] against the censure of the world, showed her that books were sweet unreproaching companions to the miserable, and that if they could not bring us to enjoy life, they would at least teach us to endure it.--O. GOLDSMITH. *The Vicar of Wakefield.*

MY DAYS AMONG THE DEAD ARE PASSED

My days among the Dead are passed;
  Around me I behold,
Where'er these casual eyes are cast,
  The mighty minds of old;
My never-failing friends are they,
With whom I converse day by day.

With them I take delight in weal,
  And seek relief in woe;
And while I understand and feel
  How much to them I owe,
My cheeks have often been bedewed
With tears of thoughtful gratitude.

My thoughts are with the Dead; with them
  I live in long-past years,
Their virtues love, their faults condemn,
  Partake their hopes and fears,
And from their lessons seek and find

Instruction with an humble mind.

My hopes are with the Dead; anon
  My place with them will be.
And I with them shall travel on
  Through all Futurity;
Yet leaving here a name, I trust,
That will not perish in the dust.

R. SOUTHEY.

A HEAVENLY DELIGHT

Talk of the happiness of getting a great prize in the lottery! What is that to the opening a box of books! The joy upon lifting up the cover must be something like what we shall feel when Peter the Porter opens the door upstairs, and says, Please to walk in, sir. That I shall never be paid for my labour according to the current value of time and labour, is tolerably certain; but if any one should offer me £10,000 to forgo that labour, I should bid him and his money go to the devil, for twice the sum could not purchase me half the enjoyment. It will be a great delight to me in the next world, to take a fly and visit these old worthies, who are my only society here, and to tell them what excellent company I found them here at the lakes of Cumberland, two centuries after they had been dead and turned to dust. In plain truth, I exist more among the dead than the living, and think more about them, and, perhaps, feel more about them.--R. SOUTHEY (Letter to S. T. Coleridge).

THE BEST OF ALL POSSIBLE COMPANY

Coleridge is gone to Devonshire, and I was going to say I am alone, but that the sight of Shakespeare, and Spenser, and Milton, and the Bible, on my table, and Castanheda, and Barros, and Osorio at my elbow, tell me I am in the best of all possible company.--R. SOUTHEY (Letter to G. C. Bedford).

Worthy books
Are not companions--they are solitudes;
We lose ourselves in them and all our cares.

P. J. BAILEY. *Festus.*

THE FELLOWSHIP OF BOOKS

What were days without such fellowship? We were alone in the world without it. Nor does our faith falter though the secret we search for and do not find in them will not commit itself to literature, still we take up the new issue with the old expectation, and again and again, as we try our friends after many failures at conversation, believing this visit will be the favoured hour and all will be told us....

One must be rich in thought and character to owe nothing to books, though preparation is necessary to profitable reading; and the less reading is better than more;--book-struck men are of all readers least wise, however knowing or learned.--A. B. ALCOTT. *Tablets.*

A COMPANY OF THE WISEST AND THE WITTIEST

There are books which are of that importance in a man's private experience, as to verify for him the fables of Cornelius Agrippa, of Michael Scott, or of the old Orpheus of Thrace,--books which take rank in our life with parents and lovers and passionate experiences, so medicinal, so stringent, so revolutionary, so authoritative,--books which are the work and the proof of faculties so comprehensive, so nearly equal to the world which they paint, that, though one shuts them with meaner ones, he feels his exclusion from them to accuse his way of living.

Consider what you have in the smallest chosen library. A company of the wisest and wittiest men that could be picked out of all civil countries, in a thousand years, have set in best order the results of their learning and wisdom. The men themselves were hid and inaccessible, solitary, impatient of interruption, fenced by etiquette; but the thought which they did not uncover to their bosom friend is here written out in transparent words to us, the strangers of another age.--R. W. EMERSON. *Books.*

We should choose our books as we would our companions, for their sterling and intrinsic merit.--C. C. COLTON. *Lacon.*

A MAGNATE IN THE REALM OF BOOKS

One, with his beard scarce silvered, bore
  A ready credence in his looks,
A lettered magnate, lording o'er
  An ever-widening realm of books.
In him brain-currents, near and far,
  Converged as in a Leyden jar;
The old, dead authors thronged him round about,
And Elzevir's grey ghosts from leathern graves looked out.

He knew each living pundit well,
  Could weigh the gifts of him or her,
And well the market value tell
  Of poet and philosopher.
But if he lost, the scenes behind,
  Somewhat of reverence vague and blind,
Finding the actors human at the best,

No readier lips than his the good he saw confessed.

His boyhood fancies not outgrown,
  He loved himself the singer's art;
Tenderly, gently, by his own
  He knew and judged an author's heart.
No Rhadamanthine brow of doom
  Bowed the dazed pedant from his room;
And bards, whose name is legion, if denied,
Bore off alike intact their verses and their pride.

Pleasant it was to roam about
  The lettered world as he had done,
And see the lords of song without
  Their singing robes and garlands on.
With Wordsworth paddle Rydal mere,
  Taste rugged Elliott's home-brewed beer,
And with the ears of Rogers, at fourscore,
Hear Garrick's buskined tread and Walpole's wit once more.

    J. G. WHITTIER. *The Tent on the Beach.*

CHOOSE an author as you choose a friend.--W. DILLON,
    EARL OF ROSCOMMON. *Essay on Translated Verse.*

MY BOOKS

All round the room my silent servants wait,--
My friends in every season, bright and dim;
Angels and seraphim
Come down and murmur to me, sweet and low,
And spirits of the skies all come and go
Early and late;
From the old world's divine and distant date,
From the sublimer few,
Down to the poet who but yester-eve
Sang sweet and made us grieve,
All come, assembling here in order due.
And here I dwell with Poesy, my mate,
With Erato and all her vernal sighs,
Great Clio with her victories elate,
Or pale Urania's deep and starry eyes.
Oh friends, whom chance and change can never harm,
Whom Death the tyrant cannot doom to die,
Within whose folding soft eternal charm
I love to lie,

And meditate upon your verse that flows,
And fertilizes whereso'er it goes....

B. W. PROCTER. *An Autobiographical Fragment.*

TO MY BOOKS

Silent companions of the lonely hour,
  Friends who can never alter or forsake,
Who for inconstant roving have no power,
  And all neglect, perforce, must calmly take,--
Let me return to *you*, this turmoil ending,
  Which worldly cares have in my spirit wrought,
And, o'er your old familiar pages bending,
  Refresh my mind with many a tranquil thought;
Till, haply meeting there, from time to time,
  Fancies, the audible echo of my own,
'Twill be like hearing in a foreign clime
  My native language spoke in friendly tone,
And with a sort of welcome I shall dwell
  On these, my unripe musings, told so well.

THE HON. CAROLINE NORTON.

ON PARTING WITH MY BOOKS

Ye dear companions of my silent hours,
Whose pages oft before my eyes would strew
So many sweet and variegated flowers--
Dear Books, awhile, perhaps for ay, adieu!
The dark cloud of misfortune o'er me lours:
No more by winter's fire--in summer's bowers,
My toil-worn mind shall be refreshed by you:
We part! sad thought! and while the damp devours
Your leaves, and the worm slowly eats them through,
Dull Poverty and its attendant ills,
Wasting of health, vain toil, corroding care,
And the world's cold neglect, which surest kills,
Must be my bitter doom; yet I shall bear
Unmurmuring, for my good perchance these evils are.

J. H. LEIGH HUNT.

TO MY BOOKS ON PARTING WITH THEM

As one who, destined from his friends to part,
Regrets his loss, yet hopes again erewhile,
To share their converse and enjoy their smile,
And tempers as he may affliction's dart,--
Thus, loved associates! chiefs of elder Art!
Teachers of wisdom! who could once beguile
My tedious hours, and lighten every toil,
I now resign you; nor with fainting heart;
For pass a few short years, or days, or hours,
And happier seasons may their dawn unfold,
And all your sacred fellowship restore;
When, freed from earth, unlimited its powers,
Mind shall with mind direct communion hold,
And kindred spirits meet to part no more.--W. ROSCOE.

TRUE FRIENDS THAT CHEER

It is a beautiful incident in the story of Mr. Roscoe's misfortunes, and one which cannot fail to interest the studious mind, that the parting with his books seems to have touched upon his tenderest feelings, and to have been the only circumstance that could provoke the notice of his Muse. The scholar only knows how dear these silent, yet eloquent, companions of pure thoughts and innocent hours become in the season of adversity. When all that is worldly turns to dross around us, these only retain their steady value. When friends grow cold, and the converse of intimates languishes into vapid civility and commonplace, these only continue the unaltered countenance of happier days, and cheer us with that true friendship which never deceived hope nor deserted sorrow.--W. IRVING. *The Sketch Book*.

MY BOOKS

Sadly as some old mediaeval knight
  Gazed at the arms he could no longer wield,
  The sword two-handed and the shining shield
Suspended in the hall, and full in sight,
While secret longings for the lost delight
  Of tourney or adventure in the field
  Came over him, and tears but half concealed
Trembled and fell upon his beard of white,
So I behold these books upon their shelf,
  My ornaments and arms of other days;
  Not wholly useless, though no longer used,
For they remind me of my other self,
  Younger and stronger, and the pleasant ways,
  In which I walked, now clouded and confused.

H. W. LONGFELLOW.

TO SIR HENRY GOODYER

When I would know thee, Goodyer, my thought looks
Upon thy well-made choice of friends, and books;
Then do I love thee, and behold thy ends
In making thy friends books, and thy books friends:
Now must I give thy life and deed the voice
Attending such a study, such a choice;
Where, though it be love that to thy praise doth move,
It was a knowledge that begat that love.

BEN JONSON.

OUR BEST ACQUAINTANCE

While you converse with lords and dukes,
I have their betters here--my books;
Fixed in an elbow chair at ease
I choose my companions as I please.
I'd rather have one single shelf
Than all my friends, except yourself;
For after all that can be said
Our best acquaintance are the dead.

T. SHERIDAN.

THE TRUE ELYSIAN FIELDS

In my garden I spend my days; in my library I spend my nights. My interests are divided
between my geraniums and my books. With the flower I am in the present; with the
book I am in the past. I go into my library, and all history unrolls before me. I breathe
morning air of the world while the scent of Eden's roses yet lingered in it, while it vibrat-
ed only to the world's first brood of nightingales, and to the laugh of Eve. I see the
pyramids building; I hear the shoutings of the armies of Alexander; I feel the ground
shake beneath the march of Cambyses. I sit as in a theatre,--the stage is time, the play is
the play of the world. What a spectacle it is! What kingly pomp, what processions file
past, what cities burn to heaven, what crowds of captives are dragged at the chariot-
wheels of conquerors! I hiss or cry 'Bravo' when the great actors come on shaking the
stage. I am a Roman Emperor when I look at a Roman coin. I lift Homer, and I shout
with Achilles in the trenches. The silence of the unpeopled Syrian plains, the out-
comings and in-goings of the patriarchs, Abraham and Ishmael, Isaac in the fields at
eventide, Rebekah at the well, Jacob's guile, Esau's face reddened by desert sun-heat,
Joseph's splendid funeral procession--all these things I find within the boards of my Old
Testament. What a silence in those old books as of a half-peopled world--what bleating

9

of flocks--what green pastoral rest--what indubitable human existence! Across brawling centuries of blood and war, I hear the bleating of Abraham's flocks, the tinkling of the bells of Rebekah's camels. O men and women, so far separated, yet so near, so strange, yet so well-known, by what miraculous power do I know ye all! Books are the true Elysian fields where the spirits of the dead converse, and into these fields a mortal may venture unappalled. What king's court can boast such company? What school of philosophy such wisdom? The wit of the ancient world is glancing and flashing there. There is Pan's pipe, there are the songs of Apollo. Seated in my library at night, and looking on the silent faces of my books, I am occasionally visited by a strange sense of the supernatural. They are not collections of printed pages, they are ghosts. I take one down and it speaks with me in a tongue not now heard on earth, and of men and things of which it alone possesses knowledge. I call myself a solitary, but sometimes I think I misapply the term. No man sees more company than I do. I travel with mightier cohorts around me than ever did Timour or Genghis Khan on their fiery marches. I am a sovereign in my library, but it is the dead, not the living, that attend my levees.--A. SMITH. *Dreamthorp.*

BOOKS AND FRIENDS

One drachma for a good book, and a thousand talents for a true
     friend;--
So standeth the market, where scarce is ever costly:
Yea, were the diamonds of Golconda common as shingles on the shore,
A ripe apple would ransom kings before a shining stone:
And so, were a wholesome book as rare as an honest friend,
To choose the book be mine: the friend let another take.

M. F. TUPPER. *Proverbial Philosophy.*

A blessed companion is a book,--a book that, fitly chosen, is a life-long friend.--D. JERROLD. *Books.*

May I a small house and large garden have!
And a few friends, and many books, both true.

A. COWLEY. *The Wish.*

THE DESIRABLE TABERNACLE

O celestial gift of divine liberality, descending from the Father of light to raise up the rational soul even to heaven!... Undoubtedly, indeed, thou hast placed thy desirable tabernacle in books, where the Most High, the Light of light, the Book of Life, hath established thee. Here then all who ask receive, all who seek find thee, to those who knock thou openest quickly. In books cherubim expand their wings, that the soul of the student may ascend and look around from pole to pole, from the rising to the setting sun, from the north and from the sea. In them the most high incomprehensible God Himself is contained and worshipped....

Let us consider how great a commodity of doctrine exists in books, how easily, how secretly, how safely they expose the nakedness of human ignorance without putting it to shame. These are the masters who instruct us without rods and ferules, without hard words and anger, without clothes or money. If you approach them, they are not asleep; if investigating you interrogate them, they conceal nothing; if you mistake them, they never grumble; if you are ignorant, they cannot laugh at you.--R. DE BURY. *Philobiblon.*

MAN'S PREROGATIVE

Books are a part of man's prerogative,
  In formal ink they thoughts and voices hold,
That we to them our solitude may give,
  And make time present travel that of old.
Our life fame pieceth longer at the end,
And books it farther backward do extend.

SIR T. OVERBURY. *The Wife.*

TO HIS BOOKS

Bright books: the perspectives to our weak sights,
The clear projections of discerning lights,
Burning and shining thoughts, man's posthume day,
The track of fled souls and their Milky Way,
The dead alive and busy, the still voice
Of enlarged spirits, kind Heaven's white decoys!
Who lives with you, lives like those knowing flowers,
Which in commerce with light spend all their hours;
Which shut to clouds, and shadows nicely shun,
But with glad haste unveil to kiss the Sun.
Beneath you, all is dark, and a dead night,
Which whoso lives in, wants both health and sight.
  By sucking you the wise, like bees, do grow
Healing and rich, though this they do most slow,
Because most choicely; for as great a store
Have we of books as bees of herbs, or more;
And the great task to try, then know, the good,
To discern weeds, and judge of wholesome food,
Is a rare scant performance: for man dies
Oft ere 'tis done, while the bee feeds and flies.
But you were all choice flowers; all set and dressed
By old sage florists, who well knew the best;
And I amidst you all am turned a weed!

11

Not wanting knowledge, but for want of heed.
Then thank thyself, wild fool, that wouldst not be
Content to know--what was too much for thee.

H. VAUGHAN.

THE LEGACIES OF GENIUS

Quod nec Iovis ira, nec ignis,
Nec poterit ferrum, nec edax abolere vetustas.--OVID.

Aristotle tells us, that the world is a copy or transcript of those ideas which are in the mind of the first Being, and that those ideas which are in the mind of man are a transcript of the world. To this we may add, that words are the transcript of those ideas which are in the mind of man, and that writing or printing is the transcript of words. As the Supreme Being has expressed, and as it were printed, his ideas in the creation, men express their ideas in books, which, by this great invention of these latter ages, may last as long as the sun and moon, and perish only in the general wreck of nature. Thus Cowley, in his poem on the Resurrection, mentioning the destruction of the universe, has these admirable lines:

Now all the wide extended sky,
And all the harmonious worlds on high
And Virgil's sacred work shall die.

There is no other method of fixing those thoughts which arise and disappear in the mind of man, and transmitting them to the last periods of time; no other method of giving a permanency to our ideas, and preserving the knowledge of any particular person, when his body is mixed with the common mass of matter, and his soul retired into the world of spirits. Books are the legacies that a great genius leaves to mankind, which are delivered down from generation to generation, as presents to the posterity of those who are yet unborn.--J. ADDISON. *Spectator*, 166.

IN PRISON

O happy be the day which gave that mind
Learning's first tincture--blest thy fostering care,
Thou most beloved of parents, worthiest sire!
Which, taste-inspiring, made the lettered page
My favourite companion: most esteemed,
And most improving! Almost from the day
Of earliest childhood to the present hour
Of gloomy, black misfortune, books, dear books,
Have been, and are, my comforts. Morn and night,
Adversity, prosperity, at home,

Abroad, health, sickness,--good or ill report,
The same firm friends; the same refreshment rich
And source of consolation. Nay, e'en here
Their magic power they lose not; still the same,
Of matchless influence in this prison-house,
Unutterably horrid; in an hour
Of woe, beyond all fancy's fictions drear.

W. DODD. *Thoughts in Prison.*

THE DEPOSITARY OF EVERYTHING HONOURABLE

Books are the depositary of everything that is most honourable to man. Literature, taken in all its bearings, forms the grand line of demarcation between the human and the animal kingdoms. He that loves reading has everything within his reach. He has but to desire; and he may possess himself of every species of wisdom to judge and power to perform....

Books gratify and excite our curiosity in innumerable ways. They force us to reflect. They hurry us from point to point. They present direct ideas of various kinds, and they suggest indirect ones. In a well-written book we are presented with the maturest reflections, or the happiest flights, of a mind of uncommon excellence. It is impossible that we can be much accustomed to such companions, without attaining some resemblance of them. When I read Thomson, I become Thomson; when I read Milton, I become Milton. I find myself a sort of intellectual chameleon, assuming the colour of the substances on which I rest. He that revels in a well-chosen library has innumerable dishes, and all of admirable flavour. His taste is rendered so acute, as easily to distinguish the nicest shades of difference. His mind becomes ductile, susceptible to every impression, and gaining new refinement from them all. His varieties of thinking baffle calculation, and his powers, whether of reason or fancy, become eminently vigorous.--W. GODWIN. *The Inquirer: Of an Early Taste for Reading.*

LOVE THAT IS LARGE

There is a period of modern times, at which the love of books appears to have been of a more decided nature than at either of these--I mean the age just before and after the Reformation, or rather all that period when book-writing was confined to the learned languages. Erasmus is the god of it. Bacon, a mighty book-man, saw, among his other sights, the great advantage of loosening the vernacular tongue, and wrote both Latin and English. I allow this is the greatest closeted age of books; of old scholars sitting in dusty studies; of heaps of 'illustrious obscure', rendering themselves more illustrious and more obscure by retreating from the 'thorny queaches' of Dutch and German names into the 'vacant interlunar caves' of appellations latinized or translated. I think I see all their volumes now, filling the shelves of a dozen German convents. The authors are bearded men, sitting in old wood-cuts, in caps and gowns, and their books are dedicated to princes and statesmen, as illustrious as themselves. My old friend Wierus, who wrote a thick book, *De Praestigiis Daemonum*, was one of them, and had a fancy worthy of his sedentary stomach. I will confess, once for all, that I have a liking for them all. It is my link with the bibliomaniacs, whom I admit into our relationship, because my love is large and my family pride nothing. But still I take my idea of books read with a gusto, of companions for bed and board, from the two ages beforementioned. The other is of too book-worm a description. There must be both a judgement and a fervour; a discrimination and a boyish eagerness; and (with all due humility) something of a point of contact between authors worth reading and the reader. How can I take Juvenal into the fields, or Valcarenghius *De Aortae Aneurismate* to bed with me? How could I expect to walk before the face of nature with the one; to tire my elbow properly with the other, before I put out my candle and turn round deliciously on the right side? Or how could I stick up *Coke upon Littleton* against something on the dinner-table, and be divided between a fresh paragraph and a mouthful of salad?--J. H. LEIGH HUNT. *My Books*.

A CATHOLIC TASTE IN BOOKS

To mind the inside of a book is to entertain one's self with the forced product of another man's brain. Now I think a man of quality and breeding may be much amused with the natural sprouts of his own. *Lord Foppington in 'The Relapse'*.

An ingenious acquaintance of my own was so much struck with this bright sally of his Lordship, that he has left off reading altogether, to the great improvement of his originality. At the hazard of losing some credit on this head, I must confess that I dedicate no inconsiderable portion of my time to other people's thoughts. I dream away my life in others' speculations. I love to lose in other men's minds. When I am not walking, I am reading; I cannot sit and think. Books think for me.

I have no repugnances. Shaftesbury is not too genteel for me, nor Jonathan Wild too low. I can read any thing which I call a *book*. There are things in that shape which I cannot allow for such.

In this catalogue of *books which are no books--biblia a-biblia--*I reckon Court Calendars, Directories, Pocket Books, Draught Boards bound and lettered at the back, Scientific Treatises, Almanacks, Statutes at Large; the works of Hume, Gibbon, Robertson, Beattie, Soame Jenyns, and, generally, all those volumes which 'no gentleman's library should be without'; the Histories of Flavius Josephus (that learned Jew), and Paley's *Moral Philosophy*. With these exceptions, I can read almost any thing. I bless my stars for a taste so catholic, so unexcluding.

I confess that it moves my spleen to see these *things in books' clothing* perched upon shelves, like false saints, usurpers of true shrines, intruders into the sanctuary, thrusting out the legitimate occupants. To reach down a well-bound semblance of a volume, and hope it is some kind-hearted play-book, then, opening what 'seem its leaves', to come bolt upon a withering Population Essay. To expect a Steele, or a Farquhar, and find-- Adam Smith. To view a well-arranged assortment of blockheaded Encyclopaedias (Anglicanas or Metropolitanas) set out in an array of Russia, or Morocco, when a tithe of that good leather would comfortably re-clothe my shivering folios; would renovate Paracelsus himself, and enable old Raymund Lully to look like himself again in the world. I never see these impostors but I long to strip them, to warm my ragged veterans in their spoils.--C. LAMB. *Detached Thoughts on Books and Reading*.

A SENSE OF HUMOUR

I am not prepared to back Charles Lamb's Index Expurgatorius. It is difficult, almost impossible, to find the book from which something either valuable or amusing may not be found, if the proper alembic be applied. I know books that are curious, and really amusing, from their excessive badness. If you want to find precisely how a thing ought not to be said, you take one of them down and make it perform the service of the intoxicated Spartan slave. There are some volumes in which, at a chance opening, you are certain to find a mere platitude delivered in the most superb and amazing climax of big words, and others in which you have a like happy facility in finding every proposition stated with its stern forward, as sailors say, or in some other grotesque mismanagement of composition. There are no better farces on or off the stage than when two or three congenial spirits ransack books of this kind, and compete with each other in taking fun out of them.--J. H. BURTON. *The Book-Hunter*.

BOOKS THE TRUE LEVELLERS

It is chiefly through books that we enjoy intercourse with superior minds, and these invaluable means of communication are in the reach of all. In the best books great men talk to us, give us their most precious thoughts, and pour their souls into ours. God be thanked for books! They are the voices of the distant and the dead, and make us heirs of the spiritual life of past ages. Books are the true levellers. They give to all, who will faithfully use them, the society, the spiritual presence, of the best and greatest of our race. No matter how poor I am. No matter though the prosperous of my own time will not enter my obscure dwelling. If the Sacred Writers will enter and take up their abode under my roof, if Milton will cross my threshold to sing to me of Paradise, and Shakespeare to open to me the worlds of imagination and the workings of the human heart, and Franklin to enrich me with his practical wisdom, I shall not pine for want of intellectual companionship, and I may become a cultivated man, though excluded from what is called the best society in the place where I live.

To make this means of culture effectual a man must select good books, such as have been written by right-minded and strong-minded men, real thinkers, who instead of diluting by repetition what others say, have something to say for themselves, and write to give relief to full, earnest souls; and these works must not be skimmed over for amusement, but read with fixed attention and a reverential love of truth. In selecting books we may be aided much by those who have studied more than ourselves. But, after all, it is best to be determined in this particular a good deal by our own tastes.--W. E. CHANNING. *Self-Culture*.

AUTHORS AS LOVERS OF BOOKS

I love an author the more for having been himself a lover of books.... We conceive of Plato as a lover of books; of Aristotle certainly; of Plutarch, Pliny, Horace, Julian, and Marcus Aurelius. Virgil, too, must have been one; and, after a fashion, Martial. May I confess that the passage which I recollect with the greatest pleasure in Cicero, is where he says that books delight us at home, *and are no impediment abroad*; travel with us, ruralize with us. His period is rounded off to some purpose: '*Delectant domi, non impediunt foris; peregrinantur, rusticantur.*' I am so much of this opinion, that I do not care to be anywhere without having a book or books at hand, and like Dr. Orkborne, in the novel of *Camilla*, stuff the coach or post-chaise with them whenever I travel. As books, however, become ancient, the love of them becomes more unequivocal and conspicuous. The ancients had little of what we call learning. They made it. They were also no very eminent buyers of books--they made books for posterity. It is true, that it is not at all necessary to love many books, in order to love them much. The scholar, in Chaucer, who would rather have

> At his beddes head
> A twenty bokes, clothed, in black and red,
> Of Aristotle and his philosophy,
> Than robès rich, or fiddle, or psaltry--

doubtless beat all our modern collectors in his passion for reading.... Dante puts Homer, the great ancient, in his Elysium, upon trust; but a few years afterwards, *Homer*, the book, made its appearance in Italy, and Petrarch, in a transport, put it upon his bookshelves, where he adored it, like 'the unknown God'. Petrarch ought to be the god of the Bibliomaniacs, for he was a collector and a man of genius, which is an union that does not often happen. He copied out, with his own precious hand, the manuscripts he rescued from time, and then produced others for time to reverence. With his head upon a book he died.--J. H. LEIGH HUNT. *My Books*.

The sweet serenity of books.--H. W. LONGFELLOW.

THE THEORY OF BOOKS

Books are the best type of the influence of the past.... The theory of books is noble. The scholar of the first age received into him the world around; brooded thereon; gave it the new arrangement of his own mind, and uttered it again. It came into him, life; it went out from him, truth. It came to him, short-lived actions; it went out from him, immortal thoughts. It came to him, business; it went from him, poetry. It was dead fact; now, it is quick thought. It can stand, and it can go. It now endures, it now flies, it now inspires. Precisely in proportion to the depth of mind from which it issued, so high does it soar, so long does it sing.--R. W. EMERSON. *The American Scholar*.

BOOKS A SUBSTANTIAL WORLD

Dreams, books, are each a world; and books, we know,
Are a substantial world, both pure and good:
Round these, with tendrils strong as flesh and blood,
Our pastime and our happiness will grow.
There find I personal themes, a plenteous store,
Matter wherein right voluble I am,
To which I listen with a ready ear;
Two shall be named, pre-eminently dear,--
The gentle Lady married to the Moor;
And heavenly Una with her milk-white Lamb....
Blessings be with them--and eternal praise,
Who gave us nobler loves, and nobler cares--
The Poets, who on earth have made us heirs
Of truth and pure delight by heavenly lays!
Oh! might my name be numbered among theirs,
Then gladly would I end my mortal days.

W. WORDSWORTH. *Personal Talk.*

TO WORDSWORTH

We both have run o'er half the space
Listed for mortal's earthly race;
We both have crossed life's fervid line,
And other stars before us shine:
May they be bright and prosperous
As those that have been stars for us!
Our course by Milton's light was sped,
And Shakespeare shining overhead:
Chatting on deck was Dryden too,
The Bacon of the rhyming crew;
None ever crossed our mystic sea
More richly stored with thought than he;
Though never tender nor sublime,
He wrestles with and conquers Time.
To learn my lore on Chaucer's knee,
I left much prouder company;
Thee gentle Spenser fondly led,
But me he mostly sent to bed.

W. S. LANDOR. *Miscellaneous Poems.*

THE SOULS OF BOOKS

I

Sit here and muse!--it is an antique room--
High-roofed, with casements, through whose purple pane
Unwilling Daylight steals amidst the gloom,
Shy as a fearful stranger.
                    There THEY reign
(In loftier pomp than waking life had known),
The Kings of Thought!--not crowned until the grave
When Agamemnon sinks into the tomb,
The beggar Homer mounts the Monarch's throne!
Ye ever-living and imperial Souls,
Who rule us from the page in which ye breathe,
All that divide us from the clod ye gave!--
Law--Order--Love--Intelligence--the Sense
Of Beauty--Music and the Minstrel's wreath!--
What were our wanderings if without your goals?
As air and light, the glory ye dispense
Becomes our being--who of us can tell
What he had been, had Cadmus never taught
The art that fixes into form the thought--
Had Plato never spoken from his cell,
Or his high harp blind Homer never strung?
Kinder all earth hath grown since genial Shakespeare sung!

II

Hark! while we muse, without the walls is heard
The various murmur of the labouring crowd,
How still, within those archive-cells interred,
The Calm Ones reign!--and yet they rouse the loud
Passions and tumults of the circling world!
From them, how many a youthful Tully caught
The zest and ardour of the eager Bar;
From them, how many a young Ambition sought
Gay meteors glancing o'er the sands afar--
By them each restless wing has been unfurled,
And their ghosts urge each rival's rushing car!
They made yon Preacher zealous for the truth;
They made yon Poet wistful for the star;
Gave Age its pastime--fired the cheek of Youth--
The unseen sires of all our beings are,--

III

And now so still! This, Cicero, is thy heart;

I hear it beating through each purple line.
This is thyself, Anacreon--yet, thou art
Wreathed, as in Athens, with the Cnidian vine.
I ope thy pages, Milton, and, behold,
Thy spirit meets me in the haunted ground!--
Sublime and eloquent, as while, of old,
'It flamed and sparkled in its crystal bound;'
These *are* yourselves--your life of life! The Wise
(Minstrel or Sage) *out* of their books are clay;
But *in* their books, as from their graves, they rise,
Angels--that, side by side, upon our way,
Walk with and warn us!
　　　　　Hark! the World so loud,
And they, the Movers of the World, so still.

What gives this beauty to the grave? the shroud
Scarce wraps the Poet, than at once there cease
Envy and Hate! 'Nine cities claim him dead,
Through which the living Homer begged his bread!'
And what the charm that can such health distil
From withered leaves--oft poisons in their bloom?
We call some books immoral! *Do they live?*
If so, believe me, TIME hath made them pure.
In Books, the veriest wicked rest in peace--
God wills that nothing evil shall endure;
The grosser parts fly off and leave the whole,
As the dust leaves the disembodied soul!
Come from thy niche, Lucretius! Thou didst give
Man the black creed of Nothing in the tomb!
Well, when we read thee, does the dogma taint?
No; with a listless eye we pass it o'er,
And linger only on the hues that paint
The Poet's spirit lovelier than his lore.
None learn from thee to cavil with their God;
None commune with thy genius to depart
Without a loftier instinct of the heart.
Thou mak'st no Atheist--thou but mak'st the mind
Richer in gifts which Atheists best confute--
FANCY AND THOUGHT! 'Tis these that from the sod
Lift us! The life which soars above the brute
Ever and mightiest, breathes from a great Poet's lute!
Lo! that grim Merriment of Hatred;--born
Of him,--the Master-Mocker of mankind,
Beside the grin of whose malignant spleen
Voltaire's gay sarcasm seems a smile serene,--
Do we not place it in our children's hands,
Leading young Hope through Lemuel's fabled lands?--
God's and man's libel in that foul Yahoo!--

Well, and what mischief can the libel do?
O impotence of Genius to belie
Its glorious task--its mission from the sky!
Swift wrote this book to wreak a ribald scorn
On aught the Man should love or Priest should mourn--
And lo! the book, from all its ends beguiled,
A harmless wonder to some happy child!

IV

All books grow homilies by time; they are
Temples, at once, and Landmarks. In them, we
Who *but* for them, upon that inch of ground
We call 'THE PRESENT', from the cell could see.
No daylight trembling on the dungeon bar,
Turn, as we list, the globe's great axle round!
And feel the Near less household than the Far!
Traverse all space, and number every star.
There is no Past, so long as Books shall live!
A disinterred Pompeii wakes again
For him who seeks you well; lost cities give
Up their untarnished wonders, and the reign
Of Jove revives and Saturn:--at our will
Rise dome and tower on Delphi's sacred hill;
Bloom Cimon's trees in Academe;--along
Leucadia's headland, sighs the Lesbian's song;
With Egypt's Queen once more we sail the Nile,
And learn how worlds are bartered for a smile:--
Rise up, ye walls, with gardens blooming o'er,
Ope but that page--lo, Babylon once more!

V

Ye make the Past our heritage and home:
And is this all? No; by each prophet sage--
No; by the herald souls that Greece and Rome
Sent forth, like hymns, to greet the Morning Star
That rose on Bethlehem--by thy golden page,
Melodious Plato--by thy solemn dreams,
World-wearied Tully!--and, above ye all,
By THIS, the Everlasting Monument
Of God to mortals, on whose front the beams
Flash glory-breathing day--our lights ye are
To the dark Bourne beyond; in you are sent
The types of Truths whose life is The TO-COME;
In you soars up the Adam from the fall;
In you the FUTURE as the PAST is given--
Even in our death ye bid us hail our birth;--

Unfold these pages, and behold the Heaven,
Without one gravestone left upon the Earth.

E. G. E. L. BULWER-LYTTON, LORD LYTTON.

USEFUL AND MIGHTY THINGS

Except a living man, there is nothing more wonderful than a book!--a message to us from the dead--from human souls whom we never saw, who lived, perhaps, thousands of miles away; and yet these, on those little sheets of paper, speak to us, amuse us, vivify us, teach us, comfort us, open their hearts to us as brothers.... I say we ought to reverence books, to look at them as useful and mighty things. If they are good and true, whether they are about religion or politics, farming, trade, or medicine, they are the message of Christ, the maker of all things, the teacher of all truth, which He has put into the heart of some man to speak, that he may tell us what is good for our spirits, for our bodies, and for our country.--C. KINGSLEY. *Village Sermons: On Books.*

AN EXTRAORDINARY DELIGHT TO STUDY

To most kind of men it is an extraordinary delight to study. For what a world of books offers itself, in all subjects, arts, and sciences, to the sweet content and capacity of the reader!... What vast tomes are extant in law, physic, and divinity, for profit, pleasure, practice, speculation, in verse or prose, &c.! their names alone are the subject of whole volumes; we have thousands of authors of all sorts, many great libraries full well furnished, like so many dishes of meat, served out for several palates; and he is a very block that is affected with none of them.--R. BURTON. *The Anatomy of Melancholy.*

SWEET AND HAPPY HOURS

BORNWELL. Learning is an addition beyond
    Nobility of birth; honour of blood
    Without the ornament of knowledge is
    A glorious ignorance.

FREDERICK. I never knew more sweet and happy hours
    Than I employed upon my books.

J. SHIRLEY. *The Lady of Pleasure.*

THE PROUDER PLEASURES OF THE MIND

Books cannot always please, however good;
Minds are not ever craving for their food;
But sleep will soon the weary soul prepare

For cares to-morrow that were this day's care:
For forms, for feasts, that sundry times have past,
And formal feasts that will for ever last.
  'But then from study will no comforts rise?'--
Yes! such as studious minds alone can prize;
Comforts, yea!--joys ineffable they find,
Who seek the prouder pleasures of the mind:
The soul, collected in those happy hours,
Then makes her efforts, then enjoys her powers;
And in those seasons feels herself repaid,
For labours past and honours long delay'd.
  No! 'tis not worldly gain, although by chance
The sons of learning may to wealth advance;
Nor station high, though in some favouring hour
The sons of learning may arrive at power;
Nor is it glory, though the public voice
Of honest praise will make the heart rejoice:
But 'tis the mind's own feelings give the joy,
Pleasures she gathers in her own employ--
Pleasures that gain or praise cannot bestow,
Yet can dilate and raise them when they flow.

    G. CRABBE. *The Borough.*

A TASTE TO BE PRAYED FOR

If I were to pray for a taste which should stand me in stead under every variety of circumstances, and be a source of happiness and cheerfulness to me through life, and a shield against its ills, however things might go amiss, and the world frown upon me, it would be a taste for reading. I speak of it of course only as a worldly advantage, and not in the slightest degree as superseding or derogating from the higher office and surer and stronger panoply of religious principles--but as a taste, an instrument and a mode of pleasurable gratification. Give a man this taste, and the means of gratifying it, and you can hardly fail of making a happy man, unless, indeed, you put into his hands a most perverse selection of books. You place him in contact with the best society in every period of history--with the wisest, the wittiest--with the tenderest, the bravest, and the purest characters who have adorned humanity. You make him a denizen of all nations--a contemporary of all ages. The world has been created for him.--SIR J. HERSCHEL. *Address to the Subscribers to the Windsor Public Library.*

MORE THAN MEAT, DRINK, AND CLOTHING

I should like you to see the additional book-room that we have fitted up, and in which I am now writing.... It would please you to see such a display of literary wealth, which is at once the pride of my eye, and the joy of my heart, and the food of my mind; indeed, more than metaphorically, meat, drink, and clothing for me and mine. I verily believe that no one in my station was ever so rich before, and I am very sure that no one in any station had ever a more thorough enjoyment of riches of any kind, or in any way. It is more delightful for me to live with books than with men, even with all the relish that I have for such society as is worth having.--R. SOUTHEY (Letter to G. C. Bedford).

THE BOOK THE HIGHEST DELIGHT

In the highest civilization the book is still the highest delight. He who has once known its satisfactions is provided with a resource against calamity. Like Plato's disciple who has perceived a truth, 'he is preserved from harm until another period.' In every man's memory, with the hours when life culminated, are usually associated certain books which met his views. Of a large and powerful class we might ask with confidence, What is the event they most desire? What gift? What but the book that shall come, which they have sought through all libraries, through all languages, that shall be to their mature eyes what many a tinsel-covered toy pamphlet was to their childhood, and shall speak to the imagination? Our high respect for a well-read man is praise enough of literature. If we encountered a man of rare intellect, we should ask him what books he read. We expect a great man to be a good reader; or in proportion to the spontaneous power should be the assimilating power. And though such are a most difficult and exacting class, they are not less eager. 'He that borrows the aid of an equal understanding,' said Burke, 'doubles his own; he that uses that of a superior elevates his own to the stature of that he contemplates.'

We prize books, and they prize them most who are themselves wise. Our debt to tradition through reading and conversation is so massive, our protest or private addition so rare and insignificant,--and this commonly on the ground of other reading or hearing,--that, in a large sense, one would say there is no pure originality. All minds quote.--R. W. EMERSON. *Quotation and Originality*.

THE PLEASURE DERIVED FROM BOOKS

It is remarkable, the character of the pleasure we derive from the best books. They impress us with the conviction that one nature wrote, and the same reads. We read the verses of one of the great English poets, of Chaucer, of Marvell, of Dryden, with the most modern joy,--with a pleasure, I mean, which is in great part caused by the abstraction of all *time* from their verses. There is some awe mixed with the joy of our surprise, when this poet, who lived in some past world, two or three hundred years ago, says that which lies close to my own soul, that which I also had wellnigh thought and said.--R. W. EMERSON. *The American Scholar*.

OUR DEBT TO A BOOK

Let us not forget the genial miraculous force we have known to proceed from a book. We go musing into the vault of day and night; no constellation shines, no muse descends, the stars are white points, the roses brick-coloured dust, the frogs pipe, mice peep, and wagons creak along the road. We return to the house and take up Plutarch or Augustine, and read a few sentences or pages, and lo! the air swims with life; the front of heaven is full of fiery shapes; secrets of magnanimity and grandeur invite us on every hand; life is made up of them. Such is our debt to a book.--R. W. EMERSON. *Thoughts on Modern Literature.*

RICH FARE

A natural turn for reading and intellectual pursuits probably preserved me from the moral shipwreck, so apt to befall those who are deprived in early life of the paternal pilotage. At the very least, my books kept me aloof from the ring, the dog-pit, the tavern, and the saloon, with their degrading orgies. For the closet associate of Pope and Addison--the mind accustomed to the noble, though silent, discourse of Shakespeare and Milton--will hardly seek, or put up with, low company and slang. The reading animal will not be content with the brutish wallowings that satisfy the unlearned pigs of the world.

Later experience enables me to depose to the comfort and blessing that literature can prove in seasons of sickness and sorrow--how powerfully intellectual pursuits can help in keeping the head from crazing, and the heart from breaking,--nay, not to be too grave, how generous mental food can even atone for a meagre diet--rich fare on the paper for short commons on the cloth.

Poisoned by the malaria of the Dutch marshes, my stomach, for many months, resolutely set itself against fish, flesh, or fowl; my appetite had no more edge than the German knife placed before me. But, luckily, the mental palate and digestion were still sensible and vigorous; and whilst I passed untasted every dish at the Rhenish *table d'hôte*, I could yet enjoy my *Peregrine Pickle*, and the feast after the manner of the ancients. There was no yearning towards calf's head *à la tortue*, or sheep's heart; but I could still relish Head *à la Brunnen* and the *Heart of Midlothian*.

Still more recently, it was my misfortune, with a tolerable appetite, to be condemned to lenten fare, like Sancho Panza, by my physician--to a diet, in fact, lower than any prescribed by the poor-law commissioners; all animal food, from a bullock to a rabbit, being strictly interdicted; as well as all fluids stronger than that which lays dust, washes pinafores, and waters polyanthus. But 'the feast of reason and the flow of soul' were still mine. Denied beef, I had *Bulwer* and *Cowper*,--forbidden mutton, there was *Lamb*,--and in lieu of pork, the great *Bacon* or *Hogg*.

Then, as to beverage, it was hard, doubtless, for a Christian to set his face like a Turk against the juice of the grape. But, eschewing wine, I had still my *Butler*; and in the absence of liquor, all the *choice spirits* from Tom Browne to Tom Moore.

Thus, though confined, physically, to the drink that drowns kittens, I quaffed mentally, not merely the best of our own home-made, but the rich, racy, sparkling growths of France and Italy, of Germany and Spain--the champagne of Molière, and the Monte Pulciano of Boccaccio, the hock of Schiller, and the sherry of Cervantes. Depressed bodily by the fluid that damps everything, I got intellectually elevated with Milton, a little merry with Swift, or rather jolly with Rabelais, whose Pantagruel, by the way, is quite equal to the best gruel with rum in it.

So far can literature palliate or compensate for gastronomical privations. But there are other evils, great and small, in this world, which try the stomach less than the head, the heart, and the temper--bowls that will not roll right--well-laid schemes that will 'gang aglee'--and ill winds that blow with the pertinacity of the monsoon. Of these, Providence has allotted me a full share; but still, paradoxical as it may sound, my *burden* has been greatly lightened by a *load of books*. The manner of this will be best understood by a feline illustration. Everybody has heard of the two Kilkenny cats, who devoured each other; but it is not so generally known that they left behind them an orphan kitten, which, true to the breed, began to eat itself up, till it was diverted from the operation by a mouse. Now, the human mind, under vexation, is like that kitten, for it is apt to *prey upon itself*, unless drawn off by a new object; and none better for the purpose than a book; for example, one of Defoe's; for who, in reading his thrilling *History of the Great Plague*, would not be reconciled to a few little ones?

Many, many a dreary, weary hour have I got over--many a gloomy misgiving postponed--many a mental or bodily annoyance forgotten, by help of the tragedies and comedies of our dramatists and novelists! Many a trouble has been soothed by the still small voice of the moral philosopher--many a dragon-like care charmed to sleep by the sweet song of the poet, for all which I cry incessantly, not aloud, but in my heart, Thanks and honour to the glorious masters of the pen, and the great inventors of the press! Such has been my own experience of the blessing and comfort of literature and intellectual pursuits; and of the same mind, doubtless, was Sir Humphry Davy, who went for 'consolations in *Travel*', not to the inn or the posting house, but to his library and his books.--T. HOOD (Letter to the Manchester Athenaeum, 1843).

POWER AND GLADNESS

Books written when the soul is at spring-tide,
When it is laden like a groaning sky
Before a thunder-storm, are power and gladness,
And majesty and beauty. They seize the reader
As tempests seize a ship, and bear him on
With a wild joy. Some books are drenchèd sands,
On which a great soul's wealth lies all in heaps,
Like a wrecked argosy. What power in books!
They mingle gloom and splendour, as I've oft,
In thunderous sunsets, seen the thunder-piles
Seamed with dull fire and fiercest glory-rents.
They awe me to my knees, as if I stood
In presence of a king. They give me tears;
Such glorious tears as Eve's fair daughters shed,
When first they clasped a Son of God, all bright
With burning plumes and splendours of the sky,
In zoning heaven of their milky arms.

How few read books aright! Most souls are shut
By sense from grandeur, as a man who snores
Night-capped and wrapt in blankets to the nose
Is shut out from the night, which, like a sea,
Breaketh for ever on a strand of stars.

A. SMITH. *A Life-Drama.*

THE COMMODITY REAPED OF BOOKS

The commerce of books comforts me in age and solaceth me in solitariness. It easeth me of the burthen of a wearisome sloth: and at all times rids me of tedious companies: it abateth the edge of fretting sorrow, on condition it be not extreme and over-insolent. To divert me from any importunate imagination or insinuating conceit, there is no better way than to have recourse unto books; with ease they allure me to them, and with facility they remove them all. And though they perceive I neither frequent nor seek them, but wanting other more essential, lively, and more natural commodities, they never mutiny or murmur at me; but still entertain me with one and self-same visage....

The sick man is not to be moaned that hath his health in his sleeve. In the experience and use of this sentence, which is most true, consisteth all the commodity I reap of books. In effect I make no other use of them than those who know them not. I enjoy them, as a miser doth his gold; to know that I may enjoy them when I list, my mind is settled and satisfied with the right of possession. I never travel without books, nor in peace nor in war: yet do I pass many days and months without using them. It shall be anon, say I, or to-morrow, or when I please; in the meanwhile the time runs away, and passeth without hurting me. For it is wonderful what repose I take, and how I continue in this consideration, that they are at my elbow to delight me when time shall serve; and in acknowledging what assistance they give unto my life. This is the best munition I have found in this human peregrination, and I extremely bewail those men of understanding that want the same. I accept with better will all other kinds of amusements, how slight soever, forsomuch as this cannot fail me.--MONTAIGNE.

BOOKS IS NURSE TO TRUTH

Condemn the days of elders great or small,
And then blur out the course of present time;
Cast one age down, and so do overthrow all,
And burn the books of printed prose or rhyme:
Who shall believe he rules, or she doth reign,
In time to come, if writers loose their pain?
The pen records time past and present both:
Skill brings forth books, and books is nurse to truth.

T. CHURCHYARD. *Worthiness of Wales.*

FOR WISDOM, PIETY, DELIGHT, OR USE

In vain that husbandman his seed doth sow,
If he his crop not in due season mow.
A general sets his army in array
In vain, unless he fight, and win the day.
'Tis virtuous action that must praise bring forth,
Without which slow advice is little worth.
Yet they who give good counsel, praise deserve,
Though in the active part they cannot serve:
In action, learnéd counsellors their age,
Profession, or disease, forbids to engage.
Nor to philosophers is praise denied,
Whose wise instructions after-ages guide;
Yet vainly most their age in study spend;
No end of writing books, and to no end:
Beating their brains for strange and hidden things,
Whose knowledge nor delight nor profit brings:
Themselves with doubt both day and night perplex,
No gentle reader please, or teach, but vex.
Books should to one of these four ends conduce
For wisdom, piety, delight, or use.
What need we gaze upon the spangled sky
Or into matter's hidden causes pry?...
If we were wise these things we should not mind
But more delight in easy matters find....
Learn to live well that thou mayst die so too,
To live and die is all we have to do.

SIR J. DENHAM. *Translation of Mancini.*

OF THE ENTERTAINMENT OF BOOKS

The diversions of reading, though they are not always of the strongest kind, yet they generally leave a better effect than the grosser satisfactions of sense: for, if they are well chosen, they neither dull the appetite nor strain the capacity. On the contrary, they refresh the inclinations, and strengthen the power, and improve under experiment: and, which is best of all, they entertain and perfect at the same time; and convey wisdom and knowledge through pleasure. By reading a man does as it were antedate his life, and makes himself contemporary with the ages past. And this way of running up beyond one's nativity is much better than Plato's pre-existence; because here a man knows something of the state and is the wiser for it; which he is not in the other.

In conversing with books we may choose our company, and disengage without ceremony or exception. Here we are free from the formalities of custom and respect: we need not undergo the penance of a dull story from a fop of figure; but may shake off the haughty, the impertinent, and the vain, at pleasure. Besides, authors, like women, commonly dress when they make a visit. Respect to themselves makes them polish their thoughts, and exert the force of their understanding more than they would or can do in ordinary conversation: so that the reader has as it were the spirit and essence in a narrow compass; which was drawn off from a much larger proportion of time, labour, and expense. Like an heir, he is born rather than made rich; and comes into a stock of sense, with little or no trouble of his own. 'Tis true, a fortune in knowledge which descends in this manner, as well as an inherited estate, is too often neglected and squandered away; because we do not consider the difficulty in raising it.

Books are a guide in youth, and an entertainment for age. They support us under solitude, and keep us from being a burthen to ourselves. They help us to forget the crossness of men and things; compose our cares and our passions; and lay our disappointments asleep. When we are weary of the living, we may repair to the dead, who have nothing of peevishness, pride, or design in their conversation. However, to be constantly in the wheel has neither pleasure nor improvement in it. A man may as well expect to grow stronger by always eating, as wiser by always reading. Too much overcharges Nature, and turns more into disease than nourishment. 'Tis thought and digestion which makes books serviceable, and gives health and vigour to the mind. Neither ought we to be too implicit or resigning to authorities, but to examine before we assent, and preserve our reason in its just liberties. To walk always upon crutches is the way to lose the use of our limbs. Such an absolute submission keeps us in a perpetual minority, breaks the spirits of the understanding, and lays us open to imposture.

But books well managed afford direction and discovery. They strengthen the organ and enlarge the prospect, and give a more universal insight into things than can be learned from unlettered observation. He who depends only upon his own experience has but a few materials to work upon. He is confined to narrow limits both of place and time: and is not fit to draw a large model and to pronounce upon business which is complicated and unusual. There seems to be much the same difference between a man of mere practice and another of learning as there is between an empiric and a physician. The first may have a good recipe, or two; and if diseases and patients were very scarce, and all alike, he might do tolerably well. But if you inquire concerning the causes of distempers, the constitution of human bodies, the danger of symptoms, and the methods of cure, upon which the success of medicine depends, he knows little of the matter. On the other side, to take measures wholly from books, without looking into men and business, is like travelling in a map, where, though countries and cities are well enough distinguished, yet villages and private seats are either overlooked, or too generally marked for a stranger to find. And therefore he that would be a master must draw by the life, as well as copy from originals, and join theory and experience together.

J. COLLIER. *Essays upon several Moral Subjects.*

INSTRUCTION OR AMUSEMENT

Books, we are told, propose to *instruct* or to *amuse.* Indeed! However, not to spend any words upon it, I suppose you will admit that this wretched antithesis will be of no service to us.... For this miserable alternative being once admitted, observe what follows. In which class of books does the *Paradise Lost* stand? Among those which instruct or those which amuse? Now, if a man answers, among those which instruct,--he lies: for there is no instruction in it, nor could be in any great poem, according to the meaning which the word must bear in this distinction, unless it is meant that it should involve its own antithesis. But if he says, 'No--amongst those which amuse,'--then what a beast must he be to degrade, and in this way, what has done the most of any human work to raise and dignify human nature. But the truth is, you see, that the idiot does not wish to degrade it; on the contrary, he would willingly tell a lie in its favour, if that would be admitted; but such is the miserable state of slavery to which he has reduced himself by his own puny distinction; for, as soon as he hops out of one of his little cells he is under a necessity of hopping into the other. The true antithesis to knowledge in this case is not *pleasure*, but power. All, that is literature, seeks to communicate power; all, that is not literature, to communicate knowledge.--T. DE QUINCEY. *Letters to a Young Man.*

EXERCISE FOR THE MIND

From my own Apartment, March 16, 1709

Reading is to the mind what exercise is to the body. As by the one health is preserved, strengthened, and invigorated; by the other, virtue (which is the health of the mind) is kept alive, cherished, and confirmed. But as exercise becomes tedious and painful when we make use of it only as the means of health, so reading is apt to grow uneasy and burdensome when we apply ourselves to it only for our improvement in virtue. For this reason the virtue which we gather from a fable or an allegory is like health we get by hunting; as we are engaged in an agreeable pursuit that draws us on with pleasure, and makes us insensible of the fatigues that accompany it.--SIR R. STEELE. *Tatler*,147.

WHY BOOKS WERE INVENTED

Books were invented to take off the odium of immediate superiority and soften the rigour of duties prescribed by the teachers and censors of human kind--setting at least those who are acknowledged wiser than ourselves at a distance. When we recollect, however, that for this very reason they are seldom consulted and little obeyed, how much cause shall his contemporaries have to rejoice that their living Johnson forced them to feel the reproofs due to vice and folly--while Seneca and Tillotson were no longer able to make impression except on our shelves.--T. PERCY.

WHY BOOKS ARE READ

It is difficult to enumerate the several motives which procure to books the honour of perusal: spite, vanity, and curiosity, hope and fear, love and hatred, every passion which incites to any other action, serves at one time or another to stimulate a reader.

Some are found to take a celebrated volume into their hands, because they hope to distinguish their penetration by finding faults that have escaped the public; others eagerly buy it in the first bloom of reputation, that they may join the chorus of praise, and not lag, as Falstaff terms it, in 'the rearward of the fashion'.

Some read for style, and some for argument: one has little care about the sentiment, he observes only how it is expressed; another regards not the conclusion, but is diligent to mark how it is inferred; they read for other purposes than the attainment of practical knowledge, and are no more likely to grow wise by an examination of a treatise of moral prudence than an architect to inflame his devotion by considering attentively the proportions of a temple.

Some read that they may embellish their conversation, or shine in dispute; some that they may not be detected in ignorance, or want the reputation of literary accomplishments: but the most general and prevalent reason of study is the impossibility of finding another amusement equally cheap or constant, equally independent of the hour or the weather. He that wants money to follow the chase of pleasure through her yearly circuit, and is left at home when the gay world rolls to Bath or Tunbridge; he whose gout compels him to hear from his chamber the rattle of chariots transporting happier beings to plays and assemblies, will be forced to seek in books a refuge from himself.--S. JOHNSON. *Adventurer*, 137.

THE INFLUENCE OF BOOKS

Every person of tolerable education has been considerably influenced by the books he has read, and remembers with a kind of gratitude several of those that made without injury the earliest and the strongest impression. It is pleasing at a more advanced period to look again into the early favourites, though the mature person may wonder how some of them had once power to absorb his passions, make him retire into a lonely wood in order to read unmolested, repel the approaches of sleep, or, when it came, infect it with visions. A capital part of the proposed task would be to recollect the books that have been read with the greatest interest, the periods when they were read, the partiality which any of them inspired to a particular mode of life, to a study, to a system of opinions, or to a class of human characters; to note the counteraction of later ones (where we have been sensible of it) to the effect produced by the former; and then to endeavour to estimate the whole and ultimate influence.

Considering the multitude of facts, sentiments, and characters, which have been contemplated by a person who has read much, the effect, one would think, must have been very great. Still, however, it is probable that a very small number of books will have the pre-eminence in our mental history. Perhaps your memory will promptly recur to six or ten that have contributed more to your present habits of feeling and thought than all the rest together.--J. FOSTER. *On a Man's Writing Memoirs of Himself.*

REMUNERATIVE READING

Cultivate above all things a taste for reading. There is no pleasure so cheap, so innocent, and so remunerative as the real, hearty pleasure and taste for reading. It does not come to every one naturally. Some people take to it naturally, and others do not; but I advise you to cultivate it, and endeavour to promote it in your minds. In order to do that you should read what amuses you and pleases you. You should not begin with difficult works, because, if you do, you will find the pursuit dry and tiresome. I would even say to you, read novels, read frivolous books, read anything that will amuse you and give you a taste for reading. On this point all persons could put themselves on an equality. Some persons would say they would rather spend their time in society; but it must be remembered that if they had cultivated a taste for reading beforehand they would be in a position to choose their society, whereas, if they had not, the probabilities were that they would have to mix with people inferior to themselves.--R. LOWE, LORD SHERBROOKE. *Speech to the Students of the Croydon Science and Art Schools*, 1869.

Books bear him up awhile, and make him try
To swim with bladders of philosophy.

> J. WILMOT, EARL OF ROCHESTER.
> *A Satire against Mankind.*

Books are men of higher stature,
And the only men that speak aloud for future times to hear.

> E. B. BROWNING. *Lady Geraldine's Courtship.*

THE MOOD FOR BOOKS

How the mood for a book sometimes rushes upon one, either one knows not why, or in consequence, perhaps, of some most trifling suggestion. Yesterday I was walking at dusk. I came to an old farmhouse; at the garden gate a vehicle stood waiting, and I saw it was our doctor's gig. Having passed, I turned to look back. There was a faint afterglow in the sky beyond the chimneys; a light twinkled at one of the upper windows. I said to myself, '*Tristram Shandy*,' and hurried home to plunge into a book which I have not opened for I dare say twenty years.

Not long ago, I awoke one morning and suddenly thought of the Correspondence between Goethe and Schiller; and so impatient did I become to open the book that I got up an hour earlier than usual. A book worth rising for; much better worth than old Burton, who pulled Johnson out of bed. A book which helps one to forget the idle or venomous chatter going on everywhere about us, and bids us cherish hope for a world 'which has such people in't'.

These volumes I had at hand; I could reach them down from my shelves at the moment when I hungered for them. But it often happens that the book which comes into my mind could only be procured with trouble and delay; I breathe regretfully and put aside the thought. Ah! the books that one will never read again. They gave delight, perchance something more; they left a perfume in the memory; but life has passed them by for ever. I have but to muse, and one after another they rise before me. Books gentle and quieting; books noble and inspiring; books that well merit to be pored over, not once but many a time. Yet never again shall I hold them in my hand; the years fly too quickly, and are too few. Perhaps when I lie waiting for the end, some of these lost books will come into my wandering thoughts, and I shall remember them as friends to whom I owed a kindness-- friends passed upon the way. What regret in that last farewell!--G. GISSING. *The Private Papers of Henry Ryecroft.*

BY DIVINE INSPIRATION

Now it is, that the minds of men are qualified with all manner of discipline, and the old sciences revived, which for many ages were extinct. Now it is, that the learned languages are to their pristine purity restored, viz. Greek, without which a man may be ashamed to account himself a scholar, Hebrew, Arabic, Chaldean, and Latin. Printing likewise is now in use, so elegant and so correct, that better cannot be imagined, although it was found out but in my time by a divine inspiration, as, by a diabolical suggestion on the other side, was the invention of ordnance. All the world is full of knowing men, of most learned schoolmasters, and vast libraries; and it appears to me as a truth, that neither in Plato's time, nor Cicero's, nor Papinian's, there was ever such conveniency for studying, as we see at this day there is. Nor must any adventure henceforward to come in public, or present himself in company, that hath not been pretty well polished in the shop of Minerva. I see robbers, hangmen, freebooters, tapsters, ostlers, and such like, of the very rubbish of the people, more learned now than the doctors and preachers were in my time. What shall I say? The very women and children have aspired to this praise and celestial manna of good learning.--RABELAIS. *The Life of Gargantua and of Pantagruel.*

PERMANENCE FOR THOUGHT

I saw a man, who bore in his hands the same instruments as our modern smith's, presenting a vase, which appeared to be made of iron, amidst the acclamations of an assembled multitude engaged in triumphal procession before the altars dignified by the name of Apollo at Delphi; and I saw in the same place men who carried rolls of papyrus in their hands and wrote upon them with reeds containing ink made from the soot of wood mixed with a solution of glue. 'See,' the genius said, 'an immense change produced in the condition of society by the two arts of which you here see the origin; the one, that of rendering iron malleable, which is owing to a single individual, an obscure Greek; the other, that of making thought permanent in written characters, an art which has gradually arisen from the hieroglyphics which you may observe on yonder pyramids.'--SIR H. DAVY. *Consolations in Travel.*

THE MIRACULOUS ART OF WRITING

Certainly the Art of Writing is the most miraculous of all things man has devised. Odin's *Runes* were the first form of the work of a Hero; *Books*, written words, are still miraculous *Runes*, the latest form! In Books lies the *soul* of the whole Past Time; the articulate audible voice of the Past, when the body and material substance of it has altogether vanished like a dream. Mighty fleets and armies, harbours and arsenals, vast cities, high-domed, many-engined,--they are precious, great: but what do they become? Agamemnon, the many Agamemnons, Pericleses, and their Greece; all is gone now to some ruined fragments, dumb mournful wrecks and blocks: but the Books of Greece! There Greece, to every thinker, still very literally lives; can be called-up again into life. No magic Rune is stranger than a Book. All that Mankind has done, thought, gained, or been: it is lying as in magic preservation in the pages of Books. They are the chosen possession of men. Do not Books still accomplish *miracles*, as *Runes* were fabled to do? They persuade men. Not the wretchedest circulating-library novel, which foolish girls thumb and con in remote villages, but will help to regulate the actual practical weddings and households of those foolish girls. So 'Celia' felt, so 'Clifford' acted: the foolish Theorem of Life, stamped into those young brains, comes out as a solid Practice one day. Consider whether any *Rune* in the wildest imagination of mythologist ever did such wonders as, on the actual firm Earth, some Books have done! What built St. Paul's Cathedral? Look at the heart of the matter, it was that divine Hebrew BOOK--the word partly of the man Moses, an outlaw tending his Midianitish herds, four thousand years ago, in the wildernesses of Sinai! It is the strangest of things, yet nothing is truer. With the art of Writing, of which Printing is a simple, an inevitable, and comparatively insignificant corollary, the true reign of miracles for mankind commenced. It related, with a wondrous new contiguity and perpetual closeness, the Past and Distant with the Present in time and place; all times and all places with this our actual Here and Now. All things were altered for men; all modes of important work of men.--T. CARLYLE. *Heroes and Hero-Worship.*

BOOKS AS MEMORIALS

In books we find the dead as it were living; in books we foresee things to come; in books warlike affairs are methodized; the rights of peace proceed from books. All things are corrupted and decayed with time. Saturn never ceases to devour those whom he generates; insomuch that the glory of the world would be lost in oblivion if God had not provided mortals with a remedy in books. Alexander the ruler of the world; Julius the invader of the world and of the city, the just who in unity of person assumed the empire in arms and arts; the faithful Fabricius, the rigid Cato, would at this day have been without a memorial if the aid of books had failed them. Towers are razed to the earth, cities overthrown, triumphal arches mouldered to dust; nor can the King or Pope be found upon whom the privilege of a lasting name can be conferred more easily than by books. A book made, renders succession to the author: for as long as the book exists, the author remaining [Greek: athanatos] immortal, cannot perish.--R. DE BURY. *Philobiblon.*

FASHION IN BOOKS

We commonly see the book that at Christmas lieth bound on the stationer's stall, at Easter to be broken in the Haberdasher's shop, which sith it is the order of proceeding, I am content this winter to have my doings read for a toy, that in summer they may be ready for trash. It is not strange when as the greatest wonder lasteth but nine days, that a new work should not endure but three months. Gentlemen use books, as gentlewomen handle their flowers, who in the morning stick them in their heads, and at night straw them at their heels. Cherries be fulsome when they be through ripe, because they be plenty, and books be stale when they be printed, in that they be common. In my mind Printers and Tailors are bound chiefly to pray for gentlemen, the one hath so many fantasies to print, the other such divers fashions to make, that the pressing iron of the one is never out of the fire, nor the printing press of the other any time lieth still. But a fashion is but a day's wearing, and a book but an hour's reading, which seeing it is so, I am of a shoemaker's mind, who careth not so the shoe hold the plucking on, nor I, so my labours last the running over. He that cometh in print because he would be known, is like the fool that cometh into the market because he would be seen.--J. LYLY. *Euphues.*

COATS FOR MACKEREL

I erect not here a statue to be set up in the market-place of a town, or in a church, or in any other public place:

> Non equidem hoc studeo, pullatis ut mihi nugis
> Pagina turgescat. (Pers. *Sat.* v. 19.)

> I study not my written leaves should grow
> Big-swoln with bubbled toys, which vain breaths blow.

> Secrete loquimur. (Pers. *Sat.* v. 21.)

> We speak alone,
> Or one to one.

It is for the corner of a library, or to amuse a neighbour, a kinsman, or a friend of mine withal, who by this image may happily take pleasure to renew acquaintance and to reconverse with me.... Notwithstanding if my posterity be of another mind, I shall have wherewith to be avenged, for they cannot make so little accompt of me, as then I shall do of them. All the commerce I have in this with the world is that I borrow the instruments of their writing, as more speedy and more easy; in requital whereof I may peradventure hinder the melting of some piece of butter in the market or a grocer from selling an ounce of pepper.

> Ne toga cordylis et paenula desit olivis (Martial).

Lest fish-fry should a fit gown want,
Lest cloaks should be for Olives scant.

Et laxas scombris saepe dabo tunicas (Catullus).

To long-tailed mackerels often I
Will side-wide (paper) coats apply.

And if it happen no man read me, have I lost my time to have entertained myself so many idle hours about so pleasing and profitable thoughts?... I have no more made my book than my book hath made me. A book consubstantial to his author: of a peculiar and fit occupation. A member of my life. Not of an occupation and end strange and foreign, as all other books.... What if I lend mine ears somewhat more attentively unto books, sith I but watch if I can filch something from them wherewith to enamel and uphold mine? I never study to make a book, yet have I somewhat studied, because I had already made it (if to nibble or pinch, by the head or feet, now one author and then another, be in any sort to study), but nothing at all to form my opinions.--MONTAIGNE.

TO HIS BOOK

Thou art a plant sprung up to wither never,
But, like a laurel, to grow green for ever.

Make haste away, and let one be
A friendly patron unto thee;
Lest rapt from hence, I see thee lie
Torn for the use of pasterie;
Or see thy injured leaves serve well
To make loose gowns for mackerel;
Or see the grocers, in a trice,
Make hoods of thee to serve out spice.

If hap it must that I must see thee lie
Absyrtus-like, all torn confusedly;
With solemn tears, and with much grief of heart,
I'll recollect thee, weeping, part by part;
And having washed thee, close thee in a chest
With spice; that done, I'll leave thee to thy rest.

The bound, almost, now of my book I see;
But yet no end of those therein or me;
Here we begin new life; while thousands quite
Are lost, and theirs, in everlasting night.

Go thou forth, my book, though late
Yet be timely fortunate.
It may chance good luck may send

Thee a kinsman or a friend
That may harbour thee, when I
With my fates neglected lie.
If thou know'st not where to dwell,
See, the fire's by. Farewell.

R. HERRICK. *Hesperides.*

IMMORTALITY IN BOOKS

Since honour from the honourer proceeds,
How well do they deserve, that memorize
And leave in books for all posterities
The names of worthies and their virtuous deeds;
When all their glory else, like water-weeds
Without their element, presèntly dies,
And all their greatness quite forgotten lies,
And when and how they flourished no man heeds!
How poor remembrances are statues, tombs,
And other monuments that men erect
To princes, which remain in closèd rooms,
Where but a few behold them, in respect
Of books, that to the universal eye
Show how they lived; the other where they lie!

S. DANIEL.

ENDURING MONUMENTS

We see then how far the monuments of wit and learning are more durable than the monuments of power or of the hands. For have not the verses of Homer continued twenty-five hundred years, or more, without the loss of a syllable or letter; during which time infinite palaces, temples, castles, cities, have been decayed and demolished? It is not possible to have the true pictures or statues of Cyrus, Alexander, Caesar, no, nor of the kings or great personages of much later years; for the originals cannot last, and the copies cannot but leese of the life and truth. But the images of men's wits and knowledges remain in books, exempted from the wrong of time and capable of perpetual renovation. Neither are they fitly to be called images, because they generate still, and cast their seeds in the minds of others, provoking and causing infinite actions and opinions in succeeding ages. So that if the invention of the ship was thought so noble, which carrieth riches and commodities from place to place, and consociateth the most remote regions in participation of their fruits, how much more are letters to be magnified, which as ships pass through the vast seas of time, and make ages so distant to participate of the wisdom, illuminations, and inventions, the one of the other?--F. BACON, LORD VERULAM. *Of the Advancement of Learning.*

THE STRANGE QUALITY OF BOOKS

Books have that strange quality, that being of the frailest and tenderest matter, they out-last brass, iron and marble; and though their habitations and walls, by uncivil hands, be many times overthrown; and they themselves, by foreign force, be turned prisoners, yet do they often, as their authors, keep their giver's names; seeming rather to change places and masters than to suffer a full ruin and total wreck. So, many of the books of Constantinople changed Greece for France and Italy; and in our time, that famous Library in the Palatinate changed Heidelberg for the Vatican. And this I think no small duty, nor mean-er gift and retribution, which I render back again to my benefactor's honest fame, being a greater matter than riches; riches being momentany and evanishing, scarce possessed by the third heir; fame immortal, and almost everlasting; by fame riches is often acquired, seldom fame by riches; except when it is their good hap to fall in the possession of some generous-minded man. And though a philosopher said of famous men, disdainfully, that they died two deaths, one in their bodies, another, long after, in their names, he must confess, that where other men live but one life, famous men live two.--W. DRUMMOND. *Bibliotheca Edinburgena Lectori.*

BOOKS ARE NOT DEAD THINGS

I deny not but that it is of greatest concernment in the Church and Commonwealth to have a vigilant eye how books demean themselves, as well as men; and thereafter to con-fine, imprison, and do sharpest justice on them as malefactors. For books are not absolutely dead things, but do contain a potency of life in them to be as active as that soul was whose progeny they are; nay, they do preserve, as in a vial, the purest efficacy and extraction of that living intellect that bred them. I know they are as lively and as vig-orously productive as those fabulous dragon's teeth; and, being sown up and down, may chance to spring up armed men. And yet, on the other hand, unless wariness be used, as good almost kill a man as kill a good book. Who kills a man kills a reasonable creature, God's image; but he who destroys a good book, kills reason itself; kills the image of God, as it were, in the eye. Many a man lives a burden to the earth; but a good book is the pre-cious life-blood of a master-spirit, embalmed and treasured up on purpose to a life beyond life. 'Tis true no age can restore a life, whereof, perhaps, there is no great loss; and revolutions of ages do not oft recover the loss of a rejected truth, for the want of which whole nations fare the worse. We should be wary, therefore, what persecution we raise against the living labours of public men, how we spill that seasoned life of man pre-served and stored up in books; since we see a kind of homicide may be thus committed, sometimes a martyrdom, and if it extend to the whole impression, a kind of massacre, whereof the execution ends not in the slaying of an elemental life, but strikes at that ethereal and fifth essence--the breath of reason itself; slays an immortality rather than a life.--J. MILTON. *Areopagitica.*

SHAKESPEARE IN HEAVEN

BOSWELL. 'There is a strange unwillingness to part with life, independent of serious fears as to futurity. A reverend friend of ours (naming him) tells me, that he feels an uneasiness at the thoughts of leaving his house, his study, his books.'

JOHNSON. 'This is foolish in ---- [Percy?]. A man need not be uneasy on these grounds; for, as he will retain his consciousness, he may say with the philosopher, *Omnia mea mecum porto*.'

BOSWELL. 'True, Sir: we may carry our books in our heads; but still there is something painful in the thought of leaving for ever what has given us pleasure. I remember, many years ago, when my imagination was warm, and I happened to be in a melancholy mood, it distressed me to think of going into a state of being in which Shakespeare's poetry did not exist. A lady whom I then much admired, a very amiable woman, humoured my fancy, and relieved me by saying, "The first thing you will meet in the other world will be an elegant copy of Shakespeare's works presented to you."'

Dr. Johnson smiled benignantly at this, and did not appear to disapprove of the notion.-- J. BOSWELL. *Life of Johnson.*

THE LIBRARIES OF HEAVEN

I cannot think the glorious world of mind,
  Embalmed in books, which I can only see
In patches, though I read my moments blind,
  Is to be lost to me.

I have a thought that, as we live elsewhere,
  So will these dear creations of the brain;
That what I lose unread, I'll find, and there
  Take up my joy again.

O then the bliss of blisses, to be freed
  From all the wants by which the world is driven;
With liberty and endless time to read
  The libraries of Heaven!

R. LEIGHTON.

THE ONLY THINGS THAT LAST FOR EVER

Actions pass away and are forgotten, or are only discernible in their effects; conquerors, statesmen, and kings live but by their names stamped on the page of history. Hume says rightly that more people think about Virgil and Homer (and that continually) than ever trouble their heads about Caesar or Alexander. In fact, poets are a longer-lived race than heroes: they breathe more of the air of immortality. They survive more entire in their thoughts and acts. We have all that Virgil or Homer did, as much as if we had lived at the same time with them: we can hold their works in our hands, or lay them on our pillows, or put them to our lips. Scarcely a trace of what the others did is left upon the earth, so as to be visible to common eyes. The one, the dead authors, are living men, still breathing and moving in their writings. The others, the conquerors of the world, are but the ashes in an urn. The sympathy (so to speak) between thought and thought is more intimate and vital than that between thought and action. Thought is linked to thought as flame kindles into flame: the tribute of admiration to the manes of departed heroism is like burning incense in a marble monument. Words, ideas, feelings, with the progress of time harden into substances: things, bodies, actions, moulder away, or melt into a sound, into thin air!--Yet though the schoolmen in the Middle Ages disputed more about the texts of Aristotle than the battle of Arbela, perhaps Alexander's Generals in his lifetime admired his pupil as much and liked him better. For not only a man's actions are effaced and vanish with him; his virtues and generous qualities die with him also: his intellect only is immortal and bequeathed unimpaired to posterity. Words are the only things that last for ever.--W. HAZLITT. *Table Talk*.

THE AUTHORS' METAMORPHOSIS

How pleasant it is to reflect, that all these lovers of books have themselves become books! What better metamorphosis could Pythagoras have desired! How Ovid and Horace exulted in anticipating theirs! And how the world have justified their exultation! They had a right to triumph over brass and marble. It is the only visible change which changes no further; which generates and yet is not destroyed. Consider: mines themselves are exhausted; cities perish; kingdoms are swept away, and man weeps with indignation to think that his own body is not immortal.

> Muoiono le città, muoiono i regni,
> E l'uom d'esser mortal par che si sdegni.

Yet this little body of thought, that lies before me in the shape of a book, has existed thousands of years, nor since the invention of the press can anything short of an universal convulsion of nature abolish it. To a shape like this, so small yet so comprehensive, so slight yet so lasting, so insignificant yet so venerable, turns the mighty activity of Homer, and, so turning, is enabled to live and warm us for ever. To a shape like this turns the placid sage of Academus: to a shape like this the grandeur of Milton, the exuberance of Spenser, the pungent elegance of Pope, and the volatility of Prior. In one small room, like the compressed spirits of Milton, can be gathered together

> The assembled souls of all that men held wise.

May I hope to become the meanest of these existences? This is a question which every author who is a lover of books asks himself some time in his life; and which must be pardoned, because it cannot be helped. I know not. I cannot exclaim with the poet,

Oh that my name were numbered among theirs,
Then gladly would I end my mortal days.

For my mortal days, few and feeble as the rest of them may be, are of consequence to others. But I should like to remain visible in this shape. The little of myself that pleases myself I could wish to be accounted worth pleasing others. I should like to survive so, were it only for the sake of those who love me in private, knowing as I do what a treasure is the possession of a friend's mind, when he is no more. At all events, nothing while I live and think can deprive me of my value for such treasures. I can help the appreciation of them while I last, and love them till I die; and perhaps, if fortune turns her face once more in kindness upon me before I go, I may chance, some quiet day, to lay my overbeating temples on a book, and so have the death I most envy.--J. H. LEIGH HUNT. *My Books.*

O BLESSED LETTERS

O blessed letters! that combine in one
All ages past, and make one live with all,
By you we do confer with who are gone,
And the dead-living unto council call;
By you the unborn shall have communion
Of what we feel and what doth us befall.

    *   *   *   *   *

What good is like to this,
To do worthy the writing, and to write
Worthy the reading, and the world's delight?

S. DANIEL. *Musophilus.*

Though they [philosophers] write *contemptu gloriae*, yet, as Hieron observes, they will put their names to their books.--R. BURTON.

A LASTING LINK OF AGES

But words are things, and a small drop of ink,
  Falling, like dew, upon a thought, produces
That which makes thousands, perhaps millions, think;
  'Tis strange, the shortest letter which man uses
Instead of speech, may form a lasting link
  Of ages; to what straits old Time reduces
Frail man, when paper--even a rag like this,
Survives himself, his tomb, and all that's his!

And when his bones are dust, his grave a blank,
  His station, generation, even his nation,
Become a thing, or nothing, save to rank
  In chronological commemoration,
Some dull MS. oblivion long has sank,
  Or graven stone found in a barrack's station
In digging the foundation of a closet,
May turn his name up, as a rare deposit.

And glory long has made the sages smile;
  'Tis something, nothing, words, illusion, wind--
Depending more upon the historian's style
  Than on the name a person leaves behind:
Troy owes to Homer what whist owes to Hoyle:
  The present century was growing blind
To the great Marlborough's skill in giving knocks,
Until his late Life by Archdeacon Coxe.

    G. GORDON, LORD BYRON. *Don Juan.*

THE VIRTUE OF A TRUE BOOK

Visible and tangible products of the Past, again, I reckon-up to the extent of three: Cities, with their Cabinets and Arsenals; then tilled Fields, to either or to both of which divisions Roads with their Bridges may belong; and thirdly--Books. In which third, truly, the last invented, lies a worth far surpassing that of the two others. Wondrous indeed is the virtue of a true Book! Not like a dead city of stones, yearly crumbling, yearly needing repair; more like a tilled field, but then a spiritual field: like a spiritual tree, let me rather say, it stands from year to year, and from age to age (we have Books that already number some hundred-and-fifty human ages); and yearly comes its new produce of leaves (Commentaries, Deductions, Philosophical, Political Systems; or were it only Sermons, Pamphlets, Journalistic Essays), every one of which is talismanic and thaumaturgic, for it can persuade men. O thou who art able to write a Book, which once in the two centuries or oftener there is a man gifted to do, envy not him whom they name City-builder, and inexpressibly pity him whom they name Conqueror or City-burner! Thou too art a Conqueror and Victor; but of the true sort, namely over the Devil: thou too hast built what will outlast all marble and metal, and be a wonder-bringing City of the Mind, a Temple and Seminary and Prophetic Mount, whereto all kindreds of the Earth will pilgrim.--T. CARLYLE. *Sartor Resartus.*

ACTION AND REACTION

Some of the well-puffed fashionable novels of eighteen hundred and twenty-nine hold the pastry of eighteen hundred and thirty; and others, which are now extolled in language almost too high-flown for the merits of *Don Quixote*, will, we have no doubt, line the trunks of eighteen hundred and thirty-one.--LORD MACAULAY. *Mr. Robert Montgomery's Poems.*

THE ULTIMATE TEST OF BOOKS

Some of the Histories that our age has produced are books in the truest sense of the word. They illustrate great periods in our own annals, and in the annals of other countries. They show what a divine discipline has been at work to form men; they teach us that there is such a discipline at work to form us into men. That is the test to which I have urged that all books must at last be brought; if they do not bear it, their doom is fixed. They may be light or heavy, the penny sheet or the vast folio; they may speak of things seen or unseen; of Science or Art; of what has been or what is to be; they may amuse us or weary us, flatter us or scorn us; if they do not assist to make us better and more substantial men, they are only providing fuel for a fire larger, and more utterly destructive, than that which consumed the Library of the Ptolemies.--F. D. MAURICE. *On Books.*

BOOKS OF THE HOUR AND OF ALL TIME

All books are divisible into two classes, the books of the hour, and the books of all time. Mark this distinction--it is not one of quality only. It is not merely the bad book that does not last, and the good one that does. It is a distinction of species. There are good books for the hour, and good ones for all time; bad books for the hour, and bad ones for all time. I must define the two kinds before I go farther.

The good book of the hour, then,--I do not speak of the bad ones--is simply the useful or pleasant talk of some person whom you cannot otherwise converse with, printed for you. Very useful often, telling you what you need to know; very pleasant often, as a sensible friend's present talk would be. These bright accounts of travels; good-humoured and witty discussions of question; lively or pathetic story-telling in the form of novel; firm fact-telling, by the real agents concerned in the events of passing history;--all these books of the hour, multiplying among us as education becomes more general, are a peculiar characteristic and possession of the present age: we ought to be entirely thankful for them, and entirely ashamed of ourselves if we make no good use of them. But we make the worst possible use, if we allow them to usurp the place of true books: for, strictly speaking, they are not books at all, but merely letters or newspapers in good print.... A book is written, not to multiply the voice merely, not to carry it merely, but to preserve it. The author has something to say which he perceives to be true and useful, or helpfully beautiful. So far as he knows, no one has yet said it; so far as he knows, no one else can say it. He is bound to say it, clearly and melodiously if he may; clearly, at all events. In the sum of his life he finds this to be the thing, or group of things, manifest to him;--this the piece of true knowledge, or sight, which his share of sunshine and earth has permitted him to seize. He would fain set it down for ever; engrave it on rock, if he could; saying, 'This is the best of me; for the rest, I ate, and drank, and slept, loved, and hated, like another; my life was as the vapour, and is not; but this I saw and knew: this, if anything of mine, is worth your memory.' That is his 'writing'; it is, in his small human way, and with whatever degree of true inspiration is in him, his inscription, or scripture. That is a 'Book'....

Now books of this kind have been written in all ages by their greatest men:--by great leaders, great statesmen, and great thinkers. These are all at your choice; and life is short. You have heard as much before; yet have you measured and mapped out this short life and its possibilities? Do you know, if you read this, that you cannot read that--that what you lose to-day you cannot gain to-morrow? Will you go and gossip with your house-maid, or your stable-boy, when you may talk with queens and kings; or flatter yourselves that it is with any worthy consciousness of your own claims to respect that you jostle with the common crowd for *entrée* here, and audience there, when all the while this eter-nal court is open to you, with its society wide as the world, multitudinous as its days, the chosen, and the mighty, of every place and time? Into that you may enter always; in that you may take fellowship and rank according to your wish; from that, once entered into it, you can never be outcast but by your own fault; by your aristocracy of companionship there, your own inherent aristocracy will be assuredly tested, and the motives with which you strive to take high place in the society of the living, measured, as to all the truth and sincerity that are in them, by the place you desire to take in this company of the Dead.--J. RUSKIN. *Sesame and Lilies.*

WHO WILL BELIEVE MY VERSE

Who will believe my verse in time to come,
If it were filled with your most high deserts?
Though yet, heaven knows, it is but as a tomb
Which hides your life and shows not half your parts.
If I could write the beauty of your eyes
And in fresh numbers number all your graces,
The age to come would say, 'This poet lies;
Such heavenly touches ne'er touched earthly faces.'
So should my papers, yellowed with their age,
Be scorned, like old men of less truth than tongue,
And your true rights be termed a poet's rage
And stretchèd metre of an antique song:
  But were some child of yours alive that time,
  You should live twice,--in it and in my rhyme.

W. SHAKESPEARE.

IMMORTALITY IN SONG

How many paltry, foolish, painted things,
That now in coaches trouble every street,
Shall be forgotten, whom no poet sings,
Ere they be well wrapped in their winding-sheet!
Where I to thee eternity shall give,

When nothing else remaineth of these days,
And queens hereafter shall be glad to live
Upon the alms of thy superfluous praise;
Virgins and matrons reading these my rhymes,
Shall be so much delighted with thy story,
That they shall grieve they lived not in these times,
To have seen thee, their sex's only glory:
  So shalt thou fly above the vulgar throng,
  Still to survive in my immortal song.

M. DRAYTON.

ONE DAY I WROTE HER NAME

One day I wrote her name upon the strand,
But came the waves and washèd it away:
Again I wrote it with a second hand,
But came the tide and made my pains his prey.
'Vain man,' said she, 'that dost in vain essay
A mortal thing so to immortalize;
For I myself shall like to this decay,
And eke my name be wipèd out likewise.'
'Not so,' quoth I; 'let baser things devise
To die in dust, but you shall live by fame;
My verse your virtues rare shall eternize,
And in the heavens write your glorious name:
  Where, whenas Death shall all the world subdue,
  Our love shall live, and later life renew.'

E. SPENSER.

WELL I REMEMBER HOW YOU SMILED

Well I remember how you smiled
  To see me write your name upon
The soft sea-sand--'O! *what a child!*
  You think you're writing upon stone!

I have since written what no tide
  Shall ever wash away, what men
Unborn shall read o'er ocean wide
  And find Ianthe's name again.

W. S. LANDOR.

THE MULTIPLICITY OF BOOKS

Solomon saith truly, Of making many books there is no end, so insatiable is the thirst of men therein; as also endless is the desire of many in buying and reading them. But we come to our rules.

1. *It is a vanity to persuade the world one hath much learning, by getting a great library.* As soon shall I believe every one is valiant that hath a well-furnished armoury. I guess good house-keeping by the smoking, not the number of the tunnels, as knowing that many of them, built merely for uniformity, are without chimneys, and more without fires. Once a dunce void of learning but full of books flouted a libraryless scholar with these words: *Salve doctor sine libris.* But the next day the scholar coming into this jeerer's study, crowded with books; *Salvete libri,* saith he, *sine doctore.*

2. *Few books, well selected, are best.* Yet, as a certain fool bought all the pictures that came out, because he might have his choice, such is the vain humour of many men in gather-ing of books: yet when they have done all, they miss their end, it being in the editions of authors as in the fashions of clothes, when a man thinks he hath gotten the latest and newest, presently another newer comes out.

3. *Some books are only cursorily to be tasted of.* Namely, first, voluminous books, the task of a man's life to read them over; secondly, auxiliary books, only to be repaired to on occa-sions; thirdly, such as are mere pieces of formality, so that if you look on them, you look through them; and he that peeps through the casement of the index sees as much as if he were in the house. But the laziness of those cannot be excused who perfunctorily pass over authors of consequence, and only trade in their tables and contents. These, like city-cheaters, having gotten the names of all country gentlemen, make silly people believe they have long lived in those places where they never were, and flourish with skill in those authors they never seriously studied.

4. *The genius of the author is commonly discovered in the dedicatory epistle.* Many place the purest grain in the mouth of the sack for chapmen to handle or buy: and from the dedication one may probably guess at the work, saving some rare and peculiar exceptions. Thus, when once a gentleman admired how so pithy, learned, and witty a dedication was matched to a flat, dull, foolish book; *In truth,* said another, *they may be well matched together, for I profess they are nothing akin.*

5. *Proportion an hour's meditation to an hour's reading of a staple author.* This makes a man mas-ter of his learning, and dispirits the book into the scholar. The king of Sweden never filed his men above six deep in one company, because he would not have them lie in useless clusters in his army, but so that every particular soldier might be drawn out into service. Books that stand thin on the shelves, yet so as the owner of them can bring forth every one of them into use, are better than far greater libraries....

But what do I, speaking against multiplicity of books in this age, who trespass in this nature myself? What was a learned man's compliment, may serve for my confession and conclusion: *Multi mei similes hoc morbo laborant, ut cum scribere nesciant tamen a scribendo tem-perare non possint.*--T. FULLER. *The Holy State and the Profane State.*

45

SUPERFLUOUS BOOKS

I have heard some with deep sighs lament the lost lines of Cicero; others with as many groans deplore the combustion of the library of Alexandria. For my own part, I think there be too many in the world, and could with patience behold the urn and ashes of the Vatican, could I, with a few others, recover the perished leaves of Solomon. I would not omit a copy of *Enoch's Pillars*, had they many nearer authors than Josephus, or did not relish somewhat of the fable. Some men have written more than others have spoken. Pineda quotes more authors in one work than are necessary in a whole world. Of those three great inventions in Germany, there are two which are not without their incommodities, and 'tis disputable whether they exceed not their use and commodities. 'Tis not a melancholy *Utinam* of mine own, but the desires of better heads that there were a general synod; not to unite the incompatible differences of religion, but for the benefit of learning, to reduce it as it lay at first, in a few and solid authors; and to condemn to the fire those swarms and millions of rhapsodies, begotten only to distract and abuse the weaker judgements of scholars, and to maintain the trade and mystery of typographers.--SIR T. BROWNE. *Religio Medici.*

MULTIPLICATION IS VEXATION

The reason that books are multiplied, in spite of the general law that beings shall not be multiplied without necessity, is, that books are made from books. A new history of France or Spain is manufactured from several volumes already printed, without adding anything new. All dictionaries are made from dictionaries; almost all new geographical books are made from other books of geography; St. Thomas's dream has brought forth two thousand large volumes of divinity; and the same race of little worms that have devoured the parent are now gnawing the children.--VOLTAIRE. *Philosophical Dictionary: Books.*

THE MULTIPLICATION OF ORIGINALS

The invention of printing has not, perhaps, multiplied books, but only the copies of them; and if we believe there were six hundred thousand in the library of Ptolemy, we shall hardly pretend to equal it by any of ours, nor, perhaps, by all put together; I mean so many originals that have lived any time, and thereby given testimony to their having been thought worth preserving. For the scribblers are infinite, that like mushrooms or flies are born and die in small circles of time; whereas books, like proverbs, receive their chief value from the stamp and esteem of ages through which they have passed.--SIR W. TEMPLE. *Ancient and Modern Learning.*

THE AUTHORS' ADVANTAGE

The circumstance which gives authors an advantage ... is this, that they can multiply their originals; or rather can make copies of their works, to what number they please, which shall be as valuable as the originals themselves. This gives a great author something like a prospect of eternity, but at the same time deprives him of those other advantages which artists meet with. The artist finds greater returns in profit, as the author in fame. What an inestimable price would a Virgil or a Homer, a Cicero or an Aristotle bear, were their works like a statue, a building, or a picture, to be confined only in one place, and made the property of a single person!--J. ADDISON. *Spectator*, 166.

AN IGNORANT AGE HATH MANY BOOKS

It is observed that *a corrupt society has many laws*; I know not whether it is not equally true, that *an ignorant age has many books*. When the treasures of ancient knowledge lie unexamined, and original authors are neglected and forgotten, compilers and plagiaries are encouraged who give us again what we had before, and grow great by setting before us what our own sloth had hidden from our view.--S. JOHNSON. *Idler*, 85.

THE DIFFUSION OF BOOKS AND ITS EFFECT ON CULTURE

Nothing can supply the place of books. They are cheering or soothing companions in solitude, illness, affliction. The wealth of both continents would not compensate for the good they impart. Let every man, if possible, gather some good books under his roof, and obtain access for himself and family to some social library. Almost any luxury should be sacrificed to this.

One of the very interesting features of our times is the multiplication of books, and their distribution through all conditions of society. At a small expense a man can now possess himself of the most precious treasures of English literature. Books, once confined to a few by their costliness, are now accessible to the multitude; and in this way a change of habits is going on in society, highly favourable to the culture of the people. Instead of depending on casual rumour and loose conversation for most of their knowledge and objects of thought; instead of forming their judgements in crowds, and receiving their chief excitement from the voice of neighbours; men are now learning to study and reflect alone, to follow out subjects continuously, to determine for themselves what shall engage their minds, and to call to their aid the knowledge, original views, and reasonings of men of all countries and ages; and the results must be, a deliberateness and independence of judgement, and a thoroughness and extent of information, unknown in former times. The diffusion of these silent teachers, books, through the whole community, is to work greater effects than artillery, machinery, and legislation. Its peaceful agency is to supersede stormy revolutions. The culture, which is to spread, whilst an unspeakable good to the individual, is also to become the stability of nations.--W. E. CHANNING. *Self-Culture*.

THE DISTRACTION OF CHOICE

Under our present enormous accumulation of books, I do affirm, that a miserable distraction of choice (which is the germ of such a madness) must be very generally incident to the times; that the symptoms of it are, in fact, very prevalent; and that one of the chief symptoms is an enormous 'gluttonism' for books, and for adding language to language; and in this way it is that literature becomes much more a source of torment than of pleasure. Nay, I will go further, and will say that of many, who escape this disease, some owe their privilege simply to the narrowness of their minds and the contracted range of their sympathies with literature--which enlarged, they would soon lose it! others, again, owe it to their situation; as, for instance, in a country town, where, books being few, a man can use up all his materials, his appetite is unpalled--and he is grateful for the loan of a MS., &c.: but bring him up to London--show him the wagon-loads of unused stores--which he is at liberty to work up--tell him that these even are but a trifle, perhaps, to what he may find in the libraries of Paris, Dresden, Milan, &c.--of religious houses--of English noblemen, &c.; and this same man, who came up to London blithe and happy, will leave it pale and sad. You have ruined his peace of mind: a subject which he fancied himself capable of exhausting, he finds to be a labour for centuries: he has no longer the healthy pleasure of feeling himself master of his materials; he is degraded into their slave.--T. DE QUINCEY. *Letters to a Young Man.*

A LIBRARY OF ONE

Were I to name, out of the times gone by,
The poets dearest to me, I should say,
Pulci for spirits, and a fine, free way;
Chaucer for manners, and close, silent eye;
Milton for classic taste, and harp strung high;
Spenser for luxury, and sweet, sylvan play;
Horace for chatting with, from day to day;
Shakespeare for all, but most, society.

But which take with me, could I take but one?
Shakespeare,--as long as I was unoppressed
With the world's weight, making sad thoughts intenser;
But did I wish, out of the common sun
To lay a wounded heart in leafy rest,
And dream of things far off and healing,--Spenser.

J. H. LEIGH HUNT.

A LIBRARY OF TWELVE

You may get the whole of Sir Thomas Browne's works more easily than the *Hydrotaphia* in a single form.... If I were confined to a score of English books, this I think would be one of them; nay, probably, it would be one if the selection were cut down to twelve. My library, if reduced to those bounds, would consist of Shakespeare, Chaucer, Spenser, and Milton; Lord Clarendon; Jackson, Jeremy Taylor, and South; Isaac Walton, Sidney's *Arcadia*, Fuller's *Church History*, and Sir Thomas Browne; and what a wealthy and well-stored mind would that man have, what an inexhaustible reservoir, what a Bank of England to draw upon for profitable thoughts and delightful associations, who should have fed upon them.--R. SOUTHEY (Letter to G. C. Bedford).

ANCIENT AND MODERN BOOKS

Whoever converses much among the old books will be something hard to please among the new; yet these must have their part, too, in the leisure of an idle man, and have, many of them, their beauties as well as their defaults. Those of story, or relations of matter of fact, have a value from their substance as much as from their form, and the variety of events is seldom without entertainment or instruction, how indifferently soever the tale is told. Other sorts of writings have little of esteem but what they receive from the wit, learning, or genius of the authors, and are seldom met with of any excellency, because they do but trace over the paths that have been beaten by the ancients, or comment, crit- ic, and flourish upon them, and are at best but copies after those originals, unless upon subjects never touched by them, such as are all that relate to the different constitutions of religions, laws, or governments in several countries, with all matters of controversy that arise upon them.--SIR W. TEMPLE. *Ancient and Modern Learning.*

THE BATTLE OF THE BOOKS

Immediately the two main bodies withdrew, under their several ensigns, to the farther parts of the library, and there entered into cabals and consults upon the present emer- gency. The Moderns were in very warm debates upon the choice of their leaders; and nothing less than the fear impending from their enemies could have kept them from mu- tinies upon this occasion. The difference was greatest among the horse, where every private trooper pretended to the chief command, from Tasso and Milton to Dryden and Wither. The light-horse were commanded by Cowley and Despreaux. There came the bowmen under their valiant leaders, Descartes, Gassendi, and Hobbes; whose strength was such that they could shoot their arrows beyond the atmosphere, never to fall down again, but turn, like that of Evander, into meteors; or, like the cannon-ball, into stars. Paracelsus brought a squadron of stinkpot-flingers from the snowy mountains of Rhae- tia. There came a vast body of dragoons, of different nations, under the leading of Harvey, their great aga: part armed with scythes, the weapons of death; part with lances and long knives, all steeped in poison; part shot bullets of a most malignant nature, and used white powder, which infallibly killed without report. There came several bodies of heavy-armed foot, all mercenaries, under the ensigns of Guiccardini, Davila, Polydore, Virgil, Buchanan, Mariana, Camden, and others. The engineers were commanded by Re- giomontanus and Wilkins. The rest was a confused multitude, led by Scotus, Aquinas, and Bellarmine; of mighty bulk and stature, but without either arms, courage, or disci- pline. In the last place came infinite swarms of calones, a disorderly rout led by L'Estrange; rogues and ragamuffins, that follow the camp for nothing but the plunder, all without coats to cover them.

The Army of the Ancients was much fewer in number; Homer led the horse, and Pindar the light-horse; Euclid was chief engineer; Plato and Aristotle commanded the bowmen;

Herodotus and Livy the foot; Hippocrates, the dragoons; the allies, led by Vossius and Temple, brought up the rear.

All things violently tending to a decisive battle, Fame, who much frequented, and had a large apartment assigned her in the regal library, fled up straight to Jupiter, to whom she delivered a faithful account of all that passed between the two parties below; for among the Gods she always tells truth. Jove, in great concern, convokes a council in the Milky Way. The senate assembled, he declares the occasion of convening them; a bloody battle just impendent between two mighty armies of ancient and modern creatures, called books, wherein the celestial interest was but too deeply concerned. Momus, the patron of the Moderns, made an excellent speech in their favour, which was answered by Pallas, the protectress of the Ancients. The assembly was divided in their affections; when Jupiter commanded the Book of Fate to be laid before him. Immediately were brought by Mercury three large volumes in folio, containing memoirs of all things past, present, and to come. The clasps were of silver double gilt, the covers of celestial turkey leather, and the paper such as here on earth might almost pass for vellum. Jupiter, having silently read the decree, would communicate the import to none, but presently shut up the book....

Meanwhile Momus, fearing the worst, and calling to mind an ancient prophecy which bore no very good face to his children the Moderns, bent his flight to the region of a malignant deity called Criticism. She dwelt on the top of a snowy mountain in Nova Zembla; there Momus found her extended in her den, upon the spoils of numberless volumes, half devoured. At her right hand sat Ignorance, her father and husband, blind with age; at her left, Pride, her mother, dressing her up in the scraps of paper herself had torn. There was Opinion, her sister, light of foot, hoodwinked, and headstrong, yet giddy and perpetually turning. About her played her children, Noise and Impudence, Dullness and Vanity, Positiveness, Pedantry, and Ill-manners.... 'Goddess,' said Momus, 'can you sit idly here while our devout worshippers, the Moderns, are this minute entering into a cruel battle, and perhaps now lying under the swords of their enemies? Who then hereafter will ever sacrifice or build altars to our divinities? Haste, therefore, to the British Isle, and, if possible, prevent their destruction; while I make factions among the gods, and gain them over to our party.' ...

The goddess and her train, having mounted the chariot, which was drawn by tame geese, flew over infinite regions, shedding her influence in due places, till at length she arrived at her beloved island of Britain; but in hovering over its metropolis, what blessings did she not let fall upon her seminaries of Gresham and Covent Garden! And now she reached the fatal plain of St. James's library, at what time the two armies were upon the point to engage; where, entering with all her caravan unseen, and landing upon a case of shelves, now desert, but once inhabited by a colony of virtuosos, she stayed awhile to observe the posture of both armies.--J. SWIFT. *The Battle of the Books.*

OLD AUTHORS TO READ

Alonso of Aragon was wont to say, in commendation of Age, that Age appeared to be best in four things; Old wood best to burn, old wine to drink, old friends to trust, and old authors to read.--F. BACON, LORD VERULAM. *Apophthegmes.*

CLASSICUS

Classicus is a man of learning, and well versed in all the best authors of antiquity. He has read them so much that he has entered into their spirit, and can very ingeniously imitate the manner of any of them. All their thoughts are his thoughts, and he can express himself in their language. He is so great a friend to this improvement of the mind that if he lights on a young scholar he never fails to advise him concerning his studies.

Classicus tells his young man he must not think that he has done enough when he has only learnt languages; but that he must be daily conversant with the best authors, read them again and again, catch their spirit by living with them, and that there is no other way of becoming like them, or of making himself a man of taste and judgement.

How wise might Classicus have been and how much good might he have done in the world, if he had but thought as justly of devotion as he does of learning!... The two testaments would not have had so much as a place amongst his books, but that they are both to be had in Greek.

Classicus thinks that he sufficiently shows his regard for the holy scriptures when he tells you that he has no other book of piety besides them.--W. LAW. *A serious Call to a devout and holy Life.*

THE DEAD ALONE CANONIZED

That critic must indeed be bold
Who pits new authors against old.
Only the ancient coin is prized,
The dead alone are canonized:
What was even Shakespeare until then?
A poet scarce compared with Ben:
And Milton in the streets no taller
Than sparkling easy-ambling Waller.
Waller now walks with rhyming crowds,
While Milton sits above the clouds,
Above the stars, his fixed abode,
And points to men their way to God.

W. S. LANDOR.

THE CLASSICS

Will nothing but from Greece or Rome
Please me? is nothing good at home?
Yes; better; but I look in vain

For a Molière or La Fontaine.
Swift in his humour was as strong,
But there was gall upon his tongue.
Bitters and acids may excite,
Yet satisfy not appetite.

W. S. LANDOR.

THE MOONS OF LITERATURE

SIR, ... we must read what the world reads at the moment. It has been maintained that this superfoetation, this teeming of the press in modern times, is prejudicial to good literature, because it obliges us to read so much of what is of inferior value, in order to be in the fashion; so that better works are neglected for want of time, because a man will have more gratification of his vanity in conversation, from having read modern books than from having read the best books of antiquity. But it must be considered, that we have now more knowledge generally diffused; all our ladies read now, which is a great extension. Modern writers are the moons of literature; they shine with reflected light, with light borrowed from the ancients. Greece appears to me to be the fountain of knowledge; Rome of elegance.--S. JOHNSON. (Boswell's *Life*.)

THE READING OF NEW BOOKS

From Lien Chi Altangi to Fum Hoam, First President of the
Ceremonial Academy at Pekin, in China

There are numbers in this city who live by writing new books; and yet there are thousands of volumes in every large library unread and forgotten. This, upon my arrival, was one of those contradictions which I was unable to account for. Is it possible, said I, that there should be any demand for new books before those already published are read? Can there be so many employed in producing a commodity with which the market is overstocked; and with goods also better than any of modern manufacture!

What at first view appeared an inconsistency is a proof at once of this people's wisdom and refinement. Even allowing the works of their ancestors better written than theirs, yet those of the moderns acquire a real value, by being marked with the impression of the times. Antiquity has been in the possession of others; the present is our own: let us first therefore learn to know what belongs to ourselves, and then, if we have leisure, cast our reflections back to the reign of Shonsu, who governed twenty thousand years before the creation of the moon.

The volumes of antiquity, like medals, may very well serve to amuse the curious; but the works of the moderns, like the current coin of a kingdom, are much better for immediate use; the former are often prized above their intrinsic value, and kept with care, the latter seldom pass for more than they are worth, and are often subject to the merciless hands of sweating critics and clipping compilers: the works of antiquity were ever praised, those of the moderns read; the treasures of our ancestors have our esteem, and we boast the passion; those of contemporary genius engage our heart, although we blush to own it. The visits we pay the former resemble those we pay the great; the ceremony is troublesome, and yet such as we would not choose to forgo; our acquaintance with modern books is like sitting with a friend; our pride is not flattered in the interview, but it gives more internal satisfaction....

In England, where there are as many new books published as in all the rest of Europe together, a spirit of freedom and reason reigns among the people; they have been often known to act like fools, they are generally found to think like men.--O. GOLDSMITH. *Letters from a Citizen of the World.*

THE CLASSICS ALWAYS MODERN

In science read, by preference, the newest works; in literature, the oldest. The classic literature is always modern. New books revive and re-decorate old ideas; old books suggest and invigorate new ideas.--E. G. E. L. BULWER-LYTTON, LORD LYTTON. *Caxtoniana.*

ON READING OLD BOOKS

I hate to read new books. There are twenty or thirty volumes that I have read over and over again, and these are the only ones that I have any desire ever to read at all. It was a long time before I could bring myself to sit down to the *Tales of My Landlord*, but now that author's works have made a considerable addition to my scanty library.... Women judge of books as they do of fashions or complexions, which are admired only 'in their newest gloss'. That is not my way. I am not one of those who trouble the circulating libraries much, or pester the booksellers for mail-coach copies of standard periodical publications. I cannot say that I am greatly addicted to black-letter, but I profess myself well versed in the marble bindings of Andrew Millar, in the middle of the last century; nor does my taste revolt at Thurloe's *State Papers*, in russia leather; or an ample impression of Sir William Temple's *Essays*, with a portrait after Sir Godfrey Kneller in front. I do not think altogether the worse of a book for having survived the author a generation or two. I have more confidence in the dead than the living.... When I take up a work that I have read before (the oftener the better), I know what I have to expect. The satisfaction is not lessened by being anticipated. When the entertainment is altogether new, I sit down to it as I should to a strange dish--turn and pick out a bit here and there, and am in doubt what to think of the composition. There is a want of confidence and security to second appetite. New-fangled books are also like made-dishes in this respect, that they are generally little else than hashes and *rifaccimentos* of what has been served up entire and in a more natural state at other times. Besides, in thus turning to a well-known author, there is not only an assurance that my time will not be thrown away, or my palate nauseated with the most insipid or vilest trash, but I shake hands with, and look an old, tried, and valued friend in the face, compare notes, and chat the hours away. It is true, we form dear friendships with such ideal guests--dearer, alas! and more lasting, than those with our most intimate acquaintance. In reading a book which is an old favourite with me (say the first novel I ever read) I not only have the pleasure of imagination and of a critical relish of the work, but the pleasures of memory added to it. It recalls the same feelings and associations which I had in first reading it, and which I can never have again in any other way. Standard productions of this kind are links in the chain of our conscious being. They bind together the different scattered divisions of our personal identity. They are landmarks and guides in our journey through life. They are pegs and loops on which we can hang up, or from which we can take down, at pleasure, the wardrobe of a moral imagination, the relics of our best affections, the tokens and records of our happiest hours. They are 'for thoughts and for remembrance'! They are like Fortunatus's Wishing Cap--they give us the best riches--those of Fancy; and transport us, not over half the globe, but (which is better) over half our lives, at a word's notice!

My father Shandy solaced himself with Bruscambille. Give me for this purpose a volume of *Peregrine Pickle* or *Tom Jones*. Open either of them anywhere--at the memoirs of Lady Vane, or the adventures at the masquerade with Lady Bellaston, or the disputes between Thwackum and Square, or the escape of Molly Seagrim, or the incident of Sophia and her muff, or the edifying prolixity of her aunt's lecture--and there I find the same delightful, busy, bustling scene as ever, and feel myself the same as when I was first introduced into the midst of it. Nay, sometimes the sight of an odd volume of these good old English authors on a stall, or the name lettered on the back among others on the shelves of a library, answers the purpose, revives the whole train of ideas, and sets 'the puppets dallying'. Twenty years are struck off the list, and I am a child again. A sage philosopher, who was not a very wise man, said, that he should like very well to be young again, if he could take his experience along with him. This ingenious person did not seem to be aware, by the gravity of his remark, that the great advantage of being young is to be without this weight of experience, which he would fain place upon the shoulders of youth, and which never comes too late with years. Oh! what a privilege to be able to let this hump, like Christian's burthen, drop from off one's back, and transport oneself, by the help of a little musty duodecimo, to the time when 'ignorance was bliss', and when we first got a peep at the raree-show of the world, through the glass of fiction--gazing at mankind, as we do at wild beasts in a menagerie, through the bars of their cages--or at curiosities in a museum, that we must not touch! For myself, not only are the old ideas of the contents of the work brought back to my mind in all their vividness, but the old associations of the faces and persons of those I then knew, as they were in their lifetime--the place where I sat to read the volume, the day when I got it, the feeling of the air, the fields, the sky--return, and all my early impressions with them. This is better to me--those places, those times, those persons, and those feelings that come across me as I retrace the story and devour the page, are to me better far than the wet sheets of the last new novel.--W. HAZLITT. *The Plain Speaker.*

ON READING NEW BOOKS

I cannot understand the rage manifested by the greater part of the world for reading new books. If the public had read all those that have gone before, I can conceive how they should not wish to read the same work twice over; but when I consider the countless volumes that lie unopened, unregarded, unread, and unthought of, I cannot enter into the pathetic complaints that I hear made that Sir Walter writes no more--that the press is idle--that Lord Byron is dead. If I have not read a book before, it is, to all intents and purposes, new to me, whether it was printed yesterday or three hundred years ago. If it be urged that it has no modern, passing incidents, and is out of date and old-fashioned, then it is so much the newer; it is farther removed from other works that I have lately read, from the familiar routine of ordinary life, and makes so much more addition to my knowledge. But many people would as soon think of putting on old armour as of taking up a book not published within the last month, or year at the utmost. There is a fashion in reading as well as in dress, which lasts only for the season. One would imagine that books were, like women, the worse for being old; that they have a pleasure in being read for the first time; that they open their leaves more cordially; that the spirit of enjoyment wears out with the spirit of novelty; and that, after a certain age, it is high time to put them on the shelf. This conceit seems to be followed up in practice.... The knowledge which so many other persons have of its contents deadens our curiosity and interest altogether. We set aside the subject as one on which others have made up their minds for us (as if we really could have ideas in their heads), and are quite on the alert for the next new work, teeming hot from the press, which we shall be the first to read, criticize, and pass an opinion on. Oh, delightful! To cut open the leaves, to inhale the fragrance of the scarcely dry paper, to examine the type to see who is the printer (which is some clue to the value that is set upon the work), to launch out into regions of thought and invention never trod till now, and to explore characters that never met a human eye before--this is a luxury worth sacrificing a dinner-party, or a few hours of a spare morning to. Who, indeed, when the work is critical and full of expectation, would venture to dine out, or to face a coterie of blue-stockings in the evening, without having gone through this ordeal, or at least without hastily turning over a few of the first pages, while dressing, to be able to say that the beginning does not promise much, or to tell the name of the heroine?

A new work is something in our power: we mount the bench, and sit in judgement on it; we can damn or recommend it to others at pleasure, can decry or extol it to the skies, and can give an answer to those who have not yet read it, and expect an account of it; and thus show our shrewdness and the independence of our taste before the world have had time to form an opinion. If we cannot write ourselves, we become, by busying ourselves about it, a kind of *accessories after the fact.*--W. HAZLITT. *Sketches and Essays.*

A PREFERENCE FOR GREAT MODELS

By the by, I observe a point in which your taste and mine differ from each other materially. It is about new publications. I read them unwillingly. You abstain from them with difficulty, and as a matter of duty and self-denial. Their novelty has very little attraction for me; and in literature I am fond of confining myself to the best company, which consists chiefly of my old acquaintance, with whom I am desirous of becoming more intimate; and I suspect that nine times out of ten it is more profitable, if not more agreeable, to read an old book over again, than to read a new one for the first time. If I hear of a new poem, for instance, I ask myself first, whether it is superior to Homer, Shakespeare, Ariosto, Virgil, or Racine; and, in the next place, whether I already have all these authors completely at my fingers' ends. And when both questions have been answered in the negative, I infer that it is better (and, to me, it is certainly pleasanter) to give such time as I have to bestow on the reading of poetry to Homer, Ariosto and Co., and so of other things.

Is it not better to try, at least, to elevate and adorn one's mind, by the constant study and contemplation of the great models, than merely to know of one's own knowledge that such a book an't worth reading?--J. W. WARD, EARL OF DUDLEY (Letter to the Bishop of Llandaff).

THE VALUE OF MODERN BOOKS

The great productions of Athenian and Roman genius are indeed still what they were. But though their positive value is unchanged, their relative value, when compared with the whole mass of mental wealth possessed by mankind, has been constantly falling. They were the intellectual all of our ancestors. They are but a part of our treasures. Over what tragedy could Lady Jane Grey have wept, over what comedy could she have smiled, if the ancient dramatists had not been in her library? A modern reader can make shift without *Oedipus* and *Medea*, while he possesses *Othello* and *Hamlet*. If he knows nothing of *Pyrgopolynices* and *Thraso*, he is familiar with *Bobadil*, and *Bessus*, and *Pistol*, and *Parolles*. If he cannot enjoy the delicious irony of Plato, he may find some compensation in that of Pascal. If he is shut out from *Nephelococcygia*, he may take refuge in *Lilliput*.... We believe that the books which have been written in the languages of Western Europe, during the last two hundred and fifty years--translations from the ancient languages of course included,--are of greater value than all the books which at the beginning of that period were extant in the world.--LORD MACAULAY. *Lord Bacon.*

A SORT OF THIRD ESTATE

Each age, it is found, must write its own books; or, rather, each generation for the next succeeding. The books of an older period will not fit this. Yet hence arises a grave mischief. The sacredness which attaches to the act of creation--the act of thought--is transferred to the record. The poet chanting, was felt to be a divine man: henceforth the chant is divine also. The writer was a just and wise spirit: henceforward it is settled, the book is perfect; as love of the hero corrupts into worship of his statue. Instantly, the book becomes noxious: the guide is a tyrant. The sluggish and perverted mind of the multitude, slow to open to the incursions of Reason, having once so opened, having once received this book, stands upon it, and makes an outcry if it is disparaged. Colleges are built on it. Books are written on it by thinkers, not by Man Thinking; by men of talent, that is, who start wrong, who set out from accepted dogmas, not from their own sight of principles. Meek young men grow up in libraries, believing it their duty to accept the views which Cicero, which Locke, which Bacon, have given, forgetful that Cicero, Locke, and Bacon were only young men in libraries when they wrote these books.

Hence, instead of Man Thinking, we have the book-worm. Hence, the book-learned class, who value books as such; not as related to nature and the human constitution, but as making a sort of Third Estate with the world and the soul. Hence, the restorers of readings, the emendators, the bibliomaniacs of all degrees.

Books are the best of things, well used; abused, among the worst.--R. W. EMERSON. *The American Scholar*.

OLD AND NEW BOOKS

Old books, as you well know, are books of the world's youth, and new books are fruits of its age. How many of all these ancient folios round me are like so many old cupels? The gold has passed out of these long ago, but their pores are full of the dross with which it was mingled.--O. W. HOLMES. *The Professor at the Breakfast-Table*.

SECURITY IN OLD BOOKS

What a sense of security in an old book which Time has criticized for us! What a precious feeling of seclusion in having a double wall of centuries between us and the heats and clamours of contemporary literature! How limpid seems the thought, how pure the old wine of scholarship that has been settling for so many generations in those silent crypts and Falernian *amphorae* of the Past! No other writers speak to us with the authority of those whose ordinary speech was that of our translation of the Scriptures; to no modern is that frank unconsciousness possible which was natural to a period when reviews were not; and no later style breathes that country charm characteristic of days ere the metropolis drew all literary activity to itself, and the trampling feet of the multitude had banished the lark and the daisy from the fresh privacies of language. Truly, as compared with the present, these old voices seem to come from the morning fields and not the paved thoroughfares of thought....

There are volumes which have the old age of Plato, rich with gathering experience, meditation, and wisdom, which seem to have sucked colour and ripeness from the genial autumns of all the select intelligences that have steeped them in the sunshine of their love and appreciation;--these quaint freaks of russet tell of Montaigne; these stripes of crimson fire, of Shakespeare; this sober gold, of Sir Thomas Browne; this purpling bloom, of Lamb;--in such fruits we taste the legendary gardens of Alcinoüs and the orchards of Atlas; and there are volumes again which can claim only the inglorious senility of Old Parr or older Jenkins, which have outlived their half-dozen of kings to be the prize of showmen and treasuries of the born-to-be-forgotten trifles of a hundred years ago....

There is to us a sacredness in a volume, however dull; we live over again the author's lonely labours and tremulous hopes; we see him, on his first appearance after parturition, 'as well as could be expected,' a nervous sympathy yet surviving between the late-severed umbilical cord and the wondrous offspring, doubtfully entering the Mermaid, or the Devil Tavern, or the Coffee-house of Will or Button, blushing under the eye of Ben or Dryden or Addison, as if they must needs know him for the author of the *Modest Enquiry into the Present State of Dramatique Poetry*, or of the *Unities briefly considered by Philomusus*, of which they have never heard and never will so much as hear the names; we see the country-gentlemen (sole cause of its surviving to our day) who buy it as a book no gentleman's library can be complete without; we see the spendthrift heir, whose horses and hounds and Pharaonic troops of friends, drowned in a Red Sea of claret, bring it to the hammer, the tall octavo in tree-calf following the ancestral oaks of the park. Such a volume is sacred to us. But it must be the original foundling of the book-stall, the engraved blazon of some extinct baronetcy within its cover, its leaves enshrining memorial-flowers of some passion smothered while the Stuarts were not yet unkinged, suggestive of the trail of laced ruffles, burnt here and there with ashes from the pipe of some dozing poet, its binding worn and weather-stained, that has felt the inquisitive finger, perhaps, of Malone, or thrilled to the touch of Lamb, doubtful between desire and the odd sixpence. When it comes to a question of reprinting we are more choice. The new duodecimo is bald and bare, indeed, compared with its battered prototype that could draw us with a single hair of association.--J. R. LOWELL. *Library of Old Authors.*

TO MY BOOK

It will be looked for, book, when some but see
  Thy title, Epigrams, and named of me,
Thou shouldst be bold, licentious, full of gall,
  Wormwood and sulphur, sharp, and toothed withal,
Become a petulant thing, hurl ink and wit
  As madmen stones; not caring whom they hit.
Deceive their malice, who could wish it so;
  And by thy wiser temper let men know
Thou art not covetous of least self-fame,
  Made from the hazard of another's shame:
Much less with lewd, profane, and beastly phrase,
  To catch the world's loose laughter, or vain gaze.
He that departs with his own honesty
  For vulgar praise, doth it too dearly buy.

BEN JONSON.

HIS PRAYER FOR ABSOLUTION

For those my unbaptizèd rhymes,
Writ in my wild unhallowed times;
For every sentence, clause, and word,
That's not inlaid with thee, my Lord,
Forgive me, God, and blot each line
Out of my book that is not thine.
But if, 'mongst all, thou findst here one
Worthy thy benediction;
That one of all the rest shall be
The glory of my work and me.

R. HERRICK. *Noble Numbers.*

BOOKS THAT DO HURT

In our forefathers' time, when papistry, as a standing pool, covered and overflowed all England, few books were read in our tongue, saving certain books of chivalry, as they said for pastime and pleasure; which, as some say, were made in monasteries by idle monks or wanton canons. As one for example, 'Morte Arthur', the whole pleasure of which book standeth in two special points, in open manslaughter and bold bawdry.... This is good stuff for wise men to laugh at, or honest men to take pleasure at: yet I know, when God's Bible was banished the court, and 'Morte Arthur' received into the prince's chamber.

What toys the daily reading of such a book may work in the will of a young gentleman, or a young maid, that liveth wealthily or idly, wise men can judge, and honest men do pity. And yet ten 'Morte Arthurs' do not the tenth part so much harm, as one of these books made in Italy and translated in England.... Suffer these books to be read, and they shall soon displace all books of godly learning.--R. ASCHAM. *The Schoolmaster.*

BOOKS AND THIEVES

A good book steals the mind from vain pretences,
From wicked cogitations and offences;
It makes us know the world's deceiving pleasures,
And set our hearts on never-ending treasures.
So when thieves steal our cattle, coin, or ware,
It makes us see how mutable they are:
Puts us in mind that we should put our trust
Where felon cannot steal or canker rust.
Bad books through eyes and ears do break and enter,
And take possession of the heart's frail centre,
Infecting all the little kingdom man
With all the poisonous mischief that they can,
Till they have robbed and ransacked him of all
Those things which men may justly goodness call;
Rob him of virtue and of heavenly grace,
And leave him beggared in a wretched state.
So of our earthly goods, thieves steal the best,
And richest jewels, and leave us the rest.
Men know not thieves from true men by their looks,
Nor by their outsides no man can know books.
Both are to be suspected, all can tell,
And wise men, ere they trust, will try them well:
Some books not worth the reading for their fruits,
Some thieves not worth the hanging, for their suits.
And as with industry, and art, and skill
One thief doth daily rob another still,

So one book from another, in this age,
Steals many a line, a sentence, or a page.
And as the veriest thief may have some friend
So the worst books some knave will still defend.

*   *   *   *   *

Still books and thieves in one conceit do join,
For, if you mark them, they are all for coin.

> J. TAYLOR. *An Arrant Thief.*

MOUNTEBANK AUTHORS

They [the Stationers] have so pestered their printing-houses and shops with fruitless volumes that the ancient and renowned authors are almost buried among them as forgotten; and that they have so much work to prefer their termly pamphlets, which they provide to take up the people's money and time, that there is neither of them left to bestow on a profitable book: so they who desire knowledge are still kept ignorant; their ignorance increaseth their affection to vain toys; their affection makes the stationer to increase his provision of such stuff, and at last you shall see nothing to be sold amongst us but Curranto's *Bevis of Southampton* or such trumpery. The Arts are already almost lost among the writings of mountebank authors. For if any one among us would study Physic, the Mathematics, Poetry, or any of the liberal sciences, they have in their warehouses so many volumes of quack-salving receipts; of false propositions; and of inartificial rhymings (of which last sort they have some of mine there, God forgive me!) that unless we be directed by some artist, we shall spend half our age before we can find those authors which are worth our readings. For what need the stationer be at the charge of printing the labours of him that is master of his art, and will require that respect which his pain deserveth, seeing he can hire for a matter of forty shillings some needy ignoramus to scribble upon the same subject, and by a large promising title, make it as vendible for an impression or two, as though it had the quintessence of all art?--G. WITHER. *The Scholler's Purgatory.*

PRINTERS GAIN BY BAD BOOKS

Learning hath gained most by those books by which the printers have lost. Arius Montanus, in printing the Hebrew Bible, commonly called the Bible of the king of Spain, much wasted himself, and was accused in the court of Rome for his good deed, and being cited thither, *Pro tantorum laborum praemio vix veniam impetravit.* Likewise Christopher Plantin, by printing of his curious interlineary Bible in Antwerp, through the unseasonable exactions of the king's officers, sunk and almost ruined his estate. And our worthy English knight, who set forth the golden-mouthed father in a silver print, was a loser by it.

Whereas foolish pamphlets prove most beneficial to the printers. When a French printer complained that he was utterly undone by printing a solid serious book of Rabelais concerning physic, Rabelais, to make him recompense, made that his jesting scurrilous work, which repaired the printer's loss with advantage. Such books the world swarms too much with. When one had set out a witless pamphlet, writing *finis* at the end thereof, another wittily wrote beneath it:

> ----*Nay there thou liest, my friend,*
> *In writing foolish books there is no end.*

And surely such scurrilous scandalous papers do more than conceivable mischief. First, their lusciousness puts many palates out of taste, that they can never after relish any solid and wholesome writers; secondly, they cast dirt on the faces of many innocent persons, which dried on by continuance of time can never after be washed off; thirdly, the pamphlets of this age may pass for records with the next, because publicly uncontrolled, and what we laugh at, our children may believe: fourthly, grant the things true they jeer at, yet this music is unlawful in any Christian church, to play upon the sins and miseries of others, the fitter object of the elegies than the satires of all truly religious.--T. FULLER. *The Holy State and the Profane State.*

THE EVIL THAT MEN DO

If writings are thus durable, and may pass from age to age throughout the whole course of time, how careful should an author be of committing anything to print that may corrupt posterity, or poison the minds of men with vice and error! Writers of great talents, who employ their parts in propagating immorality, and seasoning vicious sentiments with wit and humour, are to be looked upon as the pests of society and the enemies of mankind: they leave books behind them, as it is said of those who die in distempers which breed an ill will towards their own species, to scatter infection and destroy their posterity. They act the counterparts of a Confucius or a Socrates; and seem to have been sent into the world to deprave human nature, and sink it into the condition of brutality.--J. ADDISON. *Spectator*, 166.

He who has published an injurious book, sins, as it were, in his very grave; corrupts others while he is rotting himself.--R. SOUTH.

BOOKS BAD AND GOOD

A mind unnerved, or indisposed to bear
The weight of subjects worthiest of her care,
Whatever hopes a change of scene inspires,
Must change her nature, or in vain retires.
An idler is a watch that wants both hands,
As useless if it goes as when it stands,
Books therefore, not the scandal of the shelves,
In which lewd sensualists print out themselves;
Nor those in which the stage gives vice a blow,

With what success let modern manners show;
Nor his who, for the bane of thousands born,
Built God a church, and laughed His word to scorn,
Skilful alike to seem devout and just,
And stab religion with a sly side-thrust;
Nor those of learned philologists, who chase
A panting syllable through time and space,
Start it at home, and hunt it in the dark,
To Gaul, to Greece, and into Noah's ark;
But such as learning without false pretence,
The friend of truth, the associate of sound sense,
And such as, in the zeal of good design,
Strong judgement labouring in the scripture mine,
All such as manly and great souls produce,
Worthy to live, and of eternal use:
Behold in these what leisure hours demand,
Amusement and true knowledge hand in hand.
Luxury gives the mind a childish cast,
And while she polishes, perverts the taste;
Habits of close attention, thinking heads,
Become more rare as dissipation spreads,
Till authors hear at length, one gen'ral cry,
Tickle and entertain us, or we die.
The loud demand, from year to year the same,
Beggars invention and makes fancy lame,
Till farce itself, most mournfully jejune,
Calls for the kind assistance of a tune;
And novels (witness every month's review)
Belie their name and offer nothing new.
The mind, relaxing into needful sport,
Should turn to writers of an abler sort,
Whose wit well managed, and whose classic style,
Give truth a lustre, and make wisdom smile.
Friends (for I cannot stint, as some have done,
Too rigid in my view, that name to one;
Though one, I grant it, in the generous breast,
Will stand advanced a step above the rest:
Flowers by that name promiscuously we call,
But one, the rose, the regent of them all)--
Friends, not adopted with a school-boy's haste,
But chosen with a nice discerning taste,
Well-born, well-disciplined, who, placed apart
From vulgar minds, have honour much at heart,
And, though the world may think the ingredients odd,
The love of virtue, and the fear of God!
Such friends prevent what else would soon succeed,
A temper rustic as the life we lead,
And keep the polish of the manners clean,

As their's who bustle in the busiest scene;
For solitude, however some may rave,
Seeming a sanctuary, proves a grave,
A sepulchre in which the living lie,
Where all good qualities grow sick and die.

W. COWPER, *Retirement.*

ON CERTAIN BOOKS

Faith and fixed hope these pages may peruse,
And still be faith and hope; but, O ye winds!
Blow them far off from all unstable minds,
And foolish grasping hands of youth! Ye dews
Of heaven! be pleased to rot them where they fall,
Lest loitering boys their fancies should abuse,
And they get harm by chance, that cannot choose;
So be they stained and sodden, each and all!
And if, perforce, on dry and gusty days,
Upon the breeze some truant leaf should rise,
Brittle with many weathers, to the skies,
Or flit and dodge about the public ways--
Man's choral shout, or organ's peal of praise
Shall shake it into dust, like older lies.

C. TENNYSON TURNER.

'TO THE PURE ALL THINGS ARE PURE'

'To the pure all things are pure'; not only meats and drinks, but all kind of knowledge, whether of good or evil; the knowledge cannot defile, nor consequently the books, if the will and conscience be not defiled. For books are as meats and viands are, some of good, some of evil substance; and yet God, in that unapocryphal vision, said without exception, 'Rise, Peter, kill and eat'; leaving the choice to each man's discretion. Wholesome meats to a vitiated stomach differ little or nothing from unwholesome; and best books to a naughty mind are not unapplicable to occasions of evil. Bad meats will scarce breed good nourishment in the healthiest concoction; but herein the difference is of bad books, that they to a discreet and judicious reader serve in many respects to discover, to confute, to forewarn, and to illustrate.... If it be true that a wise man, like a good refiner, can gather gold out of the drossiest volume, and that a fool will be a fool with the best book, yea, or without book, there is no reason that we should deprive a wise man of any advantage to his wisdom, while we seek to restrain from a fool that which being restrained will be no hindrance to his folly.--J. MILTON. *Areopagitica.*

LIBERTY AND BAD BOOKS

The men who died to buy us liberty knew that it was better to let in a thousand bad books than shut out one good one. We cannot, then, silence evil books, but we can turn away our eyes from them; we can take care that what we read, and what we let others read, should be good and wholesome.--C. KINGSLEY. *Village Sermons: On Books.*

BAD BOOKS AND DEBAUCHED MINDS

Books will perhaps be found, in a less degree than is commonly imagined, the corrupters of the morals of mankind. They form an effective subsidiary to events and the contagion of vicious society: but, taken by themselves, they rarely produce vice and profligacy where virtue existed before. Everything depends upon the spirit in which they are read. He that would extract poison from them, must for the most part come to them with a mind already debauched. The power of books in generating virtue is probably much greater than in generating vice.--W. GODWIN. *The Inquirer: Of Choice in Reading.*

VIRGINIBUS PUERISQUE

To read my book, the virgin shy
May blush, while Brutus standeth by:
But when he's gone, read through what's writ,
And never stain a cheek for it.

R. HERRICK. *Hesperides.*

A WHIMSICAL SURPRISE

I should not care to be caught in the serious avenues of some cathedral alone, and reading *Candide.*

I do not remember a more whimsical surprise than having been once detected--by a familiar damsel--reclined at my ease upon the grass, on Primrose Hill (her Cythera), reading--*Pamela.* There was nothing in the book to make a man seriously ashamed at the exposure; but as she seated herself down by me, and seemed determined to read in company, I could have wished it had been--any other book. We read on very sociably for a few pages; and, not finding the author much to her taste, she got up, and--went away. Gentle casuist, I leave it to thee to conjecture, whether the blush (for there was one between us) was the property of the nymph or the swain in this dilemma. From me you shall never get the secret.--C. LAMB. *Detached Thoughts on Books and Reading.*

ROMANCES ARE PERNICIOUS

Make careful choice of the books which you read. Let the Holy Scriptures ever have the pre-eminence, and next them, the solid, lively, heavenly treatises which best expound and apply the Scriptures: and next those, the credible histories, especially of the Church, and tractates upon inferior sciences and arts: but take heed of the poison of the writings of false teachers, which would corrupt your understandings: and of vain romances, play-books, and false stories, which may bewitch your fantasies and corrupt your hearts.

To a very judicious able reader, who is fit to censure all he reads, there is no great danger in the reading of the Books of any seducers: it doth but show him how little and thin a cloak is used to cover a bad cause. But alas, young soldiers, not used to such wars, are startled at a very sophism, or at a terrible threatening of damnation to dissenters (which every censorious sect can use) or at every confident triumphant boast, or at everything that hath a fair pretence of truth or godliness.... Meddle not therefore with poison, till you better know how to use it, and may do it with less danger; as long as you have no need.

As for play-books, and romances, and idle tales, I have already showed, in my *Book of Self-denial*, how pernicious they are, especially to youth, and to frothy, empty, idle wits, that know not *what a man is*, nor what he hath to do in the world. They are powerful baits of the Devil, to keep more necessary things out of their minds, and better books out of their hands, and to poison the mind so much the more dangerously, as they are read with more delight and pleasure.--R. BAXTER. *Christian Directory*.

WHETHER 'TIS LAWFUL TO READ ROMANCES

Though we think then that the reading these Books may be lawful, and have some Convenience too, as to forming the Minds of Persons of Quality; yet we think 'em not all convenient for the Vulgar, because they give 'em extravagant Ideas of Practice, and before they have Judgement to bias their Fancies, and generally make 'em think themselves some King or Queen or other:--One Fool must be Mazares, t'other Artamen; and so for the Women, no less than Queens or Empresses will serve 'em, the Inconveniences of which are afterwards oftentimes sooner observed than remedied. Add to this, the softening of the Mind by Love, which are the greatest subject of these sort of Books, and the fooling away so many Hours and Days and Years, which might be much better employed, and which must be repented of: And upon the whole, we think Young People would do better, either not to read 'em at all, or to use 'em more sparingly than they generally do, when once they set about 'em.--From the *Athenian Mercury* (1691-7).

THE DANGER OF POETS AND ROMANCES

It is impossible for me, by any words that I can use, to express, to the extent of my thoughts, the danger of suffering young people to form their opinions from the writings of poets and romances. Nine times out of ten, the morality they teach is bad, and must have a bad tendency. Their wit is employed to *ridicule virtue*, as you will almost always find, if you examine the matter to the bottom. The world owes a very large part of its sufferings to tyrants; but what tyrant was there amongst the ancients, whom the poets did not place *amongst the gods*? Can you open an English poet without, in some part or other of his works, finding the grossest flatteries of royal and noble persons? How are young people not to think that the praises bestowed on these persons are just? Dryden, Parnell, Gay, Thomson, in short, what poet have we had, or have we, Pope only excepted, who was not, or is not, a pensioner, or a sinecure placeman, or the wretched dependant of some part of the Aristocracy? Of the extent of the power of writers in producing mischief to a nation, we have two most striking instances in the cases of Dr. Johnson and Burke.... It is, therefore, the duty of every father, when he puts a book into the hands of his son or daughter, to give the reader a true account of *who* and *what* the writer of the book was, or is.--W. COBBETT. *Advice to Young Men and (incidentally) to Young Women in the Middle and Higher Ranks of Life.*

A DAUGHTER'S FAVOURITE NOVELS

I could make neither head nor tail of it; it was neither fish, flesh, nor good red herring: it was all about my Lord, and Sir Harry, and the Captain.... The people talk such wild gibberish as no folks in their sober senses ever did talk; and the things that happen to them are not like the things that ever happen to me or any of my acquaintance. They are at home one minute, and beyond the sea the next; beggars to-day, and lords to-morrow; waiting-maids in the morning, and duchesses at night.... One would think every man in these books had the bank of England in his escritoire.... In these books (except here and there one, whom they make worse than Satan himself), every man and woman's child of them, are all wise, and witty, and generous, and rich, and handsome, and genteel, and all to the last degree. Nobody is middling, or good in one thing and bad in another, like my live acquaintance; but it is all up to the skies, or down to the dirt. I had rather read *Tom Hickathrift*, or *Jack the Giant Killer*, a thousand times.--HANNAH MORE. *The Two Wealthy Farmers.*

'ONLY A NOVEL'

'What are you reading, Miss----?' 'Oh! it's only a novel!' replies the young lady; while she lays down her book with affected indifference, or momentary shame. 'It is only *Cecilia*, or *Camilla*, or *Belinda*'; or, in short, only some work in which the greatest powers of the mind are displayed; in which the most thorough knowledge of human nature, the happiest delineation of its varieties, the liveliest effusions of wit or humour, are conveyed to the world in the best chosen language.--JANE AUSTEN. *Northanger Abbey.*

NOVELS AS ENGINES OF CIVILIZATION

The listlessness and want of sympathy with which most of the works written expressly for circulation among the labouring classes are read by them, if read at all, arises mainly from this--that the story told, or the lively or friendly style assumed, is *manifestly* and *palpably* only a cloak for the instruction intended to be conveyed--a sort of gilding of what they cannot well help fancying must be a pill, when they see so much and such obvious pains taken to wrap it up.... You will find that in the higher and better class of works of fiction and imagination duly circulated, you possess all that you require to strike your grappling-iron into their souls, and chain them, willing followers, to the car of civilization.... The novel, in its best form, I regard as one of the most powerful engines of civilization ever invented.--SIR J. HERSCHEL. *Address to the Subscribers to the Windsor Public Library.*

A NOVEL OF HIGH LIFE

Lord Harry has written a novel,
  A story of elegant life;
No stuff about love in a hovel,
  No sketch of a commoner's wife:
No trash, such as pathos and passion,
  Fine feelings, expression, and wit;
But all about people of fashion,
  Come look at his caps--how they fit!

O Radcliffe! thou once wert the charmer
  Of girls who sat reading all night;
Thy heroes were striplings in armour,
  Thy heroines damsels in white.
But past are thy terrible touches,
  Our lips in derision we curl,
Unless we are told how a Duchess
  Conversed with her cousin the Earl.

We now have each dialogue quite full
  Of titles--'I give you my word,
My lady, you're looking delightful';
  'O dear, do you think so, my lord!'
'You've heard of the marquis's marriage,
  The bride with her jewels new set,
Four horses, new travelling carriage,
  And *déjeuner à la fourchette?*'

Haut Ton finds her privacy broken,
  We trace all her ins and her outs;
The very small talk that is spoken
  By very great people at routs.
At Tenby Miss Jinks asks the loan of
  The book from the innkeeper's wife,
And reads till she dreams she is one of
  The leaders of elegant life.

        T. H. BAYLY.

LADY CONSTANCE ... guanoed her mind by reading French novels.--B. DISRAELI, EARL OF BEACONSFIELD. *Tancred.*

NOVELS ARE SWEETS

Novels are sweets. All people with healthy literary appetites love them--almost all women;--a vast number of clever, hard-headed men. Why, one of the most learned physicians in England said to me only yesterday, 'I have just read *So-and-So* for the second time' (naming one of Jones's exquisite fictions). Judges, bishops, chancellors, mathematicians, are notorious novel-readers; as well as young boys and sweet girls, and their kind, tender mothers.--W. M. THACKERAY. *Roundabout Papers: On a Lazy Idle Boy.*

EVERY MAN HIS DUE

As a good housewife out of divers fleeces weaves one piece of cloth, a bee gathers wax and honey out of many flowers, and makes a new bundle of all,

Floriferis ut apes in saltibus omnia libant,

I have laboriously collected this cento out of various authors, and that *sine injuria*: I have wronged no authors, but given every man his own; which Hierom so much commends in Nepotian; he stole not whole verses, pages, tracts, as some do nowadays, concealing their authors' names; but still said this was Cyprian's, that Lactantius, that Hilarius, so said Minutius Felix, so Victorinus, thus far Arnobius: I cite and quote mine authors (which, howsoever some illiterate scribblers account pedantical, as a cloak of ignorance, and opposite to their affected fine style, I must and will use) *sumpsi, non surripui*; and what Varro, lib. 6 de re rust., speaks of bees, *minime maleficae, nullius opus vellicantes faciunt deterius*, I can say of myself. Whom have I injured? The matter is theirs most part and yet mine: *apparet unde sumptum sit* (which Seneca approves); *aliud tamen, quam unde sumptum sit, apparet*; which nature doth with the aliment of our bodies, incorporate, digest, assimilate, I do *concoquere quod hausi*, dispose of what I take: I make them pay tribute, to set out this my Macaronican: the method only is mine own. I must usurp that of *Wecker e Ter. nihil dictum quod non dictum prius: methodus sola artificem ostendit*: we can say nothing but what hath been said, the composition and method is ours only, and shows a scholar. Oribasius, Aëtius, Avicenna, have all out of Galen, but to their own method, *diverso stylo, non diversa fide*. Our poets steal from Homer; he spews, saith Aelian, they lick it up. Divines use Austin's words *verbatim* still, and our story-dressers do as much; he that comes last is commonly best,

--donec quid grandius aetas
Postera, sorsque ferat melior.

R. BURTON. *The Anatomy of Melancholy.*

PLAGIARIE

He [King Charles I, in his *Eikon Basilike*] borrows David's Psalmes, as he charges the Assembly of Divines in his twentieth Discourse, *To have set forth old Catechisms and confessions of faith new drest.* Had he borrowed David's heart, it had been much the holier theft. For such kind of borrowing as this, if it be not bettered by the borrower, among good Authors is accounted Plagiarie. However, this was more tolerable than Pamela's prayer, stolen out of Sir Philip.--J. MILTON. *Eikonoklastes.*

TRANSPLANTATION

I number not my borrowings, but I weigh them. And if I would have made their number to prevail, I would have had twice as many. They are all, or almost all, of so famous and ancient names, that methinks they sufficiently name themselves without me. If in reasons, comparisons, and arguments, I transplant any into my soil, or confound them with mine own, I purposely conceal the author, thereby to bridle the rashness of these hasty censures that are so headlong cast upon all manner of compositions, namely, young writings of men yet living.... I will have them to give Plutarch a bob upon mine own lips, and vex themselves in wronging Seneca in me.--MONTAIGNE.

BOOK-MAKERS AND PLAGIARISTS

Some that turn over all books, and are equally searching in all papers; that write out of what they presently find or meet, without choice; by which means it happens that what they have discredited and impugned in one work, they have before or after extolled the same in another. Such are all the Essayists, even their master Montaigne. These in all they write confess still what books they have read last, and therein their own folly so much that they bring it to the stake raw and undigested; not that the place did need it neither, but that they thought themselves furnished and would vent it.

Some again, who, after they have got authority, or, which is less, opinion, by their writings, to have read much, dare presently to feign whole books and authors, and lie safely. For what never was will not easily be found, not by the most curious.

And some, by a cunning protestation against all reading, and false vendition of their own naturals, think to divert the sagacity of their readers from themselves, and cool the scent of their fox-like thefts, when yet they are so rank as a man may find whole pages together usurped from one author.--BEN JONSON. *Timber.*

A LEARNED PLAGIARY

The greatest man of the last age, Ben Jonson, was willing to give place to the classics in all things: he was not only a professed imitator of Horace, but a learned plagiary of all the others; you track him everywhere in their snow. If Horace, Lucan, Petronius Arbiter, Seneca, and Juvenal had their own from him, there are few serious thoughts which are new in him.... But he has done his robberies so openly, that one may see he fears not to be taxed by any law. He invades authors like a monarch; and what would be theft in other poets, is only victory in him.--J. DRYDEN. *Essay of Dramatic Poesy.*

Steal! to be sure they will, and, egad! serve your best thoughts as gipsies do stolen children--disfigure them to make them pass for their own.--R. B. SHERIDAN. *The Critic.*

HIDDEN TREASURE

Writers ... are apter to be beholding to books than to men, not only as the first are more in their possession, being more constant companions than dearest friends, but because they commonly make such use of treasure found in books as of other treasure belonging to the dead and hidden under ground; for they dispose of both with great secrecy, defacing the shape or images of the one as much as of the other, through fear of having the original of their stealth or abundance discovered. And the next cause why writers are more in libraries than in company is that books are easily opened, and learned men are usually shut up by a froward or envious humour of retention, or else unfold themselves so as we may read more of their weakness and vanity than wisdom, imitating the holiday-custom in great cities, where the shops of chandlery and slight wares are familiarly open, but those of solid and staple merchandise are proudly locked up.--SIR W. DAVENANT. *Gondibert.*

LITERARY COOKERY

We have been reading a treatise on the morality of Shakespeare; it is a happy and easy way of filling a book, that the present race of authors have arrived at--that of criticizing the works of some eminent poet: with monstrous extracts and short remarks. It is a species of cookery I begin to grow tired of; they cut up their authors into chops, and by adding a little crumbled bread of their own, and tossing it up a little, they present it as a fresh dish; you are to dine upon the poet;--the critic supplies the garnish; yet has the credit, as well as profit, of the whole entertainment.--HANNAH MORE. *Memoirs.*

THE MANUFACTORY OF BOOKS

To a veteran like myself, who have watched the books of forty seasons, there is nothing so old as a new book. An astonishing sameness and want of individuality pervades modern books. The ideas they contain do not seem to have passed through the mind of the writer. They have not even that originality--the only originality which John Mill in his modesty would claim for himself--'which every thoughtful mind gives to its own mode of conceiving and expressing truths which are common property'--(*Autobiography*). When you are in London step into the reading-room of the British Museum. There is the great manufactory out of which we turn the books of the season. It was so before there was any British Museum. It was so in Chaucer's time--

For out of the old fields, as men saith,
Cometh all this new corn from year to year,
And out of old books in good faith
Cometh all this new science that men lere.

It continued to be so in Cervantes' day. 'There are,' says he in *Don Quixote*, 'men who will make you books and turn them loose in the world with as much dispatch as they would do a dish of fritters.'

It is not, then, any wonder that De Quincy should account it 'one of the misfortunes of life that one must read thousands of books only to discover that one need not have read them'.... And I cannot doubt that Bishop Butler had observed the same phenomenon when he wrote, in 1729: 'The great number of books of amusement which daily come in one's way, have in part occasioned this idle way of considering things. By this means time, even in solitude, is happily got rid of without the pain of attention; neither is any part of it more put to the account of idleness, one can scarce forbear saying is spent with less thought, than great part of that which is spent in reading.'--MARK PATTISON. *Fortnightly Review: Books and Critics.*

HOW VOLUMES SWELL

The muse shall tell
How science dwindles, and how volumes swell;
  How commentators each dark passage shun,
And hold their farthing candles to the sun;
  How tortured texts to speak our sense are made,
And every vice is to the scripture laid.

E. YOUNG. *Love of Fame.*

RECIPE FOR AN ANTHOLOGY

Our modern wits are not to reckon upon the infinity of matter for a constant supply. What remains, therefore, but that our last recourse must be had to large indexes and little compendiums? Quotations must be plentifully gathered, and booked in alphabet; to this end, though authors need to be little consulted, yet critics, and commentators, and lexicons carefully must. But, above all, those judicious collectors of bright parts, and flowers, and *observandas*, are to be nicely dwelt on; by some called the sieves and coulters of learning, though it is left undetermined whether they dealt in pearls or meal, and consequently, whether we are more to value that which passed through, or what stayed behind. By these methods, in a few weeks, there starts up many a writer capable of managing the profoundest and most universal subjects. For what though his head be empty, provided his commonplace book be full? And if you will bate him but the circumstances of method, and style, and grammar, and invention; allow him but the common privileges of transcribing from others, and digressing from himself, as often as he shall see occasion; he will desire no more ingredients towards fitting up a treatise that shall make a very comely figure on a bookseller's shelf; there to be preserved neat and clean for a long eternity, adorned with the heraldry of its title fairly inscribed on a label; never to be thumbed or greased by students, nor bound to everlasting chains of darkness in a library.--J. SWIFT. *A Tale of a Tub.*

His Invention is no more than the finding out of his papers, and his few gleanings there, and his disposition of them is just as the book-binder's, a setting or glueing of them together.--J. EARLE. *Microcosmographie.*

Good God! how many dungboats full of fruitless works do they yearly foist on his Majesty's subjects; how many hundred reams of foolish, profane, and senseless ballads do they quarterly disperse abroad.--G. WITHER (1632).

TO LEIGH HUNT, ON AN OMISSION IN HIS 'FEAST OF THE POETS'

Leigh Hunt! thou stingy man, Leigh Hunt!
May Charon swamp thee in his punt,
For having, in thy list, forgotten
So many poets scarce half rotten,
Who did expect of thee at least
A few cheese-parings from thy *Feast.*
Hast thou no pity on the men
Who suck (as babes their tongues) the pen,
Until it leaves no traces where
It lighted, and seems dipped in air?
At last be generous, Hunt! and prithee
Refresh (and gratis too) in Lethe
Yonder sick Muse, surcharged with poppies
And heavier presentation-copies.
She *must* grow livelier, and the river
More potent in effect than ever.

W. S. LANDOR.

OUR MASTER, MELEAGER

Our master, Meleager, he who framed
  The first Anthology and daintiest,
Mated each minstrel with a flower, and named
  For each the blossom that beseemed him best.
'Twas then as now; garlands were somewhat rare,
  Candidates many: one in doleful strain
Lamented thus, 'This is a sad affair;

How shall I face my publisher again?
Lacking some emblem suitable for me,
  My book's undone; I shall not sell a copy.'
'Take courage, son,' quoth Phoebus, 'there must be
  Somewhere or other certainly a poppy.'

R. GARNETT.

'Tis pleasant, sure, to see one's name in print;
A book's a book, although there's nothing in't.

LORD BYRON.

THAT INVENTION OF THE ENEMY--AN ABRIDGEMENT

All my life long I have delighted in voluminous works; in other words, I have delighted in that sort of detail which permits so intimate a familiarity with the subjects of which it treats.... Even in this world of Beauties, and of Extracts, I do not believe myself quite alone in my love of the elaborate and the minute; and yet I doubt if many people contemplate very long very big books with the sense of coming enjoyment which such a prospect gives me; and few shrink, as I do, with aversion and horror from that invention of the enemy--an Abridgement. I never shall forget the shock I experienced in seeing Bruce, that opprobrium of an unbelieving age, that great and graphic traveller, whose eight or nine goodly volumes took such possession of me, that I named a whole colony of Bantams after his Abyssinian princes and princesses, calling a little golden strutter of a cock after that arch-tyrant the Ras Michael; and a speckled hen, the beauty of the poultry-yard, Ozoro Ester, in honour of the Ras's favourite wife--I never felt greater disgust than at seeing this magnificent work cut down to a thick, dumpy volume, seven inches by five; except, perhaps, when I happened to light upon another pet book--Drinkwater's *Siege of Gibraltar*, where I had first learned to tremble at the grim realities of war, had watched day by day the firing of the red-hot balls, had groped my way through the galleries, and taken refuge in the casemates,--degraded from the fair proportions of a goodly quarto into the thin and meagre pamphlet of a lending library, losing a portion of its lifelike truth with every page that was cut away.--M. R. MITFORD. *Recollections of a Literary Life.*

ORIGINAL EDITIONS

We love, we own, to read the great productions of the human mind as they were written. We have this feeling even about scientific treatises; though we know that the sciences are always in a state of progression, and that the alterations made by a modern editor in an old book on any branch of natural or political philosophy are likely to be improvements. Some errors have been detected by writers of this generation in the speculations of Adam Smith. A short cut has been made to much knowledge at which Sir Isaac Newton arrived through arduous and circuitous paths. Yet we still look with peculiar veneration on the *Wealth of Nations* and on the *Principia*, and should regret to see either of those great works garbled even by the ablest hands. But in works which owe much of their interest to the character and situation of the writers the case is infinitely stronger. What man of taste and feeling can endure *rifacimenti*, harmonies, abridgements, expurgated editions? Who ever reads a stage-copy of a play when he can procure the original? Who ever cut open Mrs. Siddons's *Milton*? Who ever got through ten pages of Mr. Gilpin's translation of John Bunyan's *Pilgrim* into modern English? Who would lose, in the confusion of a *Diatessaron*, the peculiar charm which belongs to the narrative of the disciple whom Jesus loved? The feeling of a reader who has become intimate with any great original work is that which Adam expressed towards his bride:

> 'Should God create another Eve, and I
> Another rib afford, yet loss of thee
> Would never from my heart.'

No substitute, however exquisitely formed, will fill the void left by the original. The second beauty may be equal or superior to the first; but still it is not she.--LORD MACAULAY. *Boswell's Life of Johnson.*

DEDICATIONS

Above all the rest, the gross and palpable flattery whereunto many not unlearned have abased and abused their wits and pens, turning (as Du Bartas saith) Hecuba into Helena, and Faustina into Lucretia, hath most diminished the price and estimation of learning. Neither is the modern dedication of books and writings, as to patrons, to be commended: for that books (such as are worthy the name of books) ought to have no patrons but truth and reason.--F. BACON, LORD VERULAM. *Of the Advancement of Learning.*

PRESENTATION COPIES

I want to read you some new passages from an interleaved copy of my book. You haven't read the printed part yet. I gave you a copy of it, but nobody reads a book that is given to him. Of course not. Nobody but a fool expects him to. He reads a little in it here and there, perhaps, and he cuts all the leaves if he cares enough about the writer, who will be sure to call on him some day, and if he is left alone in his library for five minutes will have hunted every corner of it until he has found the book he sent,--if it is to be found at all, which doesn't always happen, if there's a penal colony anywhere in a garret or closet for typographical offenders and vagrants.--O. W. HOLMES. *The Poet at the Breakfast-Table.*

POETS AND THEIR BIBLIOGRAPHIES

> Old poets fostered under friendlier skies,
>   Old Virgil who would write ten lines, they say,
>   At dawn, and lavish all the golden day

To make them wealthier in his readers' eyes;
And you, old popular Horace, you the wise
  Adviser of the nine-years-pondered lay,
  And you, that wear a wreath of sweeter bay,
Catullus, whose dead songster never dies;
If glancing downward on the kindly sphere
  That once had rolled you round and round the Sun,
  You see your Art still shrined in human shelves,
You should be jubilant that you flourished here
  Before the Love of Letters, overdone,
Had swampt the sacred poets with themselves.

ALFRED, LORD TENNYSON.

MEN IN THEIR NIGHTGOWNS

Writing of Lives is very profitable, both to the memory of the party, and to posterity. They do better lance into secret humours, and present men in their nightgowns, when they are truly themselves. A general may be more perfectly discovered on his pallet, than when he appears in the head of an army.--JOHN HALL. *Horae Vacivae.*

BIOGRAPHY

Oh, that mine enemy had written a book!--and that it were my life; unless indeed it provoked my friend to write another.

It has always appeared to me a strong argument for the non-existence of spirits that these friendly microscopic biographers are not haunted by the ghosts of the unfortunate men whom they persist in holding up to public contempt.--SIR A. HELPS. *Thoughts in the Cloister.*

BIOGRAPHY PREFERRED TO HISTORY

Read French authors. Read Rochefoucauld. The French writers are the finest in the world, for they clear our heads of all ridiculous ideas....

Read no history, nothing but biography, for that is life without theory.--B. DISRAELI, EARL OF BEACONSFIELD. *Contarini Fleming.*

ON READING TRANSLATIONS

The respectable and sometimes excellent translations of Bohn's Library have done for literature what railroads have done for internal intercourse. I do not hesitate to read all the books I have named, and all good books, in translations. What is really best in any book is translatable,--any real insight or broad human sentiment. Nay, I observe that, in our Bible, and other books of lofty moral tone, it seems easy and inevitable to render the rhythm and music of the original into phrases of equal melody. The Italians have a fling at translators,--*i traditori traduttori*; but I thank them. I rarely read any Latin, Greek, German, Italian, sometimes not a French book in the original, which I can procure in a good version. I like to be beholden to the great metropolitan English speech, the sea which receives tributaries from every region under heaven. I should as soon think of swimming across the Charles River when I wish to go to Boston, as of reading all my books in originals, when I have them rendered for me in my mother-tongue.--R. W. EMERSON. *Books.*

ON FIRST LOOKING INTO CHAPMAN'S HOMER

Much have I travelled in the realms of gold,
And many goodly states and kingdoms seen;
Round many western islands have I been
Which bards in fealty to Apollo hold.
Oft of one wide expanse had I been told
That deep-browed Homer ruled as his demesne;
Yet did I never breathe its pure serene
Till I heard Chapman speak out loud and bold:
Then felt I like some watcher of the skies
When a new planet swims into his ken;
Or like stout Cortez when with eagle eyes
He stared at the Pacific--and all his men
Looked at each other with a wild surmise--
Silent, upon a peak in Darien.

J. KEATS.

TRANSLATIONS FROM THE CLASSICS

Others again here livèd in my days
That have of us deservèd no less praise
For their translations than the daintiest wit
That on Parnassus thinks he highest doth sit.
And for a chair may 'mongst the Muses call
As the most curious maker of them all:
As reverent Chapman, who hath brought to us
Musaeus, Homer, and Herodotus
Out of the Greek, and by his skill hath reared
Them to that height and to our tongue endeared
That, were those poets at this day alive
To see their books thus with us to survive,

They would think, having neglected them so long,
They had been written in the English tongue.

M. DRAYTON. *To Henry Reynolds.*

It is good to have translations, because they serve as a comment, so far as the judgement of one man goes.--J. SELDEN.

TO MY WORTHY AND HONOURED FRIEND MASTER GEORGE CHAPMAN

Whose work could this be, Chapman, to refine
Old Hesiod's ore, and give it thus! but thine,
Who hadst before wrought in rich Homer's mine.

What treasure hast thou brought us! and what store
Still, still, dost thou arrive with at our shore,
To make thy honour and our wealth the more!

If all the vulgar tongues that speak this day
Were asked of thy discoveries, they must say,
To the Greek coast thine only knew the way.

Such passage hast thou found, such returns made,
As now of all men, it is called thy trade,
And who make thither else, rob or invade.

BEN JONSON.

WHEN TRANSLATIONS ARE TO BE PREFERRED

The reason the classics are not read is because there still lingers a tradition, handed down from the eighteenth century, that it is useless to read them unless in the original. A tone of sarcastic contempt is maintained towards the person who shall presume to peruse Xenophon not in the original Greek, or Virgil not in the original Latin.

In the view of these critics it is the Greek, it is the Latin, that is valuable, not the contents of the volume. Shakespeare, however, the greatest genius of England, thought otherwise. It is known that his ideas of Grecian and Roman history were derived from somewhat rude translations, yet it is acknowledged that the spirit of the ancient warriors and of the ancient luxury lives in his *Antony and Cleopatra*, and nowhere in all the ancient writers is there a poem breathing the idea of Aphrodite like his *Venus and Adonis*. The example of so great a genius may shield us in an effort to free the modern mind from this eighteenth-century incubus.

The truth is, the classics are much better understood in a good translation than in the original. To obtain a sufficient knowledge of Greek, for instance, to accurately translate is almost the work of a lifetime. Concentration upon this one pursuit gradually contracts the general perceptions, and it has often happened that an excellent scholar has been deficient in common knowledge, as shown by the singular character of his own notes. But his work of translation in itself is another matter.

It is a treasure; from it poets derive their illustrations; dramatists their plots; painters their pictures. A young mind full of intelligence, coming to such a translation, enters at once into the spirit of the ancient writer. A good translation is thus better than the original.--R. JEFFERIES. *The Dewy Morn.*

'THAT SILLY VANITY OF IMPERTINENT CITATIONS'

'Twas this vain idolizing of authors which gave birth to that silly vanity of impertinent citations, and inducing authority in things neither requiring nor deserving it. That saying was much more observable, *That men have beards and women none*, because quoted from Beza; and that other, *Pax res bona est*, because brought in with a 'said St. Austin'. But these ridiculous fooleries, to your more generous discerners, signify nothing but the pedantry of the affected sciolist. 'Tis an inglorious acquist to have our heads or volumes laden as were Cardinal Campeius his mules, with old and useless baggage.--J. GLANVILL. *The Vanity of Dogmatizing.*

QUOTATION

In quoting of books, quote such authors as are usually read; others you may read for your own satisfaction, but not name them.

Quoting of authors is most for matter of fact; and then I write them as I would produce a witness; sometimes for a free expression, and then I give the author his due, and gain myself praise by reading him.

To quote a modern Dutchman where I may use a classic author, is as if I were to justify my reputation, and I neglect all persons of note and quality that know me, and bring the testimonial of the scullion in the kitchen.--J. SELDEN. *Table Talk.*

MERIT IN QUOTATION

Next to the originator of a good sentence is the first quoter of it.... We are as much in-formed of a writer's genius by what he selects as by what he originates. We read the quotation with his eyes, and find a new and fervent sense; as a passage from one of the poets, well recited, borrows new interest from the rendering. As the journals say, 'the italics are ours.' The profit of books is according to the sensibility of the reader. The pro-foundest thought or passion sleeps as in a mine, until an equal mind and heart finds and publishes it. The passages of Shakespeare that we most prize were never quoted until within this century; and Milton's prose, and Burke, even, have their best fame within it. Every one, too, remembers his friends by their favourite poetry or other reading.

Observe, also, that a writer appears to more advantage in the pages of another book than in his own. In his own, he waits as a candidate for your approbation; in another's he is a lawgiver.--R. W. EMERSON. *Quotation and Originality.*

WHAT SHAKESPEARE HATH LEFT US

Soul of the age!
The applause, delight, the wonder of our stage,
My Shakespeare, rise! I will not lodge thee by
Chaucer, or Spenser, or bid Beaumont lie
A little further, to make thee a room:
Thou art a monument without a tomb,
And art alive still, while thy book doth live,
And we have wits to read, and praise to give.

That I not mix thee so my brain excuses;
I mean, with great but disproportioned Muses.
For, if I thought my judgement were of years,
I should commit thee, surely, with thy peers.
And tell how far thou didst our Lyly outshine
Or sporting Kyd, or Marlowe's mighty line.

And though thou hadst small Latin and less Greek,
From thence, to honour thee, I will not seek
For names; but call forth thundering Aeschylus,
Euripides, and Sophocles to us,
Paccuvius, Accius, him of Cordova dead,
To life again, to hear thy buskin tread
And shake a stage; or when thy sock was on,
Leave thee alone, for the comparison
Of all that insolent Greece or haughty Rome
Sent forth; or since did from their ashes come.

Triumph, my Britain! Thou hast one to show
To whom all scenes of Europe homage owe.
He was not of an age, but for all time!
And all the Muses still were in their prime,
When, like Apollo, he came forth to warm
Our ears, or, like a Mercury, to charm.
Nature herself was proud of his designs,
And joyed to wear the dressing of his lines,
Which were so richly spun, and woven so fit
As, since, she will vouchsafe no other wit.
The merry Greek, tart Aristophanes,

Neat Terence, witty Plautus, now not please;
But antiquated and deserted lie,
As they were not of Nature's family.

Yet must I not give Nature all! Thy art,
My gentle Shakespeare, must enjoy a part.
For though the Poet's matter Nature be
His art doth give the fashion. And that he
Who casts to write a living line, must sweat
(Such as thine are), and strike the second heat
Upon the Muses' anvil, turn the same
(And himself with it), that he thinks to frame;
Or for the laurel he may gain a scorn!
For a good Poet's made as well as born;
And such wert thou! Look how the father's face
Lives in his issue; even so, the race
Of Shakespeare's mind and manners brightly shines
In his well-turnèd and true-filèd lines;
In each of which he seems to shake a lance
As brandished at the eyes of Ignorance.
Sweet Swan of Avon! what a sight it were
To see thee in our water yet appear,
And make those flights upon the banks of Thames
That so did take Eliza, and our James!

BEN JONSON.

ON THE PORTRAIT OF SHAKESPEARE

This figure that thou here seest put,
It was for gentle Shakespeare cut,
Wherein the graver had a strife
With Nature, to outdo the life.
Oh, could he but have drawn his wit
As well in brass, as he has hit
His face, the print would then surpass
All that was ever writ in brass.
But, since he cannot, reader, look
Not on his picture, but his book.

BEN JONSON.

SHAKESPEARE'S LIVELONG MONUMENT

What needs my Shakespeare for his honoured bones,
The labour of an age in pilèd stones,

Or that his hallowed relics should be hid
Under a star-ypointing pyramid?
Dear son of Memory, great heir of Fame,
What need'st thou such weak witness of thy name?
Thou in our wonder and astonishment
Hast built thyself a livelong monument.
For whilst to the shame of slow-endeavouring art,
Thy easy numbers flow, and that each heart
Hath from the leaves of thy unvalued book,
Those Delphic lines with deep impression took,
Then thou our fancy of itself bereaving,
Dost make us marble with too much conceiving;
And so sepulchred in such pomp dost lie,
That kings for such a tomb would wish to die.

J. MILTON.

UNDER MR. MILTON'S PICTURE BEFORE HIS 'PARADISE LOST'

Three Poets, in three distant ages born,
Greece, Italy, and England did adorn.
The first in loftiness of thought surpassed,
The next in majesty, in both the last:
The force of Nature could no farther go;
To make a third she joined the former two.

J. DRYDEN.

UPON MY BROTHER'S BOOK CALLED 'THE GROUNDS, LABOUR AND
REWARD OF FAITH'

This lamp filled up, and fired by that blest spirit,
Spent his last oil in this pure heavenly flame;
Laying the grounds, walls, roof of faith: this frame
With life he ends; and now doth there inherit
What here he built, crowned with his laurel merit:
  Whose palms and triumphs once he loudly rang,
  There now enjoys what here he sweetly sang.

This is his monument, on which he drew
His spirit's image, that can never die;
But breathes in these live words, and speaks to the eye;
In these his winding-sheets he dead doth shew
To buried souls the way to live anew,
  And in his grave more powerfully now preacheth.
  Who will not learn, when that a dead man teacheth?

P. FLETCHER.

81

UPON THE BOOK AND PICTURE OF THE SERAPHICAL SAINT TERESA

Live in these conquering leaves: live all the same;
And walk through all tongues one triumphant flame;
Live here, great heart; and love, and die, and kill;
And bleed, and wound, and yield, and conquer still.
Let this immortal life where'er it comes
Walk in a crowd of loves and martyrdoms.
Let mystic deaths wait on't; and wise souls be
The love-slain witnesses of this life of thee.
O sweet incendiary! show here thy art,
Upon this carcass of a hard cold heart;
Let all thy scatter'd shafts of light, that play
Among the leaves of thy large books of day,
Combined against this breast at once break in,
And take away from me myself and sin;
This gracious robbery shall thy bounty be
And my best fortunes such fair spoils of me.
O thou undaunted daughter of desires!
By all thy dower of lights and fires;
By all the eagle in thee, all the dove;
By all thy lives and deaths of love;
By thy large draughts of intellectual day,
And by thy thirsts of love more large than they;
By all thy brim-filled bowls of fierce desire,
By thy last morning's draught of liquid fire;
By the full kingdom of that final kiss
That seized thy parting soul, and sealed thee His;
By all the Heaven thou hast in Him
(Fair sister of the seraphim!);
By all of Him we have in thee;
Leave nothing of myself in me.
Let me so read thy life, that I
Unto all life of mine may die!

R. CRASHAW.

THE SEAT OF AUTHORITY

You despise books; you, whose lives are absorbed in the vanities of ambition, the pursuit of pleasure, or in indolence; but remember that all the known world, excepting only savage nations, is governed by books. All Africa, to the limits of Ethiopia and Nigritia, obeys the book of the Koran, after bowing to the book of the Gospel. China is ruled by the moral book of Confucius, and a great part of India by the Vedah. Persia was governed for ages by the books of one of the Zoroasters.

In a law-suit or criminal process, your property, your honour, perhaps your life, depends on the interpretation of a book which you never read.... You are acquainted with neither Hippocrates nor Boerhaave nor Sydenham; but you place your body in the hands of those who can read them.--VOLTAIRE. *Philosophical Dictionary*. Books.

BOOKS PREFERRED TO PREACHERS

The writings of divines are nothing else but a preaching the Gospel to the eye, as the voice preacheth it to the ear. Vocal preaching hath the pre-eminence in moving the affections, and becometh diversified according to the state of the congregations which attend it: this way the milk cometh warmest from the breast. But books have the advantage in many other respects: you may read an able preacher when you have but a mean one to hear. Every congregation cannot hear the most judicious or powerful preachers: but every single person may read the books of the most powerful and judicious; preachers may be silenced or banished, when books may be at hand: books may be kept at a smaller charge than preachers: we may choose books which treat of that very subject which we desire to hear of; but we cannot choose what subject the preacher shall treat of. Books we may have at hand every day and hour: when we can have sermons but seldom, and at set times. If sermons be forgotten, they are gone. But a book we may read over and over till we remember it; and if we forget it, may again peruse it at our pleasure, or at our leisure. So that good books are a very great mercy to the world.--R. BAXTER. *Christian Directory*.

BOOKS OF MORALITY

Books of morality are daily written, yet its influence is still little in the world; so the ground is annually ploughed, and yet multitudes are in want of bread. But, surely, neither the labours of the moralist nor of the husbandman are vain: let them for a while neglect their tasks and their usefulness will be known; the wickedness that is now frequent would become universal, the bread that is now scarce would wholly fail.--S. JOHNSON. *Adventurer*, 137.

THE SECRET INFLUENCE OF BOOKS

Books have always a secret influence on the understanding: we cannot at pleasure obliterate ideas; he that reads books of science, though without any fixed desire of improvement, will grow more knowing; he that entertains himself with moral or religious treatises will imperceptibly advance in goodness; the ideas which are often offered to the mind will at last find a lucky moment when it is disposed to receive them.--S. JOHNSON. *Adventurer*, 137.

DEAD COUNSELLORS ARE SAFEST

It was the maxim, I think, of Alphonsus of Aragon that *dead counsellors are safest*. The grave puts an end to flattery and artifice, and the information that we receive from books is pure from interest, fear, or ambition. Dead counsellors are likewise most instructive, because they are heard with patience and with reverence. We are not unwilling to believe that man wiser than ourselves from whose abilities we may receive advantage without any danger of rivalry or opposition, and who affords us the light of his experience without hurting our eyes by flashes of insolence.--S. JOHNSON. *Rambler*, 87.

THE REAL WORKING EFFECTIVE CHURCH

But to the Church itself, as I hinted already, all is changed, in its preaching, in its working, by the introduction of Books. The Church is the working recognized Union of our Priests or Prophets, of those who by wise teaching guide the souls of men. While there was no Writing, even while there was no Easy-writing, or *Printing*, the preaching of the voice was the natural sole method of performing this. But now with Books!--He that can write a true Book, to persuade England, is not he the Bishop and Archbishop, the Primate of England and of all England? I many a time say, the writers of Newspapers, Pamphlets, Poems, Books, these *are* the real working effective Church of a modern country. Nay, not only our preaching, but even our worship, is not it too accomplished by means of Printed Books?... Fragments of a real 'Church Liturgy' and 'Body of Homilies', strangely disguised from the common eye, are to be found weltering in that huge froth-ocean of Printed Speech we loosely call Literature! Books are our Church too.

On all sides, are we not driven to the conclusion that, of the things which man can do or make here below, by far the most momentous, wonderful and worthy are the things we call Books! Those poor bits of rag-paper with black ink on them;--from the Daily Newspaper to the sacred Hebrew BOOK, what have they not done, what are they not doing!--For indeed, whatever be the outward form of the things (bits of paper, as we say, and black ink), is it not verily, at bottom, the highest act of man's faculty that produces a Book? It is the *Thought* of man; the true thaumaturgic virtue; by which man works all things whatsoever. All that he does, and brings to pass, is the vesture of a Thought. This London City, with all its houses, palaces, steam-engines, cathedrals, and huge immeasurable traffic and tumult, what is it but a Thought, but millions of Thoughts made into One;--a huge immeasurable Spirit of a THOUGHT, embodied in brick, iron, smoke, dust, Palaces, Parliaments, Hackney Coaches, Katherine Docks, and the rest of it! Not a brick was made but some man had to *think* of the making of that brick.--The thing we called 'bits of paper with traces of black ink', is the *purest* embodiment a Thought of man can have. No wonder it is, in all ways, the activest and noblest.--T. CARLYLE. *Heroes and Hero-Worship*.

BOOKS AS SIGN-POSTS

The modern scholars have their usual recourse to the Universities of their countries; some few, it may be, to those of their neighbours; and this in quest of books rather than men for their guides, though these are living and those in comparison but dead instructors, which, like a hand with an inscription, can point out the straight way upon the road, but can neither tell you the next turnings, resolve your doubts, or answer your questions, like a guide that has traced it over, and perhaps knows it as well as his chamber. And who are these dead guides we seek in our journey? They are at best but some few authors that remain among us of a great many that wrote in Greek and Latin from the age of Hippocrates to that of Marcus Antoninus, which reaches not much above six hundred years.--SIR W. TEMPLE. *Ancient and Modern Learning.*

THE NEED OF A GUIDE TO BOOKS

The colleges, whilst they provide us with libraries, furnish no professor of books; and, I think, no chair is so much wanted. In a library we are surrounded by many hundreds of dear friends, but they are imprisoned by an enchanter in these paper and leathern boxes; and, though they know us, and have been waiting two, ten, or twenty centuries for us,--some of them,--and are eager to give us a sign, and unbosom themselves, it is the law of their limbo that they must not speak until spoken to; and as the enchanter has dressed them, like battalions of infantry, in coat and jacket of one cut, by the thousand and ten thousand, your chance of hitting on the right one is to be computed by the arithmetical rule of Permutation and Combination,--not a choice out of three caskets, but out of half a million caskets all alike. But it happens in our experience, that in this lottery there are at least fifty or a hundred blanks to a prize. It seems, then, as if some charitable soul, after losing a great deal of time among the false books, and alighting upon a few true ones which made him happy and wise, would do a right act in naming those which have been bridges or ships to carry him safely over dark morasses and barren oceans, into the heart of sacred cities, into palaces and temples. This would be best done by those great masters of books who from time to time appear,--the Fabricii, the Seldens, Magliabecchis, Scaligers, Mirandolas, Bayles, Johnsons, whose eyes sweep the whole horizon of learning. But private readers, reading purely for love of the book, would serve us by leaving each the shortest note of what he found.--R. W. EMERSON. *Books.*

THE TRUE UNIVERSITY OF THESE DAYS

To look at Teaching, for instance. Universities are a notable, respectable product of the modern ages. Their existence too is modified, to the very basis of it, by the existence of Books. Universities arose while there were yet no Books procurable; while a man, for a single Book, had to give an estate of land. That, in those circumstances, when a man had some knowledge to communicate, he should do it by gathering the learners round him, face to face, was a necessity for him. If you wanted to know what Abelard knew, you must go and listen to Abelard. Thousands, as many as thirty thousand, went to hear Abelard and that metaphysical theology of his. And now for any other teacher who had also something of his own to teach, there was a great convenience opened: so many thousands eager to learn were already assembled yonder; of all places the best place for him was that. For any third teacher it was better still; and grew ever the better, the more teachers there came. It only needed now that the King took notice of this new phenomenon; combined or agglomerated the various schools into one school; gave it edifices, privileges, encouragements, and named it *Universitas*, or School of all Sciences: the University of Paris, in its essential characters, was there. The model of all subsequent Universities; which down even to these days, for six centuries now, have gone on to found themselves. Such, I conceive, was the origin of Universities. It is clear, however, that with this simple circumstance, facility of getting Books, the whole conditions of the business from top to bottom were changed. Once invent Printing, you metamorphosed all Universities, or superseded them! The Teacher needed not now to gather men personally round him, that he might *speak* to them what he knew: print it in a Book, and all learners far and wide, for a trifle, had it each at his own fireside, much more effectually to learn it!--Doubtless there is still peculiar virtue in Speech; even writers of Books may still, in some circumstances, find it convenient to speak also,--witness our present meeting here! There is, one would say, and must ever remain while man has a tongue, a distinct province for Speech as well as for Writing and Printing. In regard to all things this must remain; to Universities among others. But the limits of the two have nowhere yet been pointed out, ascertained; much less put in practice: the University which would completely take-in that great new fact, of the existence of Printed Books, and stand on a clear footing for the Nineteenth Century as the Paris one did for the Thirteenth, has not yet come into existence. If we think of it, all that a University, or final highest School, can do for us, is still but what the first School began doing--teach us to *read*. We learn to *read*, in various languages, in various sciences; we learn the alphabet and letters of all manner of Books. But the place where we are to get knowledge, even theoretic knowledge, is the Books themselves! It depends on what we read, after all manner of Professors have done their best for us. The true University of these days is a Collection of Books.--T. CARLYLE. *Heroes and Hero-Worship.*

OXFORD AND CAMBRIDGE: TWO EPIGRAMS

The King observing with judicious eyes
The state of both his Universities,
To one he sent a regiment: for why?
That learned body wanted loyalty.
To the other he sent books, as well discerning
How much that loyal body wanted learning.

J. TRAPP.

THE ANSWER

The King to Oxford sent his troop of horse,
For Tories own no argument but force;
With equal care to Cambridge books he sent,
For Whigs allow no force but argument.

SIR W. BROWNE.

Books will speak plain, when counsellors blanch.--F. BACON, LORD VERULAM. *Of Counsell.*

AGAINST WRITERS THAT CARP AT OTHER MEN'S BOOKS

The readers and the hearers like my books,
And yet some writers cannot them digest;
But what care I? for when I make a feast,
I would my guests should praise it, not the cooks.

SIR J. HARINGTON.

A CRITIC

is one that has spelt over a great many of books, and his observation is the orthography. He is the surgeon of old authors, and heals the wounds of dust and ignorance. He converses much in fragments and *Desunt multa*'s, and if he piece it up with two lines, he is more proud of that book than the author. He runs over all sciences to peruse their syntaxes, and thinks all learning comprised in writing Latin. He tastes styles, as some discreeter palaters do wine; and tells you which is genuine, which sophisticate and bastard. His own phrase is a miscellany of old words, deceased long before the Caesars, and entombed by Varro, and the modernest man he follows is Plautus. He writes *Omneis* at length, and *quicquid*, and his gerund is most inconformable. He is a troublesome vexer of the dead, which after so long sparing must rise up to the judgement of his castigations. He is one that makes all books sell dearer, whilst he swells them into folios with his comments.--J. EARLE. *Microcosmographie.*

STYLE *v.* SENSE

Others for language all their care express,
And value books, as women men, for dress:
Their praise is still,--the style is excellent:
The sense, they humbly take upon content.
Words are like leaves; and where they most abound,
Much fruit of sense beneath is rarely found.

A. POPE. *Essay on Criticism.*

WHERE FOOLS RUSH IN

The bookful blockhead, ignorantly read,
With loads of learned lumber in his head,
With his own tongue still edifies his ears,
And always listening to himself appears.

All books he reads, and all he reads assails,
From Dryden's *Fables* down to D'Urfey's *Tales*.
With him, most authors steal their works, or buy;
Garth did not write his own *Dispensary*.
Name a new play, and he's the poet's friend,
Nay, showed his faults--but when would poets mend?
No place so sacred from such fops is barred,
Nor is Paul's church more safe than Paul's churchyard.
Nay, fly to altars; there they'll talk you dead:
For fools rush in where angels fear to tread.

      A. POPE. *Essay on Criticism.*

LITERARY HYPOCRISY

There are some subjects of which almost all the world perceive the futility; yet all combine in imposing upon each other as worthy of praise. But chiefly this imposition obtains in literature, where men publicly contemn what they relish with rapture in private, and approve abroad what has given them disgust at home.--O. GOLDSMITH. *Letters from a Citizen of the World.*

IN THE SEAT OF THE SCORNER

They who are in the habit of passing sentence upon books,--and what ignoramus in our days does not deem himself fully qualified for sitting in the seat of the scorner?--are apt to think that they have condemned a work irretrievably, when they have pronounced it to be unintelligible. Unintelligible to whom? To themselves, the self-constituted judges. So that their sentence presumes their competency to pronounce it: and this, to every one save themselves, may be exceedingly questionable.

It is true, the very purpose for which a writer publishes his thoughts, is, that his readers should share them with him. Hence the primary requisite of a style is its intelligibleness: that is to say, it must be capable of being understood. But intelligibleness is a relative quality, varying with the capacity of the reader. The easiest book in a language is inaccessible to those who have never set foot within the pale of that language. The simplest elementary treatise in any science is obscure and perplexing, until we become familiar with the terminology of that science. Thus every writer is entitled to demand a certain amount of knowledge in those for whom he writes, and a certain degree of dexterity in using the implements of thought....

When a man says he sees nothing in a book, he very often means that he does not see himself in it: which, if it is not a comedy or a satire, is likely enough.--A. W. and J. C. HARE. *Guesses at Truth.*

THE FINAL VERDICT UPON BOOKS

They who make up the final verdict upon every book are not the partial and noisy readers of the hour when it appears; but a court as of angels, a public not to be bribed, not to be entreated, and not to be overawed, decides upon every man's title to fame. Only those books come down which deserve to last. Gilt edges, vellum, and morocco, and presentation copies to all the libraries, will not preserve a book in circulation beyond its intrinsic date. It must go with all Walpole's Noble and Royal Authors to its fate. Blackmore, Kotzebue, or Pollock may endure for a night, but Moses and Homer stand for ever. There are not in the world at any one time more than a dozen persons who read and understand Plato: never enough to pay for an edition of his works; yet to every generation these come duly down, for the sake of those few persons, as if God brought them in his hand. 'No book,' said Bentley, 'was ever written down by any but itself.' The permanence of all books is fixed by no effort friendly or hostile, but by their own specific gravity, or the intrinsic importance of their contents to the constant mind of man.--R. W. EMERSON. *Spiritual Laws.*

Talent alone cannot make a writer. There must be a man behind the book.--R. W. EMERSON. *Goethe.*

THE CRITICS' INFLUENCE ON THE PUBLIC

The opinion of the great body of the reading public is very materially influenced even by the unsupported assertions of those who assume a right to criticize. Nor is the public altogether to blame on this account. Most even of those who have really a great enjoyment in reading are in the same state, with respect to a book, in which a man who has never given particular attention to the art of painting is with respect to a picture. Every man who has the least sensibility or imagination derives a certain pleasure from pictures. Yet a man of the highest and finest intellect might, unless he had formed his taste by contemplating the best pictures, be easily persuaded by a knot of connoisseurs that the worst daub in Somerset House was a miracle of art.

Just such is the manner in which nine readers out of ten judge of a book. They are ashamed to dislike what men who speak as having authority declare to be good.--LORD MACAULAY. *Mr. Robert Montgomery's Poems.*

TASTE IN LITERATURE AND ART

I know many persons who have the purest taste in literature, and yet false taste in art, and it is a phenomenon which puzzles me not a little; but I have never known any one with false taste in books, and true taste in pictures. It is also of the greatest importance to you, not only for art's sake, but for all kinds of sake, in these days of book deluge, to keep out of the salt swamps of literature, and live on a little rocky island of your own, with a spring and a lake in it, pure and good. I cannot, of course, suggest the choice of your library to you: every several mind needs different books; but there are some books which we all need, and assuredly, if you read Homer, Plato, Aeschylus, Herodotus, Dante, Shakespeare, and Spenser, as much as you ought, you will not require wide enlargement of shelves to right and left of them for purposes of perpetual study.--J. RUSKIN. *The Elements of Drawing.*

'There is no book so bad,' said the bachelor, 'but something good may be found in it.'--CERVANTES.

THE FILIAL PIETY OF BOOKS

Nor is there any paternal fondness which seems to savour less of absolute instinct, and which may be so well reconciled to worldly wisdom, as this of authors for their books. These children may most truly be called the riches of their father, and many of them have with true filial piety fed their parent in his old age; so that not only the affection but the interest of the author may be highly injured by those slanderers whose poisonous breath brings his book to an untimely end.

Lastly, the slanderer of a book is, in truth, the slanderer of the author ... neither can any one give the names of sad stuff, horrid nonsense, &c., to a book, without calling the author a blockhead; which, though in a moral sense it is a preferable appellation to that of villain, is, perhaps, rather more injurious to his worldly interest.--H. FIELDING. *Tom Jones.*

THE MOTE AND THE BEAM

To complain in print of the multitude of books seems to me a self-accusing vanity, whilst the querulous reprehenders add to the cause of complaint and transgress themselves in that which they seem to wish amended. 'Tis true, the births of the press are numerous, nor is there less variety in the humours and fancies of perusers, and while the number of the one exceeds not the diversity of the other some will not think that too much which others judge superfluous. The genius of one approves what another disregardeth. And were nothing to pass the press but what were suited to the universal gusto, farewell, typography!... I seek no applause from the disgrace of others, nor will I, huckster-like, discredit any man's ware to recommend mine own. I am not angry that there are so many books already (bating only the anomalies of impiety and irreligion), nor will I plead the necessity of publishing mine from feigned importunities.--J. GLANVILL. *The Vanity of Dogmatizing.*

The foolishest book is a kind of leaky boat on the sea of wisdom; some of the wisdom will get in, anyhow.--O. W. HOLMES. *The Poet at the Breakfast-Table.*

CENSORSHIP

Popish books teach and inform; what we know, we know much out of them. The fathers, church story, school-men, all may pass for popish books; and if you take away them, what learning will you leave? Besides, who must be judge? The customer or the waiter? If he disallows a book it must not be brought into the kingdom; then Lord have mercy upon all scholars! These puritan preachers, if they have anything good, they have it out of popish books, though they will not acknowledge it, for fear of displeasing the people. He is a poor divine that cannot sever the good from the bad.--J. SELDEN. *Table Talk.*

THE IMPRIMATUR

Learning hath of late years met with an obstruction in many places which suppresses it from flourishing or increasing, in spite of all its other helps, and that is the inquisition upon the press, which prohibits any book from coming forth without an imprimatur; an old relic of popery, only necessary for the concealing of such defects of government which of right ought to be discovered and amended.--C. BLOUNT. *A Just Vindication of Learning,* 1693.

A GREAT BOOK IS A GREAT EVIL

[Greek: Méga biblíon méga kakón]

A man who publishes his works in a volume has an infinite advantage over one who communicates his writings to the world in loose tracts and single pieces. We do not expect to meet with anything in a bulky volume till after some heavy preamble, and several words of course, to prepare the reader for what follows: nay, authors have established it as a kind of rule, that a man ought to be dull sometimes, as the most severe reader makes allowances for many rests and nodding-places in a voluminous writer. This gave occasion to the famous Greek proverb which I have chosen for my motto, *That a great book is a great evil....*

An essay writer must practise in the chemical method and give the virtue of a full draught in a few drops. Were all books reduced thus to their quintessence, many a bulky author would make his appearance in a penny-paper: there would be scarce such a thing in nature as a folio: the works of an age would be contained on a few shelves, not to mention millions of volumes that would be utterly annihilated....

When knowledge, instead of being bound up in books, and kept in libraries and retirements, is thus obtruded upon the public; when it is canvassed in every assembly, and exposed upon every table; I cannot forbear reflecting upon that passage in the Proverbs, 'Wisdom crieth without, she uttereth her voice in the streets.'--J. ADDISON. *Spectator,* 124.

A LITTLE BOOK THE MOST EXCELLENT

For books we shall generally find that the most excellent in any art or science have been still the smallest and most compendious; and this not without ground, for it is an argument that the author was a master of what he wrote, and had a clear notion and a full comprehension of the subject before him. For the reason of things lies in a little compass, if the mind could at any time be so happy as to light upon it. Most of the writings and discourses in the world are but illustration and rhetoric, which signifies as much as nothing to a mind eager in pursuit after the causes and philosophical truth of things.... The truth is, there could be no such thing as art or science, could not the mind of man gather the general natures of things out of the heap of numberless particulars, and then bind them up into such short aphorisms or propositions, that so they may be made portable to the memory, and thereby become ready and at hand for the judgement to apply and make use of as there shall be occasion.--R. SOUTH. *Sermon against long extempore prayers.*

There are many books written by many men, from which two truths only are discoverable by the readers; namely, that the writers thereof wanted two things,--principle and preferment.--C. C. COLTON. *Lacon.*

BOOKS WITH ONE IDEA IN THEM

An amusing catalogue might be made of books which contain but one good passage. They would be a sort of single-speech Hamiltons; if Balaam's palfrey might not be thought a more apt counterpart to them. Killigrew's play of the Parson's Wedding, which in length of massy dullness exceeds many books, is remarkable for one little spark of liveliness. The languishing fine lady of the piece exclaims most characteristically, upon coming in tired with walking: 'I am glad I am come home, for I'm e'en as weary with this walking. For God's sake, whereabouts does the pleasure of walking lie? I swear I have often sought it till I was weary, and yet I could ne'er find it.'--Charron on Wisdom, a cumbrous piece of formality, which Pope's eulogium lately betrayed me into the perusal of, has one splendid passage, page 138, (I think) English translation. It contrasts the open honours with which we invest the sword, as the means of putting man out of the world, with the concealing and retiring circumstances that accompany his introduction into it. It is a piece of gorgeous and happy eloquence.--What could Pope mean by that line,--'sage Montaigne, or more sage Charron?' Montaigne is an immense treasure-house of observation, anticipating all the discoveries of succeeding essayists. You cannot dip in him without being struck with the aphorism, that there is nothing new under the sun. All the writers on common life since him have done nothing but echo him. You cannot open him without detecting a *Spectator* or starting a *Rambler*; besides that his own character pervades the whole, and binds it sweetly together. Charron is a mere piece of formality, scholastic dry bones, without sinew or living flesh.--C. LAMB. *Table Talk.*

BOOKS OF ONE THOUGHT

Few books have more than one thought: the generality indeed have not quite so many. The more ingenious authors of the former seem to think that, if they once get their candle lighted, it will burn on for ever. Yet even a candle gives a sorry, melancholy light unless it has a brother beside it, to shine on it and keep it cheerful. For lights and thoughts are social and sportive: they delight in playing with and into each other. One can hardly conceive a duller state of existence than sitting at whist with three dummies: and yet many of our prime philosophers have seldom done anything else.--A. W. and J. C. HARE. *Guesses at Truth.*

INDUCTIVE CRITICISM

A heedy reader shall often discover in other men's compositions perfections far differing from the author's meaning, and such as haply he never dreamed of, and illustrateth them with richer senses and more excellent constructions.--MONTAIGNE.

READING BETWEEN LINES

In hours of high mental activity we sometimes do the book too much honour, reading out of it better things than the author wrote,--reading, as we say, between the lines. You have had the like experience in conversation: the wit was in what you heard, not in what the speakers said. Our best thought came from others. We heard in their words a deeper sense than the speakers put into them, and could express ourselves in other people's phrases to finer purpose than they knew.--R. W. EMERSON. *Quotation and Originality.*

PURPLE PATCHES

There are some fine passages, I am told, in that book.

Are there? Then beware of them. Fine passages are mostly *culs de sac.* For in books also does one see

> Rich windows that exclude the light
> And passages that lead to nothing.

> A. W. and J. C. HARE. *Guesses at Truth.*

There's more ado to interpret interpretations than to interpret things, and more books upon books than upon any other subject. We do but inter-glose ourselves. All swarmeth with commentaries; of authors there is great penury.--MONTAIGNE.

THE ROYAL ROAD

ERASMUS. I am told there is a certain compendious art, that will help a man to accomplish himself with all the liberal sciences by a very little labour.

DESIDERIUS. What is that you talk of? Did you ever see the book?

ERASMUS. I did see it, and that was all, having nobody to instruct me in the use of it.

DESIDERIUS. What was the subject of the book?

ERASMUS. It treated of various forms of dragons, lions, leopards; and various circles, and words written in them, some in Greek, some in Latin, and some in Hebrew and other barbarous languages.

DESIDERIUS. Pray, in how many days' time did the title-page promise you the knowledge of the arts and sciences?

ERASMUS. In fourteen.

DESIDERIUS. In truth, a very noble promise. But did you ever know anybody that has become learned by that notable art?

ERASMUS. No.

DESIDERIUS. No, nor nobody ever did, or ever will, till we can see an alchemist grow rich.

ERASMUS. Why, is there no such art then? I wish with all my heart there was.

DESIDERIUS. Perhaps you do, because you would not be at the pains which are required to become learned.

ERASMUS. You are right.

DESIDERIUS. It seemed meet to the Divine Being that the common riches, gold, jewels, silver, palaces, and kingdoms should be bestowed on the slothful and undeserving; but the true riches, and such as are properly our own, must be gotten by labour.

ERASMUS. *Colloquies: The Notable Art.*

READERS AND WRITERS

Many books require no thought from those who read them, and for a very simple reason;--they made no such demand on those who wrote them. Those works therefore are the most valuable, that set our thinking faculties in the fullest operation.--C. C. COLTON. *Lacon.*

STUDIES

Studies serve for delight, for ornament, and for ability. Their chief use for delight, is in privateness and retiring; for ornament, is in discourse; and for ability, is in the judgement and disposition of business; for expert men can execute, and perhaps judge of particulars, one by one; but the general counsels, and the plots and marshalling of affairs come best from those that are learned. To spend too much time in studies, is sloth; to use them too much for ornament, is affectation; to make judgement wholly by their rules, is the humour of a scholar: they perfect nature, and are perfected by experience: for natural abilities are like natural plants, that need pruning by study; and studies themselves do give forth directions too much at large, except they be bounded in by experience. Crafty men contemn studies, simple men admire them, and wise men use them; for they teach not their own use; but that is a wisdom without them and above them, won by observation. Read not to contradict and confute, nor to believe and take for granted, nor to find talk and discourse, but to weigh and consider. Some books are to be tasted, others to be swallowed, and some few to be chewed and digested: that is, some books are to be read only in parts; others to be read, but not curiously; and some few to be read wholly, and with diligence and attention. Some books also may be read by deputy, and extracts made of them by others; but that would be only in the less important arguments, and the meaner sort of books; else distilled books are, like common distilled waters, flashy things. Reading maketh a full man; conference a ready man; and writing an exact man; and, therefore, if a man write little, he had need have a great memory; if he confer little, he had need have a present wit; and if he read little, he had need have much cunning, to seem to know that he doth not. Histories make men wise; poets, witty; the mathematics, subtile; natural philosophy, deep; moral, grave; logic and rhetoric, able to contend: *Abeunt studia in mores*; nay, there is no stand or impediment in the wit, but may be wrought out by fit studies: like as diseases of the body may have appropriate exercises; bowling is good for the stone and reins, shooting for the lungs and breast, gentle walking for the stomach, riding for the head and the like; so if a man's wit be wandering, let him study the mathematics; for in demonstrations, if his wit be called away never so little, he must begin again; if his wit be not apt to distinguish or find difference, let him study the schoolmen, for they are *Cymini sectores*. If he be not apt to beat over matters, and to call up one thing to prove and illustrate another, let him study the lawyers' cases: so every defect of the mind may have a special receipt.--F. BACON, LORD VERULAM. *Essays*.

HOW TO SPEND OUR DAYS

After some while meditation, I walk up to my masters and companions, my books: and, sitting down amongst them, with the best contentment, I dare not reach forth my hand to salute any of them till I have first looked up to heaven, and craved favour of Him to whom all my studies are duly referred, without whom I can neither profit nor labour. After this, out of no over-great variety, I call forth those which may best fit my occasions; wherein I am not too scrupulous of age: sometimes I put myself to school, to one of those ancients, whom the Church hath honoured with the name of Fathers, whose volumes I confess not to open without a secret reverence of their holiness and gravity: sometimes to those latter doctors, which want nothing but age to make them classical: always to God's Book. That day is lost whereof some hours are not improved in those divine monuments: others I turn over out of choice; these out of duty.--JOSEPH HALL. (Letter to Lord Denny.)

THE CHOICE OF BOOKS

In study there must be an expulsive virtue to shun all that is erroneous; and there is no science but is full of such stuff, which by direction of tutor and choice of good books must be excerned. Do not confound yourself with multiplicity of authors; two is enough upon any science, provided they be plenary and orthodox; *Philosophy* should be your substantial food, *Poetry* your banqueting stuff; *Philosophy* hath more of reality in it than any Knowledge, the *Philosopher* can fathom the deep, measure mountains, reach the stars with a staff, and bless heaven with a girdle.

But among these Studies you must not forget the *unicum necessarium*; on Sundays and Holidays let *Divinity* be the sole object of your speculation, in comparison whereof all other knowledge is but cobweb-learning.--J. HOWELL. *Familiar Letters.*

CHEWING THE CUD

Reading furnishes the mind only with materials of knowledge; it is thinking makes what we read ours. We are of the ruminating kind, and it is not enough to cram ourselves with a great load of collections; unless we chew them over again they will not give us strength and nourishment.... The memory may be stored, but the judgement is little better, and the stock of knowledge not increased, by being able to repeat what others have said or produce the arguments we have found in them. Such a knowledge as this is but knowledge by hearsay, and the ostentation of it is at best but talking by rote, and very often upon weak and wrong principles. For all that is to be found in books is not built upon true foundations, nor always rightly deduced from the principles it is pretended to be built on.... The mind is backward in itself to be at the pains to trace every argument to its original, and to see upon what basis it stands, and how firmly; but yet it is this that gives so much the advantage to one man more than another in reading. The mind should, by severe rules, be tied down to this at first uneasy task; use and exercise will give it facility. So that those who are accustomed to it, readily, as it were with one cast of the eye, take a view of the argument, and presently, in most cases, see where it bottoms. Those who have got this faculty, one may say, have got the true key of books, and the clue to lead them through the mizmaze of variety of opinions and authors to truth and certainty. This young beginners should be entered in, and showed the use of, that they might profit by their reading.... This way of thinking on and profiting by what we read will be a clog and rub to any one only in the beginning; when custom and exercise has made it familiar, it will be dispatched in most occasions, without resting or interruption in the course of our reading.--J. LOCKE. *Conduct of the Understanding.*

THE SUFFICIENCY OF HOMER

Read Homer once, and you can read no more;
For all books else appear so mean, so poor,
Verse will seem prose, but still persist to read,

And Homer will be all the books you need.

J. SHEFFIELD, DUKE OF BUCKINGHAM.
Essay on Poetry.

HOMER AND VIRGIL

Be Homer's works your study and delight,
Read them by day, and meditate by night;
Thence form your judgement, thence your maxims bring,
And trace the Muses upward to their spring.
Still with itself compared, his text peruse;
And let your comment be the Mantuan Muse.
  When first young Maro in his boundless mind
A work to outlast immortal Rome designed,
Perhaps he seemed above the critic's law,
And but from Nature's fountains scorned to draw:
But when to examine every part he came,
Nature and Homer were, he found, the same.
Convinced, amazed, he checks the bold design;
And rules as strict his laboured work confine,
As if the Stagirite o'erlooked each line.
Learn hence for ancient rules a just esteem:
To copy nature is to copy them.

A. POPE. *Essay on Criticism.*

READ WITHOUT PREJUDICE

Read boldly, and unprejudiced peruse
Each favourite modern, e'en each ancient Muse.
With all the comic salt and tragic rage,
The great stupendous genius of our stage,
Boast of our island, pride of humankind,
Had faults to which the boxes are not blind;
His frailties are to every gossip known,
Yet Milton's pedantries not shock the town.
Ne'er be the dupe of names, however high,
For some outlive good parts, some misapply.
Each elegant *Spectator* you admire,
But must you therefore swear by Cato's fire?
Masks for the court, and oft a clumsy jest
Disgraced the Muse that wrought the *Alchemist.*
'But to the ancients'--Faith! I am not clear,
For all the smooth round type of Elzevir,
That every work which lasts in prose or song

97

Two thousand years deserves to last so long:
For--not to mention some eternal blades
Known only now in academic shades,
(Those sacred groves where raptured spirits stray,
And in word-hunting waste the livelong day)
Ancients whom none but curious critics scan,--
Do read Messala's praises if you can.
Ah! who but feels the sweet contagious smart
While soft Tibullus pours his tender heart?
With him the Loves and Muses melt in tears,
But not a word of some hexameters!
'You grow so squeamish and so devilish dry
You'll call Lucretius vapid next.' Not I:
Some find him tedious, others think him lame,
But if he lags his subject is to blame.
Rough weary roads through barren wilds he tried,
Yet still he marches with true Roman pride;
Sometimes a meteor, gorgeous, rapid, bright,
He streams athwart the philosophic night.
Find you in Horace no insipid odes?--
He dared to tell us Homer sometimes nods;
And but for such a critic's hardy skill
Homer might slumber unsuspected still.

J. ARMSTRONG. *Taste.*

READING ACCORDING TO INCLINATION

He [Dr. Johnson] said, that for general improvement, a man should read whatever his immediate inclination prompts him to; though, to be sure, if a man has a science to learn, he must regularly and resolutely advance. He added, 'what we read with inclination makes a much stronger impression. If we read without inclination, half the mind is employed in fixing the attention; so there is but one half to be employed on what we read.' He told us, he read Fielding's *Amelia* through without stopping. He said, 'If a man begins to read in the middle of a book, and feels an inclination to go on, let him not quit it, to go to the beginning. He may perhaps not feel again the inclination.'

Dr. Johnson advised me to-day, to have as many books about me as I could; that I might read upon any subject upon which I had a desire for instruction at the time. 'What you read *then* (said he) you will remember; but if you have not a book immediately ready, and the subject moulds in your mind, it is a chance if you again have a desire to study it.' He added, 'If a man never has an eager desire for instruction, he should prescribe a task for himself. But it is better when a man reads from immediate inclination.'

Another admonition of his was, never to go out without some little book or other in the pocket. 'Much time,' added he, 'is lost by waiting, by travelling, &c., and this may be prevented, by making use of every possible opportunity for improvement.'--J. BOSWELL. *Life of Johnson.*

READ FEW BOOKS WELL

Read few books well. We forget names and dates; and reproach our memory. They are of little consequence. We feel our limbs enlarge and strengthen; yet cannot tell the dinner or the dish that caused the alteration. Our minds improve though we cannot name the author and have forgotten the particulars.

Read all books through; and bad books most carefully, lest you should lose one good thought, being determined never to look into them again. A man may read a great deal too much.--J. HORNE TOOKE. *Recollections of S. Rogers.*

BOOKS AS FRUITFUL TREES

Under a strong persuasion that little of real value is derived by persons in general from a wide and various reading; but still more deeply convinced as to the actual mischief of unconnected and promiscuous reading, and that it is sure, in a greater or less degree, to enervate even where it does not likewise inflate; I hope to satisfy many an ingenious mind, seriously interested in its own development and cultivation, how moderate a number of volumes, if only they be judiciously chosen, will suffice for the attainment of every wise and desirable purpose; that is, in addition to those which he studies for specific and professional purposes. It is saying less than the truth to affirm that an excellent book (and the remark holds almost equally good of a Raphael as of a Milton) is like a well-chosen and well-tended fruit-tree. Its fruits are not of one season only. With the due and natural intervals, we may recur to it year after year, and it will supply the same nourishment and the same gratification, if only we ourselves return to it with the same healthful appetite.--S. T. COLERIDGE. *Prospectus to a Course of Lectures.*

READING SEVERAL BOOKS AT A TIME

The advice I would give to any one who is disposed really to read for the sake of knowledge is, that he should have two or three books in course of reading at the same time. He will read a great deal more in that time and with much greater profit. All travels are worth reading, as subsidiary to reading, and in fact essential parts of it: old or new, it matters not--something is to be learnt from all. And the custom of making brief notes of reference to everything of interest or importance would be exceedingly useful.--R. SOUTHEY (Letter to Henry Taylor).

WHEN AND WHERE TO READ

Much depends upon *when* and *where* you read a book. In the five or six impatient minutes, before the dinner is quite ready, who would think of taking up the *Fairy Queen* for a stop-gap, or a volume of Bishop Andrewes' sermons?

Milton almost requires a solemn service of music to be played before you enter upon him. But he brings his music, to which, who listens, had need bring docile thoughts, and purged ears.

Winter evenings--the world shut out--with less of ceremony the gentle Shakespeare enters. At such a season, the *Tempest*, or his own *Winter's Tale*.--

These two poets you cannot avoid reading aloud--to yourself, or (as it chances) to some single person listening. More than one--and it degenerates into an audience.

Books of quick interest, that hurry on for incidents, are for the eye to glide over only. It will not do to read them out. I could never listen to even the better kind of modern novels without extreme irksomeness.

A newspaper, read out, is intolerable.--C. LAMB. *Detached Thoughts on Books and Reading.*

SMALL AUTHORS DANGEROUS

It is dangerous to have any intercourse or dealing with small authors. They are as troublesome to handle, as easy to discompose, as difficult to pacify, and leave as unpleasant marks on you, as small children. Cultivate on the other hand the society and friendship of the higher; first that you may learn to reverence them, which of itself is both a pleasure and a virtue, and then that on proper occasions you may defend them against the malevolent, which is a duty. And this duty cannot be well and satisfactorily performed with an imperfect knowledge, or with an inadequate esteem.--W. S. LANDOR. *Imaginary Conversations: Barrow and Newton.*

BOOKS THAT PROVOKE THOUGHT

It is wholesome and bracing for the mind, to have its faculties kept on the stretch. It is like the effect of a walk in Switzerland upon the body. Reading an Essay of Bacon's, for instance, or a chapter of Aristotle or of Butler, if it be well and thoughtfully read, is much like climbing up a hill, and may do one the same sort of good.... For my own part, I have ever gained the most profit and the most pleasure also, from the books which have made me think the most: and, when the difficulties have once been overcome, these are the books which have struck the deepest root, not only in my memory and understanding, but likewise in my affections. For this point too should be taken into account. We are wont to think slightly of that, which it costs us a slight effort to win. When a maiden is too forward, her admirer deems it time to draw back. Whereas whatever has associated itself with the arousal and activity of our better nature, with the important and memorable epochs in our lives, whether moral or intellectual, is,--to cull a sprig from the beautiful passage in which Wordsworth describes the growth of Michael's love for his native hills--

> Our living being, even more
> Than our own blood,--and could it less?--retains

Strong hold on our affections, is to us
A pleasurable feeling of blind love,
The pleasure which there is in life itself.

If you would fertilize the mind, the plough must be driven over and through it. The glid-ing of wheels is easier and rapider, but only makes it harder and more barren. Above all, in the present age of light reading, that is, of reading hastily, thoughtlessly, indiscrimi-nately, unfruitfully, when most books are forgotten as soon as they are finished, and very many sooner, it is well if something heavier is cast now and then into the midst of the literary public. This may scare and repel the weak: it will rouse and attract the stronger, and increase their strength by making them exert it. In the sweat of the brow is the mind as well as the body to eat its bread.--A. W. and J. C. HARE. *Guesses at Truth.*

RULES FOR READING

The best rule of reading will be a method from nature, and not a mechanical one of hours and pages. It holds each student to a pursuit of his native aim, instead of a desulto-ry miscellany. Let him read what is proper to him, and not waste his memory on a crowd of mediocrities. As whole nations have derived their culture from a single book,--as the Bible has been the literature as well as the religion of large portions of Europe,--as Hafiz was the eminent genius of the Persians, Confucius of the Chinese, Cervantes of the Spaniards; so, perhaps, the human mind would be a gainer, if all the secondary writers were lost--say, in England, all but Shakespeare, Milton, and Bacon--through the pro-founder study so drawn to those wonderful minds. With this pilot of his own genius, let the student read one, or let him read many, he will read advantageously....

The three practical rules, then, which I have to offer, are,--1. Never read any book that is not a year old. 2. Never read any but famed books.3. Never read any but what you like; or, in Shakespeare's phrase,

No profit goes where is no pleasure ta'en:
In brief, sir, study what you most affect.

Montaigne says, 'Books are a languid pleasure;' but I find certain books vital and spermatic, not leaving the reader what he was: he shuts the book a richer man. I would never willingly read any others than such.--R. W. EMERSON. *Books.*

A DIET OF BOOKS

I would not be hurried by any love of system, by any exaggeration of instincts, to under-rate the Book. We all know, that, as the human body can be nourished on any food, though it were boiled grass and the broth of shoes, so the human mind can be fed by any knowledge. And great and heroic men have existed, who had almost no other infor-mation than by the printed page. I only would say, that it needs a strong head to bear that diet. One must be an inventor to read well. As the proverb says, 'He that would bring home the wealth of the Indies must carry out the wealth of the Indies.' There is, then, creative reading as well as creative writing. When the mind is braced by labour and invention, the page of whatever book we read becomes luminous with manifold allusion. Every sentence is doubly significant, and the sense of our author is as broad as the world. We then see, what is always true, that, as the seer's hour of vision is short and rare among heavy days and months, so is its record, perchance, the least part of his volume. The discerning will read, in his Plato or Shakespeare, only that least part,--only the authentic utterances of the oracle; all the rest he rejects, were it never so many times Plato's and Shakespeare's.--R. W. EMERSON. *The American Scholar.*

A COURSE OF READING

Let us turn our attention to the intellectual advantages accompanying the pursuit, since the proper function of books is in the general case associated with intellectual culture and occupation. It would seem that, according to a received prejudice or opinion, there is one exception to this general connexion, in the case of the possessors of libraries, who are under a vehement suspicion of not reading their books. Well, perhaps it is true in the sense in which those who utter the taunt understand the reading of a book. That one should possess no books beyond his power of perusal--that he should buy no faster than as he can read straight through what he has already bought--is a supposition alike preposterous and unreasonable. 'Surely you have far more books than you can read,' is sometimes the inane remark of the barbarian who gets his books, volume by volume, from some circulating library or reading club, and reads them all through, one after the other, with a dreary dutifulness, that he may be sure that he has got the value of his money.

It is true that there are some books--as Homer, Virgil, Horace, Milton, Shakespeare, and Scott--which every man should read who has the opportunity--should read, mark, learn, and inwardly digest.... But is one next to read through the sixty and odd folio volumes of the Bollandist *Lives of the Saints*, and the new edition of the Byzantine historians, and the State Trials, and the *Encyclopaedia Britannica*, and Moreri, and the Statutes at large, and the *Gentleman's Magazine* from the beginning, each separately, and in succession? Such a course of reading would certainly do a good deal towards weakening the mind, if it did not create absolute insanity.

But in all these just named, even in the Statutes at large, and in thousands upon thousands of other books, there is precious honey to be gathered by the literary busy bee, who passes on from flower to flower. In fact, 'a course of reading,' as it is sometimes called, is a course of regimen for dwarfing the mind, like the drugs which dog-breeders give to King Charles spaniels to keep them small. Within the span of life allotted to man there is but a certain number of books that it is practicable to read through, and it is not possible to make a selection that will not, in a manner, wall in the mind from a free expansion over the republic of letters. The being chained, as it were, to one intellect in the perusal straight on of any large book, is a sort of mental slavery superinducing imbecility. Even Gibbon's *Decline and Fall*, luminous and comprehensive as its philosophy is, and rapid and brilliant the narrative, will become deleterious mental food if consumed straight through without variety. It will be well to relieve it occasionally with a little Boston's *Fourfold State*, or Hervey's *Meditations*, or Sturm's *Reflections for Every Day in the Year*, or *Don Juan*, or Ward's *History of Stoke-Upon-Trent*.--J. H. BURTON. *The Book-Hunter.*

OF READING

Read not Milton, for he is dry; nor Shakespeare, for he
  wrote of common life:
Nor Scott, for his romances, though fascinating, are yet
  intelligible:
Nor Thackeray, for he is a Hogarth, a photographer who
  flattereth not:
Nor Kingsley, for he shall teach thee that thou shouldest
  not dream, but do.
Read incessantly thy Burke; that Burke who, nobler than
  he of old,
Treateth of the Peer and Peeress, the truly Sublime and
  Beautiful:
Likewise study the 'creations' of 'the Prince of modern
  Romance';
Sigh over Leonard the Martyr, and smile on Pelham the
  puppy:
Learn how 'love is the dram-drinking of existence';
And how we 'invoke, in the Gadara of our still closets,
The beautiful ghost of the Ideal, with the simple wand of
  the pen.'
Listen how Maltravers and the orphan 'forgot all but
  love',
And how Devereux's family chaplain 'made and unmade
  kings':
How Eugene Aram, though a thief, a liar, a murderer,
Yet, being intellectual, was amongst the noblest of mankind.
So shalt thou live in a world peopled with heroes and
  master-spirits;
And if thou canst not realize the Ideal, thou shalt at least
  idealize the Real.

    C. S. CALVERLEY. *Proverbial Philosophy.*

POETS AS COMMENTATORS

I hold that no man can have any just conception of the history of England who has not often read, and meditated, and learnt to love the great poets of England. The greatest of them, such as Chaucer, Shakespeare, Massinger, George Herbert, Milton, Cowley, Dryden, Pope, and Burns, often throw more rich and brilliant colours, and sometimes even more clear and steady lights, on the times and doings of our forefathers, than are to be gathered out of all the chroniclers together, from the Venerable Bede to the philosophical Hume. They are at least the greatest and best commentators on those chroniclers.--

SIR JAMES STEPHEN. *Desultory and Systematic Reading.*

THE METHOD OF READING PROFANE HISTORY

In perusal of history, first, provide you some writers in chronology and cosmography. For if you be ignorant of the times and places when and where the things you read were done, it cannot choose but breed confusion in your reading, and make you many times grossly to slip and mistake in your discourse. When, therefore, you set to your book, have by you Helvicus, his *Chronology*, and a map of the country in which you are conversant; and repair unto them to acquaint you with time and place, when and where you are. If you be versing the ancient histories, then provide you Ptolemy's maps, or Ortelius, his *Conatus Geographici*: if the latter, then some of the modern cards....

Before you come to read the acts of any people, as those that intend to go to bowls will first see and view the ground upon which they are to play, so it shall not be amiss for you first to take a general view of that ground, which you mean more particularly to traverse, by reading some short epitome.... This will give you a general taste of your business, and add light unto particular authors....

From the order of reading and the matters in reading to be observed, we come to the method of observation. What order we are for our best use to keep in entering our notes into our paper-books.

The custom which hath most prevailed hitherto was commonplacing, a thing at the first original very plain and simple; but by after-times much increased, some augmenting the number of the heads, others inventing quainter forms of disposing them: till at length commonplace books became like unto the Roman Breviary or Missal. It was a great part of clerkship to know how to use them. The vastness of the volumes, the multitude of heads, the intricacy of disposition, the pains of committing the heads to memory, and last, of the labour of so often turning the books to enter the observations in their due places, are things so expensive of time and industry, that although at length the work comes to perfection, yet it is but like the silver mines in Wales, the profit will hardly quit the pains. I have often doubted with myself whether or no there were any necessity of being so exactly methodical. First, because there hath not yet been found a method of that latitude, but little reading would furnish you with some things, which would fall without the compass of it. Secondly, because men of confused, dark and cloudy understandings, no beam or light of order and method can ever rectify; whereas men of clear understanding, though but in a mediocrity, if they read good books carefully, and note diligently, it is impossible but they should find incredible profit, though their notes lie never so confusedly. The strength of our natural memory, especially if we help it, by revising our own notes; the nature of things themselves, many times ordering themselves, and *tantum non*, telling us how to range them; a mediocrity of care to see that matters lie not too chaos-like, will with very small damage save us this great labour of being over-superstitiously methodical. And what though peradventure something be lost, *Exilis domus est*, &c. It is a sign of great poverty of scholarship, where everything that is lost is missed; whereas rich and well-accomplished learning is able to lose many things with little or no inconvenience.--J. HALES. *Golden Remains.*

EPITOMES

Epitome is good privately for himself that doth work it, but ill commonly for all other that use other men's labour therein: a silly poor kind of study, not unlike to the doing of those poor folk, which neither till nor sow nor reap themselves, but glean by stealth upon other men's grounds. Such have empty barns for dear years.... Epitome hurteth most of all in divinity itself. Indeed books of commonplaces be very necessary to induce a man into an orderly general knowledge, how to refer orderly all that he readeth, *ad certa rerum capita*, and not wander in study.... But to dwell in epitomes, and books of commonplaces, and not to bind himself daily by orderly study, to read with all diligence, principally the holiest Scripture, and withal the best doctors, and so to learn to make true difference betwixt the authority of the one and the counsel of the other, maketh so many seeming and sunburnt ministers as we have; whose learning is gotten in a summer heat, and washed away with a Christmas snow again.--R. ASCHAM. *The Schoolmaster.*

ABSTRACTS OF BOOKS

My abstracts of each book were made in the French language: my observations often branched into particular essays; and I can still read, without contempt, a dissertation of eight folio pages on eight lines (287-94) of the fourth *Georgic* of Virgil....

This various reading, which I now conducted with discretion, was digested, according to the precept and model of Mr. Locke, into a large commonplace book; a practice, however, which I do not strenuously recommend. The action of the pen will doubtless imprint an idea on the mind as well as on the paper: but I much question whether the benefits of this laborious method are adequate to the waste of time; and I must agree with Dr. Johnson (*Idler*, No. 74), 'that what is twice read is commonly better remembered than what is transcribed'....

I will embrace this occasion of recommending to the young student a practice which about this time [1759] I myself adopted. After glancing my eye over the design and order of a new book, I suspended the perusal till I had finished the task of self-examination, till I had revolved, in a solitary walk, all that I knew, or believed, or had thought on the subject of the whole work, or of some particular chapter: I was then qualified to discern how much the author added to my original stock; and if I was sometimes satisfied by the agreement, I was sometimes armed by the opposition of our ideas.--E. GIBBON. *Autobiography.*

BESCRIBBLING WITH NOTES

Somewhat to aid the weakness of my memory and to assist her great defects; for it hath often been my chance to light upon books which I supposed to be new and never to have read, which I had, not understanding, diligently read and run over many years before, and all bescribbled with my notes: I have a while since accustomed myself to note at the end of my book (I mean such as I purpose to read but once) the time I made an end to read it, and to set down what censure or judgement I gave of it; that so it may at least at another time represent unto my mind the air and general idea I had conceived of the author in reading him.--MONTAIGNE.

BOOKS TO BE MARKED

If the books which you read are your own, mark with a pen or pencil the most consider-able things in them which you desire to remember. Then you may read that book the second time over with half the trouble, by your eye running over the paragraphs which your pencil has noted. It is but a very weak objection against this practice to say, 'I shall spoil my book;' for I persuade myself that you did not buy it as a bookseller, to sell it again for gain, but as a scholar, to improve your mind by it; and if the mind be improved, your advantage is abundant, though your book yields less money to your executors.--I. WATTS. *Logic.*

UNDERSCORING

'On a subsequent evening, when I called by invitation to consult some other volumes, the conversation turned on the practice of underscoring books of study. Sir William spoke highly of the practice, as attended with many advantages, especially in the saving of time and labour. Intelligent underlining gave a kind of abstract of an important work, and by the use of different coloured inks to mark a difference of contents, and discrimi-nate the doctrinal from the historical or illustrative elements of an argument or exposition, the abstract became an analysis very serviceable for ready reference. He men-tioned that this principle had been carried to a ludicrous extreme in the publication of a coloured New Testament by an Anglicized German, Wirgmann by name.... In this book, entitled *Divarication of the New Testament into Doctrine and History*, the pages were all col-oured, most of them parti-coloured, the doctrine being throughout visually separated from the history by this device; the doctrine being, if I remember rightly, blue, and the history red. The author expressed his belief that all the sects of Christendom had arisen from a confusion of these elements, and that his grand discovery in the "Divarication" would annihilate sects, establish pure Christianity as a sacred science, and become hereaf-ter a Euclid in Theology.'--SIR WILLIAM HAMILTON. *Life* by J. Veitch.

THE PARSON'S ACCESSORY KNOWLEDGE

The Country Parson hath read the Fathers also, and the Schoolmen, and the later writers, or a good proportion of all, out of all which he hath compiled a book, and Body of Di-vinity, which is the storehouse of his sermons, and which he preacheth all his life; but diversely clothed, illustrated, and enlarged. For though the world is full of such compo-sures, yet every man's own is fittest, readiest, and most savoury to him. Besides, this being to be done in his younger and preparatory times, it is an honest joy ever after to look upon his well-spent hours.--G. HERBERT. *A Priest to the Temple.*

COMMONPLACE BOOKS

For the disposition and collocation of that knowledge which we preserve in writing, it consisteth in a good digest of commonplaces, wherein I am not ignorant of the prejudice imputed to the rise of commonplace books, as causing a retardation of reading, and some sloth or relaxation of memory. But because it is but a counterfeit thing in knowledges to be forward and pregnant, except a man be deep and full, I hold the entry of commonplaces to be a matter of great use and essence in studying, as that which assureth copy of invention, and contracteth judgement to a strength. But this is true, that of the methods of commonplaces that I have seen, there is none of any sufficient worth: all of them carrying merely the face of a school, and not of a world; and referring to vulgar matters and pedantical divisions, without all life or respect to action.--F. BACON, LORD VERULAM. *Of the Advancement of Learning.*

A NEW METHOD OF A COMMONPLACE BOOK

I take a paper book of what size I please. I divide the two first pages that face one another by parallel lines into five-and-twenty equal parts, every fifth line black, the other red. I then cut them perpendicularly by other lines that I draw from the top to the bottom of the page. I put about the middle of each five spaces one of the twenty letters I design to make use of, and, a little forward in each space, the five vowels, one below another, in their natural order. This is the index to the whole volume, how big soever it may be.

The index being made after this manner, I leave a margin in all the other pages of the book, of about the largeness of an inch, in a volume in folio, or a little larger; and, in a less volume, smaller in proportion.

If I would put anything in my Commonplace Book, I find out a head to which I may refer it. Each head ought to be some important and essential word to the matter in hand, and in that word regard is to be had to the first letter, and the vowel that follows it; for upon these two letters depends all the use of the index.

I omit three letters of the alphabet as of no use to me, viz. K, Y, W, which are supplied by C, I, U, that are equivalent to them. I put the letter Q that is always followed with an u in the fifth space of Z. By throwing Q last in my index, I preserve the regularity of my index, and diminish not in the least its extent; for it seldom happens that there is any head begins with Zu. I have found none in the five-and-twenty years I have used this method.... When I meet with anything that I think fit to put into my commonplace book, I first find a proper head. Suppose, for example, that the head be EPISTOLA, I look into the index for the first letter and the following vowel, which in this instance are E i; if in the space marked E i there is any number that directs me to the page designed for words that begin with an E, and whose first vowel after the initial letter is I, I must then write under the word Epistola, in that page, what I have to remark. I write the head in large letters and begin a little way out into the margin, and I continue on the line, in writing what I have to say. I observe constantly this rule that only the head appears in the margin, and that it be continued on, without ever doubling the line in the margin, by which means the heads will be obvious at first sight....

If the head is a monosyllable and begins with a vowel, that vowel is at the same time both the first letter of the word and the characteristic vowel. Therefore I write the word Ars in A a and Os in O o....

As to the language in which one ought to express the heads I esteem the Latin tongue most commodious, provided the nominative case be always kept to.... But it is not of much consequence what language is made use of, provided there be no mixture in the heads of different languages.--W. LOCKE (Letter to Mr. Toignard).

A commonplace book contains many notions in garrison, whence the owner may draw out an army into the field on competent warning.--T. FULLER. *The Holy and the Profane State.*

Reading without thinking may indeed make a rich commonplace, but 'twill never make a clear head.--J. NORRIS. *On the Advantages of Thinking.*

MARGINAL NOTES AND COMMONPLACE BOOKS

It is the practice of many readers to note, in the margin of their books, the most important passages, the strongest arguments, or the brightest sentiments. Thus they load their minds with superfluous attention, repress the vehemence of curiosity by useless deliberation, and by frequent interruption break the current of narration or the chain of reason, and at last close the volume, and forget the passages and marks together.

Others I have found unalterably persuaded that nothing is certainly remembered but what is transcribed; and they have therefore passed weeks and months in transferring large quotations to a commonplace book. Yet, why any part of a book, which can be consulted at pleasure, should be copied, I was never able to discover. The hand has no closer correspondence with the memory than the eye. The act of writing itself distracts the thoughts, and what is read twice is commonly better remembered than what is transcribed. This method therefore consumes time without assisting memory.

The true art of memory is the art of attention. No man will read with much advantage, who is not able, at pleasure, to evacuate his mind, or who brings not to his author an intellect defecated and pure, neither turbid with care, nor agitated by pleasure. If the repositories of thought are already full, what can they receive? If the mind is employed on the past or the future, the book will be held before the eyes in vain. What is read with delight is commonly retained, because pleasure always secures attention: but the books which are consulted by occasional necessity, and perused with impatience, seldom leave any traces on the mind.--S. JOHNSON. *Idler*, 74.

THE BEE AND THE BUTTERFLY

More is got from one book on which the thought settles for a definite end in knowledge, than from libraries skimmed over by a wandering eye. A cottage flower gives honey to the bee, a king's garden none to the butterfly.--E. G. E. L. BULWER-LYTTON, LORD LYTTON. *Caxtoniana.*

SKIPPING WIT

I do not search and toss over books, but for an honester recreation to please, and pas-time to delight myself: or if I study, I only endeavour to find out the knowledge that teacheth or handleth the knowledge of myself, and which may instruct me how to die well and how to live well.

Has meus ad metas sudet oportet equus (Propertius).

My horse must sweating run,
That this goal may be won.

If in reading I fortune to meet with any difficult points, I fret not myself about them, but after I have given them a charge or two, I leave them as I found them. Should I earnestly plod upon them, I should lose both time and myself, for I have a skipping wit. What I see not at the first view, I shall less see it if I opinionate myself upon it. I do nothing without blitheness; and an over-obstinate continuation and plodding contention doth dazzle, dull, and weary the same: my sight is thereby confounded and diminished.... If one book seem tedious unto me I take another, which I follow not with any earnestness, except it be at such hours as I am idle, or that I am weary with doing nothing. I am not greatly affected to new books, because ancient authors are, in my judgement, more full and pithy: nor am I much addicted to Greek books, forasmuch as my understanding cannot well rid his work with a childish and apprentice intelligence. Amongst modern books merely pleasant, I esteem Boccaccio his *Decameron*, Rabelais, and the Kisses of John the Second (if they may be placed under this title), worth the pains-taking to read them. As for *Amadis* and such like trash of writings, they had never the credit so much as to allure my youth to delight in them. This I will say more, either boldly or rashly, that this old and heavy-paced mind of mine will no more be pleased with Aristotle, or tickled with good Ovid: his facility and quaint inventions which heretofore have so ravished me, they can nowadays scarcely entertain me.... It is neither grammatical subtilties nor logical quiddities, nor the witty contexture of choice words or arguments and syllogisms that will serve my turn.... I would not have a man go about and labour by circumlocutions to induce and win me to attention, and that (as our heralds or criers do) they shall ring out their words: Now hear me, now listen, or ho-yes. The Romans in their religion were wont to say 'Hoc age'; which in ours we say 'Sursum corda'. These are so many lost words for me. I come ready prepared from my house. I need no allurement nor sauce, my stomach is good enough to digest raw meat.--MONTAIGNE.

CHANCE READINGS

Interdum speciosa locis morataque recte
Fabula nullius veneris, sine pondere et arte,
Valdius oblectat populum meliusque moratur
Quam versus inopes rerum nugaeque canorae.--HOR.

It is the custom of the Mahometans, if they see any printed or written paper upon the ground, to take it up and lay it aside carefully, as not knowing but it may contain some piece of their Alcoran. I must confess I have so much of the Mussulman in me, that I cannot forbear looking into every printed paper which comes in my way, under whatsoever despicable circumstances it may appear; for as no mortal author, in the ordinary fate and vicissitude of things, knows to what use his works may some time or other be applied, a man may often meet with very celebrated names in a paper of tobacco. I have lighted my pipe more than once with the writings of a prelate; and know a friend of mine, who, for these several years, has converted the essays of a man of quality into a kind of fringe for his candlesticks. I remember in particular, after having read over a poem of an eminent author on a victory, I met with several fragments of it upon the next rejoicing day, which had been employed in squibs and crackers, and by that means celebrated its subject in a double capacity. I once met with a page of Mr. Baxter under a Christmas pie. Whether or no the pastry-cook had made use of it through chance or waggery, for the defence of that superstitious *viande*, I know not; but upon the perusal of it, I conceived so good an idea of the author's piety, that I bought the whole book. I have often profited by these accidental readings, and have sometimes found very curious pieces, that are either out of print, or not to be met with in the shops of our London booksellers. For this reason, when my friends take a survey of my library, they are very much surprised to find, upon the shelf of folios, two long band-boxes standing upright among my books, till I let them see that they are both of them lined with deep erudition and abstruse literature.--J. ADDISON. *Spectator*, 85.

RIDING POST

In opposition to these extremes, I meet with another sort of people, that delight themselves in reading, but it is in such a desultory way, running from one book to another, as birds skip from one bough to another, without design, that it is no marvel if they get nothing but their labour for their pains, when they seek nothing but change and diversion: they that ride post can observe but little.

It is in reading, as it is in making many books; there may be a pleasing distraction in it, but little or no profit. I would therefore do in this as merchants used to do in their trading; who, in a coasting way, put in at several ports and take in what commodities they afford, but settle their factories in those places only which are of special note: I would, by the by, allow myself a traffic with sundry authors, as I happen to light upon them, for my recreation; and I would make the best advantage that I could of them; but I would fix my study upon those only that are of most importance to fit me for action, which is the true end of all learning, and for the service of God, which is the true end of all action. Lord, teach me so to study other men's works as not to neglect mine own; and so to study Thy word, which is Thy work, that it may be 'a lamp unto my feet, and a light unto my path'--my candle to work by. Take me off from the curiosity of knowing only to know; from the vanity of knowing only to be known; and from the folly of pretending to know more than I do know; and let it be my wisdom to study to know Thee, who art life eternal. Write Thy law in my heart, and I shall be the best book here.--SIR W. WALLER. *Divine Meditations.*

APPETITE AND SATIETY

The library at Waverley-Honour, a large Gothic room, with double arches and a gallery, contained such a miscellaneous and extensive collection of volumes as had been assembled together, during the course of two hundred years, by a family which had been always wealthy, and inclined, of course, as a mark of splendour, to furnish their shelves with the current literature of the day, without much scrutiny, or nicety of discrimination. Throughout this ample realm Edward was permitted to roam at large.... With a desire of amusement, therefore, which better discipline might soon have converted into a thirst for knowledge, young Waverley drove through the sea of books, like a vessel without a pilot or a rudder. Nothing perhaps increases by indulgence more than a desultory habit of reading, especially under such opportunities of gratifying it. I believe one reason why such numerous instances of erudition occur among the lower ranks is, that, with the same powers of mind, the poor student is limited to a narrow circle for indulging his passion for books, and must necessarily make himself master of the few he possesses ere he can acquire more. Edward, on the contrary, like the epicure who only deigned to take a single morsel from the sunny side of a peach, read no volume a moment after it ceased to excite his curiosity or interest; and it necessarily happened, that the habit of seeking only this sort of gratification rendered it daily more difficult of attainment, till the passion for reading, like other strong appetites, produced by indulgence a sort of satiety.-- SIR W. SCOTT. *Waverley.*

THE HABIT OF CASUAL READING

Not to mention the multitudes who read merely for the sake of talking, or to qualify themselves for the world, or some such kind of reasons; there are, even of the few who read for their own entertainment, and have a real curiosity to see what is said, several, which is prodigious, who have no sort of curiosity to see what is true....

For the sake of this whole class of readers, for they are of different capacities, different kinds, and get into this way from different occasions, I have often wished that it had been the custom to lay before people nothing in matters of argument but premises, and leave them to draw conclusions themselves; which, though it could not be done in all cases, might in many.

The great number of books and papers of amusement, which, of one kind or another, daily come in one's way, have in part occasioned, and most perfectly fall in with and humour, this idle way of reading and considering things. By this means, time even in solitude is happily got rid of, without the pain of attention; neither is any part of it more put to the account of idleness, one can scarce forbear saying, is spent with less thought, than great part of that which is spent in reading.--J. BUTLER. Preface to *Sermons.*

JOHNSON'S CURSORY READING

Mr. Elphinston talked of a new book that was much admired, and asked Dr. Johnson if he had read it. Johnson: 'I have looked into it.' 'What (said Elphinston), have you not read it through?' Johnson, offended at being thus pressed, and so obliged to own his cursory mode of reading, answered tartly, 'No, Sir, do *you* read books *through*?'--J. BOSWELL. *Life of Johnson.*

DESULTORY READING

Desultory reading is indeed very mischievous, by fostering habits of loose, discontinuous thought, by turning the memory into a common sewer for rubbish of all sorts to float through, and by relaxing the power of attention, which of all our faculties most needs care, and is most improved by it. But a well-regulated course of study will no more weaken the mind, than hard exercise will weaken the body: nor will a strong understanding be weighed down by its knowledge, any more than an oak is by its leaves, or than Samson was by his locks. He whose sinews are drained by his hair, must already be a weakling.--A. W. and J. C. HARE. *Guesses at Truth.*

THE GREATEST CLERKS BE NOT ALWAYS THE WISEST MEN

As in the choice and reading of good books principally consists the enabling and advancement of a man's knowledge and learning; yet if it be not mixed with the conversation of discreet, able, and understanding men, they can make little use of their reading, either for themselves, or the commonwealth where they live. There is not a more common proverb than this, *That the Greatest Clerks be not always the wisest men,* and reason for it, being a very uneven rule to square all actions, and consultations, only by book precedents. Time hath so many changes, and alterations, and such variety of occasions and opportunities, intervening, and mingled, that it is impossible to go new ways in the old paths; so that though reading do furnish and direct a man's judgement, yet it doth not wholly govern it. Therefore the necessity of knowing the present time, and men, wherein we live, is so great, that it is the principal guide of our actions, and reading but supplemental.--GREY BRYDGES, LORD CHANDOS. *Horae Subsecivae.*

A BOOKISH AMBITION

Affect not, as some do, that bookish ambition, to be stored with books and have well-furnished libraries, yet keep their heads empty of knowledge: to desire to have many books, and never to use them, is like a child that will have a candle burning by him, all the while he is sleeping.--H. PEACHAM. *The Compleat Gentleman.*

FULL LIBRARIES AND EMPTY HEADS

We have a generation of people in the world, that are so far from putting themselves upon the hazard of knowing too much, that they affect a kind of Socratical knowledge (though it be the clear contrary way), a knowledge of knowing nothing; they hate learning, and wisdom, and understanding with that perfect hatred, that if one could fancy such things to be in paradise, one would think (if I may speak it, as I mean it without profaneness) that the Devil could not tempt them to come near the tree of knowledge; I cannot say these are in a state of innocency, but I am sure they are in a state of simplicity. But among those few persons (especially those of quality) that pretend to look after books, how many are there that affect rather to look upon them, than in them? Some covet to have libraries in their houses, as ladies desire to have cupboards of plate in their chambers, only for show; as if they were only to furnish their rooms, and not their minds; if the only having of store of books were sufficient to improve a man, the stationers would have the advantage of all others; but certainly books were made for use, and not for ostentation; in vain do they boast of full libraries that are contented to live with empty heads.--SIR W. WALLER. *Divine Meditations*.

TO THE GOOD OR BAD READER

Read well, and then these following lines are mine,
But read them like a botcher, they are thine.
Such virtue from some readers doth proceed,
They make the verse the better which they read:
They know their idioms, accents, emphases,
Commas, stops, colons, and parentheses,
Full points, and periods, brief apostrophes,
Good knowing readers understand all these:
But such as dares my book to take in hand,
Who scarce can read or spell or understand;
Yet, like Sir reverence Geese, they will be gagling,
And tear my lines to tatters with their hagling;
Such I request, if bachelors they be,
To leave my book, and learn their A.B.C.:
If married men they be, let them take pain
To exercise their horn-books once again.

J. TAYLOR. *Epigrams, Written on purpose to be read: with a Proviso, that they may be understood by the Reader.*

A PRETENDER TO LEARNING

... is oftener in his study than at his book.... His table is spread wide with some classic folio, which is as constant to it as the carpet, and hath lain open in the same page this half year.... He walks much alone in the posture of meditation, and has a book still before his face in the fields. His pocket is seldom without a Greek Testament, or Hebrew Bible, which he opens only in the church, and this when some stander-by looks over.... He is a great nomenclator of authors, whom he has read in general in the catalogue, and in particular in the title, and goes seldom so far as the dedication.--J. EARLE. *Microcosmographie.*

SUPERFICIAL READERS

Man has a natural desire to know,
But the one half is for interest, the other show:
As scriveners take more pains to learn the slight
Of making knots than all the hands they write:
So all his study is not to extend
The bounds of knowledge, but some vainer end;
To appear and pass for learnèd, though his claim
Will hardly reach beyond the empty name:
For most of those that drudge and labour hard,
Furnish their understandings by the yard,
As a French library by the whole is,
So much an ell for quartos and for folios;
To which they are the indexes themselves,
And understand no further than the shelves;
But smatter with their tables and editions,
And place them in their classical partitions;
When all a student knows of what he reads
Is not in 's own but under general heads
Of commonplaces not in his own power,
But, like a Dutchman's money, i' th' cantore;
Where all he can make of it, at the best,
Is hardly three per cent. for interest;
And whether he will ever get it out
Into his own possession is a doubt:
Affects all books of past and modern ages,
But reads no further than the title-pages,
Only to con the author's names by rote,
Or, at the best, those of the books they quote
Enough to challenge intimate acquaintance
With all the learnèd Moderns and the Ancients.
As Roman noblemen were wont to greet,
And compliment the rabble in the street,
Had nomenclators in their trains, to claim
Acquaintance with the meanest by his name,
And by so mean contemptible a bribe
Trepanned the suffrages of every tribe;
So learned men, by authors' names unknown,
Have gained no small improvement to their own,
And he's esteemed the learnedest of all others

That has the largest catalogue of authors.

> S. BUTLER. *Satire upon the imperfection*
> *and abuse of human learning.*

THE READING COXCOMB

Among the numerous fools, by Fate designed
Oft to disturb, and oft divert, mankind,
The reading coxcomb is of special note,
By rule a poet, and a judge by rote:
Grave son of idle Industry and Pride,
Whom learning but perverts, and books misguide.

In error obstinate, in wrangling loud,
For trifles eager, positive, and proud,
Forth steps at last the self-applauding wight,
Of points and letters, chaff and straws, to write:
Sagely resolved to swell each bulky piece
With venerable toys from Rome and Greece;
How oft, in Homer, Paris curled his hair;
If Aristotle's cap were round or square;
If in the cave, where Dido first was sped,
To Tyre she turned her heels, to Troy her head.
Hence Plato quoted or the Stagyrite,
To prove that flame ascends and snow is white:
Hence much hard study, without sense or breeding,
And all the grave impertinence of reading.
If Shakespeare says, the noon-day sun is bright,
His scholiast will remark, it then was light;
Turn Caxton, Wynkyn, each old Goth and Hun,
To rectify the reading of a pun.
Thus, nicely trifling, accurately dull,
How one may toil, and toil--to be a fool!--D. MALLET.

READING TO KILL TIME

As to the devotees of the circulating libraries, I dare not compliment their *pass-time*, or rather *kill-time*, with the name of *reading*. Call it rather a sort of beggarly daydreaming, during which the mind of the dreamer furnishes for itself nothing but laziness and a little mawkish sensibility; while the whole *material* and imagery of the doze is supplied *ab extra* by a sort of mental *camera obscura* manufactured at the printing office, which *pro tempore* fixes, reflects and transmits the moving phantasms of one man's delirium, so as to people the barrenness of an hundred other brains afflicted with the same trance or suspension of all common sense and all definite purpose. We should therefore transfer this species of *amusement* (if indeed those can be said to retire *a musis*, who were never in their company, or relaxation be attributable to those whose bows are never bent) from the genus *reading* to the comprehensive class characterized by the power of reconciling the two contrary yet co-existing propensities of human nature, namely, indulgence of sloth and hahatred of vacancy. In addition to novels and tales of chivalry in prose or rhyme (by which last I mean neither rhythm nor metre) this genus comprises as its species gaming, swinging, or swaying on a chair or gate; spitting over a bridge; smoking; snuff-taking; *tête à tête* quarrels after dinner between husband and wife; conning word by word all the advertisements of the daily advertizers in a public-house on a rainy day, &c., &c., &c.--S. T. COLERIDGE. *Biographia Literaria.*

TALKING FROM BOOKS

Dr. Johnson this day, when we were by ourselves [on the journey to the Hebrides] observed, how common it was for people to talk from books; to retail the sentiments of others, and not their own; in short, to converse without any originality of thinking. He was pleased to say, 'You and I do not talk from books.'--J. BOSWELL. *Life of Johnson.*

There are no race of people who talk about books, or perhaps, who read books, so little as literary men.--W. M. THACKERAY.

A SHORT CUT TO FAME

There is a sort of vanity some men have, of talking of and reading obscure and half-forgotten authors, because it passes as a matter of course, that he who quotes authors which are so little read, must be completely and thoroughly acquainted with those authors which are in every man's mouth. For instance, it is very common to quote Shakespeare; but it makes a sort of stare to quote Massinger. I have very little credit for being well acquainted with Virgil; but if I quote Silius Italicus, I may stand some chance of being reckoned a great scholar. In short, whoever wishes to strike out of the great road, and to make a short cut to fame, let him neglect Homer, and Virgil, and Horace, and Ariosto and Milton, and, instead of these, read and talk of Frascatorius, Sannazarius, Lorenzini, Pastorini, and the thirty-six primary sonneteers of Bettinelli;--let him neglect everything which the suffrage of ages has made venerable and grand, and dig out of their graves a set of decayed scribblers, whom the silent verdict of the public has fairly condemned to everlasting oblivion. If he complain of the injustice with which they have been treated, and call for a new trial with loud and importunate clamour, though I am afraid he will not make much progress in the estimation of men of sense, he will be sure to make some noise in the crowd, and to be dubbed a man of very curious and extraordinary erudition.--S. SMITH. *Moral Philosophy, Lecture IX. On the Conduct of the Understanding.*

TITLE-READERS

Some read to think,--these are rare; some to write,--these are common; and some read to talk,--and these form the great majority. The first page of an author not unfrequently suffices for all the purposes of this latter class: of whom it has been said, that they treat books as some do lords; they inform themselves of their *titles*, and then boast of an intimate acquaintance.--C. C. COLTON. *Lacon.*

The author who speaks about his own books is almost as bad as a mother who talks about her own children.--B. DISRAELI, LORD BEACONSFIELD.

THE BURNING OF DON QUIXOTE'S BOOKS

The priest and the barber of the place, who were Don Quixote's great friends, happened to be there [at Don Quixote's house]; and the housekeeper was saying to them aloud: What is your opinion, Señor Licentiate Pero Perez (for that was the priest's name) of my master's misfortune? for neither he, nor his horse, nor the target, nor the lance, nor the armour have been seen these six days past. Woe is me! I am verily persuaded, and it is as certainly true as I was born to die, that these cursed books of knight-errantry which he keeps, and is so often reading, have turned his brain; and now I think of it, I have often heard him say, talking to himself, that he would turn knight-errant, and go about the world in quest of adventures. The devil and Barabbas take all such books, that have thus spoiled the finest understanding in all La Mancha. The niece joined with her, and said moreover: Know, master Nicholas (for that was the barber's name), that it has often happened, that my honoured uncle has continued poring on these confounded books of disadventures two whole days and nights.... But I take the blame of all this to myself, that I did not advertise you, gentlemen, of my dear uncle's extravagances, before they were come to the height that they now are, that you might have prevented them by burning all those cursed books, of which he has so great a store, and which as justly deserve to be committed to the flames, as if they were heretical....

Whilst Don Quixote still slept on, the priest asked the niece for the keys of the chamber where the books were, those authors of the mischief; and she delivered them with a very good will. They all went in, and the housekeeper with them. They found above a hundred volumes in folio, very well bound, besides a great many small ones. And no sooner did the housekeeper see them, than she ran out of the room in great haste, and immediately returned with a pot of holy water and a bunch of hyssop, and said: Señor Licentiate, take this and sprinkle the room, lest some enchanter, of the many these books abound with, should enchant us in revenge for what we intend to do, in banishing them out of the world. The priest smiled at the housekeeper's simplicity, and ordered the barber to reach him the books one by one, that they might see what they treated of; for, perhaps, they might find some that might not deserve to be chastised by fire. No, said the niece, there is no reason why any of them should be spared.... The housekeeper said the same; so eagerly did they both thirst for the death of those innocents. But the priest would not agree to that, without first reading the titles at least....

That night the housekeeper set fire to, and burnt all the books that were in the yard [whither they had been cast], and in the house too; and some must have perished, that deserved to be treasured up in perpetual archives.--CERVANTES. *Don Quixote.*

BRAINS SQUASHED BY BOOKS

There have indeed been minds overlaid by much reading, men who have piled such a load of books on their heads, their brains have seemed to be squashed by them.--A. W. and J. C. HARE. *Guesses at Truth.*

FOLLY GENERATED BY BOOKS

Books are chiefly useful as they help us to interpret what we see and experience. When they absorb men, as they sometimes do, and turn them from observation of nature and life, they generate a learned folly, for which the plain sense of the labourer could not be exchanged but at great loss. It deserves attention that the greatest men have been formed without the studies which at present are thought by many most needful to improvement. Homer, Plato, Demosthenes, never heard the name of chemistry, and knew less of the solar system than a boy in our common schools. Not that these sciences are unimportant; but the lesson is, that human improvement never wants the means, where the purpose of it is deep and earnest in the soul.--W. E. CHANNING. *Self-Culture.*

SURCLOYING THE STOMACH

Who readeth much, and never meditates,
Is like a greedy eater of much food,
Who so surcloys his stomach with his cates,
That commonly they do him little good.

   J. SYLVESTER. *Tetrasticha.*

OVER-READING

As for the disgraces which learning receiveth from politics, they be of this nature; that learning doth soften men's minds, and makes them more unapt for the honour and exercise of arms; that it doth mar and pervert men's dispositions for matter of government and policy, in making them too curious and irresolute by variety of reading, or too peremptory or positive by strictness of rules and axioms, or too immoderate and overweening by reason of the greatness of examples, or too incompatible and differing from the times by reason of the dissimilitude of examples; or at least, that it doth divert men's travails from action and business, and bringeth them to a love of leisure and privateness; and that it doth bring into states a relaxation of discipline, whilst every man is more ready to argue than to obey and execute....

If any man be laborious in reading and study and yet idle in business and action, it groweth from some weakness of body or softness of spirit; such as Seneca speaketh of: *Quidam tam sunt umbratiles, ut putent in turbido esse quicquid in luce est,* and not of learning: well may it be that such a point of a man's nature may make him give himself to learning, but it is not learning that breedeth any such point in his nature.--F. BACON, LORD VERULAM. *Of the Advancement of Learning.*

DEEP-VERSED IN BOOKS AND SHALLOW IN HIMSELF

Many books,
Wise men have said, are wearisome; who reads
Incessantly, and to his reading brings not
A spirit and judgement, equal or superior,
(And what he brings, what needs he elsewhere seek?)
Uncertain and unsettled still remains,
Deep-versed in books, and shallow in himself;
Crude or intoxicate, collecting toys
And trifles for choice matters, worth a sponge;
As children gathering pebbles on the shore.

J. MILTON. *Paradise Regained.*

SWALLOWING THE HUSKS

The heart
May give an useful lesson to the head,
And learning wiser grow without his books.
Knowledge and wisdom, far from being one,
Have oft-times no connexion. Knowledge dwells
In heads replete with thoughts of other men;
Wisdom in minds attentive to their own.
Knowledge, a rude unprofitable mass,
The mere materials with which Wisdom builds,
Till smoothed and squared and fitted to its place,
Does but encumber whom it seems to enrich.
Knowledge is proud that he has learned so much;
Wisdom is humble that he knows no more.
  Books are not seldom talismans and spells,
By which the magic art of shrewder wits
Holds an unthinking multitude enthralled.
Some to the fascination of a name
Surrender judgement, hood-winked. Some the style
Infatuates, and through labyrinths and wilds
Of error leads them by a tune entranced.
While sloth seduces more, too weak to bear
The insupportable fatigue of thought,
And swallowing, therefore, without pause or choice,
The total grist unsifted, husks and all.
But trees, and rivulets whose rapid course

119

Defies the check of winter, haunts of deer,
And sheep-walks populous with bleating lambs,
And lanes in which the primrose ere her time
Peeps through the moss that clothes the hawthorn root,
Deceive no student. Wisdom there, and truth,
Not shy, as in the world, and to be won
By slow solicitation, seize at once
The roving thought, and fix it on themselves.

W. COWPER. *The Winter Walk at Noon.*

Much reading is like much eating, wholly useless without digestion.--R. SOUTH.

If I had read as much as other men, I should have been as ignorant as they.--T. HOBBES.

READING AND ILLITERACY

You might read all the books in the British Museum (if you could live long enough) and remain an utterly 'illiterate', uneducated person; but ... if you read ten pages of a good book, letter by letter,--that is to say, with real accuracy,--you are for evermore in some measure an educated person.--J. RUSKIN. *Sesame and Lilies.*

READING AS INTELLECTUAL INDOLENCE

Do I boast of my omnivorousness of reading, even apart from romances? Certainly no!--never, except in joke. It's against my theories and ratiocinations, which take upon themselves to assert that we all generally err by *reading too much*, or out of proportion to what we *think*. I should be wiser, I am persuaded, if I had not read half as much--should have had stronger and better exercised faculties. The fact is, that the *ne plus ultra* of intellectual indolence is this reading of books. It comes next to what the Americans call 'whittling'.--E. B. BROWNING (Letter to R. H. Horne).

BOOKS AND MEN

He that sets out on the journey of life, with a profound knowledge of books, but a shallow knowledge of men, with much sense of others, but little of his own, will find himself as completely at a loss on occasions of common and of constant recurrence, as a Dutchman without his pipe, a Frenchman without his mistress, an Italian without his fiddle, or an Englishman without his umbrella.--C. C. COLTON. *Lacon.*

Study is like the heaven's glorious sun,
  That will not be deep-searched with saucy looks;
Small have continual plodders ever won,
  Save base authority from others' books.

W. SHAKESPEARE. *Love's Labour's Lost.*

BOOKS AND LIFE

Who, loving leisure and his studious ease,
And books, and what of noblest lore they bring,
Will not confess that sometimes, called aside
To humbler work and less delightful tasks,
He has been tempted to exclaim in heart--
'How pleasant were it might we only dwell,
And ever hold sweet converse undisturbed
Thus with the choicest spirits of the world
In council, and in letters, and in arms.
Easy to live with, always at command,
They come at bidding, at our word depart,
Friends whose society not ever cloys.
Glorious it were by intercourse with these
To learn whatever men have thought or done,
And travel the great orb of knowledge round.
But oh! how most unwelcome the constraint,
How harsh the summons bidding us to pause,
And for a season turn from our high toils,
From that serener atmosphere come down,
And grow perforce acquainted with the woe,
The strife, the discord of the actual world,
And all the ignoble work beneath the sun.'

*   *   *   *   *

But other feelings occupied my heart,
And other words found utterance from my lips,
When that day's work was finished, and my feet
Again turned homeward--alteration strange
Of feeling, with a better, humbler mind.
For I was thankful now ...
                    ... that thus I was
Compelled, as by a gentle violence
Not in the pages of dead books alone,
Nor merely in the fair page nature shows,
But in the living page of human life
To look and learn--not merely left to spin

Fine webs and woofs around me like the worm,
Till in mine own coil I had hid myself
And quite shut out the light of common day,
And common air by which men breathe and live.

*　　*　　*　　*　　*

It was brought home unto my heart of hearts
There was no doom more pitiable than his,
Who at safe distance hears life's stormy waves,
Which break for ever on a rugged shore,
In which are shipwrecked mariners, for their lives
Contending some, some momently sucked up,
But as a gentle murmur afar off
To soothe his sleep, and lull him in his dreams:
Who, while he boasts he has been building up
A palace for himself, in sooth has reared
What shall be first his prison, then his tomb.

R. C. TRENCH. *Anti-Gnosticus.*

THE MIGHTY DEAD

　　　Studious let me sit,
And hold high converse with the mighty dead--
Sages of ancient time, as gods revered,
As gods beneficent, who blessed mankind
With arts and arms, and humanized a world.
Roused at the inspiring thought, I throw aside
The long-lived volume.

J. THOMSON. *The Seasons.*

THE MESSAGE OF BOOKS

If books are only dead things, if they do not speak to one, or answer one when one speaks to them, if they have nothing to do with the common things that we are busy with--with the sky over our head, and the ground under our feet--I think that they had better stay on the shelves.... What I regret is that many of us spend much of our time in reading books, and in talking of books--that we like nothing worse than the reputation of being indifferent to them, and nothing better than the reputation of knowing a great deal about them; and yet that, after all, we do not know them in the same way as we know our fellow-creatures, not even in the way we know any dumb animal that we walk with or play with. This is a great misfortune, in my opinion, and one which I am afraid is increasing as what we call 'the taste for literature' increases. It is very pleasant to think in what distant parts of the earth it [the English language] is spoken, and that in all those parts these books which are friends of ours are acknowledged as friends. And there is a living and productive power in them. They have produced an American literature, which is coming back to instruct us. They will produce by and by an Australian literature, which will be worth all the gold that is sent to us from the diggings.--F. D. MAURICE. *The Friendship of Books.*

OVERRATING THE VIRTUE OF BOOKS

In modern times instruction is communicated chiefly by means of Books. Books are no doubt very useful helps to knowledge, and in some measure also, to the practice of useful arts and accomplishments, but they are not, in any case, the primary and natural sources of culture, and, in my opinion, their virtue is not a little apt to be overrated, even in those branches of acquirement where they seem most indispensable. They are not creative powers in any sense; they are merely helps, instruments, tools; and even as tools they are only artificial tools, superadded to those with which the wise prevision of Nature has equipped us, like telescopes and microscopes, whose assistance in many researches reveals unimagined wonders, but the use of which should never tempt us to undervalue or to neglect the exercise of our own eyes. The original and proper sources of knowledge are not books, but life, experience, personal thinking, feeling, and acting. When a man starts with these, books can fill up many gaps, correct much that is inaccurate, and extend much that is inadequate; but, without living experience to work on, books are like rain and sunshine fallen on unbroken soil.--J. S. BLACKIE. *On Self-culture.*

How well he's read, to reason against reading!

W. SHAKESPEARE. *Love's Labour's Lost.*

BOOKS AN ENEMY TO HEALTH

This plodding occupation of books is as painful as any other, and as great an enemy unto health, which ought principally to be considered. And a man should not suffer himself to be inveigled by the pleasure he takes in them.... Books are delightful; but if by continual frequenting them, we in the end lose both health and cheerfulness (our best parts) let us leave them. I am one of those who think their fruit can no way countervail this loss.... As for me, I love no books but such as are pleasant and easy, and which tickle me, or such as comfort or counsel me, to direct my life and death....

If any say to me, It is a kind of vilifying the Muses to use them only for sport and recreation, he wots not as I do, what worth, pleasure, sport, and pastime is of: I had well nigh termed all other ends ridiculous. I live from hand to mouth, and, with reverence be it spoken, I live but to myself: there end all my designs. Being young I studied for ostentation; then a little to enable myself and become wiser; now for delight and recreation, never for gain.... Books have and contain divers pleasing qualities to those that can duly choose them. But no good without pains; no roses without prickles. It is a pleasure not absolutely pure and neat; no more than all others; it hath his inconveniences attending on it, and sometimes weighty ones: the mind is therein exercised, but the body (the care whereof I have not yet forgotten) remaineth there--whilst without action, and is wasted, and ensorrowed. I know no excess more hurtful for me, nor more to be avoided by me, in this declining age.--MONTAIGNE.

WHAT PROFITS IT

And yet, alas! when all our lamps are burned,
  Our bodies wasted, and our spirits spent,
When we have all the learnèd volumes turned,
  Which yield men's wits both help and ornament,
What can we know or what can we discern?

    SIR J. DAVIES. *On the Immortality of the Soul.*

BOOKS AND EYESIGHT

Why, all delights are vain; but that most vain
Which, with pain purchased doth inherit pain:
As, painfully to pore upon a book,
  To seek the light of truth; while truth the while
Doth falsely blind the eyesight of his look:
  Light seeking light doth light of light beguile:
So, ere you find where light in darkness lies,
Your light grows dark by losing of your eyes.

    W. SHAKESPEARE. *Love's Labour's Lost.*

WHEN TO READ

'Tis an honest injury to nature to steal from her some hours of repose; unsufferable to the soul to let the golden hours of the morning pass without advantage, seeing she is then more capable of culture, and seems to be renewed as well as the day. It were an excellent posture to paint Caesar in, as he swum with a book in the one hand, and a sword in the other; since he made his tent an academy, and was at leisure to read the physiognomy of the heavens in military tumults. This shows he knew how to prize time, and hated idleness as much as a superior; and indeed, to speak to Christians, we ought to look how we spend our hours here, knowing they are but the preludium of that which shall be no time but Eternity.

Judgement is long ere it be settled, experience being the best nurse of it, and we see seldom learning and wisdom concur, because the former is got *sub umbra*, but business doth winnow observations, and the better acquaintance with breathing volumes of men; it teacheth us both better to read them and to apply what we have read....

Health ought to be nicely respected by a student. For the labours of the mind are as far beyond them of the body, as the diseases of the one are above the other; and how can a spirit actuate when she is caged in a lump of fainting flesh? Unseasonable times of study are very obnoxious, as after meals, when Nature is wholly retired to concoction; or at night times, when she begins to droop for want of rest, hence so many rheums, deflux- ions, catarrhs, &c., that I have heard it spoken of one of the greatest ambulatory pieces of learning at this day, that he would redeem (if possible) his health with the loss of half his learning.--JOHN HALL. *Horae Vacivae.*

BOOKS INSTEAD OF STIMULANTS

I know what it is to have had to toil when the brain was throbbing, the mind incapable of originating a thought, and the body worn and sore with exhaustion; and I know what it is in such an hour, instead of having recourse to those gross stimulants to which all worn men, both of the higher and lower classes, are tempted, to take down my Sopho- cles or my Plato (for Plato was a poet), my Goethe, or my Dante, Shakespeare, Shelley, Wordsworth, or Tennyson; and I know what it is to feel the jar of nerve gradually cease, and the darkness in which all life had robed itself to the imagination become light, dis- cord pass into harmony, and physical exhaustion rise by degrees into a consciousness of power.--F. W. ROBERTSON. *Lectures and Addresses.*

THE PHARMACY OF BOOKS

Books, taken indiscriminately, are no cure to the diseases and afflictions of the mind. There is a world of science necessary in the taking them. I have known some people in great sorrow fly to a novel or the last light book in fashion. One might as well take a rose-draught for the plague! Light reading does not do when the heart is really heavy. I am told that Goethe, when he lost his son, took to study a science that was new to him. Ah! Goethe was a physician who knew what he was about. In a great grief like this you cannot tickle and divert the mind; you must wrench it away, abstract, absorb--bury it in an abyss, hurry it into a labyrinth. Therefore, for the irremediable sorrows of middle life and old age, I recommended a strict chronic course of science and hard reasoning-- counter-irritation. Bring the brain to act upon the heart! If science is too much against the grain (for we have not all got mathematical heads), something in the reach of the humblest understanding, but sufficiently searching to the highest--new language--Greek, Arabic, Scandinavian, Chinese, or Welsh! For the loss of fortune the dose should be ap- plied less directly to the understanding--I would administer something elegant and cordial. For as the heart is crushed and lacerated by a loss in the affections, so it is rather the head that aches and suffers by the loss of money. Here we find the higher class of poets a very valuable remedy. For observe that poets of the grander and more compre- hensive kind of genius have in them two separate men quite distinct from each other-- the imaginative man, and the practical, circumstantial man; and it is the happy mixture of these that suits diseases of the mind, half imaginative and half practical.... For hypochon- dria and satiety what is better than a brisk alterative course of travels--especially early, out-of-the-way, marvellous, legendary travels! How they freshen up the spirits! How they take you out of the humdrum yawning state you are in.... Then, for that vice of the mind which I call sectarianism--not in the religious sense of the word, but little, narrow preju-dices, that make you hate your next-door neighbour, because he has his eggs roasted when you have yours boiled; and gossiping and prying into people's affairs, and backbit-ing, and thinking heaven and earth are coming together, if some broom touch a cobweb that you have let grow over the window-sill of your brains--what like a large and gener-ous, mildly aperient course of history! How it clears away all the fumes of the head!--better than the hellebore with which the old leeches of the Middle Ages purged the cere-bellum. There, amidst all that great whirl and *sturmbad* (storm-bath), as the Germans say, of kingdoms and empires, and races and ages, how your mind enlarges beyond that little feverish animosity to John Styles: or that unfortunate prepossession of yours, that all the world is interested in your grievances against Tom Stokes and his wife!

I can only touch, you see, on a few ingredients in this magnificent pharmacy--its re-sources are boundless, but require the nicest discretion. I remember to have cured a disconsolate widower, who obstinately refused every other medicament, by a strict course of geology.... I made no less notable a cure of a young scholar at Cambridge, who was meant for the Church, when he suddenly caught a cold fit of freethinking, with great shiverings, from wading out of his depth in Spinoza.... His theological constitution, since then, has become so robust that he has eaten up two livings and a deanery! In fact, I have a plan for a library that, instead of heading its compartments, 'Philology, Natural Science, Poetry,' &c., one shall head them according to the diseases for which they are severally good, bodily and mental--up from a dire calamity, or the pangs of the gout, down to a fit of the spleen or a slight catarrh; for which last your light reading comes in with a whey-posset and barley-water. But when some one sorrow, that is yet reparable, gets hold of your mind like a monomania--when you think, because heaven has denied you this or that, on which you had set your heart, that all your life must be a blank--oh! then diet yourself well on biography--the biography of good and great men.... I have said nothing of the Book of Books, for that is the *lignum vitae*, the cardinal medicine for all. These are but the subsidiaries.--E. G. E. L. BULWER-LYTTON, LORD LYTTON. *The Caxtons.*

A LITERATURA HILARIS

Cast your eyes down any list of English writers ... and almost the only names that strike you as belonging to personally cheerful men are Beaumont and Fletcher, Suckling, Field-ing, Farquhar, Steele, O'Keefe, Andrew Marvell, and Sterne.... I am only speaking of the rarity of a certain kind of sunshine in our literature, and expressing a little rainy-day wish that we had a little more of it. It ought to be collected. There should be a joyous set of elegant extracts--a *Literatura Hilaris* or *Gaudens*,--in a score of volumes, that we could have at hand, like a cellaret of good wine, against April or November weather. Fielding should be the port, and Farquhar the champagne, and Sterne the malmsey; and whenever the possessor cast an eye on his stock he should know that he had a choice draught for himself after a disappointment, or for a friend after dinner,--some cordial extract of Par-son Adams, or Plume, or Uncle Toby, generous as heart could desire, and as wholesome for it as laughter for the lungs.--J. H. LEIGH HUNT. *Cheerful Poets.*

THE BLESSED CHLOROFORM OF THE MIND

A congenial book can be taken up by any lover of books, with the certainty of its transporting the reader within a few minutes to a region immeasurably removed from that which he desires to quit. The shape or pattern of the magic carpet whereon he flies through space and time, is of no consequence. The son of science is rapt by a problem; the philosopher by an abstruse speculation; the antiquary is carried centuries back into the chivalric past; the lover of poetry is borne upon glittering wings into the future. The charm works well for all. Books are the blessed chloroform of the mind.... It is not a very high claim that is here set forth on behalf of Literature--that of Pass-time, and yet what a blessed boon even that is! Conceive the hours of *inertia* (a thing different from idleness) that it has mercifully consumed for us! hours wherein nothing could be done, nothing, perhaps, be *thought*, of our own selves, by reason of some impending calamity. Wisely does the dentist furnish his hateful antechamber with books of all sorts. Who could abide for an hour in such an apartment with nothing to occupy his thoughts save the expectation of that wrench to come!... Indeed, it must be confessed that where Books fail as an anodyne, is rather in cases of physical than of mental pain. Through the long watches of the night, and by the bedside of some slowly dying dear one, it is easier to obtain forgetfulness--the only kind of rest that it may be safe or possible to take--by means of reading, than to do so when one is troubled with mere toothache. Nor does this arise from selfishness--since we would endure twenty toothaches, if they might give ease to the sufferer--but because the sharpness of the pang prevents our applying our mind to anything else; while the deep dull sorrow of the soul permits an intervening thought, and over it slides another, and then another, until a layer of such is formed, and the mind of the reader gets wholly free, for a brief but blessed time, partitioned off, as it were, from his real trouble.--J. PAYN. *Chambers's Journal,*1864.

LOUNGING BOOKS

I sometimes wish for a catalogue of lounging books--books that one takes up in the gout, low spirits, *ennui*, or when in waiting for company. Some novels, gay poetry, odd whimsical authors, as Rabelais, &c. A catalogue raisonné of such might be itself a good lounging book.--H. WALPOLE, EARL OF ORFORD. *Letters.*

TO DRIVE THE NIGHT AWAY

So whan I saw I might not slepe,
Til now late, this other night,
Upon my bedde I sat upright,
And bad oon reche me a book,
A romaunce, and he hit me took
To rede and dryve the night away;
For me thoghte it better play
Than playen either at chesse or tables.

    G. CHAUCER. *The Book of the Duchesse.*

READING IN BED

Since I cannot in the way of gratefulness express unto your lordship, as I would, those hearty sentiments I have of your goodness to me; I will at the last endeavour, in the way of duty and observance, to let you see how the little needle of my soul is throughly touched at the great loadstone of yours, and followeth suddenly and strongly, which way soever you beckon it. In this occasion, the magnetic motion was impatient to have the book in my hands that your lordship gave so advantageous a character of; whereupon I sent presently (as late as it was) to Paul's church-yard for this favourite of yours, *Religio Medici*: which after awhile found me in a condition fit to receive a blessing by a visit from any of such masterpieces, as you look upon with gracious eyes; for I was newly gotten into my bed. This good-natured creature I could easily persuade to be my bedfellow, and to wake with me as long as I had any edge to entertain myself with the delights I sucked from so noble a conversation. And truly, my lord, I closed not my eyes till I had enriched myself with, or at least exactly surveyed all the treasures that are lapped up in the folds of those few sheets. To return only a general commendation of this curious piece, or at large to admire the author's spirit and smartness, were too perfunctory an account, and too slight a one, to so discerning and steady an eye as yours, after so particular and en-charged a summons to read heedfully this discourse. I will therefore presume to blot a sheet or two of paper with my reflections upon sundry passages.--SIR K. DIGBY (Letter to Edward, Earl of Dorset).

READING AND MEAL TIMES

Before my meals,... and after, I let myself loose from all my thoughts; and now would forget that I ever studied. A full mind takes away the body's appetite, no less than a full body makes a dull and unwieldy mind.--JOSEPH HALL (Letter to Lord Denny).

THE DOG AND THE BONE

At Mr. Dilly's to-day [April 15, 1778] ... before dinner Dr. Johnson seized upon Mr. Charles Sheridan's *Account of the late Revolution in Sweden*, and seemed to read it ravenously, as if he devoured it, which was to all appearance his method of studying. 'He knows how to read better than any one (said Mrs. Knowles); he gets at the substance of a book di-rectly; he tears out the heart of it.' He kept it wrapt up in the tablecloth in his lap during the time of dinner, from an avidity to have one entertainment in readiness when he should have finished another; resembling (if I may use so coarse a simile) a dog who holds a bone in his paws in reserve, while he eats something else which has been thrown to him.--J. BOSWELL. *Life of Johnson*.

PROOF OF GOOD MATTER

If you find the Miltons in certain parts dirtied and soiled with a crumb of right Glouces-ter, blacked in the candle (my usual supper), or peradventure a stray ash of tobacco wafted into the crevices, look to that passage more especially: depend upon it, it contains good matter.--C. LAMB (Letter to S. T. Coleridge).

WRITING AT MEAL TIMES

... Albeit, when I did dictate [these Chronicles], I thought thereof no more than you, who possibly were drinking the whilst, as I was. For in the composing of this lordly book I never lost nor bestowed any more, nor any other time, than what was appointed to serve me for taking of my bodily refection, that is, whilst I was eating and drinking. And, indeed, that is the fittest and most proper hour, wherein to write these high matters and deep sentences: as Homer knew very well, the paragon of all philologues, and Ennius, the father of the Latin poets, as Horace calls him, although a certain sneaking jobbernol alleged that his verses smelled more of the wine than oil.--F. RABELAIS. *The Life of Gargantua and Pantagruel. Author's Prologue.*

OUT-OF-DOORS READING

I am not much a friend to out-of-doors reading. I cannot settle my spirits to it. I knew a Unitarian minister, who was generally to be seen upon Snow-hill (as yet Skinner's-street *was not*), between the hours of ten and eleven in the morning, studying a volume of Lardner. I own this to have been a strain of abstraction beyond my reach. I used to admire how he sidled along, keeping clear of secular contacts. An illiterate encounter with a porter's knot, or a bread basket, would have quickly put to flight all the theology I am master of, and have left me worse than indifferent to the five points.--C. LAMB. *Detached Thoughts on Books and Reading.*

O FOR A BOOKE

O for a Booke and a shadie nooke,
  Eyther in-a-doore or out,
With the greene leaves whisp'ring overhede,
  Or the Streete cryes all about,
Where I may Reade all at my ease,
  Both of the Newe and Olde,
For a jollie goode Booke whereon to looke,
  Is better to me than golde.

J. WILSON.

FAREWELL TO BOOKS IN SPRINGTIME

Than mote we to bokes that we finde,
Through which that olde thinges been in minde,
And to the doctrine of these olde wyse,

Yeven credence, in every skilful wyse,
And trowen on these olde aproved stories
Of holinesse, of regnes, of victories,
Of love, of hate, of other sundry thinges,
Of whiche I may not maken rehersinges.
And if that olde bokes were a-weye,
Y-loren were of remembraunce the keye.
Wel oghte us than on olde bokes leve,
Ther-as ther is non other assay by preve.
  And, as for me, though that my wit be lyte,
On bokes for to rede I me delyte,
And in myn herte have hem in reverence;
And to hem yeve swich lust and swich credence,
That ther is wel unethe game noon
That from my bokes make me to goon,
But hit be other up-on the haly-day,
Or elles in the joly tyme of May;
Whan that I here the smale foules singe,
And that the floures ginne for to springe,
Farwel my studie, as lasting that sesoun!

G. CHAUCER. *The Legend of Good Women.*

THE TABLES TURNED

Up! up! my Friend, and quit your books;
Or surely you'll grow double:
Up! up! my Friend, and clear your looks;
Why all this toil and trouble?

The sun, above the mountain's head,
A freshening lustre mellow
Through all the long green fields has spread,
His first sweet evening yellow.

Books! 'tis a dull and endless strife:
Come, hear the woodland linnet,
How sweet his music! on my life,
There's more of wisdom in it.

And hark! how blithe the throstle sings!
He, too, is no mean preacher:
Come forth into the light of things,
Let Nature be your Teacher.

She has a world of ready wealth,
Our minds and hearts to bless--

Spontaneous wisdom breathed by health,
Truth breathed by cheerfulness.

One impulse from a vernal wood
May teach you more of man,
Of moral evil and of good,
Than all the sages can.

Sweet is the love which Nature brings;
Our meddling intellect
Mis-shapes the beauteous forms of things:--
We murder to dissect.

Enough of Science and of Art;
Close up those barren leaves;
Come forth, and bring with you a heart
That watches and receives.

W. WORDSWORTH.

LEARNING

Take me to some still abode,
  Underneath some woody hill;
By some timber-skirted road,
  By some willow-shaded rill;

Where along the rocky brook
  Flying echoes sweetly sound,
And the hoarsely-croaking rook
  Builds upon the trees around.

Take me to some lofty room
  Lighted from the western sky,
Where no glare dispels the gloom
  Till the golden eve is nigh,

Where the works of searching thought,
  Chosen books, may still impart
What the wise of old have taught,
  What has tried the meek of heart.

Books in long-dead tongues, that stirred
  Living hearts in other climes;
Telling to my eyes, unheard,
  Glorious deeds of olden times.

Books that purify the thought,
  Spirits of the learned dead,
Teachers of the little taught,
  Comforters when friends are fled.

W. BARNES.

PICTURE BOOKS IN WINTER

Summer fading, winter comes--
Frosty mornings, tingling thumbs,
Window robins, winter rooks,
And the picture story-books.

Water now is turned to stone
Nurse and I can walk upon;
Still we find the flowing brooks
In the picture story-books.

All the pretty things put by,
Wait upon the children's eye,
Sheep and shepherds, trees and crooks,
In the picture story-books.

We may see how all things are,
Seas and cities, near and far,
And the flying fairies' looks
In the picture story-books.

How am I to sing your praise,
Happy chimney-corner days,
Sitting safe in nursery nooks,
Reading picture story-books?

R. L. STEVENSON. *A Child's Garden of Verses.*

THE HORN-BOOK

Hail! ancient Book, most venerable code!
Learning's first cradle, and its last abode!
The huge unnumbered volumes which we see,
By lazy plagiaries are stolen from thee.
Yet future times, to thy sufficient store,
Shall ne'er presume to add one letter more.

  Thee will I sing, in comely wainscot bound,

And golden verge enclosing thee around;
The faithful horn before, from age to age,
Preserving thy invaluable page;
Behind, thy patron saint in armour shines,
With sword and lance, to guard thy sacred lines:
Beneath his courser's feet the dragon lies
Transfixed; his blood thy scarlet cover dyes;
The instructive handle's at the bottom fixed,
Lest wrangling critics should pervert the text.

  Or if to ginger-bread thou shalt descend,
And liquorish learning to thy babes extend;
Or sugared plane, o'erspread with beaten gold,
Does the sweet treasure of thy letters hold;
Thou still shalt be my song--Apollo's choir
I scorn to invoke; Cadmus my verse inspire:
'Twas Cadmus who the first materials brought
Of all the learning which has since been taught,
Soon made complete! for mortals ne'er shall know
More than contained of old the Christ-cross row;
What masters dictate, or what doctors preach,
Wise matrons hence e'en to our children teach:
But as the name of every plant and flower
(So common that each peasant knows its power)
Physicians in mysterious cant express,
To amuse the patient, and enhance their fees;
So from the letters of our native tongue,
Put in Greek scrawls, a mystery too is sprung,
Schools are erected, puzzling grammars made,
And artful men strike out a gainful trade;
Strange characters adorn the learned gate,
And heedless youth catch at the shining bait;
The pregnant boys the noisy charms declare,
And Tau's and Delta's, make their mothers stare;
The uncommon sounds amaze the vulgar ear,
And what's uncommon never costs too dear.
Yet in all tongues the Horn-book is the same,
Taught by the Grecian master, or the English dame.

  But how shall I thy endless virtues tell,
In which thou durst all other books excel?
No greasy thumbs thy spotless leaf can soil,
Nor crooked dog-ears thy smooth corners spoil;
In idle pages no errata stand,
To tell the blunders of the printer's hand:
No fulsome dedication here is writ,
Nor flattering verse, to praise the author's wit:
The margin with no tedious notes is vexed,

Nor various readings to confound the text:
All parties in thy literal sense agree,
Thou perfect centre of concordancy!
Search we the records of an ancient date,
Or read what modern histories relate,
They all proclaim what wonders have been done
By the plain letters taken as they run:
'Too high the floods of passion used to roll,
And rend the Roman youth's impatient soul;
His hasty anger furnished scenes of blood,
And frequent deaths of worthy men ensued:
In vain were all the weaker methods tried,
None could suffice to stem the furious tide,
Thy sacred line he did but once repeat,
And laid the storm, and cooled the raging heat.'

  Thy heavenly notes, like angels' music, cheer
Departing souls, and soothe the dying ear.
An aged peasant, on his latest bed,
Wished for a friend some godly book to read:
The pious grandson thy known handle takes,
And (eyes lift up) this savoury lecture makes:
'Great A,' he gravely read: the important sound
The empty walls and hollow roof rebound:
The expiring ancient reared his drooping head,
And thanked his stars that Hodge had learned to read.
'Great B,' the younker bawls; O heavenly breath!
What ghostly comforts in the hour of death!
What hopes I feel! 'Great C,' pronounced the boy;
The grandsire dies with ecstasy of joy.

  Yet in some lands such ignorance abounds,
Whole parishes scarce know thy useful sounds.
Of Essex hundreds Fame gives this report,
But Fame, I ween, says many things in sport.
Scarce lives the man to whom thou'rt quite unknown,
Though few the extent of thy vast Empire own.
Whatever wonders magic spells can do
On earth, in air, in sea, in shades below;
What words profound and dark wise Mahomet spoke,
When his old cow an angel's figure took;
What strong enchantments sage Canidia knew,
Or Horace sung, fierce monsters to subdue,
O mighty Book, are all contained in you!
All human arts, and every science meet,
Within the limits of thy single sheet:
From thy vast root all learning's branches grow,
And all her streams from thy deep fountain flow.

And, lo! while thus thy wonders I indite,
Inspired I feel the power of which I write;
The gentler gout his former rage forgets,
Less frequent now, and less severe the fits:
Loose grow the chains which bound my useless feet;
Stiffness and pain from every joint retreat;
Surprising strength comes every moment on,
I stand, I step, I walk, and now I run.
Here let me cease, my hobbling numbers stop,
And at thy handle hang my crutches up.

T. TICKLE.

OLD STORY BOOKS

Old Story Books! Old Story Books! we owe ye much, old friends,
Bright-coloured threads in Memory's warp, of which Death holds the
    ends.
Who can forget ye? who can spurn the ministers of joy
That waited on the lisping girl and petticoated boy?
I know that ye could win my heart when every bribe or threat
Failed to allay my stamping rage, or break my sullen pet:
A 'promised story' was enough, and I turned, with eager smile,
To learn about the naughty 'pig that would not mount the stile'.

There was a spot in days of yore whereon I used to stand,
With mighty question in my head and penny in my hand;
Where motley sweets and crinkled cakes made up a goodly show,
And 'story books' upon a string appeared in brilliant row.
What should I have? the peppermint was incense in my nose,
But I had heard of 'hero Jack', who slew his giant foes:
My lonely coin was balanced long, before the tempting stall,
'Twixt book and bull's eye--but, forsooth! 'Jack' got it after all.

Talk of your 'vellum, gold embossed', 'morocco', 'roan', and 'calf',
The blue and yellow wraps of old were prettier by half;
And as to pictures--well we know that never one was made
Like that where 'Bluebeard' swings aloft his wife-destroying blade.
'Hume's England'--pshaw! what history of battles, states, and men,
Can vie with Memoirs 'all about sweet little Jenny Wren'?
And what are all the wonders that e'er struck a nation dumb,
To those recorded as performed by 'Master Thomas Thumb'?

Miss 'Riding Hood', poor luckless child! my heart grew big with dread
When the grim 'wolf', in 'grandmamma's' best bonnet, showed his head;
I shuddered when, in innocence, she meekly peeped beneath,
And made remarks about 'great eyes', and wondered at 'great teeth'.

And then the 'House that Jack built', and the 'Beanstalk' Jack cut
  down,
And 'Jack's eleven brothers', on their travels of renown;
And 'Jack', whose cracked and plastered head ensured him lyric fame,
These, these, methinks, make 'vulgar Jack' a rather classic name.

Fair 'Valentine', I loved him well; but, better still the bear
That hugged his brother in her arms with tenderness and care.
I lingered spellbound o'er the page, though eventide wore late,
And left my supper all untouched to fathom 'Orson's' fate.
Then 'Robin with his merry men', a noble band were they,
We'll never see the like again, go hunting where we may.
In Lincoln garb, with bow and barb, rapt Fancy bore me on,
Through Sherwood's dewy forest paths, close after 'Little John'.

Miss 'Cinderella' and her 'shoe' kept long their reigning powers,
Till harder words and longer themes beguiled my flying hours;
And 'Sinbad', wondrous sailor he, allured me on his track,
And set me shouting when he flung the old man from his back.
And oh! that tale--the matchless tale that made me dream at night--
Of 'Crusoe's' shaggy robe of fur, and 'Friday's' death-spurred flight;
Nay, still I read it, and again, in sleeping visions, see
The savage dancers on the sand--the raft upon the sea.

Old Story Books! Old Story Books! I doubt if 'Reason's Feast'
Provides a dish that pleases more than 'Beauty and the Beast';
I doubt if all the ledger-leaves that bear a sterling sum,
Yield happiness like those that told of 'Master Horner's plum'.
Old Story Books! Old Story Books! I never pass ye by
Without a sort of furtive glance--right loving, though 'tis sly;
And fair suspicion may arise--that yet my spirit grieves
For dear 'Old Mother Hubbard's Dog' and 'Ali Baba's Thieves'.

ELIZA COOK.

THE FIRST AUTHORS FOR YOUTH

And as it is fit to read the best authors to youth first, so let them be of the openest and clearest: as Livy before Sallust, Sidney before Donne; and beware of letting them taste Gower or Chaucer at first, lest falling too much in love with antiquity, and not apprehending the weight, they grow rough and barren in language only. When their judgements are firm and out of danger, let them read both the old and the new; but no less take heed that their new flowers and sweetness do not as much corrupt as the others' dryness and squalor, if they choose not carefully. Spenser, in affecting the ancients, writ no language: yet I would have him read for his matter, but as Virgil read Ennius. The reading of Homer and Virgil is counselled by Quintilian as the best way of informing youth and confirming man. For, besides that the mind is raised with the height and sub-limity of such a verse, it takes spirit from the greatness of the matter, and is tincted with the best things. Tragic and lyric poetry is good too; and comic with the best, if the manners of the reader be once in safety.--BEN JONSON. *Timber*.

BOOKS AND THE WORLD

A man who, without a good fund of knowledge and parts, adopts a Court life, makes the most ridiculous figure imaginable. He is a machine, little superior to the Court clock; and, as this points out the hours, he points out the frivolous employment of them. He is, at most, a comment upon the clock; and, according to the hours that it strikes, tells you, now it is levee, now dinner, now supper time, &c. The end which I propose by your education is, to unite in you all the knowledge of a scholar, with the manners of a courtier, and to join, what is seldom joined in any of my countrymen, Books and the World. They are commonly twenty years old before they have spoken to anybody above their Schoolmaster and the Fellows of their college. If they happen to have learning, it is only Greek and Latin; but not one word of Modern History or Modern Languages. Thus prepared, they go abroad, as they call it; but, in truth, they stay at home all that while; for being very awkward, confoundedly ashamed, and not speaking the languages, they go into no foreign company, at least none good; but dine and sup with one another only, at the tavern.--LORD CHESTERFIELD. *Letters to his Son*.

ADVICE TO MOTHERS

Mr. B---- has just put into my hands Mr. Locke's *Treatise on Education*, and he commands me to give him my thoughts upon it in writing. He has a very high regard for this author, and tells me that my tenderness for Billy will make me think some of the first advice given in it a little harsh, perhaps; but, although he has not read it through, only having dipped into it here and there, he believes, from the name of the author, I cannot have a better directory; and my opinion of it, after I have well considered it, will inform him, he says, of my own capacity and prudence, and how far he may rely upon both in the point of a first education.--S. RICHARDSON. *Pamela*.

GETTING A BOY FORWARD

I am always for getting a boy forward in his learning; for that is a sure good. I would let him at first read *any* English book which happens to engage his attention; because you have done a great deal when you have brought him to have entertainment from a book. He'll get better books afterwards.--S. JOHNSON. (Boswell's *Life*.)

AT LARGE IN THE LIBRARY

I would put a child into a library (where no unfit books are) and let him read at his choice. A child should not be discouraged from reading anything that he takes a liking to, from a notion that it is above his reach. If that be the case, the child will soon find it out and desist; if not, he of course gains the instruction; which is so much the more likely to come, from the inclination with which he takes up the study.--S. JOHNSON. (Boswell's *Life.*)

THE BEST BOOKS THE COMMONEST

Books are but one inlet of knowledge; and the powers of the mind, like those of the body, should be left open to all impressions. I applied too close to my studies, soon after I was of your age, and hurt myself irreparably by it. Whatever may be the value of learning, health and good spirits are of more.... By conversing with the *mighty dead*, we imbibe sentiment with knowledge. We become strongly attached to those who can no longer either hurt or serve us, except through the influence which they exert over the mind. We feel the presence of that power which gives immortality to human thoughts and actions, and catch the flame of enthusiasm from all ages and nations.... As to the books you will have to read by choice or for amusement, the best are the commonest. The names of many of them are already familiar to you. Read them as you grow up with all the satisfaction in your power, and make much of them. It is, perhaps, the greatest pleasure you will have in life; the one you will think of longest, and repent of least. If my life had been more full of calamity than it has been (much more than I hope yours will be), I would live it over again, my poor little boy, to have read the books I did in my youth.--W. HAZLITT. *On the Conduct of Life; or Advice to a Schoolboy.*

MONTAIGNE'S EARLY READING

The first taste or feeling I had of books, was of the pleasure I took in reading the fables of Ovid's *Metamorphoses*; for, being but seven or eight years old, I would steal and sequester myself from all other delights, only to read them: Forsomuch as the tongue wherein they were written was to me natural; and it was the easiest book I knew, and by reason of the matter therein contained most agreeing with my young age. For of King Arthur, of Lancelot du Lake, of Amadis, of Huon of Bordeaux, and such idle time-consuming and wit-besotting trash of books wherein youth doth commonly amuse itself, I was not so much as acquainted with their names, and to this day know not their bodies, nor what they contain, so exact was my discipline. Whereby I became more careless to study my other prescript lessons. And well did it fall out for my purpose that I had to deal with a very discreet master, who out of his judgement could with such dexterity wink at and second my untowardliness, and such other faults that were in me. For by that means I read over Virgil's *Aeneas*, Terence, Plautus, and other Italian comedies, allured thereunto by the pleasantness of their several subjects: Had he been so foolishly-severe, or so severely froward as to cross this course of mine, I think, verily, I had never brought anything from the college but the hate and contempt of books, as doth the greatest part of our nobility. Such was his discretion, and so warily did he behave himself, that he saw and would not see: he would foster and increase my longing: suffering me but by stealth and by snatches to glut myself with those books, holding ever a gentle hand over me, concerning other regular studies.--MONTAIGNE.

JOHNSON'S EARLY READING

Sir, in my early years I read very hard. It is a sad reflection, but a true one, that I knew almost as much at eighteen as I do now [then aged fifty-four]. My judgement, to be sure, was not so good; but I had all the facts. I remember very well, when I was at Oxford, an old gentleman said to me, 'Young man, ply your book diligently now and acquire a stock of knowledge; for when years come upon you, you will find that poring upon books will be but an irksome task.'--S. JOHNSON. (Boswell's *Life*.)

GIBBON'S EARLY READING

The perusal of the Roman classics was at once my exercise and reward. Dr. Middleton's *History*, which I then appreciated above its true value, naturally directed me to the writings of Cicero. The most perfect editions, that of Olivet, which may adorn the shelves of the rich, that of Ernesti, which should lie on the table of the learned, were not within my reach. For the familiar epistles I used the text and English commentary of Bishop Ross; but my general edition was that of Verburgius, published at Amsterdam in two large volumes in folio, with an indifferent choice of various notes.... Cicero in Latin, and Xenophon in Greek, are indeed the two ancients whom I would first propose to a liberal scholar....

In the infancy of my reason I turned over, as an idle amusement, the most serious and important treatise: in its maturity, the most trifling performance could exercise my taste or judgement; and more than once I have been led by a novel into a deep and instructive train of thinking.--E. GIBBON. *Autobiography*.

A BIRTH OF INTELLECT

When only eleven years old, with three pence in my pocket--my whole fortune--I perceived, at Richmond, in a bookseller's window, a little book, marked 'Price Three pence'--Swift's *Tale of a Tub*. Its odd title excited my curiosity; I bought it in place of my supper. So impatient was I to examine it, that I got over into a field at the upper corner of Kew Gardens, and sat down to read, on the shady side of a haystack. The book was so different from anything I had read before--it was something so new to my mind, that, though I could not at all understand some parts of it, still it delighted me beyond measure, and produced, what I have always considered, a sort of birth of intellect. I read on till it was dark, without any thought of supper or bed. When I could see no longer, I put it into my pocket, and fell asleep beside the stack, till the birds awaked me in the morning; and then I started off, still reading my little book. I could relish nothing beside; I carried it about with me wherever I went, till, when about twenty years old, I lost it in a box that fell overboard in the Bay of Fundy.--W. COBBETT.

WORDSWORTH'S EARLY READING

A precious treasure had I long possessed,
A little yellow, canvas-covered book,
A slender abstract of the Arabian Tales;
And, from companions in a new abode,
When first I learnt, that this dear prize of mine
Was but a block hewn from a mighty quarry--
That there were four large volumes, laden all
With kindred matter, 'twas to me, in truth,
A promise scarcely earthly. Instantly,
With one not richer than myself, I made
A covenant that each should lay aside
The moneys he possessed, and hoard up more,
Till our joint savings had amassed enough
To make this book our own. Through several months,
In spite of all temptations, we preserved
Religiously that vow; but firmness failed,
Nor were we ever masters of our wish.

  And when thereafter to my father's house
The holidays returned me, there to find
That golden store of books which I had left,
What joy was mine! How often in the course
Of those glad respites, though a soft west wind
Ruffled the waters to the angler's wish,
For a whole day together, have I lain
Down by thy side, O Derwent! murmuring stream,
On the hot stones, and in the glaring sun,
And there have read, devouring as I read,
Defrauding the day's glory, desperate!
Till with a sudden bound of smart reproach,
Such as an idler deals with in his shame,
I to the sport betook myself again.

  A gracious spirit o'er this earth presides,
And o'er the heart of man: invisibly
It comes, to works of unreproved delight,
And tendency benign, directing those
Who care not, know not, think not what they do.
The tales that charm away the wakeful night
In Araby, romances; legends penned
For solace by dim light of monkish lamps;
Fictions, for ladies of their love, devised

By youthful squires; adventures endless, spun
By the dismantled warrior in old age,
Out of the bowels of those very schemes
In which his youth did first extravagate;
These spread like day, and something in the shape
Of these will live till man shall be no more.

Dumb yearnings, hidden appetites, are ours,
And *they must* have their food. Our childhood sits,
Our simple childhood, sits upon a throne
That hath more power than all the elements.
I guess not what this tells of Being past,
Nor what it augurs of the life to come;
But so it is, and, in that dubious hour,
That twilight when we first begin to see
This dawning earth, to recognise, expect,
And, in the long probation that ensues,
The time of trial, ere we learn to live
In reconcilement with our stinted powers;
To endure this state of meagre vassalage,
Unwilling to forgo, confess, submit,
Uneasy and unsettled, yoke-fellows
To custom, mettlesome, and not yet tamed
And humbled down;--oh! then we feel, we feel,
We know where we have friends. Ye dreamers, then,
Forgers of daring tales! we bless you then,
Impostors, drivellers, dotards, as the ape
Philosophy will call you: *then* we feel
With what, and how great might ye are in league,
Who make our wish, our power, our thought a deed,
An empire, a possession,--ye whom time
And seasons serve; all Faculties to whom
Earth crouches, the elements are potter's clay,
Space like a heaven filled up with northern lights,
Here, nowhere, there, and everywhere at once.

W. WORDSWORTH. *The Prelude.*

OLD-FASHIONED VERSE

In verse alone I ran not wild
When I was hardly more than child,
Contented with the native lay
Of Pope or Prior, Swift or Gay,
Or Goldsmith, or that graver bard
Who led me to the lone churchyard.
  Then listened I to Spenser's strain,

Till Chaucer's Canterbury train
Came trooping past, and carried me
In more congenial company.
Soon my soul was hurried o'er
This bright scene: the 'solemn roar'
Of organ, under Milton's hand,
Struck me mute: he bade me stand
Where none other ambled near....
I obeyed, with love and fear.

W. S. LANDOR.

LEIGH HUNT'S EARLY READING

Cowley says that even when he was 'a very young boy at school, instead of his running about on holidays, and playing with his fellows, he was wont to steal from them and walk into the fields, either alone with a book, or with some one companion, if he could find one of the same temper'. When I was at school, I had no fields to run into, or I should certainly have gone there; and I must own to having played a great deal; but then I drew my sports as much as possible out of books, playing at Trojan wars, chivalrous encounters with coal-staves, and even at religious mysteries. When I was not at these games I was either reading in a corner, or walking round the cloisters with a book under one arm and my friend linked with the other, or with my thoughts. It has since been my fate to realize all the romantic notions I had of a friend at that time.--J. H. LEIGH HUNT. *My Books.*

A KINDLY TIE

Then, above all, we had Walter Scott, the kindly, the generous, the pure--the companion of what countless delightful hours; the purveyor of how much happiness; the friend whom we recall as the constant benefactor of our youth! How well I remember the type and the brownish paper of the old duodecimo *Tales of My Landlord*!... Oh! for a half-holiday, and a quiet corner, and one of those books again! Those books, and perhaps those eyes with which we read them; and, it may be, the brains behind the eyes! It may be the tart was good; but how fresh the appetite was!... The boy critic loves the story; grown up, he loves the author who wrote the story. Hence the kindly tie is established between writer and reader, and lasts pretty nearly for life.--W. M. THACKERAY. *Roundabout Papers.*

CHARLES DICKENS'S EARLY READING

My father had left a small collection of books in a little room upstairs, to which I had access (for it adjoined my own), and which nobody else in our house ever troubled. From that blessed little room, Roderick Random, Peregrine Pickle, Humphrey Clinker, Tom Jones, the Vicar of Wakefield, Don Quixote, Gil Blas, and Robinson Crusoe, came out, a glorious host, to keep me company. They kept alive my fancy, and my hope of something beyond that place and time,--they, and the Arabian Nights, and the Tales of the Genii--and did me no harm; for whatever harm was in some of them was not there for me; *I* knew nothing of it. It is astonishing to me now, how I found time, in the midst of my porings and blunderings over heavier themes, to read those books as I did. It is curious to me how I could ever have consoled myself under my small troubles (which were great troubles to me), by impersonating my favourite characters in them--as I did-- and by putting Mr. and Miss Murdstone into all the bad ones--which I did too. I have been Tom Jones (a child's Tom Jones, a harmless creature) for a week together. I have sustained my own idea of Roderick Random for a month at a stretch, I verily believe. I had a greedy relish for a few volumes of Voyages and Travels--I forget what, now--that were on those shelves; and for days and days I can remember to have gone about my region of our house, armed with the centrepiece out of an old set of boot-trees--the per- fect realization of Captain Somebody, of the Royal British Navy, in danger of being beset by savages, and resolved to sell his life at a great price. The Captain never lost dignity, from having his ears boxed with the Latin grammar. I did; but the Captain was a Captain and a hero, in despite of all the grammars of all the languages in the world, dead or alive.

This was my only and my constant comfort. When I think of it, the picture always rises in my mind, of a summer evening, the boys at play in the churchyard, and I sitting on my bed, reading as if for life. Every barn in the neighbourhood, every stone in the church, and every foot of the churchyard, had some association of its own, in my mind, connect- ed with these books, and stood for some locality made famous in them.--C. DICKENS. *David Copperfield.*

THE VISIONARY GLEAM

Books have in a great measure lost their power over me; nor can I revive the same inter- est in them as formerly. I perceive when a thing is good, rather than feel it. It is true,

'Marcian Colonna' is a dainty book;

and the reading of Mr. Keats's *Eve of St. Agnes* lately made me regret that I was not young again. The beautiful and tender images there conjured up, 'come like shadows--so de- part.' The 'tiger-moth's wings', which he has spread over his rich poetic blazonry, just flit across my fancy; the gorgeous twilight window which he has painted over again in his verse, to me 'blushes' almost in vain 'with blood of queens and kings'. I know how I should have felt at one time in reading such passages; and that is all. The sharp luscious flavour, the fine *aroma* is fled, and nothing but the stalk, the bran, the husk of literature is left.--W. HAZLITT. *On Reading Old Books.*

READING FOR LOVE'S SAKE

If thou survive my well-contented day,
When that churl Death my bones with dust shall cover,
And shalt by fortune once more re-survey

These poor rude lines of thy deceasèd lover,
Compare them with the bettering of the time,
And though they be outstripped by every pen,
Reserve them for my love, not for their rime,
Exceeded by the height of happier men.
O! then vouchsafe me but this loving thought:
'Had my friend's Muse grown with this growing age,
A dearer birth than this his love had brought,
To march in ranks of better equipage:
  But since he died, and poets better prove,
  Theirs for their style I'll read, his for his love.'

W. SHAKESPEARE. *Sonnet XXXII.*

VALEDICTION TO HIS BOOK

I'll tell thee now (dear love) what thou shalt do
    To anger destiny, as she doth us;
    How I shall stay, though she eloign me thus,
And how posterity shall know it too;
        How thine may out-endure
        Sibyl's glory, and obscure
        Her who from Pindar could allure,
And her, through whose help Lucan is not lame,
And her, whose book (they say) Homer did find, and name.

Study our manuscripts, those myriads
    Of letters, which have passed 'twixt thee and me;
    Thence write our annals, and in them will be
To all whom love's subliming fire invades
        Rule and example found;
        There the faith of any ground
        No schismatic will dare to wound,
That sees how Love this grace to us affords,
To make, to keep, to use, to be these his records.

This book, as long-lived as the elements,
    Or as the world's form, this all-gravèd tome
    In cypher writ, or new-made idiom;
We for Love's clergy only are instruments;
        When this book is made thus,
        Should again the ravenous
        Vandals and the Goths invade us,
Learning were safe; in this our universe,
Schools might learn sciences, spheres music, angels verse.

Here Love's divines--since all divinity

Is love or wonder--may find all they seek,
Whether abstract spiritual love they like,
Their souls exhaled with what they do not see;
    Or, loth so to amuse
    Faith's infirmity, they choose
    Something which they may see and use;
For, though mind be the heaven, where love doth sit,
Beauty a convenient type may be to figure it.

Here more than in their books may lawyers find,
    Both by what titles mistresses are ours,
    And how prerogative these states devours,
Transferred from Love himself to womankind;
    Who, though from heart and eyes,
    They exact great subsidies,
    Forsake him who on them relies;
And for the cause, honour or conscience give;
Chimeras vain as they or their prerogative.

Here statesmen--or of them, they which can read--
    May of their occupation find the grounds;
    Love, and their art, alike it deadly wounds,
If to consider what 'tis, one proceed.
    In both they do excel,
    Who the present govern well,
    Whose weakness none doth, or dares, tell;
In this thy book, such will there something see,
As in the Bible some can find out alchemy.

Thus vent thy thoughts; abroad I'll study thee,
    As he removes far off, that great heights takes;
    How great love is, presence best trial makes,
But absence tries how long this love will be;
    To take a latitude
    Sun, or stars, are fitliest viewed
    At their brightest, but to conclude
Of longitudes, what other way have we,
But to mark when and where the dark eclipses be?

        J. DONNE.

THE BOOK OF THE BRAIN

... From the table of my memory
I'll wipe away all trivial fond records,
All saws of books, all forms, all pressures past,
That youth and observation copied there;

145

And thy commandment all alone shall live
Within the book and volume of my brain.

W. SHAKESPEARE. *Hamlet.*

LOVE'S PURVEYOR

No greater grief than to remember days
Of joy, when misery is at hand. That kens
Thy learned instructor. Yet so eagerly
If thou art bent to know the primal root,
From whence our love gat being, I will do
As one, who weeps and tells his tale. One day,
For our delight we read of Lancelot,
How him love thralled. Alone we were, and no
Suspicion near us. Oft-times by that reading
Our eyes were drawn together, and the hue
Fled from our altered cheek. But at one point
Alone we fell. When of that smile we read,
The wishèd smile so rapturously kissed
By one so deep in love, then he, who ne'er
From me shall separate, at once my lips
All trembling kissed. The book and writer both
Were love's purveyors. In its leaves that day
We read no more.

DANTE. *Inferno.*

THE DOUBLE LESSON

Maiden of Padua, on thy lap
  Thus lightly let the volume lie;
And as within some pictured map
  Fair isles and waters we descry,
Trace out, with white and gliding finger,
  Along the truth-illumined page,
Its golden lines and words that linger
  In memory's cell, from youth to age.

The young Preceptor at thy side
  Had pupil ne'er before so fair;
And though that scholar be thy guide,
  He sits that fellow-learner there.
As every page unfolds its meaning,
  As every rustling leaf turns o'er,
He finds, whilst o'er thy studies leaning,

Beauty where all was dull before.

Familiar is the book to him,
  A record of heroic deed;
Yet deems he now his eyes were dim,
  And thine have taught them first to read.
Now fades in him the scholar's glory;
  For he would give the fame he sought,
With thee to read the simplest story,
  And learn what sages never taught.

The precious wealth of countless books,
  Lies stowed within his grasping mind;
Yet should he not peruse thy looks,
  He now were more than Ignorance blind.
From many a language, old, enchanting,
  Rare truths to nations he enrolls;
But one old language yet was wanting,
  The one you teach him--tis the soul's.

      *   *   *   *   *

Full long this lesson, Pupil fair!
  All pupils else hath he forsook;
He draws still nearer to thy chair,
  And bends yet closer o'er the book.
As time flies on, now fast, now fleeter,
  More slowly is the page turned o'er;
The lesson seems to both the sweeter,
  And more enchanting grows the lore.

The book now yields a tenderer theme;
  The Master loses all his art,
The Pupil droops as in a dream,
  And both are reading with one heart.
His eyes upraised a moment glisten
  With hope, and joy, and fear profound;
While thine, oh, Maiden! do they *listen*?
  They seem to *hear* his sigh's faint sound.

But hark! what sound indeed breaks through
  The silence of that life-long hour!
Melodious tinklings, such as sue
  For favour near a lady's bower.
Ah! Maid of Padua, music swelling
  In tribute to thy radiant charms,
Now greets thee in thy father's dwelling,
  To woo thee from a father's arms.

The suitor comes with song and lute,
  Youth, riches, pleasures, round him wait;
Go bid him, Paduan Maid, be mute,
  Thy lot is cast, he comes too late!
One lesson given, and one received,
  The Book prevails, the Lute's denied;
With love thy inmost heart has heaved,
  And thou shalt be a student's bride.

S. LAMAN BLANCHARD.

CUPID AND THE BOOK OF POEMS

Cadenus many things had writ:
Vanessa much esteemed his wit,
And called for his Poetic Works:
Meantime the boy in secret lurks;
And, while the book was in her hand,
The urchin from his private stand
Took aim, and shot with all his strength
A dart of such prodigious length,
It pierced the feeble volume through,
And deep transfixed her bosom too.
Some lines, more moving than the rest,
Stuck to the point that pierced her breast,
And, borne directly to her heart,
With pains unknown increased her smart.

J. SWIFT. *Cadenus and Vanessa.*

BOOKS AS SPOKESMEN

O! LET my books be then the eloquence
And dumb presagers of my speaking breast.

W. SHAKESPEARE. *Sonnet XXIII.*

TO HIS BOOK: OF HIS LADY

Happy, ye leaves, when as those lily hands,
Which hold my life in their dead doing might,
Shall handle you, and hold in love's soft bands,
Like captives trembling at the victor's sight.
And happy lines on which, with starry light,

Those lamping eyes will deign sometimes to look,
And read the sorrows of my dying spright,
Written with tears in heart's close bleeding book.
And happy rhymes bathed in the sacred brook
Of Helicon, whence she derivèd is,
When ye behold that Angel's blessèd look,
My soul's long-lackèd food, my heaven's bliss.
  Leaves, lines, and rhymes, seek her to please alone,
  Whom if ye please, I care for other none.

     E. SPENSER. *Amoretti.*

TO THE LADY LUCY, COUNTESS OF BEDFORD

And this fair course of knowledge whereunto
  Your studies, learned Lady, are addressed,
  Is the only certain way that you can go
Unto true glory, to true happiness:
  All passages on earth besides, are so
  Incumbered with such vain disturbances;
As still we lose our rest in seeking it,
  Being but deluded with appearances;
  And no key had you else that was so fit
To unlock that prison of your sex, as this;
  To let you out of weakness, and admit
  Your powers into the freedom of that bliss
That sets you there where you may oversee
  This rolling world, and view it as it is;
  And apprehend how the outsides do agree
With the inward being of the things we deem
  And hold in our ill-cast accounts, to be
  Of highest value and of best esteem;
Since all the good we have rests in the mind,
  By whose proportions only we redeem
  Our thoughts from out confusion, and do find
The measure of our selves, and of our powers.

        *   *   *   *   *

And though books, madam, cannot make this mind,
  Which we must bring apt to be set aright;
Yet do they rectify it in that kind,
  And touch it so, as that it turns that way
  Where judgement lies: and though we cannot find
The certain place of truth, yet do they stay
  And entertain us near about the same;
  And give the soul the best delight that may

Encheer it most, and most our spirits inflame
  To thoughts of glory, and to worthy ends.

S. DANIEL.

A BOOK OF FLESH AND BLOOD

There's a lady for my humour!
A pretty book of flesh and blood, and well
Bound up, in a fair letter, too. Would I
Had her, with all the Errata.

First I would marry her, that's a verb material,
Then I would print her with an *index*
Expurgatorius; a table drawn
Of her court heresies; and when she's read,
Cum privilegio, who dares call her wanton?

J. SHIRLEY. *The Cardinal.*

WOMEN'S EYES

From women's eyes this doctrine I derive:
They sparkle still the right Promethean fire;
They are the books, the arts, the academes,
That show, contain, and nourish all the world.

W. SHAKESPEARE. *Love's Labour's Lost.*

  My only books
  Were woman's looks,--
And folly's all they've taught me.

T. MOORE.

[Greek: UPOTHÊKÊ EIS EMAUTON]

Back to thy books! The swift hours spent in vain
    Are flown and gone:
Thou hast no charm to lure them, or regain
    What loss hath won.

Up from thy sleep! The dream of idle love,
    So frail and fair,

Hath vanished, and its golden wings above
    Melt in mid air.

Stand not, nor gaze astonied at the skies,
    Serenely cold:
They have no answer for thine eager eyes;
    Thy tale is told.

Fool, in all folly cradled, swathed from sense,
    To trust a toy;
To purchase from pronounced indifference
    A shallow joy;

To leave thy studious native heights untrod
    For that low soil,
Where momentary blossoms deck the sod;
    To pant and toil

In hungry chasings of the painted fly,
    That fluttered past--
Back to thy summits, where what cannot die
    Survives the blast!

There, throned in solitary calm, forget
    Who wrung thy heart:
Long hours and days of silent years may yet
    Restore a part

Of that large heritage and realm sublime,
    Which, love-elate,
Thou fain would'st barter for the fields that time
    Makes desolate.

J. A. SYMONDS.

OF A NEW MARRIED STUDENT THAT PLAYED FAST AND LOOSE

A student, at his book so placed
  That wealth he might have won,
From book to wife did flit in haste,
  From wealth to woe to run.
Now, who hath played a feater cast,
  Since juggling first begun?
In *knitting* of himself so *fast*,
  Himself he hath *undone*.

SIR T. MORE (?)

151

MARRIAGE AND BOOKS

I understand with a deep sense of sorrow of the indisposition of your Son: I fear he hath too much *mind* for his *body*, and that superabounds with fancy, which brings him to these fits of distemper, proceeding from the black humour of melancholy: moreover, I have observed that he is too much given to his study and self-society, 'specially to converse with dead men, I mean Books: you know anything in excess is naught. Now, sir, were I worthy to give you advice, I could wish he were well married, and it may wean him from that bookish and thoughtful humour.--J. HOWELL. *Familiar Letters.*

MARRIAGE! MY YEARS ARE YOUNG

Marriage, uncle! alas! my years are young,
And fitter is my study and my books
Than wanton dalliance with a paramour.

W. SHAKESPEARE. *First Part of King Henry the Sixth.*

LOVE AND THE LIBRARY

I do not know that I am happiest when alone; but this I am sure of, that I am never long even in the society of her I love without a yearning for the company of my lamp and my utterly confused and tumbled-over library.--G. GORDON, LORD BYRON.

A COUNTER ATTRACTION

So have I known a hopeful youth
Sit down in quest of lore and truth,
With tomes sufficient to confound him,
Like Tohu Bohu, heaped around him,--
Mamurra stuck to Theophrastus,
And Galen tumbling o'er Bombastus.
When lo! while all that's learned and wise
Absorbs the boy, he lifts his eyes,
And through the window of his study
Beholds some damsel fair and ruddy,
With eyes, as brightly turned upon him as
The angel's were on Hieronymus.
Quick fly the folios, widely scattered,
Old Homer's laurelled brow is battered,
And Sappho, headlong sent, flies just in
The reverend eye of St. Augustin.

Raptured he quits each dozing sage,
Oh woman, for thy lovelier page:
Sweet book!--unlike the books of art,--
Whose errors are thy fairest part:
In whom the dear errata column
Is the best page in all the volume!

    T. MOORE. *The Devil among the Scholars.*

TO COSMELIA

Some Verses, written in September, 1676, on presenting a Book.

Go, humble gift, go to that matchless saint,
Of whom thou only wast a copy meant:
And all, that's read in thee, more richly find
Comprised in the fair volume of her mind;
That living system, where are fully writ
All those high morals, which in books we meet:
Easy, as in soft air, there writ they are,
Yet firm, as if in brass they graven were.

    J. OLDHAM.

ON A PRAYER BOOK SENT TO MRS. M. R.

Lo, here a little volume, but great book!
A nest of new-born sweets,
Whose native fires disdaining
To be thus folded, and complaining
Of these ignoble sheets,
Affect more comely bands,
Fair one, from thy kind hands,
And confidently look
To find the rest
Of a rich binding in your breast!

It is in one choice handful, heaven; and all
Heaven's royal host; encamped thus small
To prove that true, schools use to tell,
A thousand angels in one point can dwell.

It is love's great artillery,
Which here contracts itself, and comes to lie
Close couched in your white bosom; and from thence,
As from a snowy fortress of defence,

Against your ghostly foes to take your part,
And fortify the hold of your chaste heart.

It is an armoury of light;
Let constant use but keep it bright,
    You'll find it yields
To holy hands and humble hearts
    More swords and shields
Than sin hath snares, or hell hath darts.
    Only be sure
    The hands be pure
That hold these weapons, and the eyes
Those of turtles, chaste and true,
    Wakeful, and wise;
Here is a friend shall fight for you;
Hold but this book before your heart,
Let prayer alone to play his part.

      R. CRASHAW.

ON GEORGE HERBERT'S 'THE TEMPLE' SENT TO A GENTLEWOMAN

Know you, fair, on what you look?
Divinest love lies in this book:
Expecting fire from your fair eyes,
To kindle this his sacrifice.
When your hands untie these strings,
Think, you've an angel by the wings;
One that gladly would be nigh,
To wait upon each morning sigh;
To flutter in the balmy air
Of your well-perfumed prayer;

These white plumes of his he'll lend you,
Which every day to heaven will send you:
To take acquaintance of each sphere,
And all your smooth-faced kindred there.
And though Herbert's name do owe
These devotions, fairest, know
While I thus lay them on the shrine
Of your white hand, they are mine.

      R. CRASHAW.

TO HELEN

Written in the first leaf of Keble's *Christian Year*, a birthday Present.

My Helen, for its golden fraught
Of prayer and praise, of dream and thought,
Where Poesy finds fitting voice
For all who hope, fear, grieve, rejoice,
Long have I loved, and studied long,
The pious minstrel's varied song.

Whence is the volume dearer now?
There gleams a smile upon your brow,
Wherein, methinks, I read how well
You guess the reason, ere I tell,
Which makes to me the single rhymes
More prized, more conned, a hundred times.

Ere vanished quite the dread and doubt
Affection ne'er was born without,
Found we not here a magic key
Opening thy secret soul to me?
Found we not here a mystic sign
Interpreting thy heart to mine?

What sympathies up-springing fast
Through all the future, all the past,
In tenderest links began to bind
Spirit to spirit, mind to mind,
As we, together wandering o'er
The little volume's precious store,

Mused, with alternate smile and tear,
On the high themes awakened here
Of fervent hope, of calm belief,
Of cheering joy, of chastening grief,
The trials borne, the sins forgiven,
The task on earth, the meed in heaven.

My Own! oh surely from above
Was shed that confidence of love,
Which in such happy moments nurst
When soul with soul had converse first,
Now through the snares and storms of life
Blesses the husband and the wife!

W. M. PRAED.

SENT WITH POEMS

Little volume, warm with wishes,
  Fear not brows that never frown!
After Byron's peppery dishes
  Matho's mild skim-milk goes down.

Change she wants not, self-concentered,
  She whom Attic graces please,
She whose Genius never entered
  Literature's gin-palaces.

W. S. LANDOR.

WOMAN AND BOOKS

Hear them [books] speak for themselves.... 'We are expelled with heart and hand from the domiciles of the clergy, apportioned to us by hereditary right, in some interior chamber of which we had our peaceful cells: but, to their shame, in these nefarious times we are altogether banished to suffer opprobrium out of doors; our places, moreover, are occupied by hounds and hawks, and sometimes by a biped beast; woman to wit,--whose cohabitation was formerly shunned by the clergy, from whom we have ever taught our pupils to fly, more than from the asp and the basilisk; wherefore this beast, ever jealous of our studies, and at all times implacable, spying us at last in a corner, protected only by the web of some long-deceased spider, drawing her forehead into wrinkles, laughs us to scorn, abuses us in virulent speeches, points us out as the only superfluous furniture lodged in the whole house; complains that we are useless for any purpose of domestic economy whatever, and recommends our being bartered away forthwith for costly head-dresses, cambric, silk, twice-dipped purple garments, woollen, linen, and furs.'--R. DE BURY. *Philobiblon.*

THE GHOST OF BETTY BARNES

I beheld a female form, with mob-cap, bib, and apron, sleeves tucked up to the elbow, a dredging-box in the one hand, and in the other a sauce-ladle. I concluded, of course, that it was my friend's cook-maid walking in her sleep; and as I knew he had a value for Sally, who could toss a pancake with any girl in the country, I got up to conduct her safely to the door. But as I approached her, she said,--'Hold, sir! I am not what you take me for;'--words which seemed so apposite to the circumstances that I should not have much minded them, had it not been for the peculiarly hollow sound in which they were uttered. 'Know, then,' she said, in the same unearthly accents, 'that I am the spirit of Betty Barnes.'--'Who hanged herself for love of the stage-coachman,' thought I; 'this is a very proper spot of work!'--'Of that unhappy Elizabeth or Betty Barnes, long cook-maid to Mr. Warburton, the painful collector, but ah! the too careless custodier, of the largest collection of ancient plays ever known--of most of which the titles only are left to glad-den the Prolegomena of the Variorum Shakespeare. Yes, stranger, it was these ill-fated hands that consigned to grease and conflagration the scores of small quartos, which, did they now exist, would drive the whole Roxburghe Club out of their senses--it was these unhappy pickers and stealers that singed fat fowls and wiped dirty trenchers with the lost works of Beaumont and Fletcher, Massinger, Jonson, Webster--what shall I say?--even of Shakespeare himself!'--SIR W. SCOTT. *Introductory Epistle to The Fortunes of Nigel.*

A CHEAP AND LASTING PLEASURE

I yet retain, and carefully cherish, my love of reading. If relays of eyes were to be hired like post-horses, I would never admit any but silent companions: they afford a constant variety of entertainment, which is almost the only one pleasing in the enjoyment, and inoffensive in the consequence.... Every woman endeavours to breed her daughter a fine lady, qualifying her for a station in which she never will appear: and at the same time incapacitating her for that retirement to which she is destined. Learning, if she has a real taste for it, will not only make her contented, but happy in it. No entertainment is so cheap as reading, nor any pleasure so lasting. She will not want new fashions, nor regret the loss of expensive diversions, or variety of company, if she can be amused with an author in her closet.... Daughter! daughter! don't call names; you are always abusing my pleasures, which is what no mortal will bear. Trash, lumber, sad stuff, are the titles you give to my favourite amusement. If I called a white staff a stick of wood, a gold key gild-ed brass, and the ensigns of illustrious orders coloured strings, this may be philosophically true, but would be very ill received. We have all our playthings; happy are they that can be contented with those they can obtain: those hours are spent in the wisest manner that can easiest shade the ills of life, and are least productive of ill consequences. I think my time better employed in reading the adventures of imaginary people, than the Duchess of Marlborough's, who passed the latter years of her life in paddling with her will, and contriving schemes of plaguing some, and extracting praise from others to no purpose; eternally disappointed and eternally fretting. The active scenes are over at my age. I indulge, with all the art I can, my taste for reading. If I would confine it to valuable books, they are almost as rare as valuable men. I must be content with what I can find. As I approach a second childhood, I endeavour to enter into the pleasures of it. Your youngest son is, perhaps, at this very moment riding on a poker with great delight, not at all regretting that it is not a gold one, and much less wishing it an Arabian horse, which he would not know how to manage; I am reading an idle tale, not expecting wit or truth in it, and am very glad it is not metaphysics to puzzle my judgement, or history to mis-lead my opinion: he fortifies his health by exercise; I calm my cares by oblivion. The methods may appear low to busy people; but if he improves his strength, and I forget my infirmities, we both attain very desirable ends.--LADY MARY WORTLEY MONTAGU. *Letters.*

THE POETS

There, obedient to her praying, did I read aloud the poems
Made to Tuscan flutes, or instruments more various of our own;

Read the pastoral parts of Spenser--or the subtle interflowings
Found in Petrarch's sonnets--here's the book--the leaf is folded
    down!

Or at times a modern volume,--Wordsworth's solemn-thoughted idyl,
Howitt's ballad-verse, or Tennyson's enchanted reverie,--
Or from Browning some 'Pomegranate', which, if cut deep down the
    middle,
Shows a heart within blood-tinctured, of a veined humanity.

      E. B. BROWNING. *Lady Geraldine's Courtship.*

THE WORLD OF BOOKS

  I sate on in my chamber green,
And lived my life, and thought my thoughts, and prayed
My prayers without the vicar; read my books,
Without considering whether they were fit
To do me good. Mark, there. We get no good
By being ungenerous, even to a book,
And calculating profits,--so much help
By so much reading. It is rather when
We gloriously forget ourselves and plunge
Soul-forward, headlong, into a book's profound,
Impassioned for its beauty and salt of truth--
'Tis then we get the right good from a book.

I read much. What my father taught before
From many a volume, Love re-emphasized
Upon the self-same pages: Theophrast
Grew tender with the memory of his eyes,
And Aelian made mine wet. The trick of Greek
And Latin, he had taught me, as he would
Have taught me wrestling or the game of fives
If such he had known,--most like a shipwrecked man
Who heaps his single platter with goats' cheese
And scarlet berries; or like any man
Who loves but one, and so gives all at once,
Because he has it, rather than because
He counts it worthy. Thus, my father gave;
And thus, as did the women formerly
By young Achilles, when they pinned the veil
Across the boy's audacious front, and swept
With tuneful laughs the silver-fretted rocks,
He wrapt his little daughter in his large
Man's doublet, careless did it fit or no....

I read books bad and good--some bad and good
At once (good aims not always make good books:
Well-tempered spades turn up ill-smelling soils
In digging vineyards even); books that prove
God's being so definitely, that man's doubt
Grows self-defined the other side the line,
Made atheist by suggestion; moral books,
Exasperating to licence; genial books,
Discounting from the human dignity;
And merry books, which set you weeping when
The sun shines,--aye, and melancholy books,
Which make you laugh that any one should weep
In this disjointed life for one wrong more.

The world of books is still the world, I write,
And both worlds have God's providence, thank God,
To keep and hearten.

       E. B. BROWNING. *Aurora Leigh*.

THE CLASSICAL EDUCATION OF WOMEN

We have often heard men who wish, as almost all men of sense wish, that women should be highly educated, speak with rapture of the English ladies of the sixteenth century, and lament that they can find no modern damsel resembling those fair pupils of Ascham and Aylmer who compared, over their embroidery, the styles of Isocrates and Lysias, and who, while the horns were sounding and the dogs in full cry, sat in the lonely oriel, with eyes riveted to that immortal page which tells how meekly and bravely the first great martyr of intellectual liberty took the cup from his weeping gaoler. But surely these complaints have very little foundation. We would by no means disparage the ladies of the sixteenth century or their pursuits. But we conceive that those who extol them at the expense of the women of our time forget one very obvious and very important circumstance. In the time of Henry the Eighth and Edward the Sixth, a person who did not read Greek and Latin could read nothing, or next to nothing. The Italian was the only modern language which possessed anything that could be called a literature. All the valuable books then extant in all the vernacular dialects of Europe would hardly have filled a single shelf. England did not yet possess Shakespeare's plays and the *Faery Queene*, nor France Montaigne's *Essays*, nor Spain *Don Quixote*. In looking round a well-furnished library, how many English or French books can we find which were extant when Lady Jane Grey and Queen Elizabeth received their education? Chaucer, Gower, Froissart, Comines, Rabelais, nearly complete the list. It was therefore absolutely necessary that a woman should be uneducated or classically educated.--LORD MACAULAY. *Lord Bacon*.

GIRLS' READING

Whether novels, or poetry, or history be read, they should be chosen, not for what is *out* of them, but for what is *in* them. The chance and scattered evil that may here and there haunt, or hide itself in, a powerful book, never does any harm to a noble girl; but the emptiness of an author oppresses her, and his amiable folly degrades her. And if she can have access to a good library of old and classical books, there need be no choosing at all. Keep the modern magazine and novel out of your girl's way: turn her loose into the old library every wet day, and let her alone. She will find what is good for her; you cannot: for there is just this difference between the making of a girl's character and a boy's--you may chisel a boy into shape, as you would a rock, or hammer him into it, if he be of a better kind, as you would a piece of bronze. But you cannot hammer a girl into anything. She grows as a flower does,--she will wither without sun; she will decay in her sheath, as the narcissus does, if you do not give her air enough; she may fall, and defile her head in dust, if you leave her without help at some moments of her life; but you cannot fetter her; she must take her own fair form and way, if she take any, and in mind as in body, must have always

> Her household motions light and free
> And steps of virgin liberty.

Let her loose in the library, I say, as you do a fawn in a field. It knows the bad weeds twenty times better than you; and the good ones too, and will eat some bitter and prickly ones, good for it, which you had not the slightest thought were good.--J. RUSKIN. *Sesame and Lilies.*

> 'Twere well with most, if books, that could engage
> Their childhood, pleased them at a riper age.

> W. COWPER. *Tirocinium.*

POETRY AND PIETY

Flavia buys all books of wit and humour, and has made an expensive collection of all our English poets. For, she says, one cannot have a true taste of any of them without being very conversant with them all.

She will sometimes read a book of piety, if it is a short one, if it is much commended for style and language, and she can tell where to borrow it.--W. LAW. *A serious Call to a devout and holy Life.*

A LADY'S LIBRARY

> Non illa colo calathisve Minervae
> Foemineas assueta manus.--VIRG.

Some months ago, my friend Sir Roger, being in the country, enclosed a letter to me, directed to a certain lady whom I shall here call by the name of Leonora, and as it contained matters of consequence, desired me to deliver it to her with my own hand. Accordingly I waited upon her ladyship pretty early in the morning, and was desired by her woman to walk into her lady's library, till such time as she was in readiness to receive me. The very sound of a lady's library gave me a great curiosity to see it; and, as it was some time before the lady came to me, I had an opportunity of turning over a great many of her books, which were ranged together in a very beautiful order. At the end of the folios (which were finely bound and gilt) were great jars of china placed one above another in a very noble piece of architecture. The quartos were separated from the octavos by a pile of smaller vessels, which rose in a delightful pyramid. The octavos were bounded by teadishes of all shapes, colours, and sizes, which were so disposed on a wooden frame, that they looked like one continued pillar indented with the finest strokes of sculpture, and stained with the greatest variety of dyes. That part of the library which was designed for the reception of plays and pamphlets, and other loose papers, was enclosed in a kind of square, consisting of one of the prettiest grotesque works that I ever saw, and made up of scaramouches, lions, monkeys, mandarins, trees, shells, and a thousand other odd figures in china ware. In the midst of the room was a little japan table, with a quire of gilt paper upon it, and upon the paper a silver snuff-box made in the shape of a little book. I found there were several other counterfeit books upon the upper shelves, which were carved in wood, and served only to fill up the number, like faggots in the muster of a regiment. I was wonderfully pleased with such a mixed kind of furniture as seemed very suitable both to the lady and the scholar, and did not know at first whether I should fancy myself in a grotto or in a library.

Upon my looking into the books I found there were some few which the lady had bought for her own use, but that most of them had been got together, either because she had heard them praised, or because she had seen the authors of them. Among several that I examined, I very well remember these that follow:

Ogilby's *Virgil*. Dryden's *Juvenal. Cassandra. Cleopatra. Astraea*. Sir Isaac Newton's works. *The Grand Cyrus*, with a pin stuck in one of the middle leaves. Pembroke's *Arcadia*. Locke of *Human Understanding*, with a paper of patches in it. A spelling-book. A dictionary for the explanation of hard words. Sherlock upon Death. *The Fifteen Comforts of Matrimony*. Sir William Temple's Essays. Father Malebranche's *Search after Truth*, translated into English. A book of Novels. *The Academy of Compliments*. Culpepper's *Midwifery. The Ladies' Calling*. Tales in Verse by Dr. D'Urfey: bound in red leather, gilt on the back, and doubled down in several places. All the Classic authors, in wood. A set of Elzevirs by the same hand. *Clelia*: which opened of itself in the place that describes two lovers in a bower. Baker's *Chronicle. Advice to a Daughter. The New Atlantis*, with a key to it. Mr. Steele's *Christian Hero*. A Prayer-book: with a bottle of Hungary water by the side of it. Dr. Sacheverell's Speech. Fielding's Trial. Seneca's *Morals*. Taylor's *Holy Living and Dying*. La Ferte's *Instructions for Country-dances*.

I was taking a catalogue in my pocket-book of these and several other authors, when Leonora entered.--J. ADDISON. *Spectator*, 37.

WOMEN'S WANT

Except some professed scholars, I have often observed that women in general read much more than men; but, for want of a plan, a method, a fixed object, their reading is of little benefit to themselves, or others.--E. GIBBON. *Autobiography*.

BOOKS FOR A LADY'S LIBRARY

Convivae prope dissentire videntur,
Poscentes vario multum diversa palato.
Quid dem? quid non dem?

HOR.

Since I have called out for help in my catalogue of a lady's library, I have received many letters upon that head, some of which I shall give an account of. In the first class I shall take notice of those which come to me from eminent booksellers, who every one of them mention with respect the authors they have printed, and consequently have an eye to their own advantage more than to that of the ladies. One tells me, that he thinks it absolutely necessary for women to have true notions of right and equity, and that therefore they cannot peruse a better book than Dalton's *Country Justice*: another thinks they cannot be without *The Compleat Jockey*. A third, observing the curiosity and desire of prying into secrets, which he tells me is natural to the fair sex, is of opinion this female inclination, if well directed, might turn very much to their advantage, and therefore recommends to me *Mr. Mede upon the Revelations*. A fourth lays it down as an unquestioned truth, that a lady cannot be thoroughly accomplished who has not read the *Secret Treaties and Negotiations of Marshal d'Estrades*. Mr. Jacob Tonson, junior, is of opinion, that *Bayle's Dictionary* might be of very great use to the ladies, in order to make them general scholars. Another, whose name I have forgotten, thinks it highly proper that every woman with child should read Mr. Wall's *History of Infant Baptism*: as another is very importunate with me to recommend to all my female readers *The Finishing Stroke: Being a Vindication of the Patriarchal Scheme*, &c.

In the second class I shall mention books which are recommended by husbands, if I may believe the writers of them. Whether or no they are real husbands or personated ones I cannot tell, but the books they recommend are as follow. *A Paraphrase on the History of Susanna. Rules to keep Lent. The Christian's Overthrow prevented. A Dissuasive from the Playhouse. The Virtues of Camphire, with Directions to make Camphire Tea. The pleasures of a Country Life. The Government of the Tongue.* A letter dated from Cheapside desires me that I would advise all young wives to make themselves mistresses of Wingate's *Arithmetic*, and concludes with a postscript, that he hopes I will not forget *The Countess of Kent's Receipts*.

I may reckon the ladies themselves as a third class among these my correspondents and privy-councillors. In a letter from one of them, I am advised to place *Pharamond* at the head of my catalogue, and, if I think proper, to give the second place to *Cassandra*. Coquetilla begs me not to think of nailing women upon their knees with manuals of devotion, nor of scorching their faces with books of housewifery. Florella desires to know if there are any books written against prudes, and entreats me, if there are, to give them a place in my library. Plays of all sorts have their several advocates: *All for Love* is mentioned in above fifteen letters; *Sophonisba, or Hannibal's Overthrow*, in a dozen; *The Innocent Adultery* is likewise highly approved of; *Mithridates, King of Pontus* has many friends; *Alexander the Great* and *Aurengzebe* have the same number of voices; but *Theodosius, or The Force of Love*, carries it from all the rest.--J. ADDISON. *Spectator*, 92.

TO A LADY FURNISHING HER LIBRARY AT *** IN WARWICKSHIRE

When just proportion in each part,
And colours mixed with nicest art,
Conspire to show the grace and mien
Of Chloe or the Cyprian queen:
With elegance throughout refined,
That speaks the passions of the mind,
The glowing canvas will proclaim
A Raphael's or a Titian's name.
  So when through every learnèd page
Each distant clime, each distant age
Display a rich variety
Of wisdom in epitome;
Such elegance and taste will tell
The hand that could select so well.
But when we all their beauties view,
United and improved by you,
We needs must own an emblem faint
To express those charms no art can paint.
Books must, with such correctness writ,
Refine another's taste and wit;
'Tis to your merit only due
That theirs can be refined by you.

R. JAGO.

LYDIA LANGUISH AND THE CIRCULATING LIBRARY

LUCY. Indeed, ma'am, I traversed half the town in search of it: I don't believe there's a circulating library in Bath I ha'n't been at.

LYDIA LANGUISH. And could not you get *The Reward of Constancy*?

LUCY. No, indeed, ma'am.

LYDIA. Nor *The Fatal Connexion?*

LUCY. No, indeed, ma'am.

LYDIA. Nor *The Mistakes of the Heart?*

LUCY. Ma'am, as ill luck would have it, Mr. Bull said Miss Sukey Saunter had just fetched it away.

LYDIA. Heigh-ho!--Did you inquire for *The Delicate Distress?*

LUCY.----Or, *The Memoirs of Lady Woodford?* Yes, indeed, ma'am. I asked everywhere for it; and I might have brought it from Mr. Frederick's, but Lady Slattern Lounger, who had just sent it home, had so soiled and dog's-eared it, it wa'n't fit for a Christian to read.

LYDIA. Heigh-ho!--Yes, I always know when Lady Slattern has been before me. She has a most observing thumb; and I believe cherishes her nails for the convenience of making marginal notes.--Well, child, what *have* you brought me?

LUCY. Oh! here, ma'am.

   [Taking books from under her cloak, and from her pockets.]

This is *The Gordian Knot*, and this *Peregrine Pickle*. Here are *The Tears of Sensibility*, and *Humphrey Clinker*. This is *The Memoirs of a Lady of Quality, written by herself*, and here the second volume of *The Sentimental Journey*.

LYDIA. Heigh-ho!--What are those books by the glass?

LUCY. The great one is only *The Whole Duty of Man*, where I press a few blonds, ma'am.

   *   *   *   *   *

... O Lud! ma'am, they are both coming upstairs....

LYDIA. Here, my dear Lucy, hide these books. Quick, quick. Fling *Peregrine Pickle* under the toilet--throw *Roderick Random* into the closet--put *The Innocent Adultery* into *The Whole Duty of Man*--thrust *Lord Aimworth* under the sofa--cram *Ovid* behind the bolster--there-- put *The Man of Feeling* into your pocket--so, so, now lay *Mrs. Chapone* in sight, and leave *Fordyce's Sermons* open on the table.

LUCY. Oh, burn it, ma'am, the hairdresser has torn away as far as *Proper Pride*.

LYDIA. Never mind--open at *Sobriety*. Fling me *Lord Chesterfield's Letters*.--Now for 'em.

[Mrs. Malaprop and Sir Anthony Absolute enter and after Lydia has been ordered to her room--]

MRS. MALAPROP. There's a little intricate hussy for you!

SIR ANTHONY. It is not to be wondered at, ma'am--all this is the natural consequence of teaching girls to read. Had I a thousand daughters, by Heaven! I'd as soon have them taught the black art as their alphabet!

MRS. MALAPROP. Nay, nay, Sir Anthony, you are an absolute misanthropy.

SIR ANTHONY. In my way hither, Mrs. Malaprop, I observed your niece's maid coming forth from a circulating library! She had a book in each hand--they were half-bound volumes, with marble covers! From that moment I guessed how full of duty I should see her mistress!

MRS. MALAPROP. Those are vile places, indeed!

SIR ANTHONY. Madam, a circulating library in a town is as an evergreen tree of diabolical knowledge! It blossoms through the year! And depend on it, Mrs. Malaprop, that they who are so fond of handling the leaves, will long for the fruit at last.--R. B. SHERIDAN. *The Rivals.*

THE OLD BACHELOR'S BOOKS

My books were changed; I now preferred the truth
To the light reading of unsettled youth;
Novels grew tedious, but by choice or chance,
I still had interest in the wild romance:
There is an age, we know, when tales of love
Form the sweet pabulum our hearts approve;
Then as we read we feel, and are indeed,
We judge, the heroic men of whom we read;
But in our after life these fancies fail,
We cannot be the heroes of the tale;
The parts that Cliffords, Mordaunts, Bevilles play
We cannot,--cannot be so smart and gay.
But all the mighty deeds and matchless powers
Of errant knights we never fancied ours,
And thus the prowess of each gifted knight
Must at all times create the same delight;
Lovelace a forward youth might hope to seem,
But Lancelot never,--that he could not dream;
Nothing reminds us in the magic page
Of old romance, of our declining age:
If once our fancy mighty dragons slew,
This is no more than fancy now can do;

But when the heroes of a novel come,
Conquered and conquering, to a drawing-room,
We no more feel the vanity that sees
Within ourselves what we admire in these,
And so we leave the modern tale, to fly
From realm to realm with Tristram or Sir Guy.
  Not quite a Quixote, I could not suppose
That queens would call me to subdue their foes;
But, by a voluntary weakness swayed,
When fancy called, I willingly obeyed.

     G. CRABBE. *Tales of the Hall.*

    The state, whereon I studied,
Is like a good thing, being often read,
Grown feared and tedious.

    W. SHAKESPEARE. *Measure for Measure.*

THE OXFORD SCHOLAR AND HIS BOOKS

A clerk ther was of Oxenford also
That un-to logik hadde long y-go.
As lene was his hors as is a rake,
And he was nat right fat, I undertake;
But loked holwe, and ther-to soberly.
Ful thredbar was his overest courtepy;
For he had geten him yet no benefyce,
Ne was so worldly for to have offyce.
For him was lever have at his beddes heed
Twenty bokes, clad in blak or reed,
Of Aristotle and his philosophye,
Than robes riche, or fithele, or gay sautrye.
But al be that he was a philosophre,
Yet hadde he but litel gold in cofre;
But al that he mighte of his freendes hente,
On bokes and on lerninge he it spente,
And bisily gan for the soules preye
Of hem that yaf him wher-with to scoleye.
Of studie took he most cure and most hede.
Noght o word spak he more than was nede,
And that was seyd in forme and reverence,
And short and quik, and ful of hy sentence.
Souninge in moral vertu was his speche,
And gladly wolde he lerne, and gladly teche.
     G. CHAUCER. *The Canterbury Tales.*

THE CHIEF FOOL

I am the first fool of all the whole navy,
To keep the poop, the helm and eke the sail.
For this is my mind, this one pleasure have I:
Of books to have great plenty and aparayle.
I take no wisdom by them, nor yet avail
Nor them preceive not: and then I them despise.
Thus am I a fool and all that sew that guise.

That in this ship the chief place I govern,
By this wide sea with fools wandering,
The cause is plain and easy to discern;
Still am I busy books assembling,
For to have plenty it is a pleasant thing,
In my conceit, and to have them ay in hand,
But what they mean do I not understand.

But yet I have them in great reverence
And honour, saving them from filth and ordure,
By often brushing and much diligence,
Full goodly bound in pleasant coverture
Of damask, satin, or else of velvet pure:
I keep them sure, fearing lest they should be lost,
For in them is the cunning wherein I me boast.

But if it fortune that any learned men
Within my house fall to disputation,
I draw the curtain to show my books then,
That they of my cunning should make probation
I care not to fall in altercation:
And while they commune, my books I turn and wind
For all is in them, and nothing in my mind.

Tholomeus the rich caused, long agone,
Over all the world good books to be sought;
Done was his commandment anon.
These books he had and in his study brought
Which passed all earthly treasure as he thought,
But nevertheless he did him not apply
Unto their doctrine, but lived unhappily.

Lo in likewise of books I have store,
But few I read, and fewer understand;
I follow not their doctrine, nor their lore,

It is enough to bear a book in hand;
It were too much to be in such a band,
For to be bound to look within the book;
I am content on the fair covering to look.

Why should I study to hurt my wit thereby,
Or trouble my mind with study excessive?
Sith many are which study right busily
And yet thereby shall they never thrive:
The fruit of wisdom can they not contrive.
And many to study so much are inclined
That utterly they fall out of their mind.

Each is not lettered that now is made a lord,
Nor each a clerk that hath a benefice;
They are not all lawyers that pleas do record,
All that are promoted are not fully wise;
On such chance now fortune throws her dice,
That though one know but the Irish game
Yet would he have a gentleman's name.

So in likewise, I am in such case,
Though I naught can, I would be called wise;
Also I may set another in my place
Which may for me my books exercise;
Or else I shall ensue the common guise,
And say *concedo* to every argument,
Lest by much speech my Latin should be spent.

    S. BRANT. *Shyp of Folys of the Worlde*, 1509.

THE ENVOY OF ALEXANDER BARCLAY, TRANSLATOR, EXHORTING THE FOOLES ACCLOYED WITH THIS VICE TO AMEND THEIR FOLLY

    Say worthy doctors and clerks curious:
What moveth you of books to have such number,
Since divers doctrines through ways contrarious
Doth man's mind dsitract and sore encumber;
Alas, blind men awake, out of your slumber,
And if ye will needs your books mutliply
With diligence endeavour you some to occupy.

    A. BARCLAY.

LETTER-FERRETS

Dionysius scoffeth at those grammarians who ploddingly labour to know the miseries of Ulysses, and are ignorant of their own.... Except our mind be the better, unless our judgement be the sounder, I had rather my scholar had employed his time in playing at tennis; I am sure his body would be the nimbler. See but one of these our university men or bookish scholars return from school, after he hath there spent ten or twelve years under a pedant's charge: who is so inapt for any matter? who so unfit for any company? who so to seek if he come into the world? all the advantage you discover in him is that his Latin and Greek have made him more sottish, more stupid, and more presumptuous, than before he went from home.... My vulgar Perigordian speech doth very pleasantly term such self-conceited wizards, letter-ferrets, as if they would say letter-stricken men, to whom (as the common saying is) letters have given a blow with a mallet.-- MONTAIGNE.

DAINTIES THAT ARE BRED OF A BOOK

Sir, he hath not fed of the dainties that are bred of a book; he hath not eat paper, as it were; he hath not drunk ink: his intellect is not replenished; he is only an animal, only sensible in the duller parts.--W. SHAKESPEARE. *Love's Labour's Lost.*

AN ANTIQUARY

He loves no library, but where there are more spiders' volumes than authors', and looks with great admiration on the antique work of cobwebs. Printed books he contemns, as a novelty of this latter age; but a manuscript he pores on everlastingly, especially if the cover be all moth-eaten, and the dust make a parenthesis between every syllable. He would give all the books in his study (which are rarities all) for one of the old Roman binding, or six lines of Tully in his own hand.--J. EARLE. *Microcosmographie.*

AN IGNORANT BOOK-COLLECTOR

With what, O Codrus! is thy fancy smit?
The flower of learning, and the bloom of wit.
Thy gaudy shelves with crimson bindings glow,
And Epictetus is a perfect beau.
How fit for thee bound up in crimson too,
Gilt, and, like them, devoted to the view!
Thy books are furniture. Methinks 'tis hard
That Science should be purchased by the yard,
And T----n, turned upholsterer, send home
The gilded leather to fit up thy room.
  If not to some peculiar end assigned,
Study's the specious trifling of the mind;
Or is at best a secondary aim,

A chase for sport alone, not game:
If so, sure they who the mere volume prize,
But love the thicket where the quarry lies.
  On buying books Lorenzo long was bent;
But found at length that it reduced his rent.
His farms were flown; when lo! a sale comes on,
A choice collection! What is to be done?
He sells his last; for he the whole will buy;
Sells even his house, nay wants whereon to lie:
So high the generous ardour of the man
For Romans, Greeks, and Orientals ran.
When terms were drawn, and brought him by the clerk,
Lorenzo signed the bargain--with his mark.
Unlearned men of books assume the care,
As eunuchs are the guardians of the fair.
  Not in his authors' liveries alone
Is Codrus' erudite ambition shown.
Editions various, at high prices bought,
Inform the world what Codrus would be thought;
And, to his cost, another must succeed,
To pay a sage, who says that he can read,
Who titles knows, and Indexes has seen;
But leaves to ---- what lies between,
Of pompous books who shuns the proud expense,
And humbly is contented with the sense.

      E. YOUNG. *The Love of Fame.*

THE BIBLIOMANIA

What wild desires, what restless torments seize
The hapless man, who feels the book-disease,
If niggard Fortune cramp his generous mind,
And Prudence quench the spark by heaven assigned!
With wistful glance his aching eyes behold
The Princeps-copy, clad in blue and gold,
Where the tall Book-case, with partition thin,
Displays, yet guards, the tempting charms within:
So great Facardin viewed, as sages tell,
Fair Crystalline immured in lucid cell.
Not thus the few, by happier fortune graced,
And blessed, like you, with talents, wealth, and taste,
Who gather nobly, with judicious hand,
The Muse's treasures from each lettered strand.
For you the Monk illumed his pictured page,
For you the press defies the spoils of age;
Faustus for you infernal tortures bore,

For you Erasmus starved on Adria's shore.
The Folio-Aldus loads your happy shelves,
And dapper Elzevirs, like fairy elves,
Show their light forms amidst the well-gilt Twelves,
In slender type the Giolitos shine,
And bold Bodoni stamps his Roman line.
For you the Louvre opes its regal doors,
And either Didot lends his brilliant stores:
With faultless types, and costly sculptures bright,
Ibarra's Quixote charms your ravished sight:
Laborde in splendid tablets shall explain
Thy beauties, glorious though unhappy Spain!
O hallowed name, the theme of future years,
Embalmed in Patriot-blood, and England's tears,
Be thine fresh honours from the tuneful tongue,
By Isis' stream which mourning Zion sung!
But devious oft from every classic Muse,
The keen Collector meaner paths will choose:
And first the margin's breadth his soul employs,
Pure, snowy, broad, the type of nobler joys.
In vain might Homer roll the tide of song,
Or Horace smile, or Tully charm the throng;
If crossed by Pallas' ire, the trenchant blade
Or too oblique, or near, the edge invade,
The Bibliomane exclaims, with haggard eye,
'No margin!' turns in haste, and scorns to buy.
He turns where Pybus rears his Atlas-head,
Or Madoc's mass conceals its veins of lead.
The glossy lines in polished order stand,
While the vast margin spreads on either hand,
Like Russian wastes, that edge the frozen deep,
Chill with pale glare, and lull to mortal sleep.
Or English books, neglected and forgot,
Excite his wish in many a dusty lot:
Whatever trash *Midwinter* gave to-day,
Or *Harper's* rhyming sons, in paper gray,
At every auction, bent on fresh supplies,
He cons his Catalogue with anxious eyes:
Where'er the slim italics mark the page,
Curious and rare his ardent mind engage.
Unlike the swans, in Tuscan song displayed,
He hovers eager o'er oblivion's shade.
To snatch obscurest names from endless night,
And give Cokain or Fletcher back to light.
In red morocco dressed he loves to boast
The bloody murder, or the yelling ghost;
Or dismal ballads, sung to crowds of old,
Now cheaply bought for thrice their weight in gold.

Yet to the unhonoured dead be Satire just;
Some flowers 'smell sweet and blossom in their dust'.
'Tis thus even Shirley boasts a golden line,
And Lovelace strikes, by fits, a note divine.
The unequal gleams like midnight-lightnings play,
And deepened gloom succeeds, in place of day.

But human bliss still meets some envious storm;
He droops to view his Paynter's mangled form:
Presumptuous grief, while pensive Taste repines
O'er the frail relics of her Attic shrines!
O for that power, for which magicians vie,
To look through earth, and secret hoards descry!
I'd spurn such gems as Marinel beheld,
And all the wealth Aladdin's cavern held,
Might I divine in what mysterious gloom
The rolls of sacred bards have found their tomb:
Beneath what mouldering tower, or waste champaign,
Is hid Menander, sweetest of the train:
Where rests Antimachus' forgotten lyre,
Where gentle Sappho's still seductive fire;
Or he, whom chief the laughing Muses own,
Yet skilled with softest accents to bemoan
Sweet Philomel in strains so like her own.
The menial train has proved the scourge of wit,
Even Omar burnt less Science than the spit.
Earthquakes and wars remit their deadly rage,
But every feast demands some fated page.
Ye Towers of Julius, ye alone remain
Of all the piles that saw our nation's stain,
When Harry's sway oppressed the groaning realm,
And Lust and Rapine seized the wavering helm.
Then ruffian-hands defaced the sacred fanes,
Their saintly statues and their storied panes;
Then from the chest, with ancient art embossed,
The penman's pious scrolls were rudely tossed;
Then richest manuscripts, profusely spread,
The brawny churls' devouring oven fed:
And thence collectors date the heavenly ire
That wrapt Augusta's domes in sheets of fire.

Taste, though misled, may yet some purpose gain,
But Fashion guides a book-compelling train.
Once, far apart from Learning's moping crew,
The travelled beau displayed his red-heeled shoe,
Till Orford rose, and told of rhyming peers,
Repeating *noble* words to polished ears;
Taught the gay crowd to prize a fluttering name,

In trifling toiled, nor 'blushed to find it fame'.
The lettered fop now takes a larger scope,
With classic furniture, designed by Hope,
(Hope whom upholsterers eye with mute despair,
The doughty pedant of an elbow-chair;)
Now warmed by Orford, and by Granger schooled
In Paper-books, superbly gilt and tooled,
He pastes, from injured volumes snipped away,
His *English Heads*, in chronicled array.
Torn from their destined page (unworthy meed
Of knightly counsel, and heroic deed)
Not Faithorne's stroke, nor Field's own types can save
The gallant Veres, and one-eyed Ogle brave.
Indignant readers seek the image fled,
And curse the busy fool, who *wants a head*.

Proudly he shows, with many a smile elate
The scrambling subjects of the *private plate*;
While Time their actions and their names bereaves,
They grin for ever in the guarded leaves.
Like poets, born, in vain collectors strive
To cross their Fate, and learn the art to thrive.
Like Cacus, bent to tame their struggling will,
The Tyrant-passion drags them backward still:
Even I, debarred of ease, and studious hours,
Confess, 'mid anxious toil, its lurking powers.
How pure the joy, when first my hands unfold
The small, rare volume, black with tarnished gold!
The eye skims restless, like the roving bee,
O'er flowers of wit, or song, or repartee,
While sweet as springs, new-bubbling from the stone,
Glides through the breast some pleasing theme unknown.
Now dipped in Rossi's terse and classic style,
His harmless tales awake a transient smile.
Now Bouchet's motley stores my thoughts arrest,
With wondrous reading, and with learnèd jest.
Bouchet whose tomes a grateful line demand,
The valued gift of Stanley's liberal hand.
Now sadly pleased, through faded Rome I stray,
And mix regrets with gentle Du Bellay;
Or turn, with keen delight, the curious page,
Where hardly Pasquin braves the Pontiff's rage.

But D----n's strains should tell the sad reverse,
When Business calls, inveterate foe to verse!
Tell how 'the Demon claps his iron hands',
'Waves his lank locks, and scours along the lands.'
Through wintry blasts, or summer's fire I go,

To scenes of danger, and to sights of woe.
Even when to Margate every Cockney roves,
And brainsick-poets long for sheltering groves,
Whose lofty shades exclude the noontide glow,
While Zephyrs breathe, and waters trill below,
The rigid Fate averts, by tasks like these,
From heavenly musings, and from lettered ease.
Such wholesome checks the better genius sends,
From dire rehearsals to protect our friends:
Else when the social rites our joys renew,
The stuffed portfolio would alarm your view,
Whence volleying rhymes your patience would o'ercome,
And, spite of kindness, drive you early home.
So when the traveller's hasty footsteps glide
Near smoking lava on Vesuvio's side,
Hoarse-muttering thunders from the depths proceed,
And spouting fires incite his eager speed.
Appalled he flies, while rattling showers invade,
Invoking every saint for instant aid:
Breathless, amazed, he seeks the distant shore,
And vows to tempt the dangerous gulf no more.

J. FERRIAR. *The Bibliomania.*

BIBLIOSOPHIA

I will begin, by designating the high and dignified passion in question by its true name--
BIBLIOSOPHIA,--which I would define--*an appetite for* COLLECTING *Books*--carefully
distinguished from, wholly unconnected with, nay, absolutely repugnant to, all idea of
READING them.

Observe, then, with merited admiration, the several points of superiority, which distinguish the *Collector*, when brought into fair and close comparison with the *Student.* As

First; the said *Collector* proceeds straight forward to his object, and (with one only exception which will hereafter be shown) under the most rational hopes of accomplishing it.
There is but a certain, and limited, number of books to which he and his inquisitive fra-
ternity have agreed to consecrate the epithet 'curious'; and all of these--with the requisite
allowance of cash, cunning, luck, patience, and time--he is within the 'potentiality' of
drawing, sooner or later, within his clutches:--whereas the *Student*, granting him the
wealth of a brewer, the cunning of a horse-dealer, the luck of a fool, the patience of Jerry
Sneak, and the longevity of the Wandering Jew, can never hope even to *taste* an hun-
dredth part of the volumes which he meditates to devour.

In the next place, the treasures of the *Collector*, when once he has submitted to the pleasing toil of procuring them, are his own;--his own, I mean, in the single sense in which he
is desirous so to call them; for he leaves them in the safe custody of his shelves, until the

arrival of that proud moment, when he shall be dared by an envious rival, to prove that the title-page of some forgotten (and thence remembered) volume, is perfect--or properly imperfect; or that it enjoys the reputation of having been printed, long before the Art had approached towards any tolerable degree of improvement; or, that it possesses some one, or more, of those curious advantages, upon which a fitter occasion for expatiating will present itself by and by:--and now, how stands the point of *possession*, with the *Student*?--unprosperously indeed!--for besides that, as already observed, he can never possibly possess, in *his* sense of that expression, more than a wretched modicum of his coveted treasures, he is doomed to a very precarious property even in those which he may have actually hoarded; inasmuch as they are entrusted to the care of that most treacherous of all librarians, *Memory*,--which, at all times, and of necessity, treats the Student's collections, as the professed Collector, occasionally, and by choice only, is tempted to treat *his*,--by casting out a great part of them for want of room.... 'Let us now be told no more,' of the superiority of the *Student* over the *Collector*.--J. BERESFORD. *Bibliosophia.*

GOLDEN VOLUMES! RICHEST TREASURES!

Golden volumes! richest treasures!
Objects of delicious pleasures!
You my eyes rejoicing please,
You my hands in rapture seize!
Brilliant wits and moving sages,
Lights who beamed through many ages,
Left to your conscious leaves their story,
And dared to trust you with their glory;
And now their hope of fame achieved,
Dear volumes!--you have not deceived!

This passion for the acquisition and enjoyment of *books* has been the occasion of their lovers embellishing their outsides with costly ornaments: a rage which ostentation may have abused; but when these volumes belong to the real man of letters, the most fanciful bindings are often the emblems of his taste and feelings. The great Thuanus was eager to procure the finest copies for his library, and his volumes are still eagerly purchased, bearing his autograph on the last page. A celebrated amateur was Grollier, whose library was opulent in these luxuries; the Muses themselves could not more ingeniously have ornamented their favourite works. I have seen several in the libraries of our own curious collectors. He embellished their outside with taste and ingenuity. They are gilded and stamped with peculiar neatness, the compartments on the binding are drawn, and painted, with different inventions of subjects, analogous to the works themselves; and they are further adorned by that amiable inscription, *Jo. Grollierii et amicorum*!--purporting that these literary treasures were collected for himself and for his friends.--I. D'ISRAELI. *Curiosities of Literature: Libraries.*

A MALADY OF WEAK MINDS

The Bibliomania, or the collecting an enormous heap of books without intelligent curiosity, has, since libraries have existed, infected weak minds, who imagine that they them-
themselves acquire knowledge when they keep it on their shelves. Their motley libraries
have been called the *madhouses of the human mind*; and again, the *tomb of books*, when the
possessor will not communicate them, and coffins them up in the cases of his library--
and as it was facetiously observed, these collections are not without a *Lock on the Human
Understanding.*--I. D'ISRAELI. *Curiosities of Literature: The Bibliomania.*

AN UNWORTHY PROFESSOR

'I will frankly confess,' rejoined Lysander, 'that I am an arrant bibliomaniac--that I love
books dearly--that the very sight, touch, and mere perusal----'

'Hold, my friend,' again exclaimed Philemon; 'you have renounced your profession--you
talk of *reading* books--do bibliomaniacs ever *read* books?'--T. F. DIBDIN. *Bibliomania.*

A BIBLIOMANIAC

You observe, my friends, said I, softly, yonder active and keen-visaged gentleman? 'Tis
Lepidus. Like Magliabechi, content with frugal fare and frugal clothing and preferring the
riches of a library to those of house-furniture, he is insatiable in his bibliomaniacal appetites. 'Long experience has made him sage:' and it is not therefore without just reason
that his opinions are courted and considered as almost oracular. You will find that he will
take his old station, commanding the right or left wing of the auctioneer; and that he will
enliven, by the gaiety and shrewdness of his remarks, the circle that more immediately
surrounds him. Some there are who will not bid till Lepidus bids; and who surrender all
discretion and opinion of their own to his universal book-knowledge. The consequence
is that Lepidus can, with difficulty, make purchases for his own library, and a thousand
dexterous and happy manoeuvres are of necessity obliged to be practised by him, whenever a rare or curious book turns up.... Justly respectable as are his scholarship and good
sense, he is not what you may call a *fashionable* collector; for old chronicles and romances
are most rigidly discarded from his library. Talk to him of Hoffman, Schoettgenius,
Rosenmuller, and Michaelis, and he will listen courteously to your conversation; but
when you expatiate, however learnedly and rapturously, upon Froissart and Prince Arthur, he will tell you that he has a heart of stone upon the subject; and that even a clean
uncut copy of an original impression of each, by Verard or by Caxton, would not bring a
single tear of sympathetic transport to his eyes.--T. F. DIBDIN. *Bibliomania.*

THE ENVIABLE BOOKWORM

The character of a scholar not unfrequently dwindles down into the shadow of a shade,
till nothing is left of it but the mere bookworm. There is often something amiable as well
as enviable in this last character. I know one such instance, at least. The person I mean

has an admiration for learning, if he is only dazzled by its light. He lives among old authors, if he does not enter much into their spirit. He handles the covers, and turns over the page, and is familiar with the names and dates. He is busy and self-involved. He hangs like a film and cobweb upon letters, or is like the dust upon the outside of knowledge, which should not be rudely brushed aside. He follows learning as its shadow; but as such, he is respectable. He browses on the husk and leaves of books, as the young fawn browses on the bark and leaves of trees. Such a one lives all his life in a dream of learning, and has never once had his sleep broken by a real sense of things. He believes implicitly in genius, truth, virtue, liberty, because he finds the names of these things in books. He thinks that love and friendship are the finest things imaginable, both in practice and theory. The legend of good women is to him no fiction. When he steals from the twilight of his cell, the scene breaks upon him like an illuminated missal, and all the people he sees are but so many figures in a *camera obscura*. He reads the world, like a favourite volume, only to find beauties in it, or like an edition of some old work which he is preparing for the press, only to make emendations in it, and correct the errors that have inadvertently slipt in. He and his dog Tray are much the same honest, simple-hearted, faithful, affectionate creatures--if Tray could but read! His mind cannot take the impression of vice: but the gentleness of his nature turns gall to milk. He would not hurt a fly. He draws the picture of mankind from the guileless simplicity of his own heart: and when he dies, his spirit will take its smiling leave, without having ever had an ill thought of others, or the consciousness of one in itself.--W. HAZLITT. *On the Conversation of Authors.*

EARS NAILED TO BOOKS

A mere scholar, who knows nothing but books, must be ignorant even of them. 'Books do not teach the use of books.' How should he know anything of a work who knows nothing of the subject of it? The learned pedant is conversant with books only as they are made of other books, and those again of others, without end. He parrots those who have parroted others. He can translate the same word into ten different languages, but he knows nothing of the *thing* which it means in any one of them. He stuffs his head with authorities built on authorities, with quotations quoted from quotations, while he locks up his senses, his understanding, and his heart. He is unacquainted with the maxims and manners of the world; he is to seek in the characters of individuals. He sees no beauty in the face of nature or of art. To him 'the mighty world of eye and ear' is hid; and 'knowledge', except at one entrance, 'quite shut out.' His pride takes part with his ignorance; and his self-importance rises with the number of things of which he does not know the value, and which he therefore despises as unworthy of his notice. He knows nothing of pictures,--'of the colouring of Titian, the grace of Raphael, the purity of Domenichino, the *corregioscity* of Correggio, the learning of Poussin, the airs of Guido, the taste of the Caracci, or the grand contour of Michael Angelo',--of all those glories of the Italian and miracles of the Flemish school, which have filled the eyes of mankind with delight, and to the study and imitation of which thousands have in vain devoted their lives. These are to him as if they had never been, a mere dead letter, a byword; and no wonder, for he neither sees nor understands their prototypes in nature. A print of Rubens' Watering-place, or Claude's Enchanted Castle may be hanging on the walls of his room for months without his once perceiving them; and if you point them out to him he will turn away from them. The language of nature, or of art (which is another nature), is one that he does not understand. He repeats indeed the names of Apelles and Phidias, because they are to be found in classic authors, and boasts of their works as prodigies, because they no longer exist; or when he sees the finest remains of Grecian art actually before him in the Elgin Marbles, takes no other interest in them than as they lead to a learned dispute, and (which is the same thing) a quarrel about the meaning of a Greek particle. He is equally ignorant of music; he 'knows no touch of it,' from the strains of the all-accomplished Mozart to the shepherd's pipe upon the mountain. His ears are nailed to his books; and deadened with the sound of the Greek and Latin tongues, and the din and smithery of school-learning.--W. HAZLITT. *On the Ignorance of the Learned.*

THE ANTIQUARY'S TREASURES

The collection was indeed a curious one, and might well be envied by an amateur. Yet it was not collected at the enormous prices of modern times, which are sufficient to have appalled the most determined as well as earliest bibliomaniac upon record, whom we take to have been none else than the renowned Don Quixote de la Mancha, as, among other slight indications of an infirm understanding, he is stated, by his veracious historian, Cid Hamet Benengeli, to have exchanged fields and farms for folios and quartos of chivalry.... Mr. Oldbuck did not follow these collectors in such excess of expenditure; but, taking a pleasure in the personal labour of forming his library, saved his purse at the expense of his time and toil.... 'Davy Wilson,' he said, 'commonly called Snuffy Davy, from his inveterate addiction to black rappee, was the very prince of scouts for searching blind alleys, cellars, and stalls, for rare volumes. He had the scent of a slow-hound, sir, and the snap of a bull-dog. He would detect you an old black-letter ballad among the leaves of a law-paper, and find an *editio princeps* under the mask of a school Corderius.' ... 'Even I, sir,' he went on, 'though far inferior in industry and discernment and presence of mind to that great man, can show you a few--a very few things, which I have collected, not by force of money, as any wealthy man might,--although, as my friend Lucian says, he might chance to throw away his coin only to illustrate his ignorance,--but gained in a manner that shows I know something of the matter. See this bundle of ballads, not one of them later than 1700, and some of them a hundred years older. I wheedled an old woman out of these, who loved them better than her psalm-book. Tobacco, sir, snuff, and the *Complete Syren*, were the equivalent! For that mutilated copy of the *Complaynt of Scotland*, I sat out the drinking of two dozen bottles of strong ale with the late learned proprietor, who, in gratitude, bequeathed it to me by his last will. These little Elzevirs are the memoranda and trophies of many a walk by night and morning through the Cowgate, the Canongate, the Bow, Saint Mary's Wynd,--wherever, in fine, there were to be found brokers and traders, those miscellaneous dealers in things rare and curious. How often have I stood haggling on a halfpenny, lest, by a too ready acquiescence in the dealer's first price, he should be led to suspect, the value I set upon the article!--how have I trembled, lest some passing stranger should chop in between me and the prize, and regarded each poor student of divinity that stopped to turn over the books at the stall, as a rival amateur, or prowling bookseller in disguise!--And then, Mr. Lovel, the sly satisfaction with which one pays the consideration, and pockets the article, affecting a cold indifference, while the hand is trembling with pleasure!--Then to dazzle the eyes of our wealthier and emulous rivals by showing them such a treasure as this' (displaying a little black smoked book about the size of a primer); 'to enjoy their surprise and envy, shrouding meanwhile, under a veil of mysterious consciousness, our own superior knowledge and dexterity;--these, my young friend, these are the white moments of life, that repay the toil, and pains, and sedulous attention, which our profession, above all others, so peculiarly demands!' ...

Here were editions esteemed as being the first, and there stood those scarcely less regarded as being the last and best; here was a book valued because it had the author's final improvements, and there another which (strange to tell!) was in request because it had them not. One was precious because it was a folio, another because it was a duodecimo; some because they were tall, some because they were short; the merit of this lay in the title-page--of that in the arrangement of the letters in the word Finis. There was, it seemed, no peculiar distinction, however trifling or minute, which might not give value to a volume, providing the indispensable quality of scarcity, or rare occurrence, was attached to it.--SIR W. SCOTT. *The Antiquary*.

I would rather be a poor man in a garret with plenty of books than a king who did not love reading.--LORD MACAULAY.

KISSING A FOLIO

Sitting, last winter, among my books, and walled round with all the comfort and protection which they and my fireside could afford me; to wit, a table of high-piled books at my back, my writing-desk on one side of me, some shelves on the other, and the feeling of the warm fire at my feet; I began to consider how I loved the authors of those books: how I loved them, too, not only for the imaginative pleasures they afforded me, but for their making me love the very books themselves, and delight to be in contact with them. I looked sideways at my Spenser, my Theocritus, and my *Arabian Nights*; then above them at my Italian poets; then behind me at my Dryden and Pope, my romances, and my Boccaccio; then on my left side at my Chaucer, who lay on a writing-desk; and thought how natural it was in C[harles] L[amb] to give a kiss to an old folio, as I once saw him do to Chapman's *Homer*.... I entrench myself in my books equally against sorrow and the weather. If the wind comes through a passage I look about to see how I can fence it off by a better disposition of my movables; if a melancholy thought is importunate, I give another glance at my Spenser. When I speak of being in contact with my books, I mean it literally. I like to lean my head against them.--J. H. LEIGH HUNT. *My Books*.

THE LITERARY HAREM

I must have my literary *harem*, my *parc aux cerfs*, where my favourites await my moments of leisure and pleasure,--my scarce and precious editions, my luxurious typographical masterpieces; my Delilahs, that take my head in their lap; the pleasant story-tellers and the like; the books I love because they are fair to look upon, prized by collectors, endeared by old associations, secret treasures that nobody else knows anything about; books, in short, that I like for insufficient reasons it may be, but peremptorily, and mean to like and to love and to cherish till death us do part.... The bookcase of Delilahs, that you have paid wicked prices for, that you love without pretending to be reasonable about it, and would bag in case of fire before all the rest.--O. W. HOLMES. *The Poet at the Breakfast-Table.*

BAYARD TAYLOR

Dead he lay among his books!
The peace of God was in his looks.

As the statues in the gloom
Watch o'er Maximilian's tomb;

So those volumes from their shelves
Watched him, silent as themselves.

Ah! his hand will never more
Turn their storied pages o'er:

Never more his lips repeat
Songs of theirs, however sweet.

Let the lifeless body rest!
He is gone, who was its guest;

Gone, as travellers haste to leave
An inn, nor tarry until eve.

Traveller! in what realms afar,
In what planet, in what star,

In what vast, aerial space,
Shines the light upon thy face?

In what gardens of delight
Rest thy weary feet to-night?

Poet! thou, whose latest verse
Was a garland on thy hearse;

Thou hast sung, with organ tone,
In Deukalion's life, thine own;

On the ruins of the Past
Blooms the perfect flower at last.

Friend! but yesterday the bells

Rang for thee their loud farewells;

And to-day they toll for thee,
Lying dead beyond the sea;

Lying dead among thy books,
The peace of God in all thy looks!

H. W. LONGFELLOW.

DEFINITIONS

To afford the reader an opportunity of noting at a glance the appropriate learned terms applicable to the different sets of persons who meddle with books, I subjoin the following definitions, as rendered in d'Israeli's *Curiosities* from the *Chasse aux Bibliographes et Antiquaires mal advisés* of Jean-Joseph Rive:

'A bibliognoste, from the Greek, is one knowing in title-pages and colophons, and in editions; the place and year when printed; the presses whence issued; and all the minutiae of a book.'

'A bibliographe is a describer of books and other literary arrangements.'

'A bibliomane is an indiscriminate accumulator, who blunders faster than he buys, cock-brained and purse-heavy.'

'A bibliophile, the lover of books, is the only one in the class who appears to read them for his own pleasure.'

'A bibliotaphe buries his books, by keeping them under lock, or framing them in glass cases.'

The accurate Peignot, after accepting of this classification with high admiration of its simplicity and exhaustiveness, is seized in his supplementary volume with a misgiving in the matter of the bibliotaphe, explaining that it ought to be translated as a grave of books, and that the proper technical expression for the performer referred to by Rive is bibliotapht. He adds to the nomenclature bibliolyte, as a destroyer of books; bibliologue, one who discourses about books; bibliotacte, a classifier of books; and bibliopée 'l'art d'écrire ou de composer des livres', or, as the unlearned would say, the function of an author.--J. H. BURTON. *The Book Hunter.*

THE LAST EDITIONS THE BEST

Buy good books, and read them; the best books are the commonest, and the last editions are always the best, if the editors are not blockheads; for they may profit of the former. But take care not to understand editions and title-pages too well. It always smells of pedantry, and not always of learning.--LORD CHESTERFIELD. *Letters to his Son.*

SIBRANDUS SCHAFNABURGENSIS

Plague take all your pedants, say I!
  He who wrote what I hold in my hand,
Centuries back was so good as to die,
  Leaving this rubbish to cumber the land;
This, that was a book in its time,
  Printed on paper and bound in leather,
Last month in the white of a matin-prime
  Just when the birds sang all together.

Into the garden I brought it to read,
  And under the arbute and laurustine
Read it, so help me grace in my need,
  From title-page to closing line.
Chapter on chapter did I count,
  As a curious traveller counts Stonehenge;
Added up the mortal amount;
  And then proceeded to my revenge.

Yonder's a plum-tree with a crevice
  An owl would build in, were he but sage;
For a lap of moss, like a fine pont-levis
  In a castle of the middle age,
Joins to a lip of gum, pure amber;
  When he'd be private, there might he spend
Hours alone in his lady's chamber:
  Into this crevice I dropped our friend.

Splash, went he, as under he ducked,
  --I knew at the bottom rain-drippings stagnate;
Next a handful of blossoms I plucked
  To bury him with, my bookshelf's magnate;
Then I went indoors, brought out a loaf,
  Half a cheese, and a bottle of Chablis;
Lay on the grass and forgot the oaf
  Over a jolly chapter of Rabelais.

Now, this morning, betwixt the moss
  And gum that locked our friend in limbo,
A spider had spun his web across,
  And sat in the midst with arms akimbo:
So, I took pity, for learning's sake,
  And, *de profundis, accentibus laetis,*
Cantate! quoth I, as I got a rake,

And up I fished his delectable treatise.

Here you have it, dry in the sun,
  With all the binding all of a blister,
And great blue spots where the ink has run,
  And reddish streaks that wink and glister
O'er the page so beautifully yellow:
  Oh, well have the droppings played their tricks!
Did he guess how toadstools grow, this fellow?
  Here's one stuck in his chapter six!

How did he like it when the live creatures
  Tickled and toused and browsed him all over,
And worm, slug, eft, with serious features,
  Came in, each one, for his right of trover?
--When the water-beetle with great blind deaf face
  Made of her eggs the stately deposit,
And the newt borrowed just so much of the preface
  As tiled in the top of his black wife's closet?

All that life and fun and romping,
  All that frisking and twisting and coupling,
While slowly our poor friend's leaves were swamping
  And clasps were cracking and covers suppling!
As if you had carried sour John Knox
  To the play-house at Paris, Vienna or Munich,
Fastened him into a front-row box,
  And danced off the ballet with trousers and tunic.

Come, old martyr! What, torment enough is it?
  Back to my room shall you take your sweet self!
Good-bye, mother-beetle; husband-eft, *sufficit*!
  See the snug niche I have made on my shelf.
A.'s book shall prop you up, B.'s shall cover you,
  Here's C. to be grave with, or D. to be gay,
And with E. on each side, and F. right over you,
  Dry-rot at ease till the Judgement-day!

R. BROWNING. *Garden Fancies.*

A STUDENT

Over an ancient scroll I bent,
Steeping my soul in wise content,
Nor paused a moment, save to chide
A low voice whispering at my side.

I wove beneath the stars' pale shine
A dream, half human, half divine;
And shook off (not to break the charm)
A little hand laid on my arm.

I read until my heart would glow,
With the great deeds of long ago;
Nor heard, while with those mighty dead,
Pass to and fro a faltering tread.

On the old theme I pondered long--
The struggle between right and wrong;
I could not check such visions high,
To soothe a little quivering sigh.

I tried to solve the problem--Life;
Dreaming of that mysterious strife,
How could I leave such reasonings wise,
To answer two blue pleading eyes?

I strove how best to give, and when,
My blood to save my fellow-men--
How could I turn aside, to look
At snowdrops laid upon my book?

Now Time has fled--the world is strange,
Something there is of pain and change;
My books lie closed upon the shelf;
I miss the old heart in myself.

I miss the sunbeams in my room--
It was not always wrapped in gloom:
I miss my dreams--they fade so fast,
Or flit unto some trivial past.

The great stream of the world goes by;
None care, or heed, or question, why
I, the lone student, cannot raise
My voice or hand as in old days.

No echo seems to wake again
My heart to anything but pain,
Save when a dream of twilight brings
The fluttering of an angel's wings!

ADELAIDE ANNE PROCTER.

OF HANDLING BOOKS

We not only set before ourselves a service to God in preparing volumes of new books, but we exercise the duties of a holy piety if we just handle so as not to injure them, then return them to their proper places, and commend them to undefiling custody that they may rejoice in their purity while held in the hand, and repose in security when laid up in their repositories....

In the first place, then, let there be a mature decorum in opening and closing of volumes, that they may neither be unclasped with precipitous haste, nor thrown aside after inspection without being duly closed; for it is necessary that a book should be much more carefully preserved than a shoe....

A stiff-necked youth, lounging sluggishly in his study ... distributes innumerable straws in various places, with the ends in sight, that he may recall by the mark what his memory cannot retain.... He is not ashamed to eat fruit and cheese over an open book, and to transfer his empty cup from side to side upon it: and because he has not his alms-bag at hand, he leaves the rest of the fragments in his books.... He next reclines with his elbows on the book, and by a short study invites a long nap; and by way of repairing the wrinkles, he twists back the margins of the leaves, to the no small detriment of the volume....

But impudent boys are to be specially restrained from meddling with books, who, when they are learning to draw the forms of letters, if copies of the most beautiful books are allowed them, begin to become incongruous annotators, and wherever they perceive the broadest margin about the text, they furnish it with a monstrous alphabet, or their unchastened pen immediately presumes to draw any other frivolous thing whatever, that occurs to their imagination.... There are also certain thieves who enormously dismember books by cutting off the side margins for letter paper, leaving only the letters or text, or the fly-leaves put in for the preservation of the book, which they take away for various uses and abuses, which sort of sacrilege ought to be prohibited under a threat of anathema.

But it is altogether befitting the decency of a scholar that washing should without fail precede reading, as often as he returns from his meals to study, before his fingers, besmeared with grease, loosen a clasp or turn over the leaf of a book.--R. DE BURY. *Philobiblon.*

DEDUCTIONS FROM SCRIPTURE

The most meek Moses instructs us about making cases for books in the neatest manner, wherein they may be safely preserved from all damage. 'Take this book,' says he, 'and put it in the side of the ark of the covenant of the Lord your God' (Deut. xxxi). O, befitting place, appropriate library, which was made of imperishable Shittim wood, and covered all over inside and out with gold! But our Saviour also, by his own example, precludes all unseemly negligence in the treatment of books, as may be read in Luke iv. For when he had read over the scriptural prophecy written about himself in a book debarred to him, he did not return it to the minister till he had first closed it with his most holy hands; by which act students are most clearly taught that they ought not in the smallest degree whatever to be negligent about the custody of books.--R. DE BURY. *Philobiblon.*

> Is not the leaf turned down
> Where I left reading?

W. SHAKESPEARE. *Julius Caesar.*

AN EDITION DE LUXE

With that of the book loosened were the clasps--
The margin was illumined all with golden rails
And bees, enpictured with grasshops and wasps,
With butterflies and fresh peacock tails,
Engloried with flowers and slimy snails;
Ennyield pictures well touched and quickly;
It would have made a man whole that had be right sickly
To behold how it was garnished and bound,
Encovered over with gold of tissue fine;
The clasps and bullions were worth a thousand pound;
With belassis and carbuncles the borders did shine;
With aurum mosaicum every other line
Was written.

JOHN SKELTON. *A Replycacion agaynst
certayne yong Scolers, &c.*

CARE AS TO BINDINGS

Have a care of keeping your books handsome, and well bound, not casting away over-much in their gilding or stringing for ostentation sake, like the prayer-books of girls and gallants, which are carried to church but for their outsides. Yet for your own use spare them not for noting or interlining (if they be printed), for it is not likely you mean to be a gainer by them, when you have done with them: neither suffer them through negligence to mould and be moth-eaten or want their strings and covers. King Alphonsus, about to lay the foundation of a castle at Naples, called for Vitruvius his book of architecture; the book was brought in very bad case, all dusty and without covers; which the king observing said, 'He that must cover us all, must not go uncovered himself'; then commanded the book to be fairly bound and brought unto him. So say I, suffer them not to lie neglected, who must make you regarded; and go in torn coats, who must apparel your mind with the ornaments of knowledge, above the robes and riches of the most magnificent princes.--H. PEACHAM. *The Compleat Gentleman.*

GOLD CLASPS AND A GOLDEN STORY

This precious book of love, this unbound lover,
To beautify him, only lacks a cover:
The fish lives in the sea, and 'tis much pride
For fair without the fair within to hide:
That book in many eyes doth share the glory,
That in gold clasps locks in the golden story.

W. SHAKESPEARE. *Romeo and Juliet.*

NOBLER THAN CONTENTS

A book? O rare one!
Be not, as is our fangled world, a garment
Nobler than that it covers: let thy effects
So follow, to be most unlike our courtiers,
As good as promise.

W. SHAKESPEARE. *Cymbeline.*

LINES HAVE THEIR LININGS, AND BOOTS THEIR BUCKRAM

As in our clothes, so likewise he who looks
Shall find much forcing buckram in our books.

R. HERRICK.

EYE-WORSHIP

While the plodding votary of *meaning* is anxiously inquiring out the sense of the oracle, his fellow-worshipper, remembering that our *eyes* were not given us for nothing, is entranced in admiration of the stately form or gorgeous vestment of the priest that utters it:--in plainer terms, he stands exploring, without end, the type, of jetty black and dazzling cut, that seems to float amidst a satin sea of cream--(it is impossible to be watching after one's metaphors on such inspiring occasions)--roves, in gazing ecstasy, from page to page, till here and there arrested by the choice vignette or richly tinctured plate: at length, 'lassatus, necdum satiatus' with the beauties of the interior, he reverently closes the superbly-plated leaves; and, turning to the sumptuous, silk-lined cover, marvels as he views the verdant, red, or purple pride of Russia, Turkey, or Morocco, glittering, in every part, with the mazy flourishes of golden decoration!--'Miror, immo etiam stupeo!' is the language of his heart--if it cannot be of his tongue.--J. BERESFORD. *Bibliosophia.*

BOOKBINDINGS

Embodied thought enjoys a splendid rest
On guardian shelves, in emblem costume dressed;
Like gems that sparkle in the parent mine,
Through crystal mediums the rich coverings shine;
Morocco flames in scarlet, blue and green,
Impressed with burnished gold, of dazzling sheen;
Arms deep embossed the owner's state declare,
Test of their worth--their age--and his kind care.
Embalmed in russia stands a valued pile,
That time impairs not, nor vile worms defile;
Russia, exhaling from its scented pores
Its saving power to these thrice-valued stores,
In order fair arranged in volumes stand,
Gay with the skill of many a modern hand;
At the expense of sinew and of bone,
The fine papyrian leaves are firm as stone:
Here all is square as by masonic rule,
And bright the impression of the burnished tool.
On some the tawny calf a coat bestows,
Where flowers and fillets beauteous forms compose:
Others in pride the virgin vellum wear,
Beaded with gold--as breast of Venus fair;
On either end the silken head-bands twine,
Wrought by some maid with skilful fingers fine--
The yielding back falls loose, the hinges play,
And the rich page lies open to the day.
Where science traces the unerring line,
In brilliant tints the forms of beauty shine;
These, in our works, as in a casket laid,
Increase the splendour by their powerful aid.

J. MACCREERY.

Hark you, sir; I'll have them very fairly bound:
All books of love, see that at any hand.

W. SHAKESPEARE. *The Taming of the Shrew.*

DISCRIMINATION IN BINDINGS

To be strong-backed and neat-bound is the desideratum of a volume. Magnificence comes after. This, when it can be afforded, is not to be lavished upon all kinds of books indiscriminately. I would not dress a set of Magazines, for instance, in full suit. The dishabille, or half-binding (with Russia backs ever) is *our* costume. A Shakespeare, or a Milton (unless the first editions), it were mere foppery to trick out in gay apparel. The possession of them confers no distinction. The exterior of them (the things themselves being so common), strange to say, raises no sweet emotions, no tickling sense of property in the owner. Thomson's *Seasons*, again, looks best (I maintain it) a little torn, and dog's-eared. How beautiful to a genuine lover of reading are the sullied leaves, and worn out appearance, nay, the very odour (beyond Russia), if we would not forget kind feelings in fastidiousness, of an old 'Circulating Library' *Tom Jones*, or *Vicar of Wakefield*! How they speak of the thousand thumbs, that have turned over their pages with delight!--of the lone sempstress, whom they may have cheered (milliner, or harder-working mantua-maker) after her long day's needle-toil, running far into midnight, when she has snatched an hour, ill spared from sleep, to steep her cares, as in some Lethean cup, in spelling out their enchanting contents! Who would have them a whit less soiled? What better condition could we desire to see them in?

In some respects the better a book is, the less it demands from binding. Fielding, Smollett, Sterne, and all that class of perpetually self-reproductive volumes--Great Nature's Stereotypes--we see them individually perish with less regret, because we know the copies of them to be 'eterne'. But where a book is at once both good and rare--where the individual is almost the species, and when *that* perishes,

We know not where is that Promethean torch
That can its light relumine--

such a book, for instance, as the *Life of the Duke of Newcastle*, by his Duchess--no casket is rich enough, no casing sufficiently durable, to honour and keep safe such a jewel.

Not only rare volumes of this description, which seem hopeless ever to be reprinted; but old editions of writers, such as Sir Philip Sidney, Bishop Taylor, Milton in his prose works, Fuller--of whom we *have* reprints, yet the books themselves, though they go about, and are talked of here and there, we know, have not endenizened themselves (nor possibly ever will) in the national heart, so as to become stock books--it is good to possess these in durable and costly covers. I do not care for a First Folio of Shakespeare. I rather prefer the common editions of Rowe and Tonson, without notes, and with *plates*, which, being so execrably bad, serve as maps, or modest remembrancers to the text; and without pretending to any supposable emulation with it, are so much better than the Shakespeare gallery *engravings*, which *did*. I have a community of feeling with my countrymen about his Plays, and I like those editions of him best, which have been oftenest tumbled about and handled.--On the contrary, I cannot read Beaumont and Fletcher but in Folio. The Octavo editions are painful to look at. I have no sympathy with them. If they were as much read as the current editions of the other poet, I should prefer them in that shape to the older one. I do not know a more heartless sight than the reprint of the *Anatomy of Melancholy*. What need was there of unearthing the bones of that fantastic old great man, to expose them in a winding-sheet of the newest fashion to modern censure? what hapless stationer could dream of Burton ever becoming popular?--The wretched Malone could not do worse, when he bribed the sexton of Stratford Church to let him white-wash the painted effigy of old Shakespeare, which stood there, in rude but lively fashion depicted, to the very colour of the cheek, the eye, the eyebrow, hair, the very dress he used to wear--the only authentic testimony we had, however imperfect, of these curious parts and parcels of him. They covered him over with a coat of white paint. By---, if I had been a justice of peace for Warwickshire, I would have clapt both commentator and sexton fast in the stocks, for a pair of meddling sacrilegious varlets.

I think I see them at their work--these sapient trouble-tombs.--C. LAMB. *Detached Thoughts on Books and Reading.*

SUITABLE BINDINGS

Books, no less than their authors, are liable to get ragged, and to experience that neglect and contempt which generally follows the outward and visible signs of poverty. We do therefore most heartily commend the man, who bestows on a tattered and shivering volume such decent and comely apparel as may protect it from the insults of the vulgar, and the more cutting slights of the fair. But if it be a rare book, 'the lone survivor of a numerous race,' the one of its family that has escaped the trunk-makers and pastry-cooks, we would counsel a little extravagance in arranging it. Let no book perish, unless it be such an one as it is your duty to throw into the fire. There is no such thing as a worthless book, though there are some far worse than worthless; no book which is not worth preserving, if its existence may be tolerated; as there are some men whom it may be proper to hang, but none who should be suffered to starve.

The binding of a book should always suit its complexion. Pages, venerably yellow, should not be cased in military morocco, but in sober brown russia. Glossy hot-pressed paper looks best in vellum. We have sometimes seen a collection of old whitey-brown blackletter ballads, &c., so gorgeously tricked out, that they remind us of the pious liberality of the Catholics, who dress in silk and gold the images of saints, part of whose saintship consisted in wearing rags and hair-cloth. The costume of a volume should also be in keeping with its subject, and with the character of its author. How absurd to see the works of William Penn in flaming scarlet, and George Fox's Journal in Bishop's purple! Theology should be solemnly gorgeous. History should be ornamented after the antique or Gothic fashion. Works of science, as plain as is consistent with dignity. Poetry, *simplex munditiis*.--HARTLEY COLERIDGE. *Biographia Borealis: William Roscoe.*

'TIS FOLLY TO BE WISE

Due attention to the inside of books, and due contempt for the outside, is the proper relation between a man of sense and his books.--LORD CHESTERFIELD. *Letters to his Son.*

THE OUTSIDE OF A BOOK

As great philosophers hold that the *esse* of things is *percipi*, so a gentleman's furniture exists to be looked at. Nevertheless, sir, there are some things more fit to be looked at than others; for instance, there is nothing more fit to be looked at than the outside of a book.

It is, as I may say, from repeated experience, a pure and unmixed pleasure to have a goodly volume lying before you, and to know that you may open it if you please, and need not open it unless you please. It is a resource against *ennui*, if *ennui* should come upon you. To have the resource and not to feel the *ennui*, to enjoy your bottle in the present, and your book in the indefinite future, is a delightful condition of human existence. There is no place, in which a man can move or sit, in which the outside of a book can be otherwise than an innocent and becoming spectacle.--T. L. PEACOCK. *Crotchet Castle.*

BOOKS YOU MAY HOLD IN YOUR HAND

Johnson used to say that no man read long together with a folio on his table. 'Books,' said he, 'that you may carry to the fire, and hold readily in your hand, are the most useful after all.'--J. BOSWELL. *Life of Johnson.*

BOOK ILLUSTRATIONS AND NIGHTMARE

Of the great passion of Henry the Seventh for fine books, even before he ascended the throne of England, there can be no doubt. I will not, however, take upon me to say that the slumbers of this monarch were disturbed in consequence of the extraordinary and frightful passages, which, accompanied with bizarre cuts, were now introduced into almost every work, both of ascetic divinity, and also of plain practical morality. His predecessor, Richard, had in all probability been alarmed by the images which the reading of these books had created; and I guess that it was from such frightful objects, rather than from the ghosts of his murdered brethren, that he was compelled to pass a sleepless night before the memorable battle of Bosworth Field. If one of those artists who used to design the horrible pictures which are engraved in many old didactic volumes of the period, had ventured to take a peep into Richard's tent, I question whether he would not have seen, lying upon an oaken table, an early edition of some of those fearful works of which he had himself aided in the embellishment, and of which Heinecken has given us such curious facsimiles: and this, in my humble apprehension, is quite sufficient to account for all the terrible workings in Richard which Shakespeare has so vividly described.--T. F. DIBDIN. *Bibliomania.*

DELIGHT IN BOOK-PRINTS

I yield to none in my love of bookstall urbanity. I have spent as happy moments over the stalls (until the woman looked out) as any literary apprentice boy who ought to be moving onwards. But I confess my weakness in liking to see some of my favourite purchases neatly bound. The books I like to have about me most are Spenser, Chaucer, the minor poems of Milton, the *Arabian Nights*, Theocritus, Ariosto, and such old good-natured speculations as Plutarch's *Morals*. For most of these I like a plain good old binding, never mind how old, provided it wears well; but my *Arabian Nights* may be bound in as fine and flowery a style as possible, and I should love an engraving to every dozen pages. Book-prints of all sorts, bad and good, take with me as much as when I was a child: and I think some books, such as Prior's *Poems*, ought always to have portraits of the authors. Prior's airy face with his cap on, is like having his company. From early association, no edition of Milton pleases me so much, as that in which there are pictures of the Devil with brute ears, dressed like a Roman General: nor of Bunyan, as the one containing the print of the Valley of the Shadow of Death, with the Devil whispering in Christian's ear, or old Pope by the wayside, and

> Vanity Fair,
> With the Pilgrims suffering there.

I delight in the recollection of the puzzle I used to have with the frontispiece of the *Tale of a Tub*, of my real horror at the sight of that crawling old man representing Avarice, at the beginning of *Enfield's Speaker*, the *Looking Glass*, or some such book; and even of the careless schoolboy hats, and the prim stomachers and cottage bonnets, of such golden-age antiquities as the *Village School*. The oldest and most worn-out woodcut, representing King Pippin, Goody Two Shoes, or the grim Soldan, sitting with three staring blots for his eyes and mouth, his sceptre in one hand, and his other five fingers raised and spread in admiration at the feats of the Gallant London Prentice, cannot excite in me a feeling of ingratitude.--J. H. LEIGH HUNT. *My Books.*

A NEAT RIVULET OF TEXT

LADY SNEERWELL. I wonder, Sir Benjamin, you never publish anything.

SIR BENJAMIN BACKBITE. To say truth, ma'am, 'tis very vulgar to print; and as my little productions are mostly satires and lampoons on particular people, I find they circulate more by giving copies in confidence to the friends of the parties. However, I have some love elegies, which, when favoured with this lady's smiles, I mean to give to the public.

CRABTREE. 'Fore Heaven, ma'am, they'll immortalize you!--you will be handed down to posterity, like Petrarch's Laura, or Waller's Sacharissa.

SIR BENJAMIN. Yes, madam, I think you will like them, when you shall see them on a beautiful quarto page, where a neat rivulet of text shall meander through a meadow of margin.--R. B. SHERIDAN. *The School for Scandal.*

THE BOOKWORMS

> Through and through the inspired leaves,
>   Ye maggots, make your windings;
> But, oh! respect his lordship's taste,
>   And spare his golden bindings.
>
>   R. BURNS.

THE BOOKWORM

Come hither, boy, we'll hunt to-day
The bookworm, ravening beast of prey,
Produced by parent Earth, at odds,
As fame reports it, with the Gods.
Him frantic hunger wildly drives
Against a thousand authors' lives:
Through all the fields of wit he flies;
Dreadful his head with clustering eyes,
With horns without, and tusks within,
And scales to serve him for a skin.
Observe him nearly, lest he climb
To wound the bards of ancient time,
Or down the vale of fancy go
To tear some modern wretch below.
On every corner fix thine eye,
Or ten to one he slips thee by.
See where his teeth a passage eat:
We'll rouse him from his deep retreat.
But who the shelter's forced to give?
'Tis sacred Virgil, as I live!
From leaf to leaf, from song to song,
He draws the tadpole form along,
He mounts the gilded edge before,
He's up, he scuds the cover o'er,
He turns, he doubles, there he passed,
And here we have him, caught at last.

Insatiate brute, whose teeth abuse
The sweetest servants of the Muse--
Nay, never offer to deny,
I took thee in the act to fly.
His roses nipped in every page,
My poor Anacreon mourns thy rage;
By thee my Ovid wounded lies;
By thee my Lesbia's Sparrow dies;
Thy rabid teeth have half destroyed
The work of love in Biddy Floyd;
They rent Belinda's locks away,
And spoiled the Blouzelind of Gay.
For all, for every single deed,
Relentless justice bids thee bleed:
Then fall a victim to the Nine,
Myself the priest, my desk the shrine.

Bring Homer, Virgil, Tasso near,
To pile a sacred altar here:

Hold, boy, thy hand outruns thy wit,
You reached the plays that Dennis writ;
You reached me Philips' rustic strain;
Pray take your mortal bards again.

Come, bind the victim,--there he lies,
And here between his numerous eyes
This venerable dust I lay
From manuscripts just swept away.
The goblet in my hand I take,
For the libation's yet to make:
A health to poets! all their days
May they have bread, as well as praise;
Sense may they seek, and less engage
In papers filled with party rage.
But if their riches spoil their vein,
Ye Muses, make them poor again.

Now bring the weapon, yonder blade
With which my tuneful pens are made.
I strike the scales that arm thee round,
And twice and thrice I print the wound;
The sacred altar floats with red,
And now he dies, and now he's dead.

How like the son of Jove I stand,
This Hydra stretched beneath the hand!
Lay bare the monster's entrails here,
And see what dangers threat the year:
Ye gods! what sonnets on a wench!
What lean translations out of French!
'Tis plain, this lobe is so unsound,
S-- prints, before the months go round.

But hold, before I close the scene
The sacred altar should be clean.
O had I Shadwell's second bays,
Or, Tate, thy pert and humble lays!
(Ye pair, forgive me, when I vow
I never missed your works till now,)
I'd tear the leaves to wipe the shrine,
That only way you please the Nine:
But since I chance to want these two,
I'll make the songs of D'Urfey do.

Rent from the corpse, on yonder pin,
I hang the scales that braced it in;
I hang my studious morning gown,

And write my own inscription down.
'This trophy from the Python won,
This robe, in which the deed was done,
These, Parnell, glorying in the feat,
Hung on these shelves, the Muses' seat.
Here Ignorance and Hunger found
Large realms of wit to ravage round;
Here Ignorance and Hunger fell,
Two foes in one I sent to hell.
Ye poets who my labours see
Come share the triumph all with me!
Ye critics, born to vex the Muse,
Go mourn the grand ally you lose!'

  T. PARNELL.

A MOTH

Here he beholds in triumph sit
The bane of beauty, sense, and wit;
Demolished distichs round his head,
Half lines and shattered stanzas spread,
While the insulting conqueror climbs
O'er mighty heaps of ruined rhymes,
And, proudly mounted, views from high,
Beneath, the harmonious fragments lie;
Boasting himself from foes secured,
In stanzas lodged, in verse immured.

  W. KING (?) *Bibliotheca.*

THE CURE FOR BOOKWORMS

There is a sort of busy worm
That will the fairest books deform,
 By gnawing holes throughout them;
Alike through every leaf they go,
Yet of its merits naught they know,
 Nor care they aught about them.

Their tasteless tooth will tear and taint
The poet, patriot, sage, or saint,
 Nor sparing wit nor learning:
Now, if you'd know the reason why,
The best of reasons I'll supply--
 'Tis bread to the poor vermin.

Of pepper, snuff, or 'bacca smoke,
And russia-calf they make a joke.
  Yet why should sons of science
These puny, rankling reptiles dread?
'Tis but to let their books be read,
  And bid the worms defiance.

J. F. M. DOVASTON.

ROYAL PATRONAGE OF BOOKS

Queen Charlotte, when discussing books with Fanny Burney and Mrs. Delany, during the former's residence at Court at Windsor, praised the work of a writer who had translated a German book into English, saying 'I wish I knew the translator,' to which Miss Burney replied, 'I wish the translator knew that!'

'Oh,' said the Queen,--'it is not--I should not like to give my name, for fear I have judged ill: I picked it up on a stall. Oh, it is amazing what good books there are on stalls.'

'It is amazing to me,' said Mrs. Delany, 'to hear that.'

'Why, I don't pick them up myself; but I have a servant very clever; and if they are not to be had at the bookseller's, they are not for me any more than for another.'--From MADAME D'ARBLAY. *Diary*.

THE TREASURE

Do you remember the brown suit, which you made to hang upon you, till all your friends cried shame upon you, it grew so thread-bare--and all because of that folio Beaumont and Fletcher, which you dragged home late at night from Barker's in Covent-garden? Do you remember how we eyed it for weeks before we could make up our minds to the purchase, and had not come to a determination till it was near ten o'clock of the Saturday night, when you set off from Islington, fearing you should be too late--and when the old bookseller with some grumbling opened his shop, and by the twinkling taper (for he was setting bed-wards) lighted out the relic from his dusty treasures--and when you lugged it home, wishing it were twice as cumbersome--and when you presented it to me--and when we were exploring the perfectness of it (*collating* you called it)--and while I was repairing some of the loose leaves with paste, which your impatience would not suffer to be left till daybreak--was there no pleasure in being a poor man? or can those neat black clothes, which you wear now, and are so careful to keep brushed, since we have become rich and finical, give you half the honest vanity, with which you flaunted it about in that over-worn suit--your old corbeau--for four or five weeks longer than you should have done, to pacify your conscience for the mighty sum of fifteen--or sixteen shillings was it?--a great affair we thought it then--which you had lavished on the old folio. Now you can afford to buy any book that pleases you, but I do not see that you ever bring me home any nice old purchases now.--C. LAMB. *Old China*.

THE MOST VALUABLE BOOK

We ought not to get books too cheaply. No book, I believe, is ever worth half so much to its reader as one that has been coveted for a year at a bookstall, and bought out of saved halfpence; and perhaps a day or two's fasting. That's the way to get at the cream of a book.--J. RUSKIN. *Political Economy of Art (A Joy for Ever)*.

THE READERS AT THE BOOKSTALL

There is a class of street-readers, whom I can never contemplate without affection--the poor gentry, who, not having wherewithal to buy or hire a book, filch a little learning at the open stalls--the owner, with his hard eye, casting envious looks at them all the while, and thinking when they will have done. Venturing tenderly, page after page, expecting every moment when he shall interpose his interdict, and yet unable to deny themselves the gratification, they 'snatch a fearful joy'. Martin B----, in this way, by daily fragments, got through two volumes of Clarissa, when the stall-keeper damped his laudable ambition, by asking him (it was in his younger days) whether he meant to purchase the work. M. declares that under no circumstances of his life did he ever peruse a book with half the satisfaction which he took in those uneasy snatches. A quaint poetess of our day has moralized upon this subject in two very touching but homely stanzas:

I saw a boy with eager eye
Open a book upon a stall,
And read, as he'd devour it all;
Which when the stall-man did espy,
Soon to the boy I heard him call,
'You, Sir, you never buy a book,
Therefore in one you shall not look.'
The boy passed slowly on and with a sigh
He wished he never had been taught to read,
Then of the old churl's books he should have had no need.

Of sufferings the poor have many,
Which never can the rich annoy:
I soon perceived another boy,
Who looked as if he'd not had any
Food, for that day at least--enjoy
The sight of cold meat in a tavern larder.
This boy's case, then thought I, is surely harder,
Thus hungry, longing, thus without a penny,
Beholding choice of dainty-dressèd meat:
No wonder if he wish he ne'er had learned to eat.

C. LAMB. *Detached Thoughts on Books and Reading.*

TETRACHORDON

A book was writ of late called Tetrachordon;
  And woven close, both matter, form and style;
  The subject new: it walked the town awhile,
  Numbering good intellects; now seldom pored on.
Cries the stall-reader, bless us! what a word on
  A title-page is this! and some in file
  Stand spelling false, while one might walk to Mile-
  End Green. Why is it harder, Sirs, than Gordon,
Colkitto, or Macdonnel, or Galasp?
  Those rugged names to our like mouths grow sleek
  That would have made Quintilian stare and gasp.
Thy age, like ours, O soul of Sir John Cheek,
  Hated not learning worse than toad or asp;
  When thou taught'st Cambridge, and King Edward Greek.

J. MILTON.

THE SECOND-HAND CATALOGUE

A Second-hand Bookseller's Catalogue is not a mere catalogue or list of saleables, as the uninitiated may fancy. Even a common auctioneer's catalogue of goods and chattels suggests a thousand reflections to a peruser of any knowledge; judge then what the case must be with a catalogue of Books; the very titles of which run the rounds of the whole world, visible and invisible; geographies--biographies-- histories--loves--hates--joys--sorrows--cookeries--sciences--fashion--and eternity! We speak on this subject from the most literal experience; for often and often have we cut open a new catalogue of old books, with all the fervour and ivory folder of a first love; often read one at tea; nay, at dinner; and have put crosses against dozens of volumes in the list, out of the pure imagination of buying them, the possibility being *out of the question*!--

Nothing delights us more than to overhaul some dingy tome, and read a chapter gratuitously. Occasionally when we have opened some very attractive old book, we have stood reading for hours at the stall, lost in a brown study and worldly forgetfulness, and should probably have read on to the end of the last chapter, had not the vendor of published wisdom offered, in a satirically polite way, to bring us out a chair--'Take a chair, sir; you must be tired.'--J. H. LEIGH HUNT. *Retrospective Review.*

THE FIND

Do you see this square old yellow Book, I toss

I' the air, and catch again, and twirl about
By the crumpled vellum covers,--pure crude fact
Secreted from man's life when hearts beat hard,
And brains, high-blooded, ticked two centuries since?
Examine it yourselves! I found this book,
Gave a *lira* for it, eightpence English just,
(Mark the predestination!) when a Hand,
Always above my shoulder, pushed me once,
One day still fierce 'mid many a day struck calm,
Across a Square in Florence, crammed with booths,
Buzzing and blaze, noontide and market-time;
Toward Baccio's marble,--ay, the basement-ledge
O' the pedestal where sits and menaces
John of the Black Bands with the upright spear,
'Twixt palace and church,--Riccardi where they lived,
His race, and San Lorenzo where they lie.
This book,--precisely on that palace-step
Which, meant for lounging knaves o' the Medici,
Now serves re-venders to display their ware,--
'Mongst odds and ends of ravage, picture-frames
White through the worn gilt, mirror-sconces chipped,
Bronze angel-heads once knobs attached to chests,
(Handled when ancient dames chose forth brocade)
Modern chalk drawings, studies from the nude,
Samples of stone, jet, breccia, porphyry
Polished and rough, sundry amazing busts
In baked earth, (broken, Providence be praised!)
A wreck of tapestry, proudly-purposed web
When reds and blues were indeed red and blue,
Now offered as a mat to save bare feet
(Since carpets constitute a cruel cost)
Treading the chill scagliola bedward: then
A pile of brown-etched prints, two *crazie* each,
Stopped by a conch a-top from fluttering forth
--Sowing the Square with works of one and the same
Master, the imaginative Sienese
Great in the scenic backgrounds--(name and fame
None of you know, nor does he fare the worse:)
From these.... Oh, with a Lionard going cheap
If it should prove, as promised, that Joconde
Whereof a copy contents the Louvre!--these
I picked this book from. Five compeers in flank
Stood left and right of it as tempting more--
A dogseared Spicilegium, the fond tale
O' the Frail One of the Flower, by young Dumas,
Vulgarized Horace for the use of schools,
The Life, Death, Miracles of Saint Somebody,
Saint Somebody Else, his Miracles, Death, and Life,--

With this, one glance at the lettered back of which,
And 'Stall!' cried I: a *lira* made it mine.

Here it is, this I toss and take again;
Small-quarto size, part print part manuscript:
A book in shape but, really, pure crude fact
Secreted from man's life when hearts beat hard,
And brains, high-blooded, ticked two centuries since.
Give it me back! The thing's restorative
I' the touch and sight.

R. BROWNING. *The Ring and the Book.*

PURCHASING AN ACT OF PIETY

When Providence throws a good book in my way, I bow to its decree and purchase it as an act of piety, if it is reasonably or unreasonably cheap. I *adopt* a certain number of books every year, out of a love for the foundlings and stray children of other people's brains that nobody seems to care for. Look here.

He took down a Greek Lexicon finely bound in calf, and spread it open.

Do you see that Hedericus? I had Greek dictionaries enough and to spare, but I saw that noble quarto lying in the midst of an ignoble crowd of cheap books, and marked with a price which I felt to be an insult to scholarship, to the memory of Homer, sir, and the awful shade of Aeschylus, I paid the mean price asked for it, and I wanted to double it, but I suppose it would have been a foolish sacrifice of coin to sentiment. I love that book for its looks and behaviour. None of your 'half-calf' economies in that volume, sir! And see how it lies open anywhere! There isn't a book in my library that has such a generous way of laying its treasures before you. From Alpha to Omega, calm, assured rest at any page that your choice or accident may light on. No lifting of a rebellious leaf like an upstart servant that does not know his place and can never be taught manners, but tranquil, well-bred repose. A book may be a perfect gentleman in its aspect and demeanour, and this book would be good company for personages like Roger Ascham and his pupils the Lady Elizabeth and the Lady Jane Grey.--O. W. HOLMES. *The Poet at the Breakfast-Table.*

A FORCED SALE

I fear that I must sell this residue
Of my father's books; although the Elzevirs
Have fly-leaves over-written by his hand,
In faded notes as thick and fine and brown
As cobwebs on a tawny monument
Of the old Greeks--*conferenda haec cum his*--
Corruptè citat--lege potiùs,

And so on, in the scholar's regal way
Of giving judgement on the parts of speech,
As if he sate on all twelve thrones up-piled,
Arraigning Israel. Ay, but books and notes
Must go together. And this Proclus too,
In quaintly dear contracted Grecian types,
Fantastically crumpled, like his thoughts
Which would not seem too plain; you go round twice
For one step forward, then you take it back,
Because you're somewhat giddy! there's the rule
For Proclus. Ah, I stained this middle leaf
With pressing in't my Florence iris-bell,
Long stalk and all: my father chided me
For that stain of blue blood,--I recollect
The peevish turn his voice took,--'Silly girls,
Who plant their flowers in our philosophy
To make it fine, and only spoil the book!
No more of it, Aurora.' Yes--no more!
Ah, blame of love, that's sweeter than all praise
Of those who love not! 'tis so lost to me,
I cannot, in such beggared life, afford
To lose my Proclus....

The kissing Judas, Wolff, shall go instead,
Who builds us such a royal book as this
To honour a chief-poet, folio-built,
And writes above, 'The house of Nobody':
Who floats in cream, as rich as any sucked
From Juno's breasts, the broad Homeric lines,
And, while with their spondaic prodigious mouths
They lap the lucent margins as babe-gods,
Proclaims them bastards. Wolff's an atheist;
And if the Iliad fell out, as he says,
By mere fortuitous concourse of old songs,
We'll guess as much, too, for the universe.

     E. B. BROWNING. *Aurora Leigh*.

THE VOCATION

One of the shop-windows he paused before was that of a second-hand book-shop, where, on a narrow table outside, the literature of the ages was represented in judicious mixture, from the immortal verse of Homer to the mortal prose of the railway novel. That the mixture was judicious was apparent from Deronda's finding in it something that he wanted--namely, that wonderful bit of autobiography, the life of the Polish Jew, Salomon Maimon; which, as he could easily slip it into his pocket, he took from its place, and entered the shop to pay for, expecting to see behind the counter a grimy personage showing that nonchalance about sales which seems to belong universally to the second-hand book-business. In most other trades you find generous men who are anxious to sell you their wares for your own welfare; but even a Jew will not urge Simson's Euclid on you with an affectionate assurance that you will have pleasure in reading it, and that he wishes he had twenty more of the article, so much is it in request. One is led to fear that a second-hand bookseller may belong to that unhappy class of men who have no belief in the good of what they get their living by, yet keep conscience enough to be morose rather than unctuous in their vocation.--G. ELIOT. *Daniel Deronda.*

TO MY BOOKSELLER

Thou that makst gain thy end, and, wisely well,
  Callst a book good, or bad, as it doth sell,
Use mine so too: I give thee leave; but crave
  For the luck's sake it thus much favour have
To lie upon thy stall, till it be sought;
  Not offered, as it made suit to be bought;
Nor have my title-leaf on posts or walls,
  Or in cleft sticks, advanced to make calls
For termers, or some clerk-like servingman,
  Who scarce can spell the hard names: whose knight less can.
If without these vile arts it will not sell,
  Send it to Bucklersbury, there 'twill well.

    BEN JONSON.

THE WRITER TO HIS BOOK

Whither thus hastes my little book so fast?
To Paul's Churchyard. What? in those cells to stand,
With one leaf like a rider's cloak put up
To catch a termer? or lie musty there
With rhymes a term set out, or two, before?
Some will redeem me. Few. Yes, read me too.
Fewer. Nay, love me. Now thou dot'st, I see.
Will not our English Athens art defend?
Perhaps. Will lofty courtly wits not aim
Still at perfection? If I grant? I fly.
Whither? To Paul's. Alas, poor book, I rue
Thy rash self-love; go, spread thy papery wings:
Thy lightness cannot help or hurt my fame.

    T. CAMPION.

AD BIBLIOPOLAM

Printer or stationer or whate'er thou prove
Shalt me record to Time's posterity:
I'll not enjoin thee, but request in love,
Thou so much deign my Book to dignify,
As, first, it be not with your ballads mixed
Next, not at play-houses 'mongst pippins sold:
Then that on posts by the ears it stand not fixt,
For every dull mechanic to behold.
Last, that it come not brought in pedler's packs,
To common fairs, of country, town, or city:
Sold at a booth 'mongst pins and almanacks;
Yet on thy hands to lie, thou'lt say 'twere pity;
  Let it be rather for tobacco rent,
  Or butchers-wives, next Cleansing-week in Lent.

     H. PARROT. *The Mastive, or Young-Whelpe*
        of the Olde-Dogge.

IN BONDAGE TO THE BOOKSELLER

Nevertheless conceive me not, I pray you, that I go about to lay a general imputation upon all stationers. For to disparage the whole profession were an act neither becoming an honest man to do, nor a prudent auditory to suffer. Their mystery, as they not untruly term it, consists of divers trades incorporated together: as printers, book-binders, clasp-makers, booksellers, &c. And of all these be some honest men, who to my knowledge are so grieved, being overborne by the notorious oppressions and proceedings of the rest, that they have wished themselves of some other calling. The printers' mystery is ingenious, painful, and profitable: the book-binders' necessary; the clasp-makers' useful. And indeed, the retailer of books, commonly called a bookseller, is a trade, which, being well governed and limited within certain bounds, might become somewhat serviceable to the rest. But as it is now, for the most part abused, the bookseller hath not only made the printer, the binder, and the clasp-maker a slave to him: but hath brought authors, yea, the whole Commonwealth, and all the liberal sciences into bondage. For he makes all professors of Art labour for his profit, at his own price, and utters it to the Commonwealth in such fashion, and at those rates, which please himself. Insomuch, that I wonder so insupportable and so impertinent a thing as a mere bookseller, considering what the profession is become now, was ever permitted to grow up in the Commonwealth.--G. WITHER. *The Schollers Purgatory.*

IN PATERNOSTER ROW

Methinks, oh vain, ill-judging book!
I see thee cast a wistful look,
Where reputations won and lost are

In famous row called *Paternoster*.
Incensed to find your precious olio
Buried in unexplored port-folio,
You scorn the prudent lock and key;
And pant, well-bound and gilt, to see
Your volume in the window set
Of Stockdale, Hookham, and Debrett.
Go then, and pass that dangerous bourne
Whence never book can back return;
And when you find--condemned, despised,
Neglected, blamed, and criticized--
Abuse from all who read you fall
(If haply you be read at all),
Sorely will you for folly sigh at,
And wish for me, and home, and quiet.

Assuming now a conjurer's office, I
Thus on your future fortune prophesy:--
Soon as your novelty is o'er,
And you are young and new no more,
In some dark dirty corner thrown,
Mouldy with damps, with cobwebs strown,
Your leaves shall be the bookworm's prey;
Or sent to chandler's shop away,
And doomed to suffer public scandal,
Shall line the trunk, or wrap the candle.

M. G. LEWIS. *The Monk*.

THE ELEPHANT AND THE BOOKSELLER

The Bookseller, who heard him speak,
And saw him turn a page of Greek,
Thought, what a genius have I found!
Then thus addressed with bow profound:
'Learned Sir, if you'd employ your pen
Against the senseless sons of men,
Or write the history of Siam,
No man is better pay than I am.
Or, since you're learned in Greek, let's see
Something against the Trinity.'
When, wrinkling with a sneer his trunk,
'Friend', quoth the Elephant, 'you're drunk:
E'en keep your money, and be wise;
Leave man on man to criticize:

204

For that you ne'er can want a pen
Among the senseless sons of men.
They unprovoked will court the fray;
Envy's a sharper spur than pay.
No author ever spared a brother;
Wits are gamecocks to one another.'

J. GAY. *Fables.*

LITERARY UPHOLSTERERS

Our booksellers here at London disgrace literature by the trash they bespeak to be written, and at the same time prevent everything else from being sold. They are little more or less than upholsterers, who sell *sets* or *bodies* of arts and sciences for furniture; and the purchasers, for I am very sure they are not readers, buy only in that view. I never thought there was much merit in reading: but yet it is too good a thing to be put upon no better footing than damask and mahogany.--H. WALPOLE. EARL OF ORFORD (Letter to Sir David Dalrymple).

No furniture so charming as books, even if you never open them or read a single word.--S. SMITH. *Memoirs.*

ON A MISCELLANY OF POEMS

To BERNARD LINTOTT

'*Ipsa varietate tentamus efficere ut alia aliis, quaedam fortasse omnibus placeant.*' *Plin. Epist.*

As when some skilful cook, to please each guest,
Would in one mixture comprehend a feast,
With due proportion and judicious care
He fills his dish with different sorts of fare,
Fishes and fowls deliciously unite,
To feast at once the taste, the smell, and sight.
So, Bernard, must a Miscellany be
Compounded of all kinds of poetry;
The Muses' olio, which all tastes may fit,
And treat each reader with his darling wit.
Wouldst thou for Miscellanies raise thy fame,
And bravely rival Jacob's mighty name,
Let all the Muses in the piece conspire;
The lyric bard must strike the harmonious lyre;
Heroic strains must here and there be found;
And nervous sense be sung in lofty sound;
Let elegy in moving numbers flow,

And fill some pages with melodious woe;
Let not your amorous songs too numerous prove,
Nor glut thy reader with abundant love;
Satire must interfere, whose pointed rage
May lash the madness of a vicious age;
Satire! the Muse that never fails to hit,
For if there's scandal, to be sure there's wit.
Tire not our patience with Pindaric lays,
Those swell the piece, but very rarely please;
Let short-breathed epigram its force confine,
And strike at follies in a single line.
Translations should throughout the work be sown,
And Homer's godlike Muse be made our own;
Horace in useful numbers should be sung,
And Virgil's thoughts adorn the British tongue.
Let Ovid tell Corinna's hard disdain,
And at her door in melting notes complain;
His tender accents pitying virgins move,
And charm the listening ear with tales of love
Let every classic in the volume shine,
And each contribute to thy great design;
Through various subjects let the reader range,
And raise his fancy with a grateful change.
Variety's the source of joy below,
From whence still fresh revolving pleasures flow.
In books and love, the mind one end pursues,
And only *change* the expiring flame renews.
  Where Buckingham will condescend to give,
That honoured piece to distant times must live;
When noble Sheffield strikes the trembling strings,
The little Loves rejoice, and clap their wings;
Anacreon lives, they cry, the harmonious swain
Retunes the lyre, and tries his wonted strain,
'Tis he--our lost Anacreon lives again.
But, when the illustrious poet soars above
The sportive revels of the God of Love,
Like Mars's Muse, he takes a loftier flight,
And towers beyond the wondering Cupid's sight.
  If thou wouldst have thy volume stand the test,
And of all others be reputed best,
Let Congreve teach the listening groves to mourn,
As when he wept o'er fair Pastora's urn.
  Let Prior's Muse with softening accents move,
Soft as the strains of constant Emma's love:
Or let his fancy choose some jovial theme,
As when he told Hans Carvel's jealous dream;
Prior the admiring reader entertains
With Chaucer's humour, and with Spenser's strains.

Waller in Granville lives; when Mira sings,
With Waller's hand he strikes the sounding strings,
With sprightly turns his noble genius shines,
And manly sense adorns his easy lines.
  On Addison's sweet lays attention waits,
And silence guards the place while he repeats;
His Muse alike on every subject charms,
Whether she paints the god of love, or arms:
In him pathetic Ovid sings again,
And Homer's *Iliad* shines in his *Campaign*.
  Whenever Garth shall raise his sprightly song,
Sense flows in easy numbers from his tongue;
Great Phoebus in his learned son we see,
Alike in physic, as in poetry.
  When Pope's harmonious Muse with pleasure roves
Amidst the plains, the murmuring streams, and groves,
Attentive Echo, pleased to hear his songs,
Through the glad shade each warbling note prolongs;
His various numbers charm our ravished ears,
His steady judgement far out-shoots his years,
And early in the youth the god appears.
  From these successful bards collect thy strains;
And praise with profit shall reward thy pains:
Then, while calf's-leather-binding bears the sway,
And sheepskin to its sleeker gloss gives way;
While neat old Elzevir is reckoned better
Than Pirate Hill's brown sheets and scurvy letter;
While print-admirers careful Aldous choose,
Before John Morphew, or the Weekly News;
So long shall live thy praise in books of fame,
And Tonson yield to Lintott's lofty name.

J. GAY.

VERSES TO BE PREFIXED BEFORE BERNARD LINTOTT'S NEW
MISCELLANY

Some Colinaeus praise, some Bleau,
Others account them but so so;
Some Plantin to the rest prefer,
And some esteem old Elzevir;
Others with Aldous would besot us;
I, for my part, admire Lintotus.--
His character's beyond compare,
Like his own person, large and fair.
They print their names in letters small,
But LINTOTT stands in capital:

Author and he with equal grace
Appear, and stare you in the face.
Stephens prints Heathen Greek, 'tis said,
Which some can't construe, some can't read;
But all that comes from Lintott's hand,
Even Rawlinson might understand.
Oft in an Aldous, or a Plantin,
A page is blotted, or leaf wanting:
Of Lintott's books this can't be said,
All fair, and not so much as read.
Their copy cost 'em not a penny
To Homer, Virgil, or to any;
They ne'er gave sixpence for two lines
To them, their heirs, or their assigns:
But Lintott is at vast expense,
And pays prodigious dear for--sense.
Their books are useful but to few,
A scholar or a wit or two;
Lintott's for general use are fit.

A. POPE.

TO MR. MURRAY

Strahan, Tonson, Lintott of the times,
Patron and publisher of rhymes,
For thee the bard up Pindus climbs,
        My Murray.

To thee, with hope and terror dumb,
The unpledged MS. authors come;
Thou printest all--and sellest some--
        My Murray.

Upon thy table's baize so green
The last new *Quarterly* is seen,--
But where is thy new Magazine,
        My Murray?

Along thy sprucest bookshelves shine
The works thou deemest most divine--
The 'Art of Cookery', and mine,
        My Murray.

Tours, Travels, Essays, too, I wist,
And Sermons, to thy mill bring grist;
And then thou hast the 'Navy List',

My Murray.

And heaven forbid I should conclude
Without 'the Board of Longitude',
Although this narrow paper would,
       My Murray.

      G. GORDON, LORD BYRON.

    TO THE EDITOR OF 'THE EVERY-DAY BOOK'

I like you, and your book, ingenuous Hone!
  In whose capacious all-embracing leaves
The very marrow of tradition's shown;
  And all that history--much that fiction--weaves.

By every sort of taste your work is graced.
  Vast stores of modern anecdote we find,
With good old story quaintly interlaced--
  The theme as various as the reader's mind.

Rome's life-fraught legends you so truly paint--
  Yet kindly,--that the half-turned Catholic
Scarcely forbears to smile at his own Saint,
  And cannot curse the candid heretic.

Rags, relics, witches, ghosts, fiends, crowd your page;
  Our father's mummeries we well-pleased behold,
And, proudly conscious of a purer age,
  Forgive some fopperies in the times of old.

Verse-honouring Phoebus, Father of bright *Days*,
  Must needs bestow on you both good and many,
Who, building trophies of his Children's praise,
  Run their rich Zodiac through, not missing any.

Dan Phoebus loves your book--trust me, friend Hone--
  The title only errs, he bids me say:
For while such art, wit, reading, there are shown,
  He swears, 'tis not a work of *every day*.

      C. LAMB.

    I love everything that is old: old friends, old times, old manners, old books, old wines.--O. GOLDSMITH.

THE BANNATYNE CLUB, OR ONE VOLUME MORE

Assist me, ye friends of Old Books and Old Wine,
To sing in the praises of sage Bannatyne,
Who left such a treasure of old Scottish lore
As enables each age to print one volume more.
  One volume more, my friends, one volume more,
  We'll ransack old Banny for one volume more.

And first, Allan Ramsay was eager to glean
From Bannatyne's *Hortus* his bright Evergreen;
Two light little volumes (intended for four)
Still leave us the task to print one volume more.
         One volume more, &c.

His ways were not ours, for he cared not a pin
How much he left out, or how much he put in;
The truth of the reading he thought was a bore,
So this accurate age calls for one volume more.
         One volume more, &c.

Correct and sagacious, then came my Lord Hailes,
And weighed every letter in critical scales,
And left out some brief words, which the prudish abhor,
And castrated Banny in one volume more.
  One volume more, my friends, one volume more;
  We'll restore Banny's manhood in one volume more.

John Pinkerton next, and I'm truly concerned
I can't call that worthy so candid as learned;
He railed at the plaid and blasphemed the claymore,
And set Scots by the ears in his one volume more.
  One volume more, my friends, one volume more,
  Celt and Goth shall be pleased with one volume more.

As bitter as gall, and as sharp as a razor,
And feeding on herbs as a Nebuchadnezzar,
His diet too acid, his temper too sour,
Little Ritson came out with his two volumes more.
  But one volume, my friends, one volume more,
  We'll dine on roast-beef and print one volume more.

The stout Gothic yeditur, next on the roll,
With his beard like a brush, and as black as a coal;

And honest Greysteel that was true to the core,
Lent their hearts and their hands each to one volume more.
      One volume more, &c.

Since by these single champions what wonders were done,
What may not be achieved by our Thirty and One?
Law, Gospel, and Commerce we count in our corps,
And the Trade and the Press join for one volume more.
      One volume more, &c.

Ancient libels and contraband books, I assure ye,
We'll print as secure from Exchequer or Jury;
Then hear your Committee and let them count o'er
The Chiels they intend in their three volumes more.
      Three volumes more, &c.

They'll produce your King Jamie, the Sapient and Sext,
And the Bob of Dumblane and her Bishops come next;
One tome miscellaneous they'll add to your store,
Resolving next year to print four volumes more.
  Four volumes more, my friends, four volumes more;
  Pay down your subscriptions for four volumes more.

    SIR W. SCOTT.

    THE BOOKSELLERS' BANQUET

Grave vendors of volumes, best friends of the Nine,
  Give ear to my song as to charm you I try;
Other bards may in vain look for audience like mine,
  For the muses they chant, for the booksellers I.
Their notes I have drawn, so 'tis nothing but fair
  That my notes should be drawn, if they please, at a beck;
Undaunted I warble--I truly declare
  My song is most valued when met by a *cheque*.

The work we've just finished went off very well;
  It was set out with *plates*, such as Finden, or Heath,
If even their professional feelings rebel,
  Must praise on account (not in spite) of their teeth.
Though by Fraser cut up, and by Murray reviewed,
  Lovegrove's articles all fit insertion have found.
We have cleared off our boards, but as business is good,
  We keep wetted for use, and for pleasure unbound.

But here not for pleasure alone are we stored
  Like holiday tomes in our gilding so bright;

Some care 'tis our duty and wish to afford
  In the moment of need to a less lucky wight,
Whose title is lost, and whose covers are torn,
  When the moth has gnawed through, dust or cobwebs surround,
And to lift on the shelf our poor brother forlorn,
  As a much damaged old folio treasured by Lowndes.

Though his back stock of life may perchance weigh him down,
  By our aid may the old heavy pressure be moved,
And new-titled we start him again on the town,
  As a second edition revised and improved.
And for dealings like this a commission will find,
  And that of a date that the primest is given,
The commission is--Strive to do good to mankind,
  And the place of its dates is no other than Heaven.

I won't keep the press waiting--my copy is gone,
  Having finished a lay which Bob Fisher, perhaps,
May out of the head of old Caxton call one,
  If not of his *Drawing*, yet *Dining-room Scraps*;
But as we all still think of Tom Talfourd's bill,
  After sixty years' date, I respectfully beg,
As a knight of the quill, here to offer for *nil*,
  My right in this song as a present to Tegg.

W. MAGINN.

WHAT A HEART-BREAKING SHOP

But what were even gold and silver, precious stones and clockwork, to the bookshops, whence a pleasant smell of paper freshly pressed came issuing forth, awakening instant recollections of some new grammar had at school, long time ago, with 'Master Pinch, Grove House Academy', inscribed in faultless writing on the fly-leaf! That whiff of russia leather, too, and all those rows on rows of volumes, neatly ranged within: what happiness did they suggest! And in the window were the spick-and-span new works from London, with the title-pages, and sometimes even the first page of the first chapter, laid wide open: tempting unwary men to begin to read the book, and then, in the impossibility of turning over, to rush blindly in, and buy it! Here too were the dainty frontispiece and trim vignette, pointing like handposts on the outskirts of great cities, to the rich stock of incident beyond; and store of books, with many a grave portrait and time-honoured name, whose matter he knew well, and would have given mines to have, in any form, upon the narrow shelf beside his bed at Mr. Pecksniff's. What a heart-breaking shop it was!--C. DICKENS. *Martin Chuzzlewit.*

GENTEEL ORNAMENTS

If people bought no more books than they intended to read, and no more swords than they intended to use, the two worst trades in Europe would be a bookseller's and a sword-cutler's; but luckily for both they are reckoned genteel ornaments.--LORD CHESTERFIELD.

MAMMON AND BOOKS

All who are affected by the love of books hold worldly affairs and money very cheap, as Jerome writes to Vigilantius (Epist. 54): 'It is not for the same man to ascertain the value of gold coins and of writings;' which somebody thus repeated in verse:

No tinker's hand shall dare a book to stain;
  No miser's heart can wish a book to gain;
The gold assayer cannot value books;
  On them the epicure disdainful looks.
One house at once, believe me, cannot hold
  Lovers of books and hoarders up of gold.

No man, therefore, can serve mammon and books.--R. DE BURY. *Philobiblon.*

THE POOR STUDENT

In the depth of college shades, or in his lonely chamber, the poor student shrunk from observation. He found shelter among books, which insult not; and studies, that ask no questions of a youth's finances. He was lord of his library, and seldom cared for looking out beyond his domains.--C. LAMB. *Poor Relations.*

NATIONAL EXPENDITURE ON BOOKS

I say first we have despised literature. What do we, as a nation, care about books? How much do you think we spend altogether on our libraries, public or private, as compared with what we spend on our horses? If a man spends lavishly on his library, you call him mad--a bibliomaniac. But you never call any one a horse-maniac, though men ruin themselves every day by their horses, and you do not hear of people ruining themselves by their books. Or, to go lower still, how much do you think the contents of the book-shelves of the United Kingdom, public and private, would fetch, as compared with the contents of its wine-cellars? What position would its expenditure on literature take, as compared with its expenditure on luxurious eating? We talk of food for the mind, as of food for the body: now a good book contains such food inexhaustibly; it is a provision for life, and for the best part of us; yet how long most people would look at the best book before they would give the price of a large turbot for it! Though there have been men who have pinched their stomachs and bared their backs to buy a book, whose libraries were cheaper to them, I think, in the end, than most men's dinners are. We are few of us put to such trial, and more the pity; for, indeed, a precious thing is all the more precious to us if it has been won by work or economy; and if public libraries were half as costly as public dinners, or books cost the tenth part of what bracelets do, even foolish men and women might sometimes suspect there was good in reading, as well as in munching and sparkling; whereas the very cheapness of literature is making even wise people forget that if a book is worth reading, it is worth buying. No book is worth anything which is not worth *much*; nor is it serviceable until it has been read, and re-read, and loved, and loved again; and marked, so that you can refer to the passages you want in it, as a soldier can seize the weapon he needs in an armoury, or a housewife bring the spice she needs from her store. Bread of flour is good; but there is bread, sweet as honey, if we would eat it, in a good book; and the family must be poor indeed which, once in their lives, cannot, for such multipliable barley-loaves, pay their baker's bill. We call ourselves a rich nation, and we are filthy and foolish enough to thumb each other's books out of circulating libraries!--J. RUSKIN. *Sesame and Lilies.*

THE VALUE OF BOOK BORROWING

I have sent you the Philosophy--books you writ to me for; anything that you want of this kind for the advancement of your studies, do but write, and I shall furnish you. When I was a student as you are, my practice was to borrow rather than buy, some sort of books, and to be always punctual in restoring them upon the day assigned, and in the interim to swallow of them as much as made for my turn. This obliged me to read them through with more haste to keep my word, whereas I had not been so careful to peruse them had they been my own books, which I knew were always ready at my dispose.--J. HOWELL. *Familiar Letters.*

ACCIDENTS TO BOOKS

Fortunate are those who only consider a book for the utility and pleasure they may derive from its possession. Those students who, though they know much, still thirst to know more, may require this vast sea of books; yet in that sea they may suffer many shipwrecks.

Great collections of books are subject to certain accidents besides the damp, the worms, and the rats; one not less common is that of the *borrowers*, not to say a word of the *purloiners*!--I. D'ISRAELI. *Curiosities of Literature.*

BORROWERS OF BOOKS

To one like Elia, whose treasures are rather cased in leather covers than closed in iron coffers, there is a class of alienators more formidable than that which I have touched upon; I mean your *borrowers of books*--those mutilators of collections, spoilers of the symmetry of shelves, and creators of odd volumes. There is Comberbatch [Coleridge], matchless in his depredations!

That foul gap in the bottom shelf facing you, like a great eye-tooth knocked out--(you are now with me in my little back study in Bloomsbury, reader!)--with the huge Switzer-like tomes on each side (like the Guildhall giants, in their reformed posture, guardant of nothing), once held the tallest of my folios, *Opera Bonaventurae*, choice and massy divinity, to which its two supporters (school divinity also, but of a lesser calibre,--Bellarmine, and Holy Thomas), showed but as dwarfs,--itself an Ascapart!--*that* Comberbatch abstracted upon the faith of a theory he holds, which is more easy, I confess, for me to suffer by than to refute, namely, that 'the title to property in a book (my Bonaventure, for instance), is in exact ratio to the claimant's powers of understanding and appreciating the same'. Should he go on acting upon this theory, which of our shelves is safe?

The slight vacuum in the left-hand case--two shelves from the ceiling--scarcely distinguishable but by the quick eye of a loser--was whilom the commodious resting-place of Browne on Urn Burial. C. will hardly allege that he knows more about that treatise than I do, who introduced it to him, and was indeed the first (of the moderns) to discover its beauties--but so have I known a foolish lover to praise his mistress in the presence of a rival more qualified to carry her off than himself.--Just below, Dodsley's dramas want their fourth volume, where Vittoria Corombona is! The remainder nine are as distasteful as Priam's refuse sons, when the Fates *borrowed* Hector. Here stood the Anatomy of Melancholy, in sober state.--There loitered the Complete Angler; quiet as in life, by some stream side.--In yonder nook, John Buncle, a widower-volume, with 'eyes closed', mourns his ravished mate.

One justice I must do my friend, that if he sometimes, like the sea, sweeps away a treasure, at another time, sea-like, he throws up as rich an equivalent to match it. I have a small under-collection of this nature (my friend's gatherings in his various calls), picked up, he has forgotten at what odd places, and deposited with as little memory as mine. I take in these orphans, the twice-deserted. These proselytes of the gate are welcome as the true Hebrews. There they stand in conjunction; natives, and naturalised. The latter seem as little disposed to inquire out their true lineage as I am.--I charge no warehouse-room for these deodands, nor shall ever put myself to the ungentlemanly trouble of advertising a sale of them to pay expenses.

To lose a volume to C. carries some sense and meaning in it. You are sure that he will make one hearty meal on your viands, if he can give no account of the platter after it. But what moved thee, wayward, spiteful K., to be so importunate to carry off with thee, in spite of tears and adjurations to thee to forbear, the Letters of that princely woman, the thrice noble Margaret Newcastle?--knowing at the time, and knowing that I knew also, thou most assuredly wouldst never turn over one leaf of the illustrious folio:--what but the mere spirit of contradiction, and childish love of getting the better of thy friend?-- Then, worst cut of all! to transport it with thee to the Gallican land--

> Unworthy land to harbour such a sweetness,
> A virtue in which all ennobling thoughts dwelt,
> Pure thoughts, kind thoughts, high thoughts, her sex's wonder!

--hadst thou not thy play-books, and books of jests and fancies, about thee, to keep thee merry, even as thou keepest all companies with thy quips and mirthful tales?--Child of the Green-room, it was unkindly done of thee. Thy wife, too, that part-French, better-part Englishwoman!--that *she* could fix upon no other treatise to bear away in kindly to-ken of remembering us, than the works of Fulke Greville, Lord Brooke--of which no Frenchman, nor woman of France, Italy, or England, was ever by nature constituted to comprehend a tittle! *Was there not Zimmerman on Solitude?*

Reader, if haply thou art blessed with a moderate collection, be shy of showing it; or if thy heart overfloweth to lend them, lend thy books; but let it be to such a one as S. T. C.--he will return them (generally anticipating the time appointed) with usury; enriched with annotations, tripling their value. I have had experience. Many are these precious MSS. of his--(in *matter* oftentimes, and almost in *quantity* not unfrequently, vying with the originals)--in no very clerky hand--legible in my Daniel; in old Burton; in Sir Thomas Browne; and those abstruser cogitations of the Greville, now, alas! wandering in Pagan lands.--I counsel thee, shut not thy heart, nor thy library, against S. T. C.--C. LAMB. *The Two Races of Men.*

BORROWING AND LENDING

I own I borrow books with as much facility as I lend. I cannot see a work that interests me on another person's shelf, without a wish to carry it off: but, I repeat, that I have been much more sinned against than sinning in the article of non-return; and am scrupulous in the article of intention.--J. H. LEIGH HUNT. *My Books.*

WEDDED TO BOOKS

If people are to be wedded to their books, it is hard that, under our present moral dispensations, they are not to be allowed the usual exclusive privileges of marriage. A friend thinks no more of borrowing a book nowadays, than a Roman did of borrowing a man's wife; and what is worse, we are so far gone in our immoral notions on this subject, that we even lend it as easily as Cato did his spouse. Now what a happy thing ought it not to be to have exclusive possession of a book,--one's Shakespeare for instance; for the finer the wedded work, the more anxious of course we should be, that it should give nobody happiness but ourselves. Think of the pleasure of not only being with it in general, of having by far the greater part of its company, but of having it entirely to oneself; of always saying internally, 'It is my property'; of seeing it well-dressed in 'black or red', purely to please one's own eyes; of wondering how any fellow could be so impudent as to propose borrowing it for an evening; of being at once proud of his admiration, and pretty certain that it was in vain; of the excitement nevertheless of being a little uneasy whenever we saw him approach it too nearly; of wishing that it could give him a cuff of the cheek with one of its beautiful boards, for presuming to like its beauties as well as ourselves; of liking other people's books, but not at all thinking it proper that they should like ours; of getting perhaps indifferent to it, and then comforting ourselves with the reflection that others are not so, though to no purpose; in short, of all the mixed transport and anxiety to which the exclusiveness of the book-wedded state would be liable; not to mention the impossibility of other people's having any literary offspring from our fair unique, and consequently of the danger of loving any compilations but our own. Really, if we could burn all other copies of our originals, as the Roman Emperor once thought of destroying Homer, this system would be worth thinking of. If we had a good library, we should be in the situation of the Turks with their seraglios, which are a great improvement upon our petty exclusivenesses. Nobody could then touch our Shakespeare, our Spenser, our Chaucer, our Greek and Italian writers. People might say, 'Those are the walls of the library!' and 'sigh, and look, and sigh again'; but they should never get in. No Retrospective rake should anticipate our privileges of quotation. Our Mary Wollstonecrafts and our Madame de Staëls--no one should know how finely they were lettered,--what soul there was in their disquisitions. We once had a glimpse of the feelings which people would have on these occasions. It was in the library of Trinity College, Cambridge. The keeper of it was from home; and not being able to get a sight of the manuscript of Milton's *Comus*, we were obliged to content ourselves with looking through a wire-work, a kind of safe, towards the shelf on which it reposed. How we winked, and yearned, and imagined we saw a corner of the all-precious sheets, to no purpose! The feelings were not very pleasant, it is true; but then as long as they were confined to others, they would of course only add to our satisfaction.--J. H. LEIGH HUNT. *Wedded to Books.*

THE ART OF BOOK-KEEPING

How hard, when those who do not wish
  To lend, that's lose, their books,
Are snared by anglers--folks that fish
  With literary hooks;

Who call and take some favourite tome,
  But never read it through;--
They thus complete their set at home,
  By making one at you.

Behold the bookshelf of a dunce
  Who borrows--never lends:
Yon work, in twenty volumes, once
  Belonged to twenty friends.

New tales and novels you may shut
  From view--'tis all in vain;
They're gone--and though the leaves are 'cut'
  They never 'come again'.

For pamphlets lent I look around,
  For tracts my tears are spilt;
But when they take a book that's bound,
  'Tis surely extra-guilt.

A circulating library
  Is mine--my birds are flown;

There's one odd volume left to be
  Like all the rest, a-lone.

I, of my Spenser quite bereft,
  Last winter sore was shaken;
Of Lamb I've but a quarter left,
  Nor could I save my Bacon.

My Hall and Hill were levelled flat,
  But Moore was still the cry;
And then, although I threw them Sprat,
  They swallowed up my Pye.

O'er everything, however slight,
  They seized some airy trammel;
They snatched my Hogg and Fox one night,
  And pocketed my Campbell.

And then I saw my Crabbe at last,
  Like Hamlet's, backward go;
And as my tide was ebbing fast,
  Of course I lost my Rowe.

I wondered into what balloon
  My books their course had bent;
And yet, with all my marvelling, soon
  I found my Marvell went.

My Mallet served to knock me down,
  Which makes me thus a talker;
And once, while I was out of town,
  My Johnson proved a Walker.

While studying o'er the fire one day
  My Hobbes amidst the smoke,
They bore my Colman clean away,
  And carried off my Coke.

They picked my Locke, to me far more
  Than Bramah's patent's worth;
And now my losses I deplore
  Without a Home on earth.

If once a book you let them lift,
  Another they conceal;
For though I caught them stealing Swift,
  As swiftly went my Steele.

Hope is not now upon my shelf,
  Where late he stood elated;
But, what is strange, my Pope himself
  Is excommunicated.

My little Suckling in the grave
  Is sunk, to swell the ravage;
And what 'twas Crusoe's fate to save
  'Twas mine to lose--a Savage.

Even Glover's works I cannot put
  My frozen hands upon;
Though ever since I lost my Foote
  My Bunyan has been gone.

My Hoyle with Cotton went; oppressed,
  My Taylor too must sail;
To save my Goldsmith from arrest,
  In vain I offered Bayle.

I Prior sought, but could not see
  The Hood so late in front;
And when I turned to hunt for Lee,
  Oh! where was my Leigh Hunt?

I tried to laugh, old care to tickle,
  Yet could not Tickell touch,
And then, alas! I missed my Mickle,
  And surely mickle's much.

'Tis quite enough my griefs to feed,
  My sorrows to excuse,
To think I cannot read my Reid,
  Nor even use my Hughes.

To West, to South, I turn my head,
  Exposed alike to odd jeers;
For since my Roger Ascham's fled,
  I ask 'em for my Rogers.

They took my Horne--and Horne Tooke, too,
  And thus my treasures flit;
I feel when I would Hazlitt view,
  The flames that it has lit.

My word's worth little, Wordsworth gone,
  If I survive its doom;
How many a bard I doated on

Was swept off--with my Broome.

My classics would not quiet lie,
　A thing so fondly hoped;
Like Dr. Primrose, I may cry,
　'My Livy has eloped!'

My life is wasting fast away--
　I suffer from these shocks;
And though I've fixed a lock on Gray,
　There's grey upon my locks.

I'm far from young--am growing pale--
　I see my Butter fly;
And when they ask about my *ail*,
　'Tis Burton! I reply.

They still, have made me slight returns,
　And thus my griefs divide;
For oh! they've cured me of my Burns,
　And eased my Akenside.

But all I think I shall not say,
　Nor let my anger burn;
For as they never found me Gay,
　They have not left me Sterne.

S. LAMAN BLANCHARD.

THE BOOK OF NATURE

Of this fair volume which we World do name,
If we the sheets and leaves could turn with care,
Of Him who it corrects, and did it frame,
We clear might read the art and wisdom rare:
Find out His power which wildest powers doth tame,
His providence extending everywhere,
His justice which proud rebels doth not spare,
In every page, no, period of the same.
But silly we, like foolish children, rest
Well pleased with coloured vellum, leaves of gold,
Fair dangling ribands, leaving what is best,
On the great Writer's sense ne'er taking hold;
Or if by chance our minds do muse on aught,
It is some picture on the margin wrought.

W. DRUMMOND.

In Nature's infinite book of secrecy
A little I can read.

    W. SHAKESPEARE. *Antony and Cleopatra.*

THE BOOK

Eternal God! Maker of all
That have lived here since the Man's fall!
The Rock of Ages! in whose shade
They live unseen when here they fade!

Thou knew'st this *paper* when it was
Mere seed, and after that but grass;
Before 'twas dressed or spun, and when
Made linen, who did *wear* it then,
What were their lives, their thoughts and deeds,
Whether good *corn*, or fruitless *weeds*.

Thou knew'st this *tree*, when a green shade
Covered it, since a *cover* made,
And where it flourished, grew, and spread,
As if it never should be dead.

Thou knew'st this harmless *beast*, when he
Did live and feed by thy decree
On each green thing; then slept, well fed,
Clothed with this *skin*, which now lies spread
A *covering* o'er this aged book,
Which makes me wisely weep, and look
On my own dust; mere dust it is,
But not so dry and clean as this.
Thou knew'st and saw'st them all, and though
Now scattered thus, dost know them so.

O knowing, glorious Spirit! when
Thou shalt restore trees, beasts and men,
When thou shalt make all new again,
Destroying only death and pain,
Give him amongst thy works a place
Who in them loved and sought thy face!

    H. VAUGHAN.

THE BOOK OF LIFE

That Life is a Comedy oft hath been shown,
By all who Mortality's changes have known;
But more like a Volume its actions appear,
Where each Day is a Page and each Chapter a year.

'Tis a Manuscript Time shall full surely unfold,
Though with Black-Letter shaded, or shining with gold;
The Initial, like youth, glitters bright on its Page,
But its text is as dark--as the gloom of old Age.
  Then Life's Counsels of Wisdom engrave on thy breast,
  And deep on thine Heart be her lessons impressed.

Though the Title stands first it can little declare
The Contents which the Pages ensuing shall bear;
As little the first day of Life can explain
The succeeding events which shall glide in its train.
The Book follows next, and, delighted, we trace
An Elzevir's beauty, a Gutenberg's grace;
Thus on pleasure we gaze with as raptured an eye,
Till, cut off like a Volume imperfect, we die!
  Then Life's Counsels of Wisdom engrave on thy breast,
  And deep on thine Heart be her lessons impressed.

Yet e'en thus imperfect, complete, or defaced,
The skill of the Printer is still to be traced;
And though death bend us early in life to his will,
The wise hand of our Author is visible still.
Like the Colophon lines is the Epitaph's lay,
Which tells of what age and what nation our day,
And, like the Device of the Printer, we bear
The form of the Founder, whose Image we wear.
  Then Life's Counsels of Wisdom engrave on thy breast,
  And deep on thine Heart be her lessons impressed.

The work thus completed its Boards shall enclose,
Till a Binding more bright and more beauteous it shows;
And who can deny, when Life's Vision hath passed,
That the dark Boards of Death shall surround us at last.
Yet our Volume illumed with fresh splendours shall rise,
To be gazed at by Angels, and read to the skies,
Reviewed by its Author, revised by his Pen,
In a fair new Edition to flourish again.
  Then Life's Counsels of Wisdom engrave on thy breast,
  And deep on thine Heart be her lessons impressed.

R. THOMSON.

THE WIND OVER THE CHIMNEY

See, the fire is sinking low,
Dusky red the embers glow,
  While above them still I cower,
While a moment more I linger,
Though the clock, with lifted finger,
  Points beyond the midnight hour.

Sings the blackened log a tune
Learned in some forgotten June
  From a school-boy at his play,
When they both were young together,
Heart of youth and summer weather
  Making all their holiday.

And the night-wind rising, hark!
How above there in the dark,
  In the midnight and the snow,
Ever wilder, fiercer, grander.
Like the trumpets of Iskander,
  All the noisy chimneys blow!

Every quivering tongue of flame
Seems to murmur some great name,
  Seems to say to me, 'Aspire!'
But the night-wind answers, 'Hollow
Are the visions that you follow,
  Into darkness sinks your fire!'

Then the flicker of the blaze
Gleams on volumes of old days,
  Written by masters of the art,
Loud through whose majestic pages
Rolls the melody of ages,
  Throb the harp-strings of the heart.

And again the tongues of flame
Start exulting and exclaim:
  'These are prophets, bards, and seers;
In the horoscope of nations,
Like ascendant constellations,
  They control the coming years.'

But the night-wind cries: 'Despair!
Those who walk with feet of air

223

Leave no long-enduring marks;
At God's forges incandescent
Mighty hammers beat incessant,
   These are but the flying sparks.

'Dust are all the hands that wrought;
Books are sepulchres of thought;
   The dead laurels of the dead
Rustle for a moment only,
Like the withered leaves in lonely
   Churchyards at some passing tread.'

Suddenly the flame sinks down;
Sink the rumours of renown;
   And alone the night-wind drear
Clamours louder, wilder, vaguer,--
"Tis the brand of Meleager
   Dying on the hearth-stone here!'

And I answer,--'Though it be,
Why should that discomfort me?
   No endeavour is in vain;
Its reward is in the doing,
And the rapture of pursuing
   Is the prize the vanquished gain.'

H. W. LONGFELLOW. *Wise Books.*

For half the truths they hold are honoured tombs.--G. ELIOT. *The Spanish Gipsy.*

A GREAT NECROMANCER

Alonso of Aragon was wont to say of himself that he was a great Necromancer, for that he used to ask counsel of the dead: meaning Books.--F. BACON, LORD VERULAM. *Apophthegmes.*

BOOKS FOR MAGIC

Resolve you, doctors, *Bacon* can by books
Make storming *Boreas* thunder from his cave,
And dim fair *Luna* to a dark Eclipse.
The great arch-ruler, potentate of hell,
Trembles, when *Bacon* bids him, or his fiends,
Bow to the force of his Pentageron.
What art can work, the frolic friar knows,

And therefore will I turn my Magic books,
And strain out Necromancy to the deep.
I have contrived and framed a head of brass
(I made *Belcephon* hammer out the stuff),
And that by art shall read Philosophy:
And I will strengthen *England* by my skill,
That if ten *Caesars* lived and reigned in *Rome*,
With all the legions *Europe* doth contain,
They should not touch a grasse of English ground:
The work that *Ninus* reared at *Babylon*,
The brazen walls framed by *Semiramis*,
Carved out like to the portal of the sun,
Shall not be such as rings the *English* strand
From *Dover* to the market place of *Rye*.

R. GREENE. *The Honourable History of
Friar Bacon and Friar Bungay.*

THE SECRET OF STRENGTH

'Tis a custom with him
I' the afternoon to sleep: there thou may'st brain him,
Having first seized his books; or with a log
Batter his skull, or paunch him with a stake,
Or cut his wezand with thy knife. Remember
First to possess his books; for without them
He's but a sot, as I am, nor hath not
One spirit to command: they all do hate him
As rootedly as I. Burn but his books.

W. SHAKESPEARE. *The Tempest.*

RED LETTERS AND CONJURING

SMITH. The clerk of Chatham: he can write and read and cast accompt.

CADE. O monstrous!

SMITH. We took him setting of boys' copies.

CADE. Here's a villain!

SMITH. Has a book in his pocket with red letters in't.

CADE. Nay, then, he is a conjurer.

W. SHAKESPEARE. *Second Part of King Henry the Sixth.*

MERLIN'S BOOK

You read the book, my pretty Vivien!
O aye, it is but twenty pages long,
But every page having an ample marge,
And every marge enclosing in the midst
A square of text that looks a little blot,
The text no larger than the limbs of fleas;
And every square of text an awful charm,
Writ in a language that has long gone by.
So long, that mountains have arisen since
With cities on their flanks--*you* read the book!
And every margin scribbled, crost, and crammed
With comment, densest condensation, hard
To mind and eye; but the long sleepless nights
Of my long life have made it easy to me.
And none can read the text, not even I;
And none can read the comment but myself;
And in the comment did I find the charm.

LORD TENNYSON. *Idylls of the King: Vivien.*

FAST AND LOOSE

Fast bind, fast find: my Bible was well bound;
A Thief came fast, and loose my Bible found:
Was't bound and loose at once? how can that be?
'Twas loose for him, although 'twas bound for me.

J. TAYLOR.

READ THE SCRIPTURES

Read the Scriptures, which Hyperius holds available of itself; 'the mind is erected thereby from all worldly cares, and hath much quiet and tranquillity.' For, as Austin well hath it, 'tis *scientia scientiarum, omni melle dulcior, omni pane suavior, omni vino hilarior.* 'tis the best nepenthe, surest cordial, sweetest alterative, presentest diverter: for neither as Chrysostom well adds, 'those boughs and leaves of trees which are plashed for cattle to stand under, in the heat of the day, in summer, so much refresh them with their acceptable shade, as the reading of the Scripture doth recreate and comfort a distressed soul, in sorrow and affliction.' Paul bids us 'pray continually'; *quod cibus corpori, lectio animae facit,* saith Seneca, 'as meat is to the body, such is reading to the soul.' 'To be at leisure without books is another hell, and to be buried alive.' Cardan calls a library the physic of the soul; 'Divine authors fortify the mind, make men bold and constant'; and (as Hyperius adds) 'godly conference will not permit the mind to be tortured with absurd cogitations.'--R. BURTON. *The Anatomy of Melancholy.*

TO THE HOLY BIBLE

O Book! Life's guide! how shall we part,
And thou so long seized of my heart?
Take this last kiss; and let me weep
True thanks to thee before I sleep.

Thou wert the first put in my hand
When yet I could not understand,
And daily didst my young eyes lead
To letters, till I learnt to read.

But as rash youths, when once grown strong,
Fly from their nurses to the throng,
Where they new consorts choose, and stick
To those till either hurt or sick;
So with the first light gained from thee
Ran I in chase of vanity,
Cried dross for gold, and never thought
My first cheap book had all I sought.
Long reigned this vogue; and thou cast by,
With meek, dumb looks didst woo mine eye,
And oft left open would'st convey
A sudden and most searching ray
Into my soul, with whose quick touch
Refining still, I struggled much.
By this mild art of love at length
Thou overcam'st my sinful strength,
And having brought me home, didst there
Show me that pearl I sought elsewhere,--
Gladness, and peace, and hope, and love,
The secret favours of the Dove;
Her quickening kindness, smiles, and kisses,
Exalted pleasures, crowning blisses,
Fruition, union, glory, life,
Thou didst lead to, and still all strife.
Living, thou wert my soul's sure ease,
And dying mak'st me go in peace:--
Thy next effects no tongue can tell;
Farewell, O Book of God! farewell!

H. VAUGHAN.

ON BUYING THE BIBLE

'Tis but a folly to rejoice or boast
How small a price thy well-bought Pen'worth cost:
Until thy death thou shalt not fully know
Whether thy purchase be good cheap, or no;
And at that day, believe 't, it will appear
If not extremely cheap, extremely dear.

F. QUARLES. *Divine Fancies.*

'I READ ONLY THE BIBLE'

Read the most useful books, and that regularly, and constantly. Steadily spend all the morning in this employ, or, at least, five hours in four-and-twenty.

'But I read only the Bible.' Then you ought to teach others to read only the Bible, and, by parity of reason, to hear only the Bible. But if so, you need preach no more. 'Just so,' said George Bell. 'And what is the fruit? Why, now he neither reads the Bible, nor anything else. This is rank enthusiasm.' If you need no book but the Bible, you are got above St. Paul. He wanted others too. 'Bring the books,' says he, 'but especially the parchments,' those wrote on parchment. 'But I have no taste for reading.' Contract a taste for it by use, or return to your trade.--J. WESLEY. *Minutes of Some Late Conversations.*

A MAN OF ONE BOOK

I want to know one thing,--the way to heaven; how to land safe on the happy shore. God himself has condescended to teach me the way. For this very end He came from heaven. He hath written it down in a book. O give me the book! At any price, give me the book of God. I have it: here is knowledge enough for me. Let me be *homo unius libri*. Here then I am, far from the busy ways of men. I sit down alone; only God is here. In His presence I open, I read His book.... And what I thus learn, that I teach.--J. WESLEY. *Preface to Sermons.*

HOMO UNIUS LIBRI

When St. Thomas Aquinas was asked in what manner a man might best become learned, he answered, 'By reading one book.' The *homo unius libri* is indeed proverbially formidable to all conversational figurantes.--R. SOUTHEY. *The Doctor.*

THE SCRIPTURES: WHAT ARE THEY?

I remember he alleged many a scripture, but those I valued not; the scriptures, thought I, what are they? A dead letter, a little ink and paper, of three or four shillings price. Alas! What is the scripture? Give me a ballad, a news-book, George on horseback, or Bevis of Southampton; give me some book that teaches curious arts, that tells of old fables; but for the holy scriptures I cared not.--J. BUNYAN. *Sighs from Hell.*

'THE PILGRIM'S PROGRESS'

I know of no book, the Bible excepted, as above all comparison, which I, according to my judgement and experience, could so safely recommend as teaching and enforcing the whole saving truth according to the mind that was in Christ Jesus, as the *Pilgrim's Progress.* It is, in my conviction, incomparably the best *summa theologiae evangelicae* ever produced by a writer not miraculously inspired.

This wonderful work is one of the few books which may be read repeatedly at different times, and each time with a new and different pleasure. I read it once as a theologian-- and let me assure you that there is great theological acumen in the work--once with de-votional feelings--and once as a poet. I could not have believed beforehand that Calvinism could be painted in such exquisitely delightful colours....

The *Pilgrim's Progress* is composed in the lowest style of English, without slang or false grammar. If you were to polish it, you would at once destroy the reality of the vision. For works of imagination should be written in very plain language; the more imaginative they are the more necessary it is to be plain.--S. T. COLERIDGE. *Table Talk.*

NO BOOK LIKE THE BIBLE

I would have you every morning read a portion of the Holy Scriptures, till you have read the Bible from the beginning to the end: observe it well, read it reverently and attentively, set your heart upon it, and lay it up in your memory and make it the direction of your life: it will make you a wise and a good man. I have been acquainted somewhat with men and books, and have had long experience in learning, and in the world: there is no book like the Bible for excellent learning, wisdom, and use; and it is want of understanding in them that think or speak otherwise.--SIR M. HALE. *A Letter to one of his Sons, after his recovery from the Smallpox.*

TO A FAMILY BIBLE

What household thoughts around thee, as their shrine,
Cling reverently!--of anxious looks beguiled,
My mother's eyes, upon thy page divine,
Each day were bent--her accents gravely mild,
Breathed out thy love: whilst I, a dreamy child,

Wandered on breeze-like fancies oft away,
To some lone tuft of gleaming spring-flowers wild,
Some fresh-discovered nook for woodland play,
Some secret nest: yet would the solemn Word
At times, with kindlings of young wonder heard,
  Fall on my wakened spirit, there to be
A seed not lost:--for which, in darker years,
O Book of Heaven! I pour, with grateful tears,
  Heart blessings on the holy dead and thee!

FELICIA D. HEMANS.

THE BOOK OF BOOKS

No man was a greater lover of books than he [Shelley]. He was rarely to be seen, unless attending to other people's affairs, without a volume of some sort, generally of Plato or one of the Greek tragedians. Nor will those who understand the real spirit of his scepticism, be surprised to hear that one of his companions was the Bible. He valued it for the beauty of some of its contents, for the dignity of others, and the curiosity of all; though the philosophy of Solomon he thought too *Epicurean*, and the inconsistencies of other parts afflicted him. His favourite part was the book of Job, which he thought the grandest of tragedies. He projected founding one of his own upon it; and I will undertake to say, that Job would have sat in that tragedy with a patience and profundity of thought worthy of the original. Being asked on one occasion, what book he would save for himself if he could save no other? he answered, 'The oldest book, the Bible.'--J. H. LEIGH HUNT. *My Books.*

A VERY PRICELESS THING

Precious temporal things are growing [in these years of peace]; priceless spiritual things. We know the Shakespeare Dramaturgy; the Rare-Ben and Elder-Dramatist affair; which has now reached its culmination. Yes; and precisely when the Wit-combats at the Mermaid are waning somewhat, and our Shakespeare is about packing up for Stratford,-- there comes out another very priceless thing; a correct Translation of the Bible; that which we still use. Priceless enough this latter; of importance unspeakable! Reynolds and Chadderton petitioned for it, at the Hampton-Court Conference, long since; and now, in 1611, by labour of Reynolds, Chadderton, Dr. Abbot, and other prodigiously learned and earnest persons, 'forty-seven in number,' it comes out beautifully printed; dedicated to the Dread Sovereign; really in part a benefit of his to us. And so we have it here to read, that Book of Books: 'barbarous enough to rouse, tender enough to assuage, and possessing how many other properties,' says Goethe;--possessing this property, inclusive of all, add we, That it is written under the eye of the Eternal; that it is of a Sincerity like very Death; the truest Utterance that ever came by Alphabetic Letters from the Soul of Man. Through which, as through a window divinely opened, all men could look, and can still look, beyond the visual Air-firmaments and mysterious Time-oceans, into the Light-sea of Infinitude, into the stillness of Eternity; and discern in glimpses, with such emotions and practical suggestions as there may be, their far-distant, longforgotten Home.--T. CARLYLE. *Historical Sketches.*

MATERIAL FOR POESY

What can we imagine more proper for the ornaments of wit and learning in the story of Deucalion than in that of Noah? Why will not the actions of Samson afford as plentiful matter as the labours of Hercules? Why is not Jephthah's daughter as good a woman as Iphigenia? and the friendship of David and Jonathan more worthy celebration than that of Theseus and Pirithous? Does not the passage of Moses and the Israelites into the Holy Land yield incomparably more poetic variety than the voyages of Ulysses or Aeneas? Are the obsolete, threadbare tales of Thebes and Troy half so stored with great, heroical, and supernatural actions (since verse will needs find or make such) as the wars of Joshua, of the Judges, of David, and divers others?... All the books of the Bible are either already most admirable and exalted pieces of poesy, or are the best material in the world for it.-- A. COWLEY. *Preface to Davideis.*

SACRED AND PROFANE WRITERS

Let those who will, hang rapturously o'er
The flowing eloquence of Plato's page,
Repeat, with flashing eye, the sounds that pour
From Homer's verse as with a torrent's rage;
Let those who list, ask Tully to assuage
Wild hearts with high-wrought periods, and restore
The reign of rhetoric; or maxims sage
Winnow from Seneca's sententious lore.
Not these, but Judah's hallowed bards, to me
Are dear: Isaiah's noble energy;
The temperate grief of Job; the artless strain
Of Ruth and pastoral Amos; the high songs
Of David; and the tale of Joseph's wrongs,
Simply pathetic, eloquently plain.

SIR AUBREY DE VERE.

A STANDARD FOR LANGUAGE

It is your lordship's observation, that if it were not for the Bible and Common Prayer Book in the vulgar tongue, we should hardly be able to understand anything that was written among us a hundred years ago; which is certainly true: for those books, being perpetually read in churches, have proved a kind of standard for language, especially to the common people.... As to the greatest parts of our liturgy, compiled long before the translation of the Bible now in use, and little altered since, these seem to be in as great strains of true sublime eloquence as are anywhere to be found in our language.--J.

SWIFT. *A proposal for correcting, improving and ascertaining the English Tongue* (Letter to the Earl of Oxford).

THE GRAND MINE OF DICTION

... He [the translator of Homer] will find one English book and one only, where, as in the *Iliad* itself, perfect plainness of speech is allied with perfect nobleness; and that book is the Bible. No one could see this more clearly than Pope saw it: 'This pure and noble simplicity,' he says, 'is nowhere in such perfection as in the Scripture and Homer': yet even with Pope a woman is a 'fair', a father is a 'sire', and an old man a 'reverend sage', and so on through all the phrases of that pseudo-Augustan, and most unbiblical, vocabulary. The Bible, however, is undoubtedly the grand mine of diction for the translator of Homer; and, if he knows how to discriminate truly between what will suit him and what will not, the Bible may afford him also invaluable lessons of style.--M. ARNOLD. *On Translating Homer.*

THE ENGLISH OF THE BIBLE

Who will say that the uncommon beauty and marvellous English of the Protestant Bible is not one of the great strongholds of heresy in this country? It lives on in the ear, like a music that never can be forgotten, like the sound of church bells which the convert hardly knows how he can forgo. Its felicities seem often to be almost things rather than mere words. It is part of the national mind, and the anchor of the national seriousness.... Nay, it is worshipped with a positive idolatry, in extenuation of whose grotesque fanaticism its intrinsic beauty pleads availingly with the man of letters and the scholar. The memory of the dead passes into it. The potent traditions of childhood are stereotyped in its verses. The power of all the griefs and trials of a man is hidden beneath its words. It is the representative of his best moments, and all that there has been about him of soft, and gentle, and pure, and penitent, and good, speaks to him for ever out of his English Bible. It is his sacred thing which doubt never dimmed and controversy never soiled. In the length and breadth of the land there is not a Protestant, with one spark of religiousness about him, whose spiritual biography is not his Saxon Bible.--F. W. FABER. *The Interest and Characteristics of the Lives of the Saints.*

THE BIBLE AND BURNS

Search Scotland over, from the Pentland to the Solway, and there is not a cottage-hut so poor and wretched as to be without its Bible; and hardly one that, on the same shelf, and next to it, does not treasure a Burns. Have the people degenerated since their adoption of this new manual? Has their attachment to the Book of Books declined? Are their hearts less firmly bound, than were their fathers', to the old faith and the old virtues? I believe he that knows the most of the country will be the readiest to answer all these questions, as every lover of genius and virtue would desire to hear them answered.... Extraordinary ... has been the unanimity of his critics. While differing widely in their estimates of his character and *morale*, they have, without a single exception, expressed a lofty idea of his powers of mind and of the excellence of his poetry. Here, as on the subject of Shakespeare, and on scarcely any other, have Whigs and Tories, Infidels and Christians, bigoted Scotchmen and bigoted sons of John Bull, the high and the low, the rich and the poor, the prosaic and the enthusiastic lovers of poetry, the strait-laced and the morally lax, met and embraced each other.--J. G. LOCKHART. *Life of Burns.*

THE BIG HA'-BIBLE

The cheerfu' supper done, wi' serious face,
  They round the ingle form a circle wide;
The sire turns o'er, wi' patriarchal grace,
  The big ha'-bible, ance his father's pride:

*   *   *   *   *

The priest-like father reads the sacred page,
  How Abram was the friend of God on high;
Or Moses bade eternal warfare wage
  With Amalek's ungracious progeny;
  Or how the royal Bard did groaning lie
Beneath the stroke of Heaven's avenging ire;
  Or Job's pathetic plaint, and wailing cry;
Or rapt Isaiah's wild, seraphic fire;
Or other holy seers that tune the sacred lyre.

R. BURNS. *The Cotter's Saturday Night.*

'OF THE IMITATION OF CHRIST'

She read on and on in the old book, devouring eagerly the dialogues with the invisible Teacher, the pattern of sorrow, the source of all strength; returning to it after she had been called away, and reading till the sun went down behind the willows. With all the hurry of an imagination that could never rest in the present, she sat in the deepening twilight forming plans of self-humiliation and entire devotedness; and, in the ardour of first discovery, renunciation seemed to her the entrance into that satisfaction which she had so long been craving in vain. She had not perceived--how could she until she had lived longer?--the inmost truth of the old monk's outpourings, that renunciation remains sorrow, though a sorrow borne willingly. Maggie was still panting for happiness, and was in ecstasy because she had found the key to it. She knew nothing of doctrines and systems--of mysticism or quietism; but this voice out of the far-off middle ages was the direct communication of a human soul's belief and experience, and came to Maggie as an unquestioned message.

I suppose that is the reason why the small old-fashioned book, for which you need only pay sixpence at a bookstall, works miracles to this day, turning bitter waters into sweetness; while expensive sermons and treatises, newly issued, leave all things as they were

233

before. It was written down by a hand that waited for the heart's prompting; it is the chronicle of a solitary, hidden anguish, struggle, trust and triumph--not written on velvet cushions to teach endurance to those who are treading with bleeding feet on the stones. And so it remains to all time a lasting record of human needs and human consolations: the voice of a brother who, ages ago, felt and suffered and renounced--in the cloister, perhaps, with serge gown and tonsured head, with much chanting and long fasts, and with a fashion of speech different from ours--but under the same silent far-off heavens, and with the same passionate desires, the same strivings, the same failures, the same weariness.--G. ELIOT. *The Mill on the Floss.*

LITERARY GEOGRAPHY

Scotland.

The globe we inhabit is divisible into two worlds; one hardly less tangible, and far more known than the other,--the common geographical world, and the world of books; and the latter may be as geographically set forth. A man of letters, conversant with poetry and romance, might draw out a very curious map, in which this world of books should be delineated and filled up, to the delight of all genuine readers, as truly as that in Guthrie or Pinkerton. To give a specimen, and begin with Scotland,--Scotland would not be the mere territory it is, with a scale of so many miles to a degree, and such and such a population. Who (except a patriot or cosmopolite) cares for the miles or the men, or knows that they exist, in any degree of consciousness with which he cares for the never-dying population of books? How many generations of men have passed away, and will pass, in Ayrshire or Dumfries, and not all the myriads be as interesting to us as a single Burns? What have we known of them, or shall ever know, whether lairds, lords, or ladies, in comparison with the inspired ploughman? But we know of the bards and the lasses, and the places which he has recorded in song; we know the scene of 'Tam o' Shanter's' exploit; we know the pastoral landscapes ... and the scenes immortalized in Walter Scott and the old ballads; and, therefore, the book-map of Scotland would present us with the most prominent of these. We should have the Border, with its banditti, towns, and woods; Tweedside, Melrose, and Roslin, 'Edina,' otherwise called Edinburgh and Auld Reekie, or the town of Hume, Robertson, and others; Woodhouselee, and other classical and haunted places; the bower built by the fair hands of 'Bessie Bell' and 'Mary Gray'; the farm-houses of Burns's friends; the scenes of his loves and sorrows; the land of 'Old Mortality', of the 'Gentle Shepherd', and of 'Ossian'. The Highlands, and the great blue billowy domains of heather, would be distinctly marked out, in their most poetical regions; and we should have the tracks of Ben Jonson to Hawthornden, of 'Rob Roy' to his hiding-places, and of 'Jeanie Deans' towards England. Abbotsford, be sure, would not be left out; nor the house of the 'Antiquary'--almost as real a man as his author. Nor is this all: for we should have older Scotland, the Scotland of James the First, and of 'Peeblis at the Play', and Gawin Douglas, and Bruce, and Wallace; we should have older Scotland still, the Scotland of Ariosto, with his tale of 'Ginevra', and the new 'Andromeda', delivered from the sea-monster at the Isle of Ebuda (the Hebrides); and there would be the residence of the famous 'Launcelot of the Lake', at Berwick, called the Joyeuse Garde, and other ancient sites of chivalry and romance; nor should the nightingale be left out in 'Ginevra's' bower, for Ariosto has put it there, and there, accordingly, it is and has been heard, let ornithology say what it will; for what ornithologist knows so much of the nightingale as a poet? We would have an inscription put on the spot--'Here the nightingale sings, contrary to what has been affirmed by White and others.' This is the Scotland of books, and a beautiful place it is. I will venture to affirm, Sir, even to yourself, that it is a more beautiful place than the other Scotland, always excepting to an exile or a lover.

England.

Book-England, on the map, would shine as the Albion of the old Giants; as the 'Logres' of the Knights of the Round Table; as the scene of Amadis of Gaul, with its *island* of Windsor; as the abode of fairies, of the Druids, of the divine Countess of Coventry, of Guy, Earl of Warwick, of 'Alfred' (whose reality was a romance), of the Fair Rosamond, of the *Arcades* and *Comus*, of Chaucer and Spenser, of the poets of the Globe and the Mermaid, the wits of Twickenham and Hampton Court. Fleet Street would be Johnson's Fleet Street; the Tower would belong to Julius Caesar; and Blackfriars to Suckling, Vandyke, and the *Dunciad.* Chronology and the mixture of truth and fiction, that is to say, of one sort of truth and another, would come to nothing in a work of this kind; for, as it has been before observed, things are real in proportion as they are impressive. And who has not as 'gross, open, and palpable' an idea of 'Falstaff' in Eastcheap, as of 'Captain Grose' himself, beating up his quarters? A map of fictitious, literary, and historical London, would, of itself, constitute a great curiosity.

Ireland.

Swift speaks of maps, in which they

   Place elephants for want of towns.

Here would be towns and elephants too, the popular and the prodigious. How much would not Swift do for Ireland, in this geography of wit and talent! What a figure would not St. Patrick's Cathedral make! The other day, mention was made of a 'Dean of St. Patrick's' *now living,* as if there was, or ever could be, more than one Dean of St. Patrick's! In the Irish maps we should have the Saint himself driving out all venomous creatures (what a pity that the most venomous retain a property as absentees!); and there would be the old Irish kings, and O'Donoghue with his White Horse, and the lady of the 'gold wand' who made the miraculous virgin pilgrimage, and all the other marvels of lakes and ladies, and the Round Towers still remaining to perplex the antiquary, and Goldsmith's 'Deserted Village', and Goldsmith himself, and the birthplaces of Steele and Sterne, and the brief hour of poor Lord Edward Fitzgerald, and Carolan with his harp, and the schools of the poor Latin boys under the hedges, and Castle Rackrent, and Edgeworth's-town, and the Giant's Causeway, and Ginleas and other classical poverties, and Spenser's castle on the river Mulla, with the wood-gods whom his pipe drew round him.--J. H. LEIGH HUNT. *The World of Books.*

ON 'CORYAT'S CRUDITES'

Tom Coryat, I have seen thy Crudities,
And, methinks, very strangely brewed--it is
With piece and patch together glued--it is
And how, like thee, ill-favoured hued--it is
In many lines I see that lewd--it is
And therefore fit to be subdued--it is

Within thy broiling brain-pan stewed--it is
And 'twixt thy grinding jaws well chewed--it is
Within thy stomach closely mewed--it is
And last, in Court and Country spewed--it is
But now by wisdom's eye that viewed--it is
They all agree that very rude--it is
With foolery so full endued--it is

That wondrously by fools pursued--it is
As sweet as gall's amaritude--it is
And seeming full of pulchritude--it is
But more to write, but to intrude--it is
And therefore wisdom to conclude--it is.

J. TAYLOR. *The World's Eighth Wonder.*

LITERATURE FOR DESOLATE ISLANDS

I've thought very often 'twould be a good thing
In all public collections of books, if a wing
Were set off by itself, like the seas from the dry lands,
Marked *Literature suited to desolate islands,*
And filled with such books as could never be read
Save by readers of proofs, forced to do it for bread,--
Such books as one's wrecked on in small country taverns,
Such as hermits might mortify over in caverns,
Such as Satan, if printing had then been invented,
As a climax of woe, would to Job have presented,
Such as Crusoe might dip in, although there are few so
Outrageously cornered by fate as poor Crusoe;

*   *   *   *   *

I propose to shut up every doer of wrong
With these desperate books, for such term, short or long,
As by statute in such cases made and provided,
Shall be by you wise legislators decided.

J. R. LOWELL. *A Fable for Critics.*

I have sometimes heard of an Iliad in a nutshell; but it has been my fortune to have much oftener seen a nutshell in an Iliad.--J. SWIFT. *A Tale of a Tub.*

BOOKS FOR THE SALON

I am sure that if Madame de Sablé lived now, books would be seen in her salon as part of its natural indispensable furniture; not brought out, and strewed here and there when 'company was coming', but as habitual presences in her room, wanting which, she would want a sense of warmth and comfort and companionship. Putting out books as a sort of preparation for an evening, as a means for making it pass agreeably, is running a great risk. In the first place, books are by such people, and on such occasions, chosen more for their outside than their inside. And in the next, they are the 'mere material with which wisdom (or wit) builds'; and if persons don't know how to use the material, they will suggest nothing. I imagine Madame de Sablé would have the volumes she herself was reading, or those which, being new, contained any matter of present interest, left about, as they would naturally be. I could also fancy that her guests would not feel bound to talk continually, whether they had anything to say or not, but that there might be pauses of not unpleasant silence--a quiet darkness out of which they might be certain that the little stars would glimmer soon. I can believe that in such pauses of repose, some one might open a book, and catch on a suggestive sentence, might dash off again into a full flow of conversation. But I cannot fancy any grand preparations for what was to be said among people, each of whom brought the best dish in bringing himself; and whose own store of living, individual thought and feeling, and mother-wit, would be infinitely better than any cut-and-dry determination to devote the evening to mutual improvement. If people are really good and wise, their goodness and their wisdom flow out unconsciously, and benefit like sunlight. So, books for reference, books for impromptu suggestion, but never books to serve for texts to a lecture.--ELIZABETH C. GASKELL. *Company Manners.*

Far more seemly were it for thee to have thy study full of books, than thy purse full of money.--J. LYLY. *Euphues.*

THE LIBRARY AND THE GRAVE

TO SIR H. G.

Sir,--This letter hath more merits than one of more diligence, for I wrote it in bed, and with much pain. I have occasion to sit late some nights in my study (which your books make a pretty library) and now I find that that room hath a wholesome emblematic use: for having under it a vault, I make that promise me that I shall die reading; since my book and a grave are so near.--JOHN DONNE. *Letters to Several Persons of Honour.*

THE LIBRARY A GLORIOUS COURT

That place, that does contain
My books, the best companions, is to me
A glorious court, where hourly I converse
With the old sages and philosophers.
And sometimes, for variety, I confer
With kings and emperors, and weigh their counsels;
Calling their victories, if unjustly got,
Unto a strict account: and in my fancy,
Deface their ill-planned statues. Can I then
Part with such constant pleasures, to embrace
Uncertain vanities? No: be it your care
To augment your heap of wealth; it shall be mine
To increase in knowledge. Lights there for my study!

J. FLETCHER. *The Elder Brother.*

THE LIBRARY AS STUDY

I like a great library next my study; but for the study itself, give me a small snug place, almost entirely walled with books. There should be only one window in it, looking upon trees. Some prefer a place with few, or no books at all--nothing but a chair or a table, like Epictetus; but I should say that these were philosophers, not lovers of books, if I did not recollect that Montaigne was both. He had a study in a round tower, walled as aforesaid. It is true, one forgets one's books while writing--at least they say so. For my part, I think I have them in a sort of sidelong mind's eye; like a second thought, which is none--like a waterfall, or a whispering wind.

I dislike a grand library to study in. I mean an immense apartment, with books all in Museum order, especially wire-safed. I say nothing against the Museum itself, or public libraries. They are capital places to go to, but not to sit in; and talking of this, I hate to read in public, and in strange company. The jealous silence; the dissatisfied looks of the messengers; the inability to help yourself; the not knowing whether you really ought to trouble the messengers, much less the Gentleman in black, or brown, who is, perhaps, half a trustee; with a variety of other jarrings between privacy and publicity, prevent one's settling heartily to work.... A grand private library, which the master of the house also makes his study, never looks to me like a real place of books, much less of authorship. I cannot take kindly to it. It is certainly not out of envy; for three parts of the books are generally trash, and I can seldom think of the rest and the proprietor together. It reminds me of a fine gentleman, of a collector, of a patron, of Gil Blas and the Marquis of Marialva; of anything but genius and comfort. I have a particular hatred of a round table (not *the* Round Table, for that was a dining one) covered and irradiated with books, and never met with one in the house of a clever man but once. It is the reverse of Montaigne's Round Tower. Instead of bringing the books around you, they all seem turning another way, and eluding your hands.

Conscious of my propriety and comfort in these matters, I take an interest in the book-cases as well as the books of my friends. I long to meddle and dispose them after my own notions.--J. H. LEIGH HUNT. *My Books.*

Come, and take choice of all my library.

W. SHAKESPEARE. *Titus Andronicus.*

Libraries are the wardrobes of literature, whence men, properly informed, might bring forth something for ornament, much for curiosity, and more for use.--G. DYER.

THE STUDY

Here, while the night-wind wreaked its frantic will
On the loose ocean and the rock-bound hill,
Rent the cracked topsail from its quivering yard,
And rived the oak a thousand storms had scarred,
Fenced by these walls the peaceful taper shone,
Nor felt a breath to slant its trembling cone.

Not all unblessed the mild interior scene
Where the red curtain spread its falling screen;
O'er some light task the lonely hours were passed,
And the long evening only flew too fast;
Or the wide chair its leathern arms would lend
In genial welcome to some easy friend,
Stretched on its bosom with relaxing nerves,
Slow moulding, plastic, to its hollow curves;
Perchance indulging, if of generous creed,
In brave Sir Walter's dream-compelling weed.
Or, happier still, the evening hour would bring
To the round table its expected ring,
And while the punch-bowl's sounding depths were stirred,--
Its silver cherubs, smiling as they heard,--
Our hearts would open, as at evening's hour
The close-sealed primrose frees its hidden flower.

Such the warm life this dim retreat has known,
Not quite deserted when its guests were flown;
Nay, filled with friends, an unobtrusive set,
Guiltless of calls and cards and etiquette,
Ready to answer, never known to ask,
Claiming no service, prompt for every task.

On those dark shelves no housewife hand profanes,
O'er his mute files the monarch folio reigns;
A mingled race, the wreck of chance and time,
That talk all tongues and breathe of every clime,
Each knows his place, and each may claim his part
In some quaint corner of his master's heart.
This old Decretal, won from Kloss's hoards,
Thick-leaved, brass-cornered, ribbed with oaken boards,
Stands the grey patriarch of the graver rows,
Its fourth ripe century narrowing to its close;
Not daily conned, but glorious still to view,
With glistening letters wrought in red and blue.
There towers Stagira's all-embracing sage,
The Aldine anchor on his opening page;
There sleep the births of Plato's heavenly mind,
In yon dark tomb by jealous clasps confined.
Olim e libris (dare I call it mine?)
Of Yale's grave Head and Killingworth's divine!
In those square sheets the songs of Maro fill
The silvery types of smooth-leaved Baskerville;
High over all, in close, compact array,
Their classic wealth the Elzevirs display.

In lower regions of the sacred space
Range the dense volumes of a humbler race;
There grim chirurgeons all their mysteries teach,
In spectral pictures, or in crabbèd speech;
Harvey and Haller, fresh from Nature's page,
Shoulder the dreamers of an earlier age,
Lully and Geber, and the learnèd crew
That loved to talk of all they could not do.
Why count the rest,--those names of later days
That many love, and all agree to praise,--
Or point the titles, where a glance may read
The dangerous lines of party or of creed?
Too well, perchance, the chosen list would show
What few may care and none can claim to know.
Each has his features, whose exterior seal
A brush may copy, or a sunbeam steal;
Go to his study,--on the nearest shelf
Stands the mosaic portrait of himself.

What though for months the tranquil dust descends,
Whitening the heads of these mine ancient friends,
While the damp offspring of the modern press
Flaunts on my table with its pictured dress;
Not less I love each dull familiar face,
Nor less should miss it from the appointed place;

I snatch the book, along whose burning leaves
His scarlet web our wild romancer weaves,
Yet, while proud Hester's fiery pangs I share,
My old MAGNALIA must be standing *there*!

O. W. HOLMES.

THE CONSULTING ROOM OF A WISE MAN

The great consulting room of a wise man is a library. When I am in perplexity about life, I have but to come here, and, without fee or reward, I commune with the wisest souls that God has blessed the world with. If I want a discourse on immortality Plato comes to my help. If I want to know the human heart Shakespeare opens all its chambers. Whatever be my perplexity or doubt, I know exactly the great man to call to me, and he comes in the kindest way, he listens to my doubts and tells me his convictions. So that a library may be regarded as the solemn chamber in which a man can take counsel with all that have been wise and great and good and glorious amongst the men that have gone before him. If we come down for a moment and look at the bare and immediate utilities of a library we find that here a man gets himself ready for his calling, arms himself for his profession, finds out the facts that are to determine his trade, prepares himself for his examination. The utilities of it are endless and priceless. It is too a place of pastime; for man has no amusement more innocent, more sweet, more gracious, more elevating, and more fortifying than he can find in a library.--GEORGE DAWSON. *Address at the opening of the Birmingham Free Reference Library*, 1866.

THE LIBRARY A KEY TO CHARACTER

The first thing, naturally, when one enters a scholar's study or library, is to look at his books. One gets a notion very speedily of his tastes and the range of his pursuits by a glance round his bookshelves.

Of course, you know there are many fine houses where a library is a part of the upholstery, so to speak. Books in handsome binding kept locked under plate-glass in showy dwarf bookcases are as important to stylish establishments as servants in livery, who sit with folded arms, are to stylish equipages. I suppose those wonderful statues with the folded arms do sometimes change their attitude, and I suppose those books with the gilded backs do sometimes get opened, but it is nobody's business whether they do or not, and it is best not to ask too many questions.

This sort of thing is common enough, but there is another case that may prove deceptive if you undertake to judge from appearances. Once in a while you will come on a house where you will find a family of readers and almost no library. Some of the most indefatigable devourers of literature have very few books. They belong to book clubs, they haunt the public libraries, they borrow of friends, and somehow or other get hold of everything they want, scoop out all it holds for them, and have done with it.--O. W. HOLMES. *The Poet at the Breakfast-Table.*

THE SCENT OF BOOKS

I know men who say they had as lief read any book in a library copy as in one from their own shelf. To me that is unintelligible. For one thing, I know every book of mine by its *scent*, and I have but to put my nose between the pages to be reminded of all sorts of things. My Gibbon, for example, my well-bound eight-volume Milman edition, which I have read and read and read again for more than thirty years--never do I open it but the scent of the noble pages restores to me all the exultant happiness of that moment when I received it as a prize. Or my Shakespeare, the great Cambridge Shakespeare--it has an odour which carries me yet further back in life; for these volumes belonged to my father, and before I was old enough to read them with understanding, it was often permitted me, as a treat, to take down one of them from the bookcase, and reverently to turn the leaves. The volumes smell exactly as they did in that old time, and what a strange tenderness comes upon me when I hold one of them in hand. For that reason I do not often read Shakespeare in this edition.--G. GISSING. *The Private Papers of Henry Ryecroft.*

    Of his gentleness,
Knowing I loved my books, he furnished me,
From mine own library with volumes that
I prize above my dukedom.

   W. SHAKESPEARE. *The Tempest.*

AN EPISCOPAL LIBRARY

Here, duly placed on consecrated ground,
The studied works of many an age are found,
The ancient Fathers' reverend remains;
The Roman Laws, which freed a world from chains;
Whate'er of law passed from immortal Greece
To Latin lands, and gained a rich increase;
All that blessed Israel drank in showers from heaven,
Or Afric sheds, soft as the dew of even.

   ALCUIN.

A MODERN LIBRARY

The Doctor with himself decreed
To nod--or, much the same, to read.
He always seemed a wondrous lover
Of painted leaf and Turkey cover,
While no regard at all was had

To sots in homely russet clad,
Concluding he must be within
A calf, that wore without his skin.

But, though his thoughts were fixed to read,
The treatise was not yet decreed:
Uncertain to devote the day
To politics or else to play;
What theme would best his genius suit,
Grave morals or a dull dispute,
Where both contending champions boast
The victory which neither lost;
As chiefs are oft in story read
Each to pursue, when neither fled.
  He enters now the shining dome
Where crowded authors sweat for room;
So close a man could hardly say
Which were more fixed, the shelves or they.

     *   *   *   *   *

To please the eye, the highest space
A set of wooden volumes grace;
Pure timber authors that contain
As much as some that boast a brain;
That Alma Mater never viewed,
Without degrees to writers hewed:
Yet solid thus just emblems show
Of the dull brotherhood below,
Smiling their rivals to survey,
As great and real blocks as they.
Distinguished then in even rows,
Here shines the Verse and there the Prose;
(For, though Britannia fairer looks
United, 'tis not so with books):
The champions of each different art
Had stations all assigned apart,
Fearing the rival chiefs might be
For quarrels still, nor dead agree.
The schoolmen first in long array
Their bulky lumber round display;
Seemed to lament their wretched doom,
And heave for more convenient room;
While doctrine each of weight contains
To crack his shelves as well as brains;
Since all with him were thought to dream,
That flagged before they filled a ream:
His authors wisely taught to prize,

Not for their merit, but their size;
No surer method ever found
Than buying writers by the pound;
For heaven must needs his breast inspire,
That scribbling filled each month a quire,
And claimed a station on his shelves,
Who scorned each sot who fooled in twelves.

W. KING. (?) *Bibliotheca.*

SAFE AND UNTOUCHED

'In another century it may be impossible to find a collection of the whole [Greek trage-dies] unless some learned and rich man, like Pericles, or some protecting King, like Hiero, should preserve them in his library.' 'Prudently have you considered how to pre-serve all valuable authors. The cedar doors of a royal library fly open to receive them: aye, there they will be safe ... and untouched.'--W. S. LANDOR. *Pericles and Aspasia.*

CIBBER'S LIBRARY

Next o'er his books his eyes began to roll,
In pleasing memory of all he stole,
How here he sipped, how there he plundered snug,
And sucked all o'er, like an industrious bug.
Here lay poor Fletcher's half-eat scenes, and here
The frippery of crucified Moliere;
There hapless Shakespeare, yet of Tibbald sore,
Wished he had blotted for himself before.
The rest on outside merit but presume,
Or serve (like other fools) to fill a room;
Such with their shelves as due proportion hold,
Or their fond parents dressed in red and gold;
Or where the pictures for the page atone
And Quarles is saved by beauties not his own.
Here swells the shelf with Ogilby the great;
There, stamped with arms, Newcastle shines complete:
Here all his suffering brotherhood retire,
And 'scape the martyrdom of jakes and fire:
A Gothic Library! of Greece and Rome
Well purged, and worthy Settle, Banks, and Broome.
But, high above, more solid learning shone,
The classics of an age that heard of none;
There Caxton slept, with Wynkyn at his side,
One clasped in wood, and one in strong cow-hide;
There saved by spice, like mummies, many a year,
Dry Bodies of Divinity appear;

De Lyra there a dreadful front extends,
And here the groaning shelves Philemon bends.
  Of these twelve volumes, twelve of amplest size,
Redeemed from tapers and defrauded pies,
Inspired he seizes; these an altar raise;
An hecatomb of pure unsullied lays
That altar crowns; a folio Commonplace
Founds the whole pile, of all his works the base;
Quartos, octavos, shape the lessening pyre;
A twisted birthday ode completes the spire.

A. POPE. *The Dunciad.*

MR. SHANDY'S LIBRARY

Few men of great genius had exercised their parts in writing books upon the subject of great noses: by the trotting of my lean horse, the thing is incredible! and I am quite lost in my understanding, when I am considering what a treasure of precious time and talents together has been wasted upon worse subjects--and how many millions of books in all languages, and in all possible types and bindings, have been fabricated upon points not half so much tending to the unity and peace-making of the world. What was to be had, however, he set the greater store by; and though my father would ofttimes sport with my uncle Toby's library--which, by the by, was ridiculous enough--yet at the very same time he did it, he collected every book and treatise which had been systematically wrote upon noses, with as much care as my honest uncle Toby had done those upon military architecture.... My father's collection was not great, but, to make amends, it was curious; and consequently he was some time in making it ... he got hold of Prignitz--purchased Scroderus, Andrea Paraeus, Bouchet's Evening Conferences, and above all, the great and learned Hafen Slawkenbergius.... To do justice to Slawkenbergius, he has entered the list with a stronger lance, and taken a much larger career in it than any one man who had ever entered it before him--and indeed, in many respects, deserves to be en-niched as a prototype for all writers, of voluminous works at least, to model their books by--for he has taken in, Sir, the whole subject--examined every part of it dialectically----then brought it into full day; dilucidating it with all the light which either the collision of his own natural parts could strike--or the profoundest knowledge of the sciences had empowered him to cast upon it--collating, collecting, and compiling--begging, borrowing, and stealing, as he went along, all that had been wrote or wrangled thereupon in the schools and porticoes of the learned: so that Slawkenbergius his book may properly be considered, not only as a model--but as a thorough-stitched digest and regular institute of noses, comprehending in it all that is or can be needful to be known about them.

For this cause it is that I forbear to speak of so many (otherwise) valuable books and treatises of my father's collecting, wrote either, plump upon noses--or collaterally touching them;----such for instance as Prignitz, now lying upon the table before me, who with infinite learning, and from the most candid and scholar-like examination of above four thousand different skulls, in upwards of twenty charnel-houses in Silesia, which he had rummaged----has informed us, that the mensuration and configuration of the osseous or bony parts of human noses, in any given tract of country, except Crim Tartary, where they are all crushed down by the thumb, so that no judgement can be formed upon them--are much nearer alike, than the world imagines.--L. STERNE. *Tristram Shandy.*

DOMINIE SAMPSON IN THE LIBRARY

Dominie Sampson was occupied, body and soul, in the arrangement of the late bishop's library, which had been sent from Liverpool by sea, and conveyed by thirty or forty carts from the seaport at which it was landed. Sampson's joy at beholding the ponderous contents of these chests arranged upon the floor of the large apartment, from whence he was to transfer them to the shelves, baffles all description. He grinned like an ogre, swung his arms like the sails of a windmill, shouted 'Prodigious' till the roof rung to his raptures. 'He had never,' he said, 'seen so many books together, except in the College Library;' and now his dignity and delight in being superintendent of the collection, raised him, in his own opinion, almost to the rank of the academical librarian, whom he had always regarded as the greatest and happiest man on earth. Neither were his transports diminished upon a hasty examination of the contents of these volumes. Some, indeed, of belles lettres, poems, plays, or memoirs, he tossed indignantly aside, with the implied censure of 'psha', or 'frivolous'; but the greater and bulkier part of the collection bore a very different character. The deceased prelate, a divine of the old and deeply-learned cast, had loaded his shelves with volumes which displayed the antique and venerable attributes so happily described by a modern poet:

> That weight of wood, with leathern coat o'erlaid;
> Those ample clasps, of solid metal made;
> The close-pressed leaves unoped for many an age;
> The dull red edging of the well-filled page;
> On the broad back the stubborn ridges rolled,
> Where yet the title stands in tarnished gold.

Books of theology and controversial divinity, commentaries, and polyglots, sets of the Fathers, and sermons, which might each furnish forth ten brief discourses of modern date, books of science, ancient and modern, classical authors in their best and rarest forms; such formed the late bishop's venerable library, and over such the eye of Dominie Sampson gloated with rapture. He entered them in the catalogue in his best running hand, forming each letter with the accuracy of a lover writing a valentine, and placed each individually on the destined shelf with all the reverence which I have seen a lady pay to a jar of old china. With all this zeal his labours advanced slowly. He often opened a volume when half-way up the library-steps, fell upon some interesting passage, and, without shifting his inconvenient posture, continued immersed in the fascinating perusal until the servant pulled him by the skirts to assure him that dinner waited. He then repaired to the parlour, bolted his food down his capacious throat in squares of three inches, answered aye or no at random to whatever question was asked at him, and again hurried back to the library as soon as his napkin was removed, and sometimes with it hanging round his neck like a pinafore--

How happily the days

Of Thalaba went by!

SIR W. SCOTT. *Guy Mannering.*

Me, poor man,--my library
Was dukedom large enough.

W. SHAKESPEARE. *The Tempest.*

THE PEASANT'S LIBRARY

On shelf of deal beside the cuckoo-clock,
Of cottage-reading rests the chosen stock;
Learning we lack, not books, but have a kind
For all our wants, a meat for every mind:
The tale for wonder and the joke for whim,
The half-sung sermon and the half-groaned hymn.
No need of classing; each within its place,
The feeling finger in the dark can trace;
'First from the corner, farthest from the wall,'
Such all the rules, and they suffice for all.
There pious works for Sunday's use are found;
Companions for the Bible newly bound;
That Bible, bought by sixpence weekly saved,
Has choicest prints by famous hands engraved;
Has choicest notes by many a famous head,
Such as to doubt have rustic readers led;
Have made them stop to reason *why?* and *how?*
And, where they once agreed, to cavil now.
Oh! rather give me commentators plain,
Who with no deep researches vex the brain;
Who from the dark and doubtful love to run,
And hold their glimmering tapers to the sun;
Who simple truth with nine-fold reason back,
And guard the point no enemies attack.
Bunyan's famed Pilgrim rests the shelf upon;
A genius rare but rude was honest John:
Not one who, early by the Muse beguiled,
Drank from her well the waters undefiled;
Not one who slowly gained the hill sublime,
Then often sipped and little at a time;
But one who dabbled in the sacred springs,
And drank them muddy, mixed with baser things.
Here to interpret dreams we read the rules,
Science our own! and never taught in schools;
In moles and specks we Fortune's gifts discern,

And Fate's fixed will from Nature's wanderings learn.
  Of Hermit Quarle we read, in island rare,
Far from mankind and seeming far from care;
Safe from all want, and sound in every limb;
Yes! there was he, and there was care with him.
  Unbound and heaped, these valued works beside,
Lay humbler works, the pedlar's pack supplied;
Yet these, long since, have all acquired a name;
The Wandering Jew has found his way to fame;
And fame, denied to many a laboured song,
Crowns Thumb the great and Hickerthrift the strong.
  There too is he, by wizard-power upheld,
Jack, by whose arm the giant-brood were quelled:
His shoes of swiftness on his feet he placed;
His coat of darkness on his loins he braced;
His sword of sharpness in his hand he took,
And off the heads of doughty giants stroke:
Their glaring eyes beheld no mortal near;
No sound of feet alarmed the drowsy ear;
No English blood their pagan sense could smell,
But heads dropped headlong, wondering why they fell.
  These are the peasant's joy, when, placed at ease,
Half his delighted offspring mount his knees.

    G. CRABBE. *The Parish Register.*

THE LIBRARY IN THE GARRET

      Books, books, books!
I had found the secret of a garret-room
Piled high with cases in my father's name;
Piled high, packed large,--where, creeping in and out
Among the giant fossils of my past,
Like some small nimble mouse between the ribs
Of a mastodon, I nibbled here and there
At this or that box, pulling through the gap,
In heats of terror, haste, victorious joy,
The first book first. And how I felt it beat
Under my pillow, in the morning's dark,
An hour before the sun would let me read!
My books!

    E. B. BROWNING. *Aurora Leigh.*

    Every library should try to be complete on something, if it were only on the history of pin-heads.--O. W. HOLMES. *The Poet at the Breakfast-Table.*

MONTAIGNE'S LIBRARY

At home I betake me somewhat the oftener to my library, whence all at once I command and survey all my household. It is seated in the chief entry of my house, thence I behold under me my garden, my base court, my yard, and look even into most rooms of my house. There without order, without method, and by piece-meals I turn over and ransack, now one book and now another. Sometimes I muse and rave; and walking up and down I indite and enregister these my humours, these my conceits. It is placed on the third story of a tower. The lowermost is my chapel; the second a chamber with other lodgings, where I often lie, because I would be alone. Above it is a great wardrobe. It was in times past the most unprofitable place of all my house. There I pass the greatest part of my life's days, and wear out most hours of the day. I am never there a nights. Next unto it is a handsome neat cabinet, able and large enough to receive fire in winter, and very pleasantly windowen. And if I feared not care more than cost (care which drives and diverts me from all business), I might easily join a convenient gallery of a hundred paces long and twelve broad on each side of it, and upon one floor; having already, for some other purpose, found all the walls raised unto a convenient height. Each retired place requireth a walk. My thoughts are prone to sleep if I sit long. My mind goes not alone, as if ledges did move it. Those that study without books are all in the same case. The form of it is round, and hath no flat side, but what serveth for my table and chair: in which bending or circling manner, at one look it offereth me the full sight of all my books, set round about upon shelves or desks, five ranks one upon another. It hath three bay-windows, of a far-extending, rich and unresisted prospect, and is in diameter sixteen paces void. In winter I am less continually there: for my house (as the name of it importeth) is perched upon an over-peering hillock; and hath no part more subject to all weathers than this: which pleaseth me the more, both because the access unto it is somewhat troublesome and remote, and for the benefit of the exercise which is to be respected; and that I may the better seclude myself from company, and keep encroachers from me: There is my seat, that is my throne. I endeavour to make my rule therein absolute, and to sequester that only corner from the community of wife, of children, and of acquaintance. Elsewhere I have but a verbal authority, of confused essence. Miserable in my mind is he who in his own home hath nowhere to be to himself; where he may particularly court, and at his pleasure hide or withdraw self.--MONTAIGNE.

A COLLOQUY IN A LIBRARY

I was in my library, making room upon the shelves for some books which had just arrived from New England, removing to a less conspicuous station others which were of less value and in worse dress, when Sir Thomas entered. You are employed, said he, to your heart's content. Why, Montesinos, with these books, and the delight you take in their constant society, what have you to covet or desire?

Montesinos

Nothing, ... except more books.

Sir Thomas More

Crescit, indulgens sibi, dirus hydrops.

Montesinos

Nay, nay, my ghostly monitor, this at least is no diseased desire! If I covet more, it is for the want I feel and the use which I should make of them.

'Libraries,' says my good old friend George Dyer, a man as learned as he is benevolent, ... 'libraries are the wardrobes of literature, whence men, properly informed, might bring forth something for ornament, much for curiosity, and more for use.' These books of mine, as you well know, are not drawn up here for display, however much the pride of the eye may be gratified in beholding them; they are on actual service. Whenever they may be dispersed, there is not one among them that will ever be more comfortably lodged, or more highly prized by its possessor; and generations may pass away before some of them will again find a reader.... It is well that we do not moralize too much upon such subjects, ...

> For foresight is a melancholy gift,
> Which bares the bald, and speeds the all-too-swift.

But the dispersion of a library, whether in retrospect or in anticipation, is always to me a melancholy thing.

Sir Thomas More

How many such dispersions must have taken place to have made it possible that these books should thus be brought together here among the Cumberland mountains!

Montesinos

Many, indeed; and in many instances most disastrous ones. Not a few of these volumes have been cast up from the wreck of the family or convent libraries during the late Revolution. Yonder Acta Sanctorum belonged to the Capuchines, at Ghent. This book of St. Bridget's Revelations, in which not only all the initial letters are illuminated, but every capital throughout the volume was coloured, came from the Carmelite Nunnery at Bruges. That copy of Alain Chartier, from the Jesuits' College at Louvain; that *Imago Primi Saeculi Societatis*, from their college at Ruremond. Here are books from Colbert's library; here others from the Lamoignon one.... A book is the more valuable to me when I know to whom it has belonged, and through what 'scenes and changes' it has past.

Sir Thomas More

You would have its history recorded in the fly-leaf, as carefully as the pedigree of a race-horse is preserved.

Montesinos

I confess that I have much of that feeling in which the superstition concerning relics has originated; and I am sorry when I see the name of a former owner obliterated in a book, or the plate of his arms defaced. Poor memorials though they be, yet they are something saved for awhile from oblivion; and I should be almost as unwilling to destroy them, as to efface the *Hic jacet* of a tombstone. There may be sometimes a pleasure in recognizing them, sometimes a salutary sadness....

Sir Thomas More

How peaceably they stand together,--Papists and Protestants side by side!

Montesinos

Their very dust reposes not more quietly in the cemetery. Ancient and Modern, Jew and Gentile, Mahommedan and Crusader, French and English, Spaniards and Portuguese, Dutch and Brazilians, fighting their old battles, silently now, upon the same shelf: Fernand Lopez and Pedro de Ayala; John de Laet and Barlaeus, with the historians of Joam Fernandes Vieira; Foxe's Martyrs and the Three Conversions of Father Parsons; Cranmer and Stephen Gardiner; Dominican and Franciscan; Jesuit and *Philosophe* (equally misnamed); Churchmen and Sectarians; Roundheads and Cavaliers

> Here are God's conduits, grave divines; and here
> Is nature's secretary, the philosopher:
> And wily statesman, which teach how to tie
> The sinews of a city's mystic body;
> Here gathering chroniclers: and by them stand
> Giddy fantastic poets of each land.

Here I possess these gathered treasures of time, the harvest of so many generations, laid up in my garners: and when I go to the window, there is the lake, and the circle of the mountains, and the illimitable sky.... Never can any man's life have been passed more in accord with his own inclinations, nor more answerably to his own desires. Excepting that peace which, through God's infinite mercy, is derived from a higher source, it is to literature, humanly speaking, that I am beholden, not only for the means of subsistence, but for every blessing which I enjoy; ... health of mind and activity of mind, contentment, cheerfulness, continual employments, and therewith continual pleasure. *Suavissima vita indies sentire se fieri meliorem*; and this, as Bacon has said, and Clarendon repeated, is the benefit that a studious man enjoys in retirement. To the studies which I have faithfully pursued, I am indebted for friends with whom, hereafter, it will be deemed an honour to have lived in friendship; and as for the enemies which they have procured to me in sufficient numbers, ... happily I am not of the thin-skinned race, ... they might as well fire small shot at a rhinoceros, as direct their attacks upon me. *In omnibus requiem quaesivi*, said Thomas à Kempis, *sed non inveni nisi in angulis et libellis*. I too have found repose where he did, in books and retirement, but it was there alone I sought it: to these my nature, under the direction of a merciful Providence, led me betimes, and the world can offer nothing which should tempt me from them.--R. SOUTHEY. *Sir Thomas More: or, Colloquies on the Progress and Prospects of Society. Colloquy xiv: 'The Library.'*

CHARLES LAMB'S LIBRARY

His library, though not abounding in Greek or Latin (which are the only things to help some persons to an idea of literature), is anything but superficial. The depths of philosophy and poetry are there, the innermost passages of the human heart. It has some Latin too. It has also a handsome contempt for appearance. It looks like what it is, a selection made at precious intervals from the book-stalls; now a Chaucer at nine and twopence; now a Montaigne or a Sir Thomas Browne at two shillings; now a Jeremy Taylor; a Spinoza; an old English Dramatist, Prior, and Sir Philip Sidney; and the books are 'neat as imported'. The very perusal of the backs is a 'discipline of humanity'. There Mr. Southey takes his place again with an old Radical friend: there Jeremy Collier is at peace with Dryden: there the lion, Martin Luther, lies down with the Quaker lamb, Sewell: there Guzman d'Alfarache thinks himself fit company for Sir Charles Grandison, and has his claims admitted. Even the 'high fantastical' Duchess of Newcastle, with her laurel on her head, is received with grave honours, and not the less for declining to trouble herself with the constitutions of her maids.--J. H. LEIGH HUNT. *My Books.*

STANZAS COMPOSED IN THE REV. J. MITFORD'S LIBRARY

O! I methinks could dwell content
  A spell-bound captive here;
And find, in such imprisonment,
  Each fleeting moment dear;--
Dear, not to outward sense alone,
But thought's most elevated tone.

The song of birds, the hum of bees,
  Their sweetest music make;
The March winds, through the lofty trees,
  Their wilder strains awake;
Or from the broad magnolia leaves
A gentler gale its spirit heaves.

Nor less the eye enraptured roves
  O'er turf of freshest green,
O'er bursting flowers, and budding groves,
  And sky of changeful mien,
Where sunny glimpses, bright and blue,
The fleecy clouds are peeping through.

Thus soothed, in every passing mood,
  How sweet each gifted page,
Rich with the mind's ambrosial food,
  The Muse's brighter age!

How sweet, communion here to hold
With them, the mighty bards of old.

With them--whose master spirits yet
  In deathless numbers dwell,
Whose works defy us to forget
  Their still-surviving spell;--
That spell, which lingers in a name,
Whose every echo whispers Fame!

Could aught enhance such hours of bliss,
  It were in converse known
With him who boasts a scene like this,
  An Eden of his own;
Whose taste and talent gave it birth,
And well can estimate its worth.

B. BARTON.

THE SHRINES OF THE ANCIENT SAINTS

The works or acts of merit towards learning are conversant about three objects; the places of learning, the books of learning, and the persons of the learned.... The works touching books are two: first, libraries which are as the shrines where all the relics of the ancient saints, full of true virtue, and that without delusion or imposture, are preserved and reposed; secondly, new editions of authors, with more correct impressions, more faithful translations, more profitable glosses, more diligent annotations, and the like.--F. BACON, LORD VERULAM. *Of the Advancement of Learning.*

A MOST HORRIBLE INFAMY

Never had we been offended for the loss of our libraries, being so many in number, and in so desolate places for the most part, if the chief monuments and most notable works of our excellent writers had been reserved. If there had been in every shire of England but one Solempne Library, to the preservation of those noble works, and preferment of good learning in our posterity, it had been yet somewhat. But to destroy all without consideration is, and will be, unto England for ever, a most horrible infamy among the grave seniors of other nations. A great number of them which purchased those superstitious mansions, reserved of those library-books, some to serve the jakes, some to scour their candlesticks, and some to rub their boots. Some they sold to the grocers and soap-sellers; some they sent over sea to the bookbinders, not in small number, but at times whole ships full, to the wondering of the foreign nations. Yea, the universities of this realm are not all clear of this detestable fact. But, cursed is that belly which seeketh to be fed with such ungodly gains, and shameth his natural country. I know a merchant-man, which shall at this time be nameless, that bought the contents of two noble libraries for forty shillings price; a shame it is to be spoken! This stuff hath he occupied in the stead of gray paper, by the space of more than ten years, and yet he hath store enough for as many years to come!--J. BALE. *Preface to the Laboryouse Journey of Leland.*

LIBRARIES FOR EVERY CITY

I hope it will not be long before royal or national libraries will be founded in every considerable city, with a royal series of books in them; the same series in every one of them, chosen books, the best in every kind, prepared for that national series in the most perfect way possible; their text printed all on leaves of equal size, broad of margin, and divided into pleasant volumes, light in the hand, beautiful, and strong, and thorough as examples of binders' work; and that these great libraries will be accessible to all clean and orderly persons at all times of the day and evening; strict law being enforced for this cleanliness and quietness.--J. RUSKIN. *Sesame and Lilies.*

THE LIBRARY

'Let there be light!' God spake of old,
And over chaos dark and cold,
And through the dead and formless frame
Of nature, life and order came.

Faint was the light at first that shone
On giant fern and mastodon,
On half-formed plant and beast of prey,
And man as rude and wild as they.

Age after age, like waves, o'erran
The earth, uplifting brute and man;
And mind, at length, in symbols dark
Its meanings traced on stone and bark.

On leaf of palm, on sedge-wrought roll,
On plastic clay and leathern scroll,
Man wrote his thoughts; the ages passed,
And lo! the Press was found at last!

Then dead souls woke; the thoughts of men
Whose bones were dust revived again;
The cloister's silence found a tongue,
Old prophets spake, old poets sung.

And here, to-day, the dead look down,
The kings of mind again we crown;
We hear the voices lost so long,
The sage's word, the sibyl's song.

Here Greek and Roman find themselves
Alive along these crowded shelves;
And Shakespeare treads again his stage,
And Chaucer paints anew his age.

As if some Pantheon's marbles broke
Their stony trance, and lived and spoke,
Life thrills along the alcoved hall,
The lords of thought await our call!

J. G. WHITTIER.

THE REFERENCE LIBRARY

One of the great offices of a Reference Library is to keep at the service of everybody what everybody cannot keep at home for his own service. It is not convenient to every man to have a very large telescope; I may wish to study the skeleton of a whale but my house is not large enough to hold one; I may be curious in microscopes but I may have no money to buy one of my own. But provide an institution like this and here is the telescope, here is the microscope, and here the skeleton of the whale. Here are the great picture, the mighty book, the ponderous atlas, the great histories of the world. They are here always ready for the use of every man without his being put to the cost of purchase or the discomfort of giving them house-room. Here are books that we only want to consult occasionally and which are very costly. These are the books proper for a Library like this--mighty cyclopaedias, prodigious charts, books that only Governments can publish. It is almost the only place where I would avoid cheapness as a plague and run away from mean printing and petty pages with disgust.--GEORGE DAWSON. *Address at the opening of the Birmingham Free Reference Library*, 1866.

IN THE BRITISH MUSEUM LIBRARY

The shade deepens as I turn from the portico to the hall and vast domed house of books. The half-hearted light under the dome is stagnant and dead. For it is the nature of light to beat and throb; it has a pulse and undulation like the swing of the sea. Under the trees in the woodlands it vibrates and lives; on the hills there is a resonance of light.... It is renewed and fresh every moment, and never twice do you see the same ray. Stayed and checked by the dome and book-built walls, the beams lose their elasticity, and the ripple ceases in the motionless pool. The eyes, responding, forget to turn quickly, and only partially see. Deeper thought and inspiration quit the heart, for they can only exist where the light vibrates and communicates its tone to the soul. If any imagine they shall find thought in many books, certainly they will be disappointed. Thought dwells by the stream and sea, by the hill and in the woodland, in the sunlight and free wind, where the wild dove haunts. Walls and roof shut it off as they shut off the undulation of light. The very lightning cannot penetrate here. A murkiness marks the coming of the cloud, and the dome becomes vague, but the fierce flash is shorn to a pale reflection, and the thunder is no more than the rolling of a heavier truck loaded with tomes. But in closing out the sky, with it is cut off all that the sky can tell you with its light, or in its passion of storm.

Sitting at these long desks and trying to read, I soon find that I have made a mistake; it is not here I shall find that which I seek. Yet the magic of books draws me here time after time, to be as often disappointed. Something in a book tempts the mind as pictures tempt the eye; the eye grows weary of pictures, but looks again. The mind wearies of books, yet cannot forget that once when they were first opened in youth they gave it hope of knowledge. Those first books exhausted, there is nothing left but words and covers. It seems as if all the books in the world--really books--can be bought for £10. Man's whole thought is purchaseable at that small price, for the value of a watch, of a good dog. For the rest it is repetition and paraphrase.--R. JEFFERIES. *The Life of the Fields: The Pigeons at the British Museum.*

THE LIBRARY AN HERACLEA

Now behold us, ... settled in all the state and grandeur of our own house in Russell Street, Bloomsbury: the library of the Museum close at hand. My father spends his mornings in those *lata silentia*, as Virgil calls the world beyond the grave. And a world beyond the grave we may well call that land of the ghosts, a book collection.

'Pisistratus,' said my father, one evening as he arranged his notes before him, and rubbed his spectacles. 'Pisistratus, a great library is an *awful* place! There, are interred all the remains of men since the Flood.'

'It is a burial-place!' quoth my Uncle Roland, who had that day found us out.

'It is an Heraclea!' said my father.

'Please, not such hard words,' said the Captain, shaking his head.

'Heraclea was the city of necromancers, in which they raised the dead. Do I want to speak to Cicero?--I invoke him. Do I want to chat in the Athenian market-place, and hear news two thousand years old?--I write down my charm on a slip of paper, and a grave magician calls me up Aristophanes.... But it is not *that* which is awful. It is the presuming to vie with these "spirits elect": to say to them, "Make way--I too claim place with the chosen. I too would confer with the living, centuries after the death that consumes my dust."'--E. G. E. L. BULWER-LYTTON, LORD LYTTON. *The Caxtons.*

BOOKS IN A NEW LIGHT

I should explain that I cannot write unless I have a sloping desk, and the reading-room of the British Museum, where alone I can compose freely, is unprovided with sloping desks. Like every other organism, if I cannot get exactly what I want, I make shift with the next thing to it; true, there are no desks in the reading-room, but, as I once heard a visitor from the country say, 'it contains a large number of very interesting works.' I know it was not right, and hope the Museum authorities will not be severe upon me if any one of them reads this confession; but I wanted a desk, and set myself to consider which of the many very interesting works which a grateful nation places at the disposal of its would-be authors was best suited for my purpose.

For mere reading I suppose one book is pretty much as good as another: but the choice of a desk-book is a more serious matter. It must be neither too thick nor too thin; it must be large enough to make a substantial support; it must be strongly bound so as not to yield or give; it must not be too troublesome to carry backwards and forwards; and it must live on shelf C, D, or E, so that there need be no stooping or reaching too high.... For weeks I made experiments upon sundry poetical and philosophical works, whose names I have forgotten, but could not succeed in finding my ideal desk, until at length, more by luck than cunning, I happened to light upon Frost's *'Lives of Eminent Christians'*, which I had no sooner tried than I discovered it to be the very perfection and *ne plus ultra* of everything that a book should be.... On finding myself asked for a contribution to the *Universal Review*, I went, as I have explained, to the Museum, and presently repaired to bookcase No. 2008 to get my favourite volume. Alas! it was in the room no longer. It was not in use, for its place was filled up already; besides, no one ever used it but my-self.... Till I have found a substitute I can write no more, and I do not know how to find even a tolerable one. I should try a volume of Migne's *Complete Course of Patrology*, but I do not like books in more than one volume, for the volumes vary in thickness, and one nev-er can remember which one took; the four volumes, however, of Bede in Giles's *Anglican Fathers* are not open to this objection, and I have reserved them for favourable considera-tion. Mather's *Magnalia* might do, but the binding does not please me; Cureton's *Corpus Ignatianum* might also do if it were not too thin. I do not like taking Norton's *Genuineness of the Gospels*, as it is just possible some one may be wanting to know whether the Gospels are genuine or not, and be unable to find out because I have got Mr. Norton's book. Baxter's *Church History of England*, Lingard's *Anglo-Saxon Church*, and Cardwell's *Documen-tary Annals*, though none of them as good as Frost, are works of considerable merit; but on the whole I think Arvine's *Cyclopaedia of Moral and Religious Anecdote* is perhaps the one book in the room which comes within measurable distance of Frost.... Some successor I must find, or I must give up writing altogether, and this I should be sorry to do.--S. BUTLER. *Essays on Life, Art, and Science.*

ON THE SIGHT OF A GREAT LIBRARY

What a world of wit is here packed up together! I know not, whether this sight doth more dismay, or comfort me: it dismays me, to think that here is so much that I cannot know; it comforts me, to think that this variety yields so good helps, to know what I should. There is no truer word than that of Solomon: 'There is no end of making many books.' This sight verifies it. There is no end: it were pity there should. God hath given to man a busy soul; the agitation whereof cannot but, through time and experience, work out many hidden truths: to suppress these, would be no other than injurious to mankind, whose minds like unto so many candles should be kindled by each other. The thoughts of our deliberation are most accurate: these we vent into our papers. What a happiness is it, that, without all offence of necromancy, I may here call up any of the ancient worthies of learning, whether human or divine, and confer with them of all my doubts! that I can, at pleasure, summon whole synods of reverend fathers and acute doctors from all the coasts of the earth, to give their well-studied judgements, in all points of question, which I propose! Neither can I cast my eye casually upon any of these silent masters, but I must learn somewhat. It is a wantonness, to complain of choice. No law binds us to read all: but the more we can take in and digest, the better-liking must the mind needs be. Blessed be God, that set up so many clear lamps in his Church: now, none, but the wilfully blind, can plead darkness. And blessed be the memory of those his faithful servants, that have left their blood, their spirits, their lives, in these precious papers; and have willingly wasted themselves into these during monuments, to give light unto others.--JOSEPH HALL. *Occasional Meditations.*

REFLECTIONS IN A LIBRARY

There are more ways to derive instruction from books than the direct and chief one of applying the attention to what they contain. Things connected with them, by natural or casual association, will sometimes suggest themselves to a reflective and imaginative reader, and divert him into secondary trains of ideas. In these, the mind may, indeed, float along in perfect indolence and acquire no good; but a serious disposition might regulate them to a profitable result....

Even in the most cursory notice of them, when the attention is engaged by no one in particular, ideas may be started of a tendency not wholly foreign to instruction. A reflective person, in his library, in some hour of intermittent application, when the mind is surrendered to vagrant musing, may glance along the ranges of volumes with a slight recognition of the authors, in long miscellaneous array of ancients and moderns. And that musing may become shaped into ideas like these:--What a number of our busy race have deemed themselves capable of informing and directing the rest of mankind! What a vast amount is collected here of the results of the most strenuous and protracted exertions of so many minds! What were in each of these claimants that the world should think as they did, the most prevailing motives? How many of them sincerely loved truth, honestly sought it, and faithfully, to the best of their knowledge, declared it? What might be the circumstances and influences which determined in the case of that one author, and the next, and the next again, their own modes of opinion?

And how much have they actually done for truth and righteousness in the world? Do not the contents of these accumulated volumes constitute a chaos of all discordant and contradictory principles, theories, representations of facts, and figurings of imaginations? Could I not instantly place beside each other the works of two noted authors, who maintain for truth directly opposite doctrines, or systems of doctrine; and then add a third book which explodes them both? I can take some one book in which the prime spirits of the world, through all time, are brought together, announcing the speculations which they, respectively, proclaimed to be the essence of all wisdom, protesting, with solemn censure or sneering contempt, against the dogmas and theories of one another, and conflicting in a huge Babel of all imaginable opinions and vagaries....

Thus far the instructive reflections which even the mere exterior of an accumulation of books may suggest are supposed to occur in the way of thinking of the *authors*. But the same books may also excite some interesting ideas through their less obvious but not altogether fanciful association with the persons who may have been their *readers* or *possessors*. The mind of a thoughtful looker over a range of volumes of many dates, and a considerable portion of them old, will sometimes be led into a train of conjectural questions:--Who were they that, in various times and places, have had these in their possession? Perhaps many hands have turned over the leaves, many eyes have passed along the lines. With what measure of intelligence, and of approval or dissent, did those persons respectively follow the train of thoughts? How many of them were honestly intent on becoming wise by what they read? How many sincere prayers were addressed by them to the Eternal Wisdom during the perusal? How many have been determined, in their judgement or their actions, by these books? What emotions, temptations, or painful occurrences, may have interrupted the reading of this book, or of that?--J. FOSTER. *Introductory Essay to Doddridge's Rise and Progress of Religion in the Soul.*

THOUGHTS IN A LIBRARY

A great library! What a mass of human misery is here commemorated!--how many buried hopes surround us!

The author of that work was the greatest natural philosopher that ever enlightened mankind. His biographers are now disputing whether at one period of his life he was not of unsound mind--but all agree that he was afterwards able to understand his own writings.

The author of those numerous volumes was logician, metaphysician, natural historian, philosopher; his sanity was never doubted, and with his last breath he regretted his birth, mourned over his life, expressed his fear of death, and called upon the Cause of causes to pity him. His slightest thoughts continued to domineer over the world for ages, until they were in some measure silenced by those works which contain the unfettered meditations of a very great man, who, being more careless than corrupt in the administration of his high office, has gone down to posterity, as

'The wisest, brightest, meanest, of mankind.'

For his wisdom has embalmed his meanness.

Those volumes contain the weighty, if not wise opinions of one who, amidst penury and wretchedness, first learnt to moralize with companions as poor and wretched as himself. Even in his latter years, when sought by a monarch, and listened to with submission by all who approached him, his life can scarcely be called a happy one; yet he must have enjoyed some moments of triumph, if not of happiness, in contemplating the severe but well-merited rebuke which he inflicted upon that courtier, who could behold his difficulties with all the indifference that belongs to good breeding, and then thought fit, in the hour of his success, to encumber him with paltry praises.

Those poems were the burning words of one

'... Cradled into poetry by wrong,

Who learnt in suffering what he taught in song.'

The slightest foibles of this unhappy man have been brought into odious prominence, for he was the favourite author of his age, and therefore the property of the public.

That boyish book absolved its author from a father's cares; and he was one to whom those cares would have been dearest joys, who loved to look upon a poor man's child. Listen to the music of his sadness--

'I see the deep's untrampled floor
  With green and purple seaweeds strown;
I see the waves upon the shore,
  Like light dissolv'd in star-showers, thrown:
I sit upon the sands alone,
  The lightning of the noon-tide ocean
Is flashing round me, and a tone
  Arises from its measured motion,
How sweet! did any heart now share in my emotion!'

The sharp arrows of criticism were successfully directed against that next volume, and are said to have been the means of hurrying its author to that world of dreams and shadows, for which, in the critic's opinion, he was so pre-eminently fitted.

'Where is the youth, for deeds immortal born,
Who loved to whisper to the embattled corn,
And clustered woodbines, breathing o'er the stream
Endymion's beauteous passion for a dream?'

You already smile, my friend; but to know the heights and the depths, you must turn your attention to those numberless, unread, unheard-of volumes. Their authors did not suffer from the severity of the critic or the judge, but were only neglected. If Mephistopheles ever requires rest and seclusion--But, hark! is there not a laugh? and that grotesque face in the carved woodwork, how scoffingly it is looking down upon us!--SIR A. HELPS. *Thoughts in a Cloister.*

THE TRUE POEM ON THE LIBRARY

Let us compare the different ways in which Crabbe and Foster (certainly a *prose* poet) deal with a library. Crabbe describes minutely and successfully the outer features of the volumes, their colours, clasps, the stubborn ridges of their bindings, the illustrations which adorn them, so well that you feel yourself among them, and they become sensible to touch almost as to sight. But there he stops, and sadly fails, we think, in bringing out the living and moral interest which gathers around a multitude of books, or even around a single volume. This Foster has amply done. The speaking silence of a number of books, where, though it were the wide Bodleian or Vatican, not one whisper could be heard, and yet where, as in an antechamber, so many great spirits are waiting to deliver their messages--their churchyard stillness continuing even when their readers are moving to their pages, in joy or agony, as to the sound of martial instruments--their awaking, as from deep slumber, to speak with miraculous organ, like the shell which has only to be lifted, and 'pleased it remembers its august abodes, and murmurs as the ocean murmurs there'--their power of drawing tears, kindling blushes, awakening laughter, calming or quickening the motions of the life's-blood, lulling to repose, or rousing to restlessness--the meaning which radiates from their quiet countenances--the tale of shame or glory which their title-pages tell--the memories suggested by the character of their authors, and of the readers who have throughout successive centuries perused them--the thrilling thoughts excited by the sight of names and notes inscribed on their margins or blank pages by hands long since mouldered in the dust, or by those dear to us as our life's-blood, who have been snatched from our sides--the aspects of gaiety or of gloom connected with the bindings and the age of volumes--the effects of sunshine playing as if on a congregation of happy faces, making the duskiest shine and the gloomiest be glad--or of shadow suffusing a sombre air over all--the joy of the proprietor of a large library, who feels that Nebuchadnezzar watching great Babylon, or Napoleon reviewing his legions, will not stand comparison with himself seated amid the broad maps, and rich prints, and numerous volumes which his wealth has enabled him to enjoy--all such hieroglyphics of interest and meaning has Foster included and interpreted in one gloomy but noble meditation, and his introduction to Doddridge is the true 'Poem on the Library'.--G. GILFILLAN. *Gallery of Literary Portraits: George Crabbe.*

THE LIBRARY

When the sad soul, by care and grief oppressed,
Looks round the world, but looks in vain for rest;
When every object that appears in view,
Partakes her gloom and seems dejected too;
Where shall affliction from itself retire?
Where fade away and placidly expire?
Alas! we fly to silent scenes in vain;
Care blasts the honours of the flowery plain:
Care veils in clouds the sun's meridian beam,
Sighs through the grove and murmurs in the stream;
For when the soul is labouring in despair,
In vain the body breathes a purer air:
No storm-tossed sailor sighs for slumbering seas,--
He dreads the tempest, but invokes the breeze;
On the smooth mirror of the deep resides
Reflected woe, and o'er unruffled tides
The ghost of every former danger glides.
Thus, in the calms of life, we only see
A steadier image of our misery;
But lively gales and gently-clouded skies
Disperse the sad reflections as they rise;
And busy thoughts and little cares avail
To ease the mind, when rest and reason fail.
When the dull thought, by no designs employed,

Dwells on the past, or suffered or enjoyed,
We bleed anew in every former grief,
And joys departed furnish no relief.

 Not Hope herself, with all her flattering art,
Can cure this stubborn sickness of the heart:
The soul disdains each comfort she prepares,
And anxious searches for congenial cares;
Those lenient cares, which, with our own combined,
By mixed sensations ease the afflicted mind,
And steal our grief away and leave their own behind;
A lighter grief! which feeling hearts endure
Without regret, nor e'en demand a cure.

 But what strange art, what magic can dispose
The troubled mind to change its native woes?
Or lead us willing from ourselves, to see
Others more wretched, more undone than we?
This, books can do;--nor this alone; they give
New views to life, and teach us how to live;
They soothe the grieved, the stubborn they chastise,
Fools they admonish, and confirm the wise:
Their aid they yield to all: they never shun
The man of sorrow, nor the wretch undone:
Unlike the hard, the selfish, and the proud,
They fly not sullen from the suppliant crowd;
Nor tell to various people various things,
But show to subjects, what they show to kings.

 Come, Child of Care! to make thy soul serene,
Approach the treasures of this tranquil scene;
Survey the dome, and, as the doors unfold,
The soul's best cure, in all her cares, behold!
Where mental wealth the poor in thought may find,
And mental physic the diseased in mind;
See here the balms that passion's wounds assuage;
See coolers here, that damp the fire of rage;
Here alteratives, by slow degrees control
The chronic habits of the sickly soul;
And round the heart and o'er the aching head,
Mild opiates here their sober influence shed.
Now bid thy soul man's busy scenes exclude,
And view composed this silent multitude:--
Silent they are, but, though deprived of sound,
Here all the living languages abound;
Here all that live no more; preserved they lie,
In tombs that open to the curious eye.

Blessed be the gracious Power, who taught mankind
To stamp a lasting image of the mind!--
Beasts may convey, and tuneful birds may sing,
Their mutual feelings, in the opening spring;
But man alone has skill and power to send
The heart's warm dictates to the distant friend:
'Tis his alone to please, instruct, advise
Ages remote, and nations yet to rise.

In sweet repose, when labour's children sleep,
When joy forgets to smile and care to weep,
When passion slumbers in the lover's breast,
And fear and guilt partake the balm of rest,
Why then denies the studious man to share
Man's common good, who feels his common care?

Because the hope is his, that bids him fly
Night's soft repose, and sleep's mild power defy;
That after-ages may repeat his praise,
And fame's fair meed be his, for length of days.
Delightful prospect! when we leave behind
A worthy offspring of the fruitful mind!
Which, born and nursed through many an anxious day,
Shall all our labour, all our care repay.

Yet all are not these births of noble kind,
Not all the children of a vigorous mind;
But where the wisest should alone preside,
The weak would rule us, and the blind would guide;
Nay, man's best efforts taste of man, and show
The poor and troubled source from which they flow:
Where most he triumphs, we his wants perceive,
And for his weakness in his wisdom grieve.
But though imperfect all; yet wisdom loves
This seat serene, and virtue's self approves:--
Here come the grieved, a change of thought to find;
The curious here, to feed a craving mind;
Here the devout their peaceful temple choose;
And here the poet meets his favouring muse.

With awe, around these silent walks I tread;
These are the lasting mansions of the dead:--
'The dead,' methinks a thousand tongues reply;
'These are the tombs of such as cannot die!
Crowned with eternal fame, they sit sublime,
And laugh at all the little strife of time.'

Hail, then, immortals! ye who shine above,

Each, in his sphere, the literary Jove;
And ye the common people of these skies,
A humbler crowd of nameless deities;
Whether 'tis yours to lead the willing mind
Through history's mazes, and the turnings find;
Or whether, led by science, ye retire,
Lost and bewildered in the vast desire;
Whether the Muse invites you to her bowers,
And crowns your placid brows with living flowers;
Or godlike wisdom teaches you to show
The noblest road to happiness below;
Or men and manners prompt the easy page
To mark the flying follies of the age:
Whatever good ye boast, that good impart;
Inform the head and rectify the heart.

  Lo! all in silence, all in order stand
And mighty folios first, a lordly band;
Then quartos their well-ordered ranks maintain.
And light octavos fill a spacious plain:
See yonder, ranged in more frequented rows,
A humbler band of duodecimos;
While undistinguished trifles swell the scene,
The last new play and frittered magazine.
Thus 'tis in life, where first the proud, the great,
In leagued assembly keep their cumbrous state;
Heavy and huge, they fill the world with dread,
Are much admired, and are but little read:
The commons next, a middle rank, are found;
Professions fruitful pour their offspring round:
Reasoners and wits are next their place allowed,
And last, of vulgar tribes a countless crowd.

  First, let us view the form, the size, the dress;
For these the manners, nay the mind express;
That weight of wood, with leathern coat o'erlaid;
Those ample clasps, of solid metal made;
The close-pressed leaves, unclosed for many an age;
The dull red edging of the well-filled page;
On the broad back the stubborn ridges rolled,
Where yet the title stands in tarnished gold;
These all a sage and laboured work proclaim,
A painful candidate for lasting fame:
No idle wit, no trifling verse can lurk
In the deep bosom of that weighty work;
No playful thoughts degrade the solemn style,
Nor one light sentence claims a transient smile.

264

Hence, in these times, untouched the pages lie,
And slumber out their immortality:
They *had* their day, when, after all his toil,
His morning study, and his midnight oil,
At length an author's ONE great work appeared,
By patient hope, and length of days, endeared:
Expecting nations hailed it from the press;
Poetic friends prefixed each kind address;
Princes and kings received the ponderous gift,
And ladies read the work they could not lift.
Fashion, though Folly's child, and guide of fools,
Rules e'en the wisest, and in learning rules;
From crowds and courts to Wisdom's seat she goes,
And reigns triumphant o'er her mother's foes.

For lo! these favourites of the ancient mode
Lie all neglected like the Birth-day Ode;
Ah! needless now this weight of massy chain;
Safe in themselves, the once-loved works remain;
No readers now invade their still retreat,
None try to steal them from their parent-seat;
Like ancient beauties, they may now discard
Chains, bolts, and locks, and lie without a guard.
Our patient fathers trifling themes laid by,
And rolled o'er laboured works the attentive eye;
Page after page, the much-enduring men
Explored, the deeps and shallows of the pen;
Till, every former note and comment known,
They marked the spacious margin with their own:
Minute corrections proved their studious care,
The little index, pointing, told us where;
And many an emendation showed the age
Looked far beyond the rubric title-page.

Our nicer palates lighter labours seek,
Cloyed with a folio-*Number* once a week;
Bibles, with cuts and comments, thus go down:
E'en light Voltaire is *numbered* through the town:
Thus physic flies abroad, and thus the law,
From men of study, and from men of straw;
Abstracts, abridgements, please the fickle times,
Pamphlets and plays, and politics and rhymes:
But though to write be now a task of ease,
The task is hard by manly arts to please,
When all our weakness is exposed to view,
And half our judges are our rivals too.

Amid these works, on which the eager eye

Delights to fix, or glides reluctant by,
When all combined, their decent pomp display,
Where shall we first our early offering pay?----

  To thee, DIVINITY! to thee, the light
And guide of mortals, through their mental night;
By whom we learn our hopes and fears to guide;
To bear with pain, and to contend with pride;
When grieved, to pray; when injured, to forgive;
And with the world in charity to live.

  Not truths like these inspired that numerous race,
Whose pious labours fill this ample space;
But questions nice, where doubt on doubt arose,
Awaked to war the long-contending foes.
For dubious meanings, learned polemics strove,
And wars on faith prevented works of love;
The brands of discord far around were hurled,
And holy wrath inflamed a sinful world:--
Dull though impatient, peevish though devout,
With wit disgusting and despised without;
Saints in design, in execution men,
Peace in their looks, and vengeance in their pen.

  Methinks I see, and sicken at the sight,
Spirits of spleen from yonder pile alight;
Spirits who prompted every damning page,
With pontiff pride and still-increasing rage:
Lo! how they stretch their gloomy wings around,
And lash with furious strokes the trembling ground!
They pray, they fight, they murder, and they weep,--
Wolves in their vengeance, in their manners sheep;
Too well they act the prophet's fatal part,
Denouncing evil with a zealous heart;
And each, like Jonas, is displeased if God
Repent his anger, or withhold his rod.
But here the dormant fury rests unsought,
And Zeal sleeps soundly by the foes she fought;
Here all the rage of controversy ends,
And rival zealots rest like bosom-friends:
An Athanasian here, in deep repose,
Sleeps with the fiercest of his Arian foes;
Socinians here with Calvinists abide,
And thin partitions angry chiefs divide;
Here wily Jesuits simple Quakers meet,
And Bellarmine has rest at Luther's feet.
Great authors, for the church's glory fired,
Are, for the church's peace, to rest retired;

And close beside, a mystic, maudlin race,
Lie, 'Crums of Comfort for the Babes of Grace.'

Against her foes Religion well defends
Her sacred truths, but often fears her friends;
If learned, their pride, if weak, their zeal she dreads,
And their hearts' weakness, who have soundest heads:
But most she fears the controversial pen,
The holy strife of disputatious men;
Who the blessed Gospel's peaceful page explore,
Only to fight against its precepts more.

Near to these seats, behold yon slender frames,
All closely filled and marked with modern names;
Where no fair science ever shows her face,
Few sparks of genius, and no spark of grace;
There sceptics rest, a still-increasing throng,
And stretch their widening wings ten thousand strong:
Some in close fight their dubious claims maintain;
Some skirmish lightly, fly and fight again;
Coldly profane, and impiously gay,
Their end the same, though various in their way.

When first Religion came to bless the land,
Her friends were then a firm believing band;
To doubt was, then, to plunge in guilt extreme,
And all was gospel that a monk could dream;
Insulted Reason fled the grovelling soul,
For fear to guide, and visions to control:
But now, when Reason has assumed her throne,
She, in her turn, demands to reign alone;
Rejecting all that lies beyond her view,
And, being judge, will be a witness too:
Insulted Faith then leaves the doubtful mind,
To seek for truth, without a power to find:
Ah! when will both in friendly beams unite,
And pour on erring man resistless light?

Next to the seats, well stored with works divine,
An ample space, PHILOSOPHY! is thine;
Our reason's guide, by whose assisting light
We trace the moral bounds of wrong and right;
Our guide through nature, from the sterile clay,
To the bright orbs of yon celestial way!
'Tis thine, the great, the golden chain to trace,
Which runs through all, connecting race with race;
Save where those puzzling, stubborn links remain,
Which thy inferior light pursues in vain:--

How vice and virtue in the soul contend;
How widely differ, yet how nearly blend!
What various passions war on either part,
And now confirm, now melt the yielding heart:
How Fancy loves around the world to stray,
While Judgement slowly picks his sober way;
The stores of memory, and the flights sublime
Of genius, bound by neither space nor time;--
All these divine Philosophy explores,
Till, lost in awe, she wonders and adores.
From these, descending to the earth, she turns,
And matter, in its various form, discerns;
She parts the beamy light with skill profound,
Metes the thin air, and weighs the flying sound;
'Tis hers, the lightning from the clouds to call,
And teach the fiery mischief where to fall.

Yet more her volumes teach,--on these we look
As abstracts drawn from Nature's larger book:
Here, first described, the torpid earth appears,
And next, the vegetable robe it wears;
Where flowery tribes, in valleys, fields and groves,
Nurse the still flame, and feed the silent loves;
Loves, where no grief, nor joy, nor bliss, nor pain,
Warm the glad heart or vex the labouring brain;
But as the green blood moves along the blade,
The bed of Flora on the branch is made;
Where, without passion, love instinctive lives,
And gives new life, unconscious that it gives.
Advancing still in Nature's maze, we trace,
In dens and burning plains, her savage race;
With those tame tribes who on their lord attend,
And find, in man, a master and a friend:
Man crowns the scene, a world of wonders new,
A moral world, that well demands our view.

This world is here; for, of more lofty kind,
These neighbouring volumes reason on the mind;
They paint the state of man ere yet endued
With knowledge;--man, poor, ignorant, and rude;
Then, as his state improves, their pages swell,
And all its cares, and all its comforts, tell:
Here we behold how inexperience buys,
At little price, the wisdom of the wise;
Without the troubles of an active state,
Without the cares and dangers of the great,
Without the miseries of the poor, we know

What wisdom, wealth, and poverty bestow;
We see how reason calms the raging mind,
And how contending passions urge mankind:
Some, won by virtue, glow with sacred fire;
Some, lured by vice, indulge the low desire;
Whilst others, won by either, now pursue
The guilty chase, now keep the good in view;
For ever wretched, with themselves at strife,
They lead a puzzled, vexed, uncertain life;
For transient vice bequeaths a lingering pain
Which transient virtue seeks to cure in vain.

Whilst thus engaged, high views enlarge the soul,
New interests draw, new principles control:
Nor thus the soul alone resigns her grief,
But here the tortured body finds relief;
For see where yonder sage Arachnè shapes
Her subtile gin, that not a fly escapes!
There PHYSIC fills the space, and far around,
Pile above pile, her learned works abound:
Glorious their aim--to ease the labouring heart;
To war with death, and stop his flying dart;
To trace the source whence the fierce contest grew,
And life's short lease on easier terms renew;
To calm the frenzy of the burning brain;
To heal the tortures of imploring pain;
Or, when more powerful ills all efforts brave,
To ease the victim no device can save,
And smooth the stormy passage to the grave.

But man, who knows no good unmixed and pure,
Oft finds a poison where he sought a cure;
For grave deceivers lodge their labours here,
And cloud the science they pretend to clear:
Scourges for sin, the solemn tribe are sent;
Like fire and storms, they call us to repent;
But storms subside, and fires forget to rage,
These are eternal scourges of the age:
'Tis not enough that each terrific hand
Spreads desolation round a guilty land;
But, trained to ill, and hardened by its crimes,
Their pen relentless kills through future times.

Say ye, who search these records of the dead,
Who read huge works, to boast what ye have read;
Can all the real knowledge ye possess,
Or those (if such there are) who more than guess,
Atone for each impostor's wild mistakes,

And mend the blunders pride or folly makes?

What thought so wild, what airy dream so light,
That will not prompt a theorist to write?
What art so prevalent, what proof so strong,
That will convince him his attempt is wrong?
One in the solids finds each lurking ill,
Nor grants the passive fluids power to kill;
A learned friend some subtler reason brings,
Absolves the channels, but condemns their springs;
The subtile nerves, that shun the doctor's eye,
Escape no more his subtler theory;
The vital heat, that warms the labouring heart,
Lends a fair system to these sons of art;
The vital air, a pure and subtile stream,
Serves a foundation for an airy scheme,
Assists the doctor, and supports his dream.
Some have their favourite ills, and each disease
Is but a younger branch that kills from these:
One to the gout contracts all human pain,
He views it raging in the frantic brain;
Finds it in fevers all his efforts mar,
And sees it lurking in the cold catarrh:
Bilious by some, by others nervous seen,
Rage the fantastic demons of the spleen;
And every symptom of the strange disease
With every system of the sage agrees.

Ye frigid tribe, on whom I wasted long
The tedious hours, and ne'er indulged in song;
Ye first seducers of my easy heart,
Who promised knowledge ye could not impart;
Ye dull deluders, truth's destructive foes;
Ye sons of fiction, clad in stupid prose;
Ye treacherous leaders, who, yourselves in doubt,
Light up false fires, and send us far about;--
Still may yon spider round your pages spin,
Subtile and slow, her emblematic gin!
Buried in dust and lost in silence, dwell,
Most potent, grave, and reverend friends--farewell!

Near these, and where the setting sun displays,
Through the dim window, his departing rays,
And gilds yon columns, there, on either side,
The huge abridgements of the LAW abide;
Fruitful as vice the dread correctors stand,
And spread their guardian terrors round the land;
Yet, as the best that human care can do,

Is mixed with error, oft with evil too,
Skilled in deceit, and practised to evade,
Knaves stand secure, for whom these laws were made;
And justice vainly each expedient tries,
While art eludes it, or while power defies.
'Ah! happy age,' the youthful poet sings,
'When the free nations knew not laws nor kings;
When all were blessed to share a common store,
And none were proud of wealth, for none were poor;
No wars nor tumults vexed each still domain,
No thirst for empire, no desire of gain;
No proud great man, nor one who would be great,
Drove modest merit from its proper state;
Nor into distant climes would avarice roam,
To fetch delights for luxury at home:
Bound by no ties which kept the soul in awe,
They dwelt at liberty, and love was law!'

'Mistaken youth! each nation first was rude,
Each man a cheerless son of solitude,
To whom no joys of social life were known,
None felt a care that was not all his own;
Or in some languid clime his abject soul
Bowed to a little tyrant's stern control;
A slave, with slaves his monarch's throne he raised,
And in rude song his ruder idol praised;
The meaner cares of life were all he knew;
Bounded his pleasures, and his wishes few:
But when by slow degrees the Arts arose,
And Science wakened from her long repose;
When Commerce, rising from the bed of ease,
Ran round the land, and pointed to the seas;
When Emulation, born with jealous eye,
And Avarice, lent their spurs to industry;
Then one by one the numerous laws were made
Those to control, and these to succour trade;
To curb the insolence of rude command,
To snatch the victim from the usurer's hand;
To awe the bold, to yield the wronged redress,
And feed the poor with Luxury's excess.'

Like some vast flood, unbounded, fierce, and strong,
His nature leads ungoverned man along;
Like mighty bulwarks made to stem that tide,
The laws are formed and placed on every side:
Whene'er it breaks the bounds by these decreed,
New statutes rise, and stronger laws succeed;
More and more gentle grows the dying stream,

More and more strong the rising bulwarks seem;
Till, like a miner working sure and slow,
Luxury creeps on, and ruins all below;
The basis sinks, the ample piles decay;
The stately fabric shakes and falls away;
Primeval want and ignorance come on,
But freedom, that exalts the savage state, is gone.

  Next, HISTORY ranks;--there full in front she lies,
And every nation her dread tale supplies;
Yet History has her doubts, and every age
With sceptic queries marks the passing page;
Records of old nor later date are clear,
Too distant those, and these are placed too near;
There time conceals the objects from our view,
Here our own passions and a writer's too:
Yet, in these volumes, see how states arose!
Guarded by virtue from surrounding foes;
Their virtue lost, and of their triumphs vain,
Lo! how they sunk to slavery again!
Satiate with power, of fame and wealth possessed,
A nation grows too glorious to be blessed;
Conspicuous made, she stands the mark of all,
And foes join foes to triumph in her fall.

  Thus speaks the page that paints ambition's race,
The monarch's pride, his glory, his disgrace;
The headlong course, that maddening heroes run,
How soon triumphant, and how soon undone;
How slaves, turned tyrants, offer crowns to sale,
And each fallen nation's melancholy tale.

  Lo! where of late the Book of Martyrs stood,
Old pious tracts, and Bibles bound in wood;
There, such the taste of our degenerate age,
Stand the profane delusions of the STAGE:
Yet virtue owns the TRAGIC MUSE a friend,
Fable her means, morality her end;
For this she rules all passions in their turns;
And now the bosom bleeds, and now it burns,
Pity with weeping eye surveys her bowl,
Her anger swells, her terror chills the soul;
She makes the vile to virtue yield applause,
And own her sceptre while they break her laws;
For vice in others is abhorred of all,
And villains triumph when the worthless fall.

  Not thus her sister COMEDY prevails,

Who shoots at folly, for her arrow fails;
Folly, by dulness armed, eludes the wound,
And harmless sees the feathered shafts rebound;
Unhurt she stands, applauds the archer's skill,
Laughs at her malice, and is folly still.
Yet well the Muse portrays in fancied scenes,
What pride will stoop to, what profession means;
How formal fools the farce of state applaud,
How caution watches at the lips of fraud;
The wordy variance of domestic life;
The tyrant husband, the retorting wife;
The snares for innocence, the lie of trade,
And the smooth tongue's habitual masquerade.

With her the virtues too obtain a place,
Each gentle passion, each becoming grace;
The social joy in life's securer road,
Its easy pleasure, its substantial good;
The happy thought that conscious virtue gives,
And all that ought to live, and all that lives.

But who are these? Methinks a noble mien
And awful grandeur in their form are seen,
Now in disgrace: what though by time is spread
Polluting dust o'er every reverend head;
What though beneath yon gilded tribe they lie,
And dull observers pass insulting by:
Forbid it shame, forbid it decent awe,
What seems so grave, should no attention draw!
Come, let us then with reverend step advance,
And greet--the ancient worthies of ROMANCE.

Hence, ye profane! I feel a former dread,
A thousand visions float around my head:
Hark! hollow blasts through empty courts resound,
And shadowy forms with staring eyes stalk round;
See! moats and bridges, walls and castles rise,
Ghosts, fairies, demons, dance before our eyes;
Lo! magic verse inscribed on golden gate,
And bloody hand that beckons on to fate:--
'And who art thou, thou little page, unfold?
Say, doth thy lord my Claribel withhold?
Go tell him straight, Sir Knight, thou must resign
The captive queen;--for Claribel is mine.'
Away he flies; and now for bloody deeds,
Black suits of armour, masks, and foaming steeds;
The giant falls; his recreant throat I seize,
And from his corslet take the massy keys:--

Dukes, lords, and knights in long procession move,
Released from bondage with my virgin love:--
She comes! she comes! in all the charms of youth,
Unequalled love and unsuspected truth!

  Ah! happy he who thus, in magic themes,
O'er worlds bewitched, in early rapture dreams,
Where wild Enchantment waves her potent wand,
And Fancy's beauties fill her fairy land;
Where doubtful objects strange desires excite,
And Fear and Ignorance afford delight.

  But lost, for ever lost, to me these joys,
Which Reason scatters, and which Time destroys;
Too dearly bought: maturer judgement calls
My busied mind from tales and madrigals;
My doughty giants all are slain or fled,
And all my knights, blue, green, and yellow, dead!
No more the midnight fairy tribe I view,
All in the merry moonshine tippling dew;
E'en the last lingering fiction of the brain,
The church-yard ghost, is now at rest again;
And all these wayward wanderings of my youth
Fly Reason's power and shun the light of truth.

  With fiction then does real joy reside,
And is our reason the delusive guide?
Is it then right to dream the syrens sing?
Or mount enraptured on the dragon's wing?
No, 'tis the infant mind, to care unknown,
That makes the imagined paradise its own;
Soon as reflections in the bosom rise,
Light slumbers vanish from the clouded eyes:
The tear and smile, that once together rose,
Are then divorced; the head and heart are foes.
Enchantment bows to Wisdom's serious plan,
And Pain and Prudence make and mar the man.

  While thus, of power and fancied empire vain,
With various thoughts my mind I entertain;
While books my slaves, with tyrant hand I seize,
Pleased with the pride that will not let them please;
Sudden I find terrific thoughts arise,
And sympathetic sorrow fills my eyes;
For, lo! while yet my heart admits the wound,
I see the CRITIC army ranged around.

  Foes to our race! if ever ye have known

A father's fears for offspring of your own;--
If ever, smiling o'er a lucky line,
Ye thought the sudden sentiment divine,
Then paused and doubted, and then, tired of doubt,
With rage as sudden dashed the stanza out;--
If, after fearing much and pausing long,
Ye ventured on the world your laboured song,
And from the crusty critics of those days
Implored the feeble tribute of their praise;
Remember now the fears that moved you then,
And, spite of truth, let mercy guide your pen.

What venturous race are ours! what mighty foes
Lie waiting all around them to oppose!
What treacherous friends betray them to the fight!
What dangers threaten them!--yet still they write:
A hapless tribe! to every evil born,
Whom villains hate, and fools affect to scorn:
Strangers they come, amid a world of woe,
And taste the largest portion ere they go.

Pensive I spoke, and cast mine eyes around;
The roof, methought, returned a solemn sound;
Each column seemed to shake, and clouds like smoke,
From dusty piles and ancient volumes broke;
Gathering above, like mists condensed they seem,
Exhaled in summer from the rushy stream;
Like flowing robes they now appear, and twine
Round the large members of a form divine;
His silver beard, that swept his aged breast,
His piercing eye, that inward light expressed,
Were seen,--but clouds and darkness veiled the rest.
Fear chilled my heart: to one of mortal race,
How awful seemed the Genius of the place!
So in Cimmerian shores, Ulysses saw
His parent-shade, and shrunk in pious awe;
Like him I stood, and wrapt in thought profound,
When from the pitying power broke forth a solemn sound:--

'Care lives with all; no rules, no precepts save
The wise from woe, no fortitude the brave;
Grief is to man as certain as the grave:
Tempests and storms in life's whole progress rise,
And hope shines dimly through o'erclouded skies;
Some drops of comfort on the favoured fall,
But showers of sorrow are the lot of *all*:
Partial to talents, then, shall Heaven withdraw
The afflicting rod, or break the general law?

Shall he who soars, inspired by loftier views,
Life's little cares and little pains refuse?
Shall he not rather feel a double share
Of mortal woe, when doubly armed to bear?

  'Hard is his fate who builds his peace of mind
On the precarious mercy of mankind;
Who hopes for wild and visionary things,
And mounts o'er unknown seas with venturous wings:
But as, of various evils that befall
The human race, some portion goes to all;
To him perhaps the milder lot's assigned,
Who feels his consolation in his mind;
And, locked within his bosom, bears about
A mental charm for every care without.
E'en in the pangs of each domestic grief,
Or health or vigorous hope affords relief;
And every wound the tortured bosom feels,
Or virtue bears, or some preserver heals;
Some generous friend, of ample power possessed;
Some feeling heart, that bleeds for the distressed;
Some breast that glows with virtues all divine;
Some noble RUTLAND, Misery's friend and thine.

  'Nor say, the Muse's song, the Poet's pen,
Merit the scorn they meet from little men.
With cautious freedom if the numbers flow,
Not wildly high, nor pitifully low;
If vice alone their honest aims oppose,
Why so ashamed their friends, so loud their foes?
Happy for men in every age and clime,
If all the sons of vision dealt in rhyme.
Go on then, Son of Vision! still pursue
Thy airy dreams; the world is dreaming too.
Ambition's lofty views, the pomp of state,
The pride of wealth, the splendour of the great,
Stripped of their mask, their cares and troubles known,
Are visions far less happy than thy own:
Go on! and, while the sons of care complain,
Be wisely gay and innocently vain;
While serious souls are by their fears undone,
Blow sportive bladders in the beamy sun,
And call them worlds! and bid the greatest show
More radiant colours in their worlds below:
Then, as they break, the slaves of care reprove,
And tell them, Such are all the toys they love.'

             G. CRABBE.

THE LIBRARY

Here, e'en the sturdy democrat may find,
Nor scorn their rank, the nobles of the mind;
While kings may learn, nor blush at being shown
How Learning's patents abrogate their own.
A goodly company and fair to see;
Royal plebeians; earls of low degree;
Beggars whose wealth enriches every clime;
Princes who scarce can boast a mental dime;
Crowd here together like the quaint array
Of jostling neighbours on a market day.
Homer and Milton,--can we call them blind?--
Of godlike sight, the vision of the mind;
Shakespeare, who calmly looked creation through,
'Exhausted worlds, and then imagined new';
Plato the sage, so thoughtful and serene,
He seems a prophet by his heavenly mien;
Shrewd Socrates, whose philosophic power
Xantippe proved in many a trying hour;
And Aristophanes, whose humour run
In vain endeavour to be-'cloud' the sun;
Majestic Aeschylus, whose glowing page
Holds half the grandeur of the Athenian stage;
Pindar, whose odes, replete with heavenly fire,
Proclaim the master of the Grecian lyre;
Anacreon, famed for many a luscious line,
Devote to Venus and the god of wine.
I love vast libraries; yet there is a doubt
If one be better with them or without--
Unless he use them wisely, and, indeed,
Knows the high art of what and how to read.
At Learning's fountain it is sweet to drink,
But 'tis a nobler privilege to think;
And oft, from books apart, the thirsting mind
May make the nectar which it cannot find.
'Tis well to borrow from the good and great;
'Tis wise to learn; 'tis godlike to create!

J. G. SAXE.

OF LIBRARIES: THE BODLEIAN

What oweth Oxford, nay this Isle, to the most worthy Bodley, whose Library, perhaps, containeth more excellent books than the ancients by all their curious search could find?... To such a worthy work all the lovers of learning should conspire and contribute; and of small beginnings who is ignorant what great effects may follow? If, perhaps, we will consider the beginnings of the greatest libraries of Europe (as Democritus said of the world, that it was made up of atoms), we shall find them but small; for how great soever in their present perfection they are now, these Carthages were once Magalia. Libraries are as forests, in which not only tall cedars and oaks are to be found, but bushes too and dwarfish shrubs; and as in apothecaries' shops all sorts of drugs are permitted to be, so may all sorts of books be in a library. And as they out of vipers and scorpions, and poisoning vegetables, extract often wholesome medicaments, for the life of mankind; so out of whatsoever book, good instructions and examples may be acquired.--WILLIAM DRUMMOND. *Of Libraries.*

ON THE DEATH OF SIR THOMAS BODLEY

One Homer was enough to blazon forth
  In a full lofty style Ulysses' praise,
Caesar had Lucan to enrol his worth
Unto the memory of endless days.
  Of thy deeds, Bodley, from thine own pure spring
  A thousand Homers and sweet Lucans sing.
One volume was a monument to bound
The large extent of their deserving pains,
In learning's commonwealth was never found
So large a decade to express thy strains,
  Which who desires to character aright,
  Must read more books than they had lines to write.
Yet give this little river leave to run,
Into the boundless ocean of thy fame;
Had they first ended I had not begun,
Sith each is a Protogenes to frame
  So curiously the picture of thy worth
  That when all's done, art wants to set it forth.

PETER PRIDEAUX (Exeter College, 1613).

TO BE CHAINED WITH GOOD AUTHORS

King James, 1605, when he came to see our University of Oxford, and amongst other edifices now went to view that famous library, renewed by Sir Thomas Bodley in imitation of Alexander at his departure, brake out into that noble speech, 'If I were not a king, I would be a University man: and if it were so that I must be a prisoner, if I might have my wish, I would desire to have no other prison than that library, and to be chained together with so many good authors, *et mortuis magistris.*' So sweet is the delight of study, the more learning they have (as he that hath a dropsy, the more he drinks the thirstier he is) the more they covet to learn, and the last day is *prioris discipulus*; harsh at first learning is, *radices amarae*, but *fructus dulces*, according to that of Isocrates, pleasant at last; the longer they live, the more they are enamoured with the Muses. Heinsius, the keeper of the library at Leyden, in Holland, was mewed up in it all the year long; and that which to thy thinking should have bred a loathing, caused in him a greater liking. 'I no sooner (saith he) come into the library, but I bolt the door to me, excluding lust, ambition, avarice, and all such vices, whose nurse is Idleness, the mother of Ignorance, and Melancholy herself, and in the very lap of eternity, amongst so many divine souls, I take my seat with so lofty a spirit and sweet content, that I pity all our great ones, and rich men that know not this happiness.'

I am not ignorant in the meantime (notwithstanding this which I have said) how barbarously and basely, for the most part, our ruder gentry esteem of libraries and books, how they neglect and contemn so great a treasure, so inestimable a benefit, as Aesop's cock did the jewel he found in the dunghill; and all through error, ignorance, and want of education.--R. BURTON. *The Anatomy of Melancholy.*

AN ODE ADDRESSED TO MR. JOHN ROUSE

LIBRARIAN, OF THE UNIVERSITY OF OXFORD

On a lost volume of my poems, which he desired me to replace, that he might add them to my other works deposited in the library.

Strophe.

My two-fold book! single in show,
    But double in contents,
Neat, but not curiously adorned,
  Which, in his early youth,
A poet gave, no lofty one in truth,
Although an earnest wooer of the Muse--
Say while in cool Ausonian shades
  Or British wilds he roamed,
Striking by turns his native lyre,
  By turns the Daunian lute,
  And stepped almost in air,--

Antistrophe.

Say, little book, what furtive hand
Thee from thy fellow-books conveyed,
What time, at the repeated suit
  Of my most learnèd friend,
I sent thee forth, an honoured traveller,
From our great city to the source of Thames,
  Caerulian sire!
Where rise the fountains, and the raptures ring,
  Of the Aonian choir,

Durable as yonder spheres,
And through the endless lapse of years
  Secure to be admired?

  Strophe II.

  Now what God, or Demigod
For Britain's ancient Genius moved,
    (If our afflicted land
Have expiated at length the guilty sloth
  Of her degenerate sons)
  Shall terminate our impious feuds,
And discipline, with hallowed voice, recall?
  Recall the Muses too,
  Driven from their ancient seats
In Albion, and well nigh from Albion's shore,
  And with keen Phoebean shafts,
  Piercing the unseemly birds,
    Whose talons menace us,
Shall drive the Harpy race from Helicon afar?

  Antistrophe.

But thou, my book, though thou hast strayed,
    Whether by treachery lost
Or indolent neglect, thy bearer's fault,
    From all thy kindred books,
To some dark cell or cave forlorn,
  Where thou endurest, perhaps
The chafing of some hard untutored hand,
    Be comforted--
For lo! again the splendid hope appears
  That thou mayest yet escape,
The gulfs of Lethe, and on oary wings
Mount to the everlasting courts of Jove!

  Strophe III.

Since Rouse desires thee, and complains
  That, though by promise his,
  Thou yet appear'st not in thy place
Among the literary noble stores,
    Given to his care,
But, absent, leavest his numbers incomplete:
  He, therefore, guardian vigilant
  Of that unperishing wealth,
Calls thee to the interior shrine, his charge,
Where he intends a richer treasure far

Than Iön kept (Iön, Erectheus' son
Illustrious, of the fair Creüsa born)
In the resplendent temple of his God,
Tripods of gold, and Delphic gifts divine.

Antistrophe.

  Haste, then, to the pleasant groves,
    The Muses' favourite haunt;
Resume thy station in Apollo's dome,
    Dearer to him
Than Delos, or the forked Parnassian hill!
    Exulting go,
Since now a splendid lot is also thine,
And thou art sought by my propitious friend;
  For there thou shalt be read
  With authors of exalted note,
The ancient glorious lights of Greece and Rome.

Epode.

Ye, then, my works, no longer vain,
  And worthless deemed by me!
Whate'er this sterile genius has produced
Expect, at last, the rage of envy spent,
  An unmolested happy home,
Gift of kind Hermes, and my watchful friend,
  Where never flippant tongue profane
    Shall entrance find,
And whence the coarse unlettered multitude
    Shall babble far remote.
  Perhaps some future distant age,
Less tinged with prejudice, and better taught,
    Shall furnish minds of power
    To judge more equally.
  Then, malice silenced in the tomb,
    Cooler heads and sounder hearts,
    Thanks to Rouse, if aught of praise
I merit, shall with candour weigh the claim.

    W. COWPER. *Translated from Milton.*

PINDARIC ODE

Hail! Learning's Pantheon! Hail, the sacred Ark,
Where all the world of science does embark!
Which ever shall withstand, and hast so long withstood,

Insatiate time's devouring flood!
Hail, Tree of Knowledge! thy leaves fruit! which well
Dost in the midst of Paradise arise,
  Oxford, the Muses' Paradise!
From which may never Sword the blest expel.
Hail, Bank of all past ages, where they lie
To enrich with interest posterity!
  Hail, Wit's illustrious Galaxy,
Where thousand lights into one brightness spread,
Hail, living University of the Dead!

Unconfused Babel of all Tongues, which e'er
The mighty linguist, Fame, or Time, the mighty traveller,
That could speak or this could hear!
Majestic Monument and Pyramid,
Where still the shapes of parted souls abide
Embalmed in verse! exalted souls, which now,
Enjoy those Arts they wooed so well below!
Which now all wonders printed plainly see
  That have been, are, or are to be,
  In the mysterious Library,
The Beatific Bodley of the Dead!

Will ye into your sacred throng admit
  The meanest British wit?
Ye General Council of the Priests of Fame,
Will ye not murmur and disdain
  That I a place amongst ye claim
  The humblest Deacon of her train?
Will ye allow me the honourable chain?
  The chain of ornament, which here
  Your noble prisoners proudly wear?
A chain which will more pleasant seem to me
Than all my own Pindaric liberty.
Will ye to bind me with these mighty names submit
  Like an Apocrypha with Holy Writ?
Whatever happy Book is chainèd here,
No other place or people needs to fear;
His chain's a passport to go everywhere.

  As when a seat in Heaven
Is to an unmalicious sinner given,
  Who casting round his wondering Eye
Does none but Patriarchs and Apostles there espy,
  Martyrs who did their lives bestow
  And Saints who Martyrs lived below,
With trembling and amazement he begins
To recollect his frailties past and sins,

He doubts almost his station there,
His soul says to itself, 'How came I here?'
  It fares no otherwise with me
When I myself with conscious wonder see
Amidst this purified elected company;
  With hardship they and pain
  Did to their happiness attain.
No labours I or merits can pretend;
I think, Predestination only was my friend.

Ah! if my author had been tied like me,
To such a place and such a company,
Instead of several countries, several men,
  And business, which the Muses hate!
He might have then improved that small estate
Which Nature sparingly did to him give,
  He might perhaps have thriven then,
And settled upon me, his child, somewhat to live;
It had happier been for him, as well as me.
  For when all, alas, is done,
We Books, I mean you Books, will prove to be
The best and noblest conversation.
  For though some errors will get in,
  Like tinctures of original sin,
  Yet sure we from our Father's wit
  Draw all the strength and spirits of it,
Leaving the grosser parts for conversation,
As the best blood of man's employed on generation.

A. COWLEY.

ON SIR THOMAS BODLEY'S LIBRARY, THE AUTHOR BEING THEN IN OXFORD

Boast not, proud Golgotha, that thou canst show
The ruins of mankind and let us know
How frail a thing is flesh! though we see there
But empty skulls, the Rabbins still live here.
They are not dead, but full of blood again,
I mean the sense, and every line a vein.
Triumph not o'er their dust; whoever looks
In here, shall find their brains all in their books.
  Nor is't old Palestine alone survives,
Athens lives here, more than in Plutarch's Lives.
The stones which sometimes danced unto the strain
Of Orpheus, here do lodge his muse again.
And you the Roman spirits, Learning has

Made your lives longer than your empire was.
Caesar had perished from the world of men,
Had not his sword been rescued by his pen.
Rare Seneca! how lasting is thy breath!
Though Nero did, thou could'st not bleed to death.
How dull the expert tyrant was, to look
For that in thee, which livèd in thy book!
Afflictions turn our blood to ink, and we
Commence, when writing, our eternity.
Lucilius here I can behold, and see
His counsels and his life proceed from thee.
But what care I to whom thy Letters be?
I change the name, and thou dost write to me;
And in this age, as sad almost as thine,
Thy stately Consolations are mine.
Poor earth! what though thy viler dust enrolls
The frail enclosures of these mighty souls?
Their graves are all upon record; not one
But is as bright and open as the sun,
And though some part of them obscurely fell
And perished in an unknown, private cell,
Yet in their books they found a glorious way
To live unto the Resurrection-day!
Most noble Bodley! we are bound to thee
For no small part of our eternity.
Thy treasure was not spent on horse and hound,
Nor that new mode, which doth old States confound.
Thy legacies another way did go,
Nor were they left to those would spend them so.
Thy safe, discreet expense on us did flow;
Walsam is in the midst of Oxford now.
Thou hast made us all thine heirs; whatever we
Hereafter write, 'tis thy posterity.
This is thy monument! here thou shalt stand
Till the times fail in their last grain of sand.
And wheresoe'er thy silent relics keep,
This tomb will never let thine honour sleep.
Still we shall think upon thee; all our fame
Meets here to speak one letter of thy name.
Thou canst not die! Here thou art more than safe,
Where every book is thy large epitaph.

    H. VAUGHAN.

THE BODLEIANS OF OXFORD

Above all thy rarities, old Oxenford, what do most arride and solace me, are thy repositories of mouldering learning, thy shelves--

What a place to be in is an old library! It seems as though all the souls of all the writers, that have bequeathed their labours to these Bodleians, were reposing here, as in some dormitory, or middle state. I do not want to handle, to profane the leaves, their winding-sheets. I could as soon dislodge a shade. I seem to inhale learning, walking amid their foliage; and the odour of their old moth-scented coverings is fragrant as the first bloom of those sciential apples which grew amid the happy orchard.--C. LAMB. *Oxford in the Vacation.*

THE BODLEIAN: A DEAD SEA OF BOOKS

Few places affected me more than the Libraries, and especially the Bodleian Library, re-puted to have half a million printed books and manuscripts. I walked solemnly and reverently among the alcoves and through the halls, as if in the pyramid of embalmed souls. It was their life, their heart, their mind, that they treasured in these book-urns. Si-lent as they are, should all the emotions that went to their creation have utterance, could the world itself contain the various sound? They longed for fame? Here it is--to stand silently for ages, moved only to be dusted and catalogued, valued only as units in the ambitious total, and gazed at, occasionally, by men as ignorant as I am, of their name, their place, their language, and their worth. Indeed, unless a man can link his written thoughts with the everlasting wants of men, so that they shall draw from them as from wells, there is no more immortality to the thoughts and feelings of the soul than to the muscles and the bones. A library is but the soul's burial-ground. It is the land of shad-ows.

Yet one is impressed with the thought, the labour, and the struggle, represented in this vast catacomb of books. Who could dream, by the placid waters that issue from the level mouths of brooks into the lake, all the plunges, the whirls, the divisions, and foaming rushes that had brought them down to the tranquil exit? And who can guess through what channels of disturbance, and experiences of sorrow, the heart passed that has emp-tied into this Dead Sea of books?--HENRY WARD BEECHER. *Star Papers.*

A COLLEGE LIBRARY

A churchyard with a cloister running round
And quaint old effigies in act of prayer,
And painted banners mouldering strangely there
Where mitred prelates and grave doctors sleep,
Memorials of a consecrated ground!
Such is this antique room, a haunted place
Where dead men's spirits come, and angels keep
Long hours of watch with wings in silence furled.
Early and late have I kept vigil here;
And I have seen the moonlight shadows trace
Dim glories on the missal's blue and gold,

The work of my scholastic sires, that told
Of quiet ages men call dark and drear,
For Faith's soft light is darkness to the world.

F. W. FABER.

MERTON LIBRARY

Quaint gloomy chamber, oldest relic left
Of monkish quiet, like a ship thy form,
Stranded keel upward by some sudden storm;
Now that a safe and polished age hath cleft
Locks, bars and chains, that saved thy tomes from theft,
May Time, a surer robber, spare thine age,
And reverence each huge black-lettered page,
Of real boards and gilt-stamped leather reft.
Long may ambitious students here unseal
The secret mysteries of classic lore;
Though urged not by that blind and aimless zeal
With which the Scot within these walls of yore
Transcribed the Bible without breaking fast,
Toiled through each word and perished at the last.

J. B. NORTON.

OXFORD NIGHTS

About the august and ancient *Square*,
Cries the wild wind; and through the air,
The blue night air, blows keen and chill:
Else, all the night sleeps, all is still.
Now, the lone *Square* is blind with gloom:
Now, on that clustering chestnut bloom,
A cloudy moonlight plays, and falls
In glory upon *Bodley's* walls:
Now, wildlier yet, while moonlight pales,
Storm the tumultuary gales.
O rare divinity of Night!
Season of undisturbed delight:
Glad interspace of day and day!
Without, a world of winds at play:
Within, I hear what dead friends say.
Blow, winds! and round that perfect *Dome*,
Wail as you will, and sweep, and roam:
Above *Saint Mary's* carven home,
Struggle, and smite to your desire

The sainted watchers on her spire:
Or in the distance vex your power
Upon mine own *New College* tower:
You hurt not these! On me and mine,
Clear candlelights in quiet shine:
My fire lives yet! nor have I done
With *Smollett*, nor with *Richardson*:
With, gentlest of the martyrs! *Lamb*,
Whose lover I, long lover, am:
With *Gray*, whose gracious spirit knew
The sorrows of art's lonely few:
With *Fielding*, great, and strong, and tall;
Sterne, exquisite, equivocal;
Goldsmith, the dearest of them all:
While *Addison's* demure delights
Turn *Oxford*, into *Attic*, nights.
Still *Trim* and *Parson Adams* keep
Me better company, than sleep:
Dark sleep, who loves not me; nor I
Love well her nightly death to die,
And in her haunted chapels lie.
Sleep wins me not: but from his shelf
Brings me each wit his very self:
Beside my chair the great ghosts throng,
Each tells his story, sings his song:
And in the ruddy fire I trace
The curves of each *Augustan* face.
I sit at *Doctor Primrose'* board:
I hear *Beau Tibbs* discuss a lord.
Mine, *Matthew Bramble's* pleasant wrath;
Mine, all the humours of the *Bath*.
Sir Roger and the *Man in Black*
Bring me the *Golden Ages* back.
Now white *Clarissa* meets her fate,
With virgin will inviolate:
Now *Lovelace* wins me with a smile,
Lovelace, adorable and vile.
I taste, in slow alternate way,
Letters of *Lamb*, letters of *Gray*:
Nor lives there, beneath Oxford towers,
More joy, than in my silent hours.
Dream, who love dreams! forget all grief:
Find, in sleep's nothingness, relief:
Better my dreams! Dear, human books,
With kindly voices, winning looks!
Enchaunt me with your spells of art,
And draw me homeward to your heart:
Till weariness and things unkind

Seem but a vain and passing wind:
Till the grey morning slowly creep
Upward, and rouse the birds from sleep:
Till *Oxford* bells the silence break,
And find me happier, for your sake.
Then, with the dawn of common day,
Rest you! But I, upon my way,
What the fates bring, will cheerlier do,
In days not yours, through thoughts of you!

L. JOHNSON.

ON THE LIBRARY AT CAMBRIDGE

In that great maze of books I sighed, and said,--
  'It is a grave-yard, and each tome a tomb;
Shrouded in hempen rags, behold the dead,
  Coffined and ranged in crypts of dismal gloom,--
Food for the worm and redolent of mould,
Traced with brief epitaph in tarnished gold.'--
  Ah, golden-lettered hope!--Ah, dolorous doom!
Yet, mid the common death, when all is cold,
  And mildewed pride in desolation dwells,
A few great Immortalities of old
  Stand brightly forth;--not tombs but living shrines,
Where from high saint or martyr virtue wells,
Which on the living yet works miracles,
  Spreading a relic wealth, richer than golden mines.

J. M.

THE SOUL'S VIATICUM

Books looked on as to their readers or authors do at the very first mention challenge pre-eminence above the world's admired fine things. Books are the glass of council to dress ourselves by. They are life's best business: vocation to these hath more emolument coming in than all the other busy terms of life. They are fee-less councillors, no delaying patrons, of easy access, and kind expedition, never sending away empty any client or petitioner. They are for company the best friends; in doubts, counsellors; in damp, comforters; Time's perspective; the home traveller's ship, or horse, the busy man's best recreation; the opiate of idle weariness; the mind's best ordinary; Nature's garden and seed-plot of Immortality. Time spent, needlessly, from them is consumed, but with them twice gained. Time captivated and snatched from thee by incursions of business, thefts of visitants, or by thy own carelessness lost, is by these redeemed in life; they are the soul's viaticum; and against death its cordial. In a true verdict, no such treasure as a library.--B. WHITELOCKE.

NOTES

PAGE 1. *Lamb.*--The extracts from the works of Charles Lamb are from the Oxford edition, edited by T. Hutchinson. Not content with 'grace' before Milton and Shakespeare, Lamb suggests elsewhere (see p. 100) a solemn service.

P. 1. *Petrarch.*--When the love-sick Petrarch retired from Avignon to Vaucluse, in 1338, his only companions were his books; for his friends rarely visited him, alleging that his mode of life was unnatural. Petrarch replied as in the text, which is quoted from Mrs. S. Dodson's *Life.* On another occasion, however, Petrarch wrote: 'Many have found the multitude of their books a hindrance to learning, and abundance has bred want, as sometimes happens. But if the many books are at hand, they are not to be cast aside, but to be gleaned, and the best used; and care should be taken that those which might have proved seasonable auxiliaries do not become hindrances out of season.' See Leigh Hunt's reference on page 17 to Petrarch as 'the god of the Bibliomaniacs'.

P. 2. *Waller.*--Carlyle, aged 22, wrote to Robert Mitchell that, lacking society, he found 'books are a ready and effectual resource'. 'It is lawful,' he added, 'for the solitary wight to express the love he feels for those companions so steadfast and unpresuming--that go or come without reluctance, and that, when his fellow-animals are proud or stupid or peevish, are ever ready to cheer the languor of his soul, and gild the barrenness of life with the treasures of bygone times.'

Walter Pater, in *Appreciations: Style*, observes that 'different classes of persons, at different times, make, of course, very various demands upon literature. Still, scholars, I suppose, and not only scholars but all disinterested lovers of books, will always look to it, as to all other fine art, for a refuge, a sort of cloistral refuge, from a certain vulgarity in the actual world. A perfect poem like *Lycidas*, a perfect fiction like *Esmond*, the perfect handling of a theory like Newman's *Idea of a University*, has for them something of the uses of a religious "retreat".'

P. 3. *Chesterfield.*--Folio, a book whose sheets are folded into two leaves; quarto, sheets folded into four leaves, abbreviated into 4to; octavo, sheets folded into eight leaves, 8vo; duodecimo, sheets folded into twelve leaves, 12mo. The first three words come to us from the Italian, through the French; the last is from the Latin *duodecim*.

P. 4. *Southey.*--

> Better than men and women, friend,
>   That are dust, though dear in our joy and pain,
> Are the books their cunning hands have penned,
>   For they depart, but the books remain....
> When others fail him, the wise man looks
> To the sure companionship of books.--R. H. STODDARD.

P. 4. *Southey* ('A heavenly delight').--See p. 250.

P. 4. *Southey* ('The best of all possible company').--Castanheda died in 1559, Barros in 1570, Osorio (da Fonseca) in 1580. They were Portuguese historians.

P. 5. *Emerson.*

> There comes Emerson first, whose rich words, every one,
> Are like gold nails in temples to hang trophies on.--J. R. LOWELL.

P. 6. *Whittier.*--The poet explains that the 'lettered magnate' was his friend Fields (James Thomas, 1817-81), who edited the *Atlantic Monthly*. Among Fields's friends were Leigh Hunt, Barry Cornwall, Miss Mitford, and Dickens. Longfellow's 'Auf Wiedersehen' was written 'in memory of J. T. F.', and Whittier himself wrote some elegiac verse after his death.

It may be noted that Elzevir was the name of a famous family of Dutch printers, whose books were chiefly issued between 1592 and 1681. Louis Elzevir (? 1540-1617) was the first to make the name famous.

P. 8. *Roscoe.*--The sale of Roscoe's library, necessary on account of financial failure, took place in August and September 1816. This Roscoe is the historian of the Medici.

Washington Irving quotes Roscoe's sonnet in his reference to the incident.

P. 8. *Longfellow.*--These valedictory lines were written in December 1881. In the following year Longfellow died.

P. 9. *Jonson.*--Goodyer or Goodier (spelt Goodyere by Herrick) was the friend of Donne and of many other literary men, and he wrote verses on his own account. His father, Sir Henry Goodyer, was the patron of Michael Drayton.

P. 9. *Sheridan.*--Written to Dean Swift, then in London.

P. 10. *Tupper.*--'Next to possessing a true, wise, and victorious friend seated by your fireside, it is blessed to have the spirit of such a friend embodied--for spirit can assume any embodiment--on your bookshelves. But in the latter case the friendship is all on one side. For full friendship your friend must love you, and know that you love him.'--GEORGE

MACDONALD.

Compare C. S. C.'s parody on page 104; and Goethe's statement that he only hated paro-
dies 'because they lower the beautiful, noble, and great'.

P. 11. *de Bury.*--Richard de Bury was born near Bury St. Edmunds in1287, his father being Sir Richard Aungervile. He had a distinguished career at Oxford, and was the tutor of
Edward III. Sent as ambassador to the papal court at Avignon, he formed a friendship
with Petrarch (see pp. 1 and 369). While Bishop of Durham, he was for a short time
Lord Chancellor and also Treasurer of England. He finished the *Philobiblon* less than
three months before he died, in 1345. Thomas Fuller says that he had more books than
all the other English bishops in that age put together. He had a library at each of his resi-
dences, and Mr. E. C. Thomas tells us, on the authority of William de Chambre, that
wherever he was residing so many books lay about his bedchamber that it was hardly
possible to stand or move without treading upon them. All the time he could spare from
business was devoted either to religious offices or to books, and daily at table he would
have a book read to him. The *Philobiblon* was printed first at Cologne in 1473, then ten
years later at Spires, and in 1500 at Paris. The first edition printed in England appeared in
1598, and it was a product of the Oxford Press. It was not until 1832 that any English
translation was published. This, although the name was not divulged in the book, was the
work of John Bellingham Inglis. More than half a century passed before another translation was made--that of Mr. Thomas, who personally examined or collated twenty-eight
MSS. Inglis's translation, according to his successor, is a work of more spirit than accuracy, but it is the spirit that quickeneth, and it is the 1832 volume which I have used.

P. 12. *Addison.*--Ovid, *Met.* xv. 871:

--which nor dreads the rage
Of tempests, fire, or war, or wasting age.--WELSTED.

Fielding says in *Tom Jones*:--'I question not but the ingenious author of the *Spectator* was
principally induced to prefix Greek and Latin mottoes to every paper, from the same
consideration of guarding against the pursuit of those scribblers who, having no talents
of a writer but what is taught by the writing-master, are yet not more afraid nor ashamed
to assume the same titles with the greatest genius, than their good brother in the fable
was of braying in the lion's skin. By the device, therefore, of his motto, it became imprac-
ticable for any man to presume to imitate the *Spectators*, without understanding at least
one sentence in the learned languages.'

'No praise of Addison's style,' Lord Lytton declares, 'can exaggerate its merits. Its art is
perfectly marvellous. No change of time can render the workmanship obsolete. His
manner has that nameless urbanity in which we recognize the perfection of manner--
courteous, but not courtier-like; so dignified, yet so kindly; so easy, yet so high-bred. Its
form of English is fixed--a safe and eternal model, of which all imitation pleases--to
which all approach is scholarship--like the Latin of the Augustan age.'

So much for style. For the rest Hazlitt remarks that 'it is the extremely moral and didactic
tone of the *Spectator* which makes us apt to think of Addison (according to Mandeville's

sarcasm) as "a parson in a tie-wig"'. How often history repeats itself.

P. 12. *Dodd.*--His *Beauties of Shakespeare*, published in 1752, is still well known. Dodd was hanged for forgery, despite many efforts, including those of Dr. Johnson, on his behalf.

P. 13. *Hunt.*--The periods referred to by Leigh Hunt are 'the dark ages, as they are called', and 'the gay town days of Charles II, or a little afterwards'. In the first the essayist imagines 'an age of iron warfare and energy, with solitary retreats, in which the monk or the hooded scholar walks forth to meditate, his precious volume under his arm. In the other, I have a triumphant example of the power of books and wit to contest the victory with sensual pleasure:--Rochester staggering home to pen a satire in the style of Monsieur Boileau; Butler, cramming his jolly duodecimo with all the learning that he laughed at; and a new race of book poets come up, who, in spite of their periwigs and petit-maîtres, talk as romantically of "the bays" as if they were priests of Delphos.'

In Chapman's translation of Homer occur the words: 'The fortresses of thorniest queaches.' A queach is a thick bushy plot, or a quickset hedge.

> You will see Hunt--one of those happy souls
> Which are the salt of the earth, and without whom
> This world would smell like what it is--a tomb.
>
> SHELLEY. *Letter to Maria Gisborne.*

P. 14. *Lamb.*--

> What youth was in thy years,
> What wisdom in thy levity, what truth
> In every utterance of that purest soul!
> Few are the spirits of the glorified
>
> W. S. LANDOR.

> Encumbered dearly with old books,
> Thou, by the pleasant chimney nooks,
> Didst laugh, with merry-meaning looks,
>   Thy griefs away.--LIONEL JOHNSON.

P. 15. *Burton.*--Compare the remark of the 'Hammock School' reviewers in Mr. G. K. Chesterton's *The Napoleon of Notting Hill*--'Next to authentic goodness in a book (and that, alas! we never find) we desire a rich badness.'

P. 15. *Channing.*--An address introductory to the Franklin lectures delivered at Boston, 1838. Channing's influence increased after his death, which occurred in 1842. In the seventies nearly 50,000 copies of his *Complete Works* were circulated in America and Europe.

P. 26. *Hunt.*--The novel *Camilla* is Madame D'Arblay's; the entire passage relating to the Oxford scholar's books is given on page 167. Petrarch is quoted on pages 1 and 289.

P. 17. *Landor.*--See 'Old-Fashioned Verse'.

P. 21. *Burton.*--Lord Byron is reported by Moore to have said: 'The book, in my opinion, most useful to a man who wishes to acquire the reputation of being well read, with the least trouble, is Burton's *Anatomy of Melancholy*, the most amusing and instructive medley of quotations and classical anecdotes I ever perused. But a superficial reader must take care, or his intricacies will bewilder him. If, however, he has patience to go through his volumes, he will be more improved for literary conversation than by the perusal of any twenty other works with which I am acquainted, at least in the English language.'

Dr. Johnson, while admitting that the *Anatomy* is a valuable work, suggests that it is over-loaded with quotation. But he adds, 'It is the only book that ever took me out of bed two hours sooner than I wished to rise.'

P. 22. *Southey.*--'Southey's appearance is *Epic*; and he is the only existing entire man of letters. All the others have some pursuit annexed to their authorship'.--LORD BYRON.

> Ye, loved books, no more
> Shall Southey feed upon your precious lore,
> To works that ne'er shall forfeit their renown,
> Adding immortal labours of his own.--WORDSWORTH.
> (Inscription for a monument in Crosthwaite Church).

P. 26. *Montaigne.*--Michel Eyquem, Seigneur de Montaigne, began to write his essays in his château at Montaigne in Périgord in 1572, at the age of thirty-nine. The essays were published in 1580, and five editions had appeared before his death in 1592.

The Essayes of Michael Lord of Montaigne translated by John Florio were first published in 1603. The translator was born in London about 1553, and he died in 1625. It is this translation from which my excerpts are given, and it is the only book known to have been in Shakespeare's library; the volume contains his autograph, and is now in the British Museum.

Emerson classes Montaigne in his *Representative Men* as the Sceptic. He calls to mind that Gibbon reckoned, in the bigoted times of the period, but two men of liberality in France--Henry IV and Montaigne--and adds, 'Though a Biblical plainness, coupled with a most uncanonical levity, may shut his pages to many sensitive readers, yet the offence is superficial.... I know not anywhere the book that seems less written. It is the language of conversation transferred to a book.'

P. 36. *Denham.*--Dominico Mancini wrote the *Libellus de quattuor Virtutibus*, published in Paris, 1484.

P. 30. *Johnson.*--The excerpts from Johnson and from Boswell's *Life* are taken, where possible, from Dr. Birkbeck Hill's Oxford edition.

P. 32. *Rabelais.*--The translation is that of Peter Anthony Motteux (1660-1718) and of Sir

Thomas Urquhart (1611-1660).

It may be remembered that Pantagruel on his travels found in Paris 'the library of St. Victor, a very stately and magnificent one, especially in some books which were there', of which the Repertory or Catalogue is given. A few of the titles are:--*The Pomegranate of Vice*, *The Henbane of the Bishops*, *The Crucible of Contemplation*, *The Flimflams of the Law*, *The Pleasures of the Monachal Life*, *Sixty-nine fat Breviaries*, and *The Chimney-sweeper of Astrology*. Some of the titles are too 'Rabelaesian', or what some booksellers call 'curious', to print. A certain number of the books appear to have actually existed outside the author's imagination.

P. 35. *Herrick*.--These are, of course, separate poems, scattered fruit of the *Hesperides*.

'Absyrtus-like': an allusion, of course, to the story of Medea, who took her brother Absyrtus with her when she fled with Jason. Being nearly overtaken by her father, Medea murdered Absyrtus, and strewed the road with pieces of his body so that the pursuit might be stayed.

P. 36. *Daniel*.--This sonnet was prefaced to the second edition of Florio's *Montaigne* (1613), and is often ascribed to the translator; but the weight of criticism credits the authorship to Daniel. Mr. Locker-Lampson was tempted to write a couple of verses for the fly-leaf of the Rowfant Montaigne, which not only belonged to Shakespeare, but was also given by Pope to Gay and enjoyed by Johnson:

For me the halycon days have passed,
I'm here and with a dunce at last.

See note on previous page.

P. 37. *Milton*.--Milton's prose masterpiece was printed, in a modified form, by Mirabeau, under the title *Sur la Liberté de la Presse*, imité de l'Anglais, de Milton.

P. 38. *Leighton*.--

Methinks in that refulgent sphere
  That knows not sun or moon,
An earth-born saint might long to hear
  One verse of 'Bonnie Doon'.--O. W. HOLMES.

P. 39. *Hazlitt*.--'Because they both wrote essays and were fond of the Elizabethans,' Mr. Augustine Birrell says, 'it became the fashion to link Hazlitt's name with Lamb's. Hazlitt suffered by the comparison.'

P. 40. *Hunt*.--The poet is Wordsworth and the lines 'Oh that my name' are found in 'Personal Talk'. See page 18.

P. 42. *Carlyle*.--In *The Hero as Priest* Carlyle wrote of Luther's written works: 'The dialect of these speculations is now grown obsolete for us; but one still reads them with a singular attraction. And indeed the mere grammatical diction is still legible enough; Luther's merit in literary history is of the greatest; his dialect became the language of all writing. They are not well written, these Four-and-twenty Quartos of his; written hastily, with quite other than literary objects. But in no Books have I found a more robust, genuine, I will say noble faculty of a man than in these. A rugged honesty, homeliness, simplicity; a rugged sterling sense and strength. He flashes-out illumination from him; his smiting idiomatic phrases seem to cleave into the very secret of the matter. Good humour too, nay, tender affection, nobleness, and depth: this man could have been a Poet too! He had to *work* an Epic Poem, not write one.'

> Beneath the rule of men entirely great
> The pen is mightier than the sword. Behold
> The arch-enchanter's wand!--itself a nothing.--
> But taking sorcery from the master-hand
> To paralyse the Caesars, and to strike
> The loud earth breathless!--Take away the sword--
> States can be saved without it!

LYTTON. *Richelieu*, Act II, sc. ii.

P. 43. *Macaulay.*--'Macaulay is like a book in breeches.'--SYDNEY SMITH.

P. 43. *Maurice.*--The first Ptolemy founded the famous Alexandrian Library which is supposed to have been partly destroyed by Christian fanatics in 391 A.D., the Arabs in 641 completing the work of destruction.

P. 45. *Fuller.*--'Fuller's language!' Coleridge writes: 'Grant me patience, Heaven! A tithe of his beauties would be sold cheap for a whole library of our classical writers, from Addison to Johnson and Junius inclusive. And Bishop Nicolson!--a painstaking old charwoman of the Antiquarian and Rubbish Concern! The venerable rust and dust of the whole firm are not worth an ounce of Fuller's earth!'

The rest of this essay will be found on page 61. The learned man referred to in the last paragraph is Erasmus.

P. 47. *Browne.*--Pineda in *Monarchica Ecclesiastica* mentions 1,040authors. See the note above on Maurice.

P. 48. *Addison.*--'The multiplication of readers is the multiplication of loaves. On the day when Christ created that symbol, he caught a glimpse of printing. His miracle is this marvel. Behold a book. I will nourish with it five thousand souls--a million souls--all humanity. In the action of Christ bringing forth the loaves, there is Gutenberg bringing forth books. One sower heralds the other.... Gutenberg is for ever the auxiliary of life; he is the permanent fellow-workman in the great work of civilization. Nothing is done without him. He has marked the transition of the man-slave to the free man. Try and deprive civilization of him, you become Egypt.'--VICTOR HUGO on Shakespeare.

P. 48. *De Quincey.*--'The few shelves which would hold all the true classics extant might receive as many more of the like as there is any chance that the next two or three centuries could produce, without burthening the select and leisurely scholar with a sense of how much he had to read.'--C. PATMORE. *Principle in Art: William Barnes.*

P. 50. *Temple.*--Sir William Temple's historic dispute with Wotton and Bentley, in which he had the assistance of Charles Boyle, afterwards Earl of Orrery, provoked Swift's *Battle of the Books.* Compare Boileau's *La Lutrin.*

P. 50. *Swift.*--'"The Battle of the Books" is the fancy of a lover of libraries.'--LEIGH HUNT.

The royal library at St. James's alluded to was one of the nine privileged libraries which received copies of new books under the Copyright Act of Anne. The privilege passed to the British Museum in1757, when George II made over the royal collection to the nation.

P. 52. *Bacon.*--Sir William Temple in his *Essay on the Ancient and Modern Learning* (pp. 47, 50) concludes 'with a Saying of Alphonsus Sirnamed the Wise, King of Aragon: That among so many things as are by Men possessed or pursued in the Course of their Lives, all the rest are Bawbles, Besides Old Wood to Burn, Old Wine to Drink, Old Friends to Converse with, and Old Books to Read'.

P. 53. *Goldsmith.*--Horace Walpole wrote to the Rev. William Cole (Letter 2337; Oxford edition): 'There is a chapter in Voltaire that would cure anybody of being a great man even in his own eyes. It is the chapter in which a Chinese goes into a bookseller's shop, and marvels at not finding any of his own country's classics.'

P. 54. *Hazlitt.*--'William Hazlitt, I believe, has no books, except mine; but he has Shakespeare and Rousseau by heart.'--LEIGH HUNT.

P. 55. *Hazlitt.*--Hazlitt wrote this essay in Florence, on his honeymoon, and it opens with a quotation from Sterne: 'And what of this new book, that the whole world make such a rout about?' Lord Byron had died in the previous year, 1824.

'Laws are not like women, the worse for being old.'--The Duke of Buckingham's speech in the House of Lords in Charles the Second's time (Hazlitt's note).

P. 56. *Dudley.*--Rogers is reported to have said, 'When a new book comes out I read an old one.'

P. 57. *Macaulay.*--Pyrgopolynices (Plautus: *Miles Gloriosus*); Thraso (Terence: *Eunuch*); Bobadil (Ben Jonson: *Every Man in his Humour*); Bessus (Beaumont and Fletcher: *A King and no King*); Pistol (*The Merry Wives of Windsor*); Parolles (*All's Well that Ends Well*); Nephelococcygia (Aristophanes: *The Birds*--the cuckoos' town in the clouds); Lilliput (Swift: *Gulliver's Travels*--the pygmies' country).

P. 60. *Ascham.*--Thomas Blundeville wrote some lines in praise of Roger Ascham's Latin grammar:--

Of English books as I could find,
I have perused many a one:
Yet so well done unto my mind,
As this is, yet have I found none.

The words of matter here do rise,
So fitly and so naturally,
As heart can wish or wit devise,
In my conceit and fantasy.

The words well chosen and well set,
Do bring such light unto the sense:
As if I lacked I would not let
To buy this book for forty pence.

This was published in 1561.

P. 61. *Wither.*--Bevis of Hampton, a hero of early mediaeval romance. The story has been published by the Early English Text Society.

Compare 'The common rabble of scribblers and blur-papers which nowadays stuff stationers' shops.'--MONTAIGNE.

P. 61. *Fuller.*--The other portion of this essay will be found on page 57. Arius Montanus was the court chaplain of Philip II of Spain, and he personally superintended the printing of the *Biblia Polyglotta* (8vols., 1569-73), the most famous of the books printed by Christophe Plantin. The printing office is one of the sights of Antwerp, whose council bought the property from Plantin's descendants in 1876 for £48,000.

Compare also: 'Evil books corrupt at once both our manners and our taste.'--FIELDING.

P. 62. *Addison.*--Addison 'takes off the severity of this speculation' with an anecdote of an atheistical author who was sick unto death. A curate, to comfort him, said he did not believe any besides the author's particular friends or acquaintance had ever been at the pains of reading his book, or that anybody after his death would ever inquire after it. 'The dying Man had still so much the Frailty of an Author in him, as to be cut to the Heart with these Consolations; and without answering the good Man, asked his Friends about him (with a Peevishness that is natural to a sick Person) where they had picked up such a Blockhead?' It seems that the author recovered, 'and has since written two or three other Tracts with the same Spirit, and very luckily for his poor Soul with the same success.'

P. 65. *Milton.*--'For he [Pliny the Elder] read no book which he did not make extracts from. He used to say that "no book was so bad but some good might be got out of it."'--PLINY THE YOUNGER.

P. 65. *Baxter.*--'Richard, Richard, dost thou think we will let thee poison the court? Richard, thou art an old knave. Thou hast written books enough to load a cart, and every book as full of sedition as an egg is full of meat.'--Judge Jeffreys' address at Baxter's trial.

P. 66. *Athenian Mercury.*--An 'answer to correspondents'--the question 'Whether 'tis lawful to read Romances?' being asked in *The Athenian Mercury*. This, the first popular periodical published in this country, was started in 1691, and written by John Dunton, R. Sault, and Samuel (the father of John) Wesley; the last number appeared in 1697, and Dunton collected into three volumes the most valuable questions and answers under the title of *The Athenian Oracle*.

Gray's wish was to be always lying on sofas, reading 'eternal new novels of Crébillon and Marivaux'.

P. 67. *Cobbett.*--Cobbett attacks Dr. Johnson, because in a pamphlet he urged war on the American colonies; Burke, because in another pamphlet he urged war on revolutionary France. 'The first war lost us America, the last cost us six hundred millions of money, and has loaded us with forty millions a year of taxes.'

P. 67. *More.*--Tom Hickathrift, who killed a giant at Tylney, Norfolk, with a cartwheel. He dates from the Conquest, and was made governor of Thanet.

P. 67. *Austen.*--*Cecilia* and *Camilla*, both by Mme. D'Arblay; *Belinda*, by Miss Edgeworth.

'She [Diana] says of Romance: "The young who avoid that region escape the title of Fool at the cost of a celestial crown."'-GEORGE MEREDITH. *Diana of the Crossways*.

P. 67. *Herschel.*--'The most influential books, and the truest in their influence, are works of fiction.'--R. L. STEVENSON.

P. 69. *Burton.*--'They lard their lean books with the fat of others' works.'--BURTON.

P. 70. *Milton.*--South said that *Eikon Basilike* was 'composed with such an unfailing majesty of diction, that it seems to have been written with a sceptre rather than a pen'.

Milton condemns the king for having 'so little care of truth in his last words, or honour to himself, or to his friends, or sense of his afflictions, or of that sad hour which was upon him, as immediately before his death to pop into the hand of that grave bishop [Juxon] who attended him, for a special relic of his saintly exercises, a prayer stolen word for word from the mouth of a heathen woman praying to a heathen god; and that in no serious book, but the vain amatorious poem of Sir Philip Sidney's *Arcadia*'.

P. 91. *Dryden.*--Hazlitt, who could not 'much relish Ben Jonson', describes him as 'a great borrower from the works of others, and a plagiarist even from nature; so little freedom is there in his imitations of her, and he appears to receive her bounty like an alms'. J. A. Symonds, stating that Jonson 'held the prose writers and poets of antiquity in solution in his spacious memory', points out that such looting on his part of classical treasuries of wit and wisdom was accounted no robbery in his age.

P. 71. *Sheridan.*--Churchill has the same thought in *The Apology*:

Like gypsies, lest the stolen brat be known,
Defacing first, then claiming for their own.

P. 72. *Pattison.*--Matthew Arnold, in the preface to *Literature and Dogma* (1873), points out that 'To read to good purpose we must read a great deal, and be content not to use a great deal of what we read. We shall never be content not to use the whole, or nearly the whole, of what we read, unless we read a great deal.'

P. 74. *Mitford.*--'Every abridgement of a good book is a stupid abridgement.'--MONTAIGNE.

P. 98. *Tennyson.*--J. J. Jusserand, in the first annual Shakespeare lecture before the British Academy (July 5, 1911), used eloquent language which might be said to justify bibliographies:--'Books, like their authors, have their biography. They live their own lives. Some behave like honourable citizens of the world of thought, do good, propagate sound views, strengthen heart and courage, assuage, console, improve those men to whose hearths they have been invited. Others corrupt or debase, or else turn minds towards empty frivolities. In proportion to their fame, and to the degree of their perenniality, is the good or evil that they do from century to century, eternal benefactors of mankind or deathless malefactors. Posted on the road followed by humanity, they help or destroy the passers-by; they deserve gratitude eternal, or levy the toll of some of our life's blood, leaving us weaker; highwaymen or good Samaritans. Some make themselves heard at once and continue to be listened to for ever; others fill the ears for one or two generations, and then begin an endless sleep; or, on the contrary, long silent or misunderstood, they awake from their torpor, and astonished mankind discovers with surprise long-concealed treasures like those trodden upon by the unwary visitor of unexplored ruins.'

P. 76. *Helps.*--'My desire is ... that mine adversary had written a book.'--The Author of Job, ch. 31.

'Curll, Pope's victim and accomplice ... hit on one of those epoch-making ideas which are so simple when once they are conceived, so difficult, save for the loftiest genius, in their first conception. It occurred to him that, in a world governed by the law of mortality, men might be handsomely entertained on one another's remains. He lost no time in putting his theory into action. During the years of his activity he published some forty or fifty separate *Lives*, intimate, anecdotal, scurrilous sometimes, of famous and notorious persons who had the ill-fortune to die during his lifetime.... His books commanded a large sale, and modern biography was established.'--SIR W. RALEIGH. *Six Essays on Johnson.*

It is related in *The Percy Anecdotes* that 'A gentleman calling on Archbishop Tillotson observed in his library one shelf of books of various forms and sizes, all richly bound, finely gilt and lettered. He inquired what favourite authors these were that had been so remarkably distinguished by his Grace. "These," said the Archbishop, "are my own personal friends; and what is more I have made them such (for they were avowedly my enemies), by the use I have made of those hints which their malice had suggested to me. From these I have received more profit than from the advice of my best and most cordial friends; and therefore you see I have rewarded them accordingly.'"

P. 76. *Disraeli.*--Compare Emerson: 'There is properly no history, only biography; and Carlyle: 'History is the essence of innumerable biographies.'

'Those that write of men's lives,' says Montaigne, 'forasmuch as they amuse and busy themselves more about counsels than events, more about that which cometh from within than that which appeareth outward; they are fittest for me.'

P. 79. *Glanvill.*--An original Fellow of the Royal Society, and in many ways an interesting divine, probably best known in these days through Matthew Arnold's 'Scholar-Gypsy', whose story is told in *The Vanity of Dogmatizing* (1661), from which this quotation and that on page 118 are made.

P. 79. *Jonson.*--The poem 'To the Memory of my Beloved Master William Shakespeare, and what he hath left us' appeared in 1623.

P. 79. *Jonson.*--This was printed in the First Folio of Shakespeare's works, 1623, on the page opposite the Droeshout portrait.

P. 81. *Milton.*--These lines were printed anonymously in the Second Folio Shakespeare, 1632, and, it is believed, this was Milton's first appearance as a poet.

P. 82. *Dryden.*--This was printed under the engraving in Tonson's folio edition of *Paradise Lost* (1688). Mr. F. A. Mumby, in *The Romance of Bookselling*, recalls that in Moseley's first edition of Milton's poems there was an atrocious portrait of the poet by William Marshall. Milton wrote four lines in Greek, which the artist, innocent of that language, gravely cut into the plate, lines that Dr. Masson has thus translated:

That an unskilful hand had carved this print
You'd say at once, seeing the living face;
But, finding here no jot of me, my friends,
Laugh at the botching artist's mis-attempt.

P. 83. *Fletcher.*--The subject of this poem was Giles Fletcher, the author of *Christ's Victory and Triumph*, 'equally beloved of the Muses and Graces.'

P. 83. *Crashaw.*--From *The Flaming Heart*. 'His masterpiece, one of the most astonishing things in English or any literature, comes without warning at the end of *The Flaming Heart*. For page after page the poet has been playing on some trifling conceit ... and then in a moment, in the twinkling of an eye, without warning of any sort, the metre changes, the poet's inspiration catches fire, and then rushes up into the heaven of poetry the marvellous rocket of song: "Live in these conquering leaves," &c. The contrast is perhaps unique as regards the colourlessness of the beginning and the splendid colour of the end. But contrasts like it occur all over Crashaw's work.'--PROFESSOR SAINTSBURY. *History of Elizabethan Literature.*

As an interesting example of Crashaw's conceits it may be noted that, when alluding to Mary Magdalene, he speaks of her eyes as 'Portable and compendious oceans.'

P. 83. *Voltaire.*--The philosopher also remarks, in the same article, that 'there is hardly a single philosophical or theological book in which heresies and impieties may not be found by misinterpreting, or adding to, or subtracting from, the sense'.

P. 86. *Carlyle.*--Abelard, born 1079, died 1142, is less known now as a famous teacher at the University of Paris than as the lover of Héloise.

P. 88. *Trapp and Browne.*--When George I sent a present of some books, in November 1715, to the University of Cambridge, he sent at the same time a troop of horse to Oxford. This inspired Dr. Trapp and provoked the rejoinder from Sir William Browne.

P. 88. *Earle.*--Mr. A. S. West, in his edition of Earle's *Microcosmographie; or a Piece of the World discovered; in Essayes and Characters*, says: 'The critic supposed that *omneis* was the original form of the accusative plural of *omnis*, and that the forms *omnes* and *omnis* had taken its place. In order to adhere to the older spelling "he writes *omneis* at length". *Quicquid* is cited as an instance of pedantry because the ordinary man wrote the word as *quidquid*, and doubtless so pronounced it. The critic's gerund may be described as "inconformable" because it resists attraction--remains a gerund and does not become a gerundive. Or Earle may have had in view passages in which the gerund of transitive verbs with *est* govern an object.'

P. 89. *Goldsmith.*--'When Dr. Johnson is free to confess that he does not admire Gray's *Elegy*, and Macaulay to avow that he sees little to praise in Dickens and Wordsworth, why should not humbler folks have the courage of their opinions?' Such is the question asked by James Payn in the *Nineteenth Century* (March 1880), his article being entitled 'Sham Admiration in Literature'. Mr. Payn noted that 'curiously enough, it is women who have the most courage in the expression of their literary opinions', instancing the authoress of *Jane Eyre*, who 'did not derive much pleasure from the perusal of the works of the other Jane [Austen]', and Harriet Martineau, who confessed to him that she could see no beauties in *Tom Jones*.

'There is no ignorance more shameful than to admit as true that which one does not understand: and there is no advantage so great as that of being set free from error.'--XENOPHON. *Memorabilia.*

P. 91. *Fielding.*--'What a master of composition Fielding was! Upon my word, I think the *Oedipus Tyrannus*, *The Alchemist*, and *Tom Jones*, the three most perfect plots ever planned.... How charming, how wholesome, Fielding always is!'--S. T. COLERIDGE. *Table Talk.*

P. 95. *Erasmus.*--The translation is the work of Nathaniel Bailey, lexicographer and schoolmaster, who died in 1742. Desiderius and Erasmus are Latin and Greek for Gerhard 'the beloved', the name of the scholar's father.

P. 95. *Colton.*--Compare R. B. Sheridan's: 'Easy writing's curst hard reading.'

P. 95. *Bacon.*--Mr. A. S. Gaye, in the new Clarendon Press edition of the *Essays*, points out that on almost every page the reader will find quotations from the Bible and from the Greek and Latin classics, especially Tacitus, Plutarch, Cicero, Virgil, Seneca, and Ovid, besides frequent allusions to biblical, classical, and mediaeval history. 'It is also remarkable that the quotations are more often than not inaccurate, not only in words but in sense.... Bacon furnished in himself an exception to the rule which he laid down in his Essay "Of Studies"; for though "reading" made him "a full man", "writing" did not make him "an exact man".'

P. 98. *Boswell.*--One of Mrs. Piozzi's anecdotes of Dr. Johnson is that he asked 'Was there ever yet anything written by mere man that was wished longer by its readers excepting *Don Quixote*, *Robinson Crusoe*, and the *Pilgrim's Progress*?' Johnson declared that the work of Cervantes was the greatest in the world, 'speaking of it, I mean, as a book of entertainment.'

P. 102. *Emerson.*--Shakespeare's phrase: *Taming of the Shrew*, Act I, sc. i.

P. 102. *Emerson.*--O. W. Holmes applies the proverb to the Bible. 'What you bring away from the Bible depends to some extent on what you carry to it.'

P. 104. *Calverley.*--See Tupper's lines on page 12. The allusions are, of course, to the creations of Bulwer-Lytton.

P. 106. *Gibbon.*--F. W. Robertson's opinion is worth recording: 'It is very surprising to find how little we retain of a book, how little we have really made our own, when we come to interrogate ourselves as to what account we can give of it, however we may seem to have mastered it by understanding it. Hundreds of books read once have passed as completely from us as if we had never read them; whereas the discipline of mind got by writing down, not copying, an abstract of a book which is worth the trouble, fixes it on the mind for years, and, besides, enables one to read other books with more attention and more profit.'

P. 107. *Hamilton.*--'This assumes that the book to be operated on is your own, and perhaps is rather too elaborate a counsel of perfection for most of us.'--LORD MORELY.

P. 107. *Addison.*--Hor. *Ars Poet.* 1. 319:--

  When the sentiments and manners please,
And all the characters are wrought with ease,
Your tale, though void of beauty, force, and art,
More strongly shall delight and warm the heart;
Than where a lifeless pomp of verse appears,
And with sonorous trifles charms our ears.--FRANCIS

Butler, writing of 'A small poet' (*Characters*), says: 'There was one that lined a hat-case with a paper of Benlowe's poetry: Prynne bought it by chance, and put a new demicastor into it. The first time he wore it he felt a singing in his head, which within two days turned to a vertigo.' A 'demicastor' is a hat.

P. 112. *Scott.*--Mr. W. J. Courthope, in his Warton Lecture on English Poetry before the British Academy, read on October 25, 1911, observes that 'the best illustration of historic change in "romantic" temper is perhaps to be found in a comparison of Cervantes' account of the character of Don Quixote [see p. 118] with Walter Scott's representation of the romanticism of the hero of *Waverley.* Don Quixote's "fancy", says Cervantes, "grew full of what he used to read about in his books, enchantments, battles, challenges, wounds, wooings, loves, agonies, and all sorts of impossible nonsense; and it so possessed his mind that the whole fabric of invention and fancy he read of was true, that to him no history in the world had more reality in it." ... "My intention," says Scott, "is not to follow the steps of the inimitable Cervantes in describing such total perversion of intellect as misconstrues the objects actually presented to the senses, but the more common aberration from sound judgement, which apprehends occurrences indeed in their reality, but communicates to them a tincture of its own romantic colouring."' Scott expatiates at length on Waverley's reading in the third chapter of his novel.

P. 113. *Boswell.*--Macaulay writes in his review of Southey's edition of *The Pilgrim's Progress:* 'Doctor Johnson, all whose studies were desultory, and who hated, as he said, to read books through, made an exception in favour of *The Pilgrim's Progress.* That work was one of the two or three works which he wished longer. It was by no common merit that the illiterate sectary extracted praise like this from the most pedantic of critics and the most bigoted of Tories.'

Boswell relates that Dr. Johnson 'had a peculiar facility in seizing at once what was valuable in any book, without submitting to the labour of perusing it from beginning to end.'

P. 114. *Chandos.*--The authorship of *Horae Subsecivae* is not absolutely known, but it is attributed to James I's favourite courtier. It was published in 1620, the year before Chandos died.

P. 114. *Waller.*--'A library well chosen cannot be too extensive, but some there are who amass a great quantity of books, which they keep for show, and not for service. Of such persons, Louis XI of France aptly enough observed, that "they resembled *hunch-backed* people, who carried a great burden, which *they never saw*".'--W. KEDDIE. *Cyclopaedia.*

P. 116. *Coleridge.*--The most deadly thing that Coleridge wrote was when he classed the patrons of the circulating libraries as lower in the scale than that reading public nine-tenths of whose reading is confined to periodicals and 'Beauties, elegant Extracts and Anas [Anecdotes]'.

P. 117. *Boswell.*--Dr. Birkbeck Hill points out that Boswell alludes to this opinion in one of his letters, modestly adding: 'I am afraid I have not read books enough to be able to talk from them.' Johnson particularized Langton as talking from books, 'and Garrick would if he talked seriously.'

P. 118. *S. Smith.*--Bettinelli, a scholar and a Jesuit (1718-1808), who attacked the reputation of Dante and Petrarch.

Coventry Patmore wrote: 'If you want to shine as a diner-out, the best way is to know something which others do not know, and not to know many things which everybody knows. This takes much less reading, and is doubly effective, inasmuch as it makes you a really good, that is, an interested listener, as well as a talker.'--(*On Obscure Books.*)

P. 118. *Colton.*--'Methinks 'tis a pitiful piece of knowledge that can be learnt from an index and a poor ambition to be rich in the inventory of another's treasure.'--J. GLANVILL. *The Vanity of Dogmatizing.*

P. 118. *Cervantes.*--A whole chapter is devoted to the destruction of Don Quixote's library. (Part i, chap, vi.) The books that, condemned by the priest, were passed into the housekeeper's hands and thence into the fire were:--*Adventures of Esplandian*; *Amadis of Greece*; *Don Olivante de Laura*; *Florismarte of Hyrcania*; *The Knight Platir*; *The Knight of the Cross*; *Bernardo del Carpio*; *Roncesvalles*; *Palmerin de Oliva*; *Diana*, called the Second, by Salmantino; *The Shepherd of Iberia*; *The Nymphs of Henares*; and *The Curse of Jealousy*. The priest, however, put by for further examination or determined to save: *Amadis de Gaul*; *The Mirror of Chivalry*, and 'all other books that shall be found treating of French matters'; *Palmerin of England*; *Don Belianis*; *Tirante the White*; *Diana*, of Montemayor, and its continuation by Gil Polo; *Ten Books of the Fortune of Love*; *The Shepherd of Filida*; *The Treasure of Divers Poems* (de Padilla); *Book of Songs*, by Lopez Maldonado; *Galatea*, by Cervantes; *Araucana*; *Austriada*; *Monserrate*; and the *Tears of Angelica*. The curious reader will find these volumes traced in the admirable notes in J. Fitzmaurice-Kelly's edition of *Don Quixote* in 'The World's Classics'. Cervantes, Mr. Fitzmaurice-Kelly says, devoured in his wandering youth, 'those folios of chivalrous adventures which he, and he alone, has saved from the iniquity of oblivion'. The early association of Barabbas and books will be noticed.

It is the translation by Charles Jervas, first published in 1742, which is here employed.

The Renowned Romance of Amadis of Gaul, by Vasco Lobeira, which was expressly condemned by Montaigne (see p. 110) was translated from the Spanish version of Garciodonez de Montalvo by Southey.

P. 121. *Ruskin.*--As Mr. Frederic Harrison points out, 'Books are no more education than laws are virtue; and, just as profligacy is easy within the strict limits of law, a boundless knowledge of books may be found with a narrow education.'

P. 121. *E. B. Browning.*--This letter was written to 'Orion' Horne three years before Mrs. Browning's marriage in 1843, when she was thirty-seven. Compare Matthew Arnold in the preface to *Literature and Dogma* (1873): 'Nothing can be truer than what Butler says, that really, in general, no part of our time is more idly spent than the time spent in reading. Still, culture is indispensably necessary, and culture is reading; but reading with a purpose to guide it, and with system.'

P. 123. *Maurice.*--This is better than Sydney Smith's attitude expressed in the question, 'Who reads an American book, or goes to an American play, or looks at an American picture or statue?'

P. 124. *Blackie.*--'Reading is seeing by proxy--is learning indirectly through another man's faculties, instead of directly through one's own faculties; and such is the prevailing bias, that the indirect learning is thought preferable to the direct learning, and usurps the name of cultivation.'--HERBERT SPENCER. *The Study of Sociology.*

P. 124. *Montaigne.*--'Montesquieu used to say that he had never known a pain or a distress which he could not soothe by half an hour of a good book.'--LORD MORLEY.

P. 125. *Davies.*--

What is the end of Fame? 'Tis but to fill
  A certain portion of uncertain paper ...
To have, when the original is dust,
A name, a wretched picture, and worse bust.

  LORD BYRON, *Don Juan.*

P. 124. *Hall.*--'Hard students are commonly troubled with gouts, catarrhs, rheums, cachexia, bradiopepsia, bad eyes, stone and colic, crudities, oppitations, vertigo, winds, consumptions, and all such diseases as come by overmuch sitting; they are most part lean, dry, ill-coloured, spend their fortunes, lose their wits, and many times their lives, and all through immoderate pains, and extraordinary studies.'--R. BURTON. *The Anatomy of Melancholy.*

P. 126. *Lytton.*--'I look upon a library as a kind of mental chemist's shop, filled with the crystals of all forms and hues which have come from the union of individual thought with local circumstances or universal principles.'--O. W. HOLMES. *The Professor at the Breakfast-Table.*

P. 129. *Walpole.*--Mr. Augustine Birrell in *Obiter Dicta: The Office of Literature* writes that the author's office is to make the reader happy:--

'Cooks, warriors, and authors must be judged by the effects they produce: toothsome dishes, glorious victories, pleasant books--these are our demands....

'Literature exists to please--to lighten the burden of men's lives; to make them for a short while forget their sorrows and their sins, their silenced hearths, their disappointed hopes, their grim futures--and those men of letters are the best loved who have best performed literature's truest office.'

P. 129. *Chaucer.*--The book referred to is Ovid's *Metamorphoses.*

P. 129. *Digby.*--Sir Kenelm Digby's 'observations' are generally printed with *Religio Medici*, although in a letter to Sir T. Browne, who had written to him on the subject, he explained that the hastily set down notes did not merit the press, and would 'serve only for a private letter, or a familiar discourse with lady-auditors'.

To Sir Thomas Browne, 'a library,' says Coleridge, 'was a living world, and every book a man, absolute flesh and blood.'

P. 129. *Boswell.*--'Who is he that is now wholly overcome with idleness, or otherwise in-volved in a labyrinth of worldly cares, troubles, and discontents, that will not be much lightened in his mind by reading of some enticing story, true or feigned, where as in a glass he shall observe what our forefathers have done, the beginnings, ruins, ends, falls of commonwealths, private men's actions displayed to the life, &c. Plutarch therefore calls them *secundas mensas et bellaria*, the second courses and junkets, because they were usually read at noblemen's feasts.'--R. BURTON. *Anatomy.*

P. 130. *Rabelais.*--

Whence is thy learning? Hath thy toil
O'er books consumed the midnight oil?--J. GAY.

P. 130. *Wilson.*--This is often taken to be an antique. As a matter of fact, Mr. John Wil-son, a London bookseller, stated to Mr. Austin Dobson that he wrote the lines as a motto for one of his second-hand catalogues. Wilson, Mr. Dobson tells us, was amused at the vogue the lines eventually obtained.

P. 131. *Chaucer.*--This is the earlier version, and to be preferred to the later, in which the passage ends:

Farwel my book and my devocioun!

wel unethe=scarcely any.

P. 133. *Tickle.*--'Written in a fit of the gout.'

'And laid the storm,' &c.: the advice given to Augustus by Athenodorus the Stoic philos-opher.

See Shakespeare's *Love's Labour's Lost*, Act v, sc. i. Holofernes 'teaches boys the horn-book'.

P. 138. *Richardson.*--In his preface to *Pamela* Richardson claims to give 'practical examples worthy to be followed in the most critical and affecting cases by the modest virgin, the chaste bride, and the obliging wife'. The heroine becomes Mrs. B----, and Billy is the first-born. Locke's treatise was published in 1693, or forty-seven years before Richard-son's novel, and the philosopher observes 'That most Children's Constitutions are either spoiled, or at least harmed, by *Cockering and Tenderness*'. 'Mr. B.' recommended better than he knew.

P. 138. *Johnson* ('At large in the library').--Ruskin gives the same advice. See p. 160.

P. 140. *Gibbon.*--The *Autobiography*, in Sir Archibald Alison's opinion, is 'the most perfect account of an eminent man's life, from his own hand, which exists in any language'.

P. 141. *Landor.*--See the poem to Wordsworth on p. 18.

P. 141. *Hunt.*--The friend referred to was Shelley.

P. 143. *Dickens.*--Of this passage, Forster says in the *Life of Dickens*, 'It is one of the many passages in *Copperfield* which are literally true.... Every word of this personal recollection had been written down as fact, some years before it found its way into *David Copperfield*; the only change in the fiction being his omission of the name of a cheap series of novelists then in course of publication, by means of which his father had become happily the owner of so large a lump of literary treasure in his small collection of books.'

Apropos of Defoe, Macaulay, who could not 'understand the mania of some people about Defoe', admitted that 'he certainly wrote an excellent book--the first part of *Robinson Crusoe* ... my delight before I was five years old'.

P. 144. *Hazlitt.*--It is reported (Dibdin relates in *Bibliomania*) that a certain man, of the name of Similis, who fought under the Emperor Hadrian, became so wearied and disgusted with the number of troublesome events which he met with in that mode of life, that he retired and devoted himself wholly to leisure and reading, and to meditations upon divine and human affairs, after the manner of Pythagoras. In this retirement, Similis was wont frequently to exclaim that '*now* he began to *live*': at his death he desired the following inscription to be placed upon his tomb.

> Here lies Similis;
> In the seventieth year of his age
> But only the seventh of his life.

In a note it is stated that 'This story is related by Dion Cassius and from him told by Spizelius in his *Infelix Literarius*'.

P. 145. *Donne.*--This is the title given by Donne's editors, but is nonsense. Grosart explains that Pindar's instructress was Corinna the Theban, and that Lucan's 'help' is probably his helpmeet--Argentaria Polla, his wife who survived him.

P. 147. *Dante.*--This is the famous passage in Canto V referring to Paolo and Francesca.-- (Cary's translation.)

P. 151. *Moore.*--

> For where is any author in the world
> Teaches such beauty as a woman's eye?

SHAKESPEARE. *Love's Labour's Lost*, Act IV. Sc. iii.

P. 198. *More.*--Warton thinks it probable that Sir Thomas More--'one of the best jokers of the age'--may have written this epigram, which he considers the first pointed epigram in our language. But by some the lines are credited to Henry Howard, Earl of Surrey, who is memorable, among other things, for introducing the sonnet from Italy into England, a distinction which he shares with Wyatt.

P. 154. *Moore.*--'Mamurra was a dogmatic philosopher, who never doubted about anything, except who was his father; Bombastus, one of the names of the great scholar and quack Paracelsus. St. Jerome was scolded by an angel for reading Cicero, as Gratia tells the story in his *Concordantia discordantium Canonum*, and says, that for this reason bishops were not allowed to read the classics'.

P. 157. *Scott.*--The Roxburgh Club was inaugurated on the day of the sale of the Duke of Roxburgh's library in 1812 in order to print for members rare books or manuscripts. The club had numerous offspring, including the Bannatyne Club (see p. 211, and the note thereon). The Duke of Roxburgh's library, which was celebrated for its Caxtons, sold for £23,341.

P. 158. *E. B. Browning.*--

Here with a Loaf of Bread beneath the Bough,
A Flask of Wine, a Book of Verse--and Thou
  Beside me singing in the Wilderness--
And Wilderness is Paradise enow.

      E. FITZGERALD. *Omar Khayyám.*

P. 160. *Macaulay.*--'Neither we nor divinity require much learning in women; Francis, Duke of Brittany, son to John V, when he was spoke unto for a marriage between him and Isabel, a daughter of Scotland, and some told him she was meanly brought up, and without any instruction of learning, answered he loved her the better for it, and that a woman was wise enough if she could but make a difference between the shirt and doublet of her husband's.'--MONTAIGNE.

P. 161. *Ruskin.*--Compare Johnson's advice on page 138.

P. 161. *Addison.*--Virgil *Aeneid*, vii. 805:

Unused to spinning, in the loom unskilled.--DRYDEN.

The *Virgil* of Ogilby, or Ogilvy, originally a dancing-master, was published in 1649, and was the first complete English translation (Ogilby is mentioned by Pope, see page 313); *Cassandra, Cleopatra, Astraea, The Grand Cyrus* and *Clelia* were French romances translated into English. Sidney called his pastoral romance *The Countess of Pembroke's Arcadia*; Sherlock's *Discourse on Death* passed through forty editions; *The Fifteen Comforts*, a translation of a French satirical work of the fifteenth century; Sir Richard Baker's *Chronicle of the Kings of England from the time of the Romans' Government unto the Death of King James* (1641); Mrs. Manley was tried for libelling the nobility in her *Secret Memoirs and Manners of several Persons of Quality of both Sexes from the New Atlantis* (1707); the Fielding referred to is Beau Fielding, tried at the Old Bailey in 1706 for a bigamous marriage with the Duchess of Cleveland.

In Addison's time, Dr. Johnson wrote, 'in the female world, any acquaintance with books was distinguished only to be censured.'

P. 162. *Addison.*--Hor. 2 *Ep.* ii. 61:

> What would you have me do,
> When out of twenty I can please not two?--
> One likes the pheasant's wing, and one the leg;
> The vulgar boil, the learned roast an egg;
> Hard task, to hit the palate of such guests.--POPE.

The *Vindication* was the work of Charles Leslie, the non-juror; *Pharamond*, a romance dealing with the Frankish empire, by La Calprenède; *Cassandra* is wrong--the French work, also by La Calprenède, was *Cassandre* (the son of Antipater); *All for Love*, Dryden's play; *Sophonisba*, by Lee; *The Innocent Adultery*, the second name of Sotherne's *The Fatal Marriage*; *Mithridates* was by Lee, who also wrote *The Rival Queens, or The Death of Alexander the Great*, and *Theodosius*; *Aureng-Zebe*, Dryden's tragedy. (T. Arnold's *Addison*: Clarendon Press).

P. 164. *Sheridan.*--The first reference to a circulating library given in the *Oxford English Dictionary* is an advertisement, June 12, 1742--'Proposals for erecting a Public Circulating Library in London.' Joseph Knight, in the Oxford edition of Sheridan's *Plays*, annotates this passage fully. Dillingham, sending his Latin translation of Herbert's *Porch* to Sancroft, says: 'I know that if these should be once published, it would be too late then to prevent, if not to correct a fault; I therefore shall take it as a great kindness if you will please to put on your critical naile, and to give your impartial censure on these papers while they are yet in the tireing roome; and I shall endeavour to amend them with one great or more lesser blotts.' Sancroft replies: 'I greedily took your original in one hand, and your copy in the other, of which I had suffered one nayl (though it pretends not to be a critical one) to grow ever since you bespoke its service.'

Compare Herrick:--

> Be bold, my book, nor be abashed, or fear
> The cutting thumb-nail, or the brow severe;
> But by the Muses swear, all here is good,
> If but, well read or ill read, understood.

Blonds=blond laces, produced from unbleached silk.

All the works mentioned have been identified. The *Innocent Adultery* is the alternative title of Sotherne's *Fatal Marriage*; *The Whole Duty of Man* was by Allestree, once Provost of Eton; the 'admirable Mrs. Chapone', an admirer of Richardson, and a contributor to the *Rambler*; 'Under the most repulsive exterior that any woman ever possessed she concealed very superior attainments and extensive knowledge'; Fordyce was Johnson's friend, and his sermons were specially addressed to young women.

P. 167. *Chaucer.*--holwe=hollow; courtepy=short upper coat of a coarse material; fithele=fiddle; sautrye=psaltery; hente=borrow; yaf=gave; scoleye=to attend school;

sentence=sentiment; souninge in=conducing to.

P. 168. *Brant*.--Sebastian Brant's *Narrenschiff*, published in 1497, at Basle, was the first printed book that treated of contemporaneous events and living persons, instead of old German battles and French knights. Barclay's translation, Professor Max Müller points out, 'was not made from the original but from Locher's Latin translation. It reproduces the matter, but not the marrow of the original satire ... in some parts his translation is an improvement on the original.' *The Ship of Fools* in its original form, and in numerous translations, had an enormous success, edition after edition being printed.

aparayle=apparatus.

P. 170. *Young*.--T--n=Tonson.

P. 171. *Ferriar*.--The first edition of this poem was issued as a quarto pamphlet in 1809. It is reprinted in the second volume of the second edition of Ferriar's *Illustrations of Sterne, and other Essays*,1812, with some 140 additional lines.

'He, whom chief the laughing Muses own' is Aristophanes; the lines that follow refer to the fire of London. D--n=Dryden.

'On one of these occasions [a book-auction] a succession of valuable fragments of early English poetry brought prices so high and far beyond those of ordinary expensive books in the finest condition, that it seemed as if their imperfections were their merit; and the auctioneer, momentarily carried off with this feeling, when the high prices began to sink a little, remonstrated thus, "Going so low as thirty shillings, gentlemen,--this curious book--so low as thirty shillings--and *quite imperfect*!"'--J. H. BURTON. *The Book-Hunter*.

Ferriar mentions incidentally most of the famous printers of olden time. Aldine editions were those printed by Aldo Manuzio and his family in Venice from 1490 to 1597. The Elzevir family became famous on account of its duodecimos.

P. 175. *Beresford*.--*Bibliosophia; or Book-wisdom*, by the Rev. J. Beresford, was written as 'a feeling remonstrance against the *prose* work, lately published by the Reverend T. F. Dibdin under the title of *Bibliomania; or Book-madness*', quoted in successive pages.

P. 176. *d'Israeli*.--The verse is imitated from the Latin of 'Henry Rantzau, a Danish gentleman, the founder of the great library at Copenhagen, whose days were dissolved in the pleasures of reading', who 'discovers his taste and ardour in the following elegant effusion'.

P. 177. *d'Israeli*.--'An allusion and pun which occasioned the French translator of the present work an unlucky blunder: puzzled no doubt by my *facetiously*, he translates "mettant comme on l'a *très judicieusement* fait observer, l'entendement humain sous la clef". The book, and the author alluded to, quite escaped him.'--I. D'ISRAELI. *Curiosities of Literature: The Bibliomania, note*.

P. 177. *Dibdin*.--Magliabechi was born at Florence, October 29, 1633. 'He had never learned to read; and yet he was perpetually poring over the leaves of old books that were used in his master's shop. A bookseller, who lived in the neighbourhood, and who had often observed this, and knew the boy could not read, asked him one day "what he meant by staring so much on printed paper?" Magliabechi said that he did not know how it was, but that he loved it of all things. The consequence was that he was received, with tears of joy in his eyes, into the bookseller's shop; and hence rose, by a quick succession, into posts of literary honour, till he became librarian to the Grand Duke of Tuscany.'

P. 181. *Longfellow*.--Bayard Taylor, born 1825, died 1878. The allusion is to the famous monument of the Emperor Maximilian in the Franciscan church, or Hofkirche, at Innsbruck, where a kneeling figure of Maximilian is surrounded by statues of his contemporaries and ancestors. The emperor is buried actually at Wiener-Neustadt. Taylor published *Prince Deukalion: a lyrical drama*, in 1878.

P. 183. *Browning*.--Sibrandus Schafnaburgensis 'is apparently', Mrs. Orr says, without adding to our store of knowledge, 'the name of an old pedant who has written a tiresome book.'

P. 185. *de Bury*.--J. H. Burton, in *The Book-Hunter*, tells the following story:--It was Thomson, I believe, who used to cut the leaves with his snuffers. Perhaps an event in his early career may have soured him of the proprieties. It is said that he had an uncle, a clever active mechanic, who could do many things with his hands, and contemplated James's indolent, dreamy, 'feckless' character with impatient disgust. When the first of *The Seasons--Winter* it was, I believe--had been completed at press, Jamie thought, by a presentation copy, to triumph over his uncle's scepticism, and to propitiate his good opinion he had the book handsomely bound. The old man never looked inside, or asked what the book was about, but turning it round and round with his fingers in gratified admiration, exclaimed: 'Come, is that really our Jamie's doin' now? Weel, I never thought the cratur wad hae had the handicraft to do the like!'

P. 191. *H. Coleridge*.--See Roscoe's poem to his books on parting with them, p. 8.

P. 192. *Dibdin*.--'There are shrewd books, with dangerous frontispieces set to sale; who shall prohibit them? shall twenty licensers?'--MILTON. *Areopagitica*.

P. 193. *Burns*.--Mr. Andrew Lang states that Burns saw a splendidly bound but sadly neglected copy of Shakespeare in the library of a nobleman in Edinburgh, and he wrote these lines on the ample margin of one of its pages, where they were found long after the poet's death.

P. 194. *Parnell*.--'It was supposed that a binding of Russian leather secured books against insects, but the contrary was recently demonstrated at Paris by two volumes pierced in every direction. The first bookbinder in Paris, Bozerian, told me he knew of no remedy except to steep the blank leaves in muriatic acid.'--PINKERTON'S *Recollections of Paris*. Parnell's poem is translated from Theodore Beza.

'Smith was very comical about a remedy of Lady Holland's for the bookworms in the library at Holland House, having the books washed with some mercurial preparation. He said it was Sir Humphry Davy's opinion that the air would become charged with the mercury, and that the whole family would be salivated, adding, "I shall see Allen some day, with his tongue hanging out, speechless, and shall take the opportunity to stick a few principles into him.'"--*Bon-Mots* of Sydney Smith, edited by W. Jerrold.

John Allen, M.D., was the librarian, described by Byron as 'the best informed and one of the ablest men I know--a perfect Magliabechi; a devourer, a *heluo* of books'. His scepticism earned him the title of 'Lady Holland's atheist'.

P. 196. *King*.--This is from J. Nichols's Collection of Poems, vol. iii, *Bibliotheca*, and is ascribed 'upon conjecture only' to Dr. W. King. *See* p. 343.

P. 197. *d'Arblay*.--Macaulay notes that Miss Burney 'describes this conversation as delightful; and, indeed, we cannot wonder that, with her literary tastes, she should be delighted at hearing in how magnificent a manner the greatest lady in the land encouraged literature'. The conversation took place at Windsor in December, 1785.

P. 198. *Lamb*.--Walter Pater says of Charles Lamb: 'He was a true "collector", delighting in the personal finding of a thing, in the colour an old book or print gets for him by the little accidents which attest previous ownership. Wither's *Emblems*, "that old book and quaint," long-desired, when he finds it at last, he values none the less because a child had coloured the plates with his paints.'

P. 199. *Milton*.--'The call for books was not in Milton's age what it is in the present. To read was not then a general amusement; neither traders, nor often gentlemen, thought themselves disgraced by ignorance. The women had not then aspired to literature nor was every house supplied with a closet of knowledge.'--DR. JOHNSON.

P. 199. *Browning*.--The statue referred to is that of Giovanni delle Bande Nere, father of Cosimo de' Medici, in the Piazza San Lorenzo. The imaginative Sienese is Ademollo; the 'Frail one of the Flower' will be recognized as *La Dame aux Camélias*. Browning 'translates' the title-page of his 'find' thus:--

> A Roman murder-case:
> Position of the entire criminal cause
> Of Guido Franceschini, nobleman,
> With certain Four the cutthroats in his pay,
> Tried, all five, and found guilty and put to death
> By heading or hanging as befitted ranks,
> At Rome on February Twenty Two,
> Since our salvation Sixteen Ninety Eight:
> Wherein it is disputed if, and when,
> Husbands may kill adulterous wives, yet 'scape
> The customary forfeit.'

P. 202. *Eliot.--*

> I often wonder what the Vintners buy
> One half so precious as the stuff they sell.

> E. FITZGERALD. *Rubaiyát of Omar Khayyám.*

P. 204. *Lewis.--*This is a portion of an imitation of Horace. *Ep.* 20, Bk. i.

P. 206. *Gay.--*The authorship of this and the following poem cannot be decided definite-ly, but it is presumed that they were written by Gay and Pope respectively, and they have been so credited in the text.

P. 210. *Lamb.--*This appeared originally in *The London Magazine*, and was reprinted by Hone in *The Every-Day Book*. It was in Hone's *Table Book* that Lamb's extracts from the Elizabethan dramatists were published.

P. 210. *Goldsmith.--*See Bacon, on p. 51, and the note thereon.

P. 211. *Scott.--*Sir Walter was the first President of the Bannatyne Club, and he wrote these lines for the anniversary dinner in 1823. The club had been founded in the previ-ous year with the object of printing works on the history and antiquities of Scotland. Bannatyne himself, whose name was given to the club, achieved immortality by copying out nearly all the ancient poetry of Scotland in 1568, at a time when the country was rav-aged by plague, and the records of Scottish literature were also in danger of destruction. Of the other names mentioned here, Ritson had written a vegetarian book. The 'yeditur' was the name given by Lord Eldon to James Sibbald. 'Greysteel' was a romance that Da-vid Herd sought in vain, and it gave him his nickname.

P. 212. *Maginn.--*Sung at the Booksellers' Annual Dinner, Blackwall, June 7, 1840. Fraser, whose name lives in his magazine, died in the following year.

It is very tempting to give more passages about booksellers but I must refrain as it would be foreign to the purpose of this volume, and the subject has been recently treated with great fullness and greater ability by Mr. Frank A. Mumby in *The Romance of Bookselling*.

P. 214. *de Bury.--*'Would it not grieve a man of a good spirit to see Hobson finde more money in the tayles of 12 jades than a scholler in 200 bookes?'--*The Pilgrimage to Parnassus*. Hobson, the carrier, celebrated by Milton, is the hero of 'Hobson's choice'.

P. 214. *Lamb.--*'The motto I proposed for the [*Edinburgh*] *Review* was: Tenui Musam meditamur avena--"we cultivate literature upon a little oatmeal."'--SYDNEY SMITH.

P. 214. *Ruskin.--*Mark Pattison said that nobody who respected himself could have less than 1,000 volumes, and that this number of octavo volumes could be stacked in a book-case 13 feet by 10 feet and 6 inches deep. He complained that the bookseller's bill in the ordinary middle-class family is shamefully small, and he thought it monstrous that a man who is earning £1,000 a year should spend less than £1 a week on books. 'A shilling in the pound to be spent on books,' is Lord Morley's comment, 'by a clerk who earns a couple of hundred pounds a year, or by a workman who earns a quarter of that sum, is rather more, I think, than can be reasonably expected.'

P. 215. *Lamb.*--Comberbatch was the name in which Coleridge enlisted in the Dragoons. *The Life and Opinions of John Buncle, Esq.*, was by Thomas Amory. Leigh Hunt describes Buncle as 'a kind of innocent Henry VIII of private life'.

Charles Lamb, who at last grew tired of lending his books, threatened to chain Wordsworth's poems to his shelves, adding:--'For of those who borrow, some read slow; some mean to read, but don't read; and some neither read nor mean to read, but borrow to leave you an opinion of their sagacity. I must do my money-borrowing friends the justice to say that there is nothing of this caprice or wantonness of alienation in them. When they borrow my money they never fail to make use of it.'--SIR T. N. TALFOURD.

P. 226. *Shakespeare.*--Also in a later scene of the same play:--'Thou hast most traitorously corrupted the youth of the realm in erecting a grammar-school; and whereas, before, our forefathers had no other books but the score and the tally, thou hast caused printing to be used; and, contrary to the king, his crown, and dignity, thou hast built a paper-mill. It will be proved to thy face that thou hast men about thee that usually talk of a noun and a verb, and such abominable words as no Christian ear can endure to hear.'

P. 230. *Wesley.*--'Next morning he was still better: ... he desired to be drawn into the library, and placed by the central window, that he might look down upon the Tweed. Here he expressed a wish that I should read to him, and when I asked from what book, he said--"Need you ask? There is but one."'--J. G. LOCKHART. *Life of Sir Walter Scott.*

'It is our *duty* to live among books, especially to live by ONE BOOK, and a very old one.'--JOHN HENRY NEWMAN in *Tracts for the Times.*

P. 232. *De Vere.*--Addison speaks of Horace and Pindar as showing, when confronted with the Psalms, 'an absurdity and confusion of style,' and 'a comparative poverty of imagination'.

Coleridge has left on record his opinion that, 'after reading Isaiah or St. Paul's Epistle to the Hebrews, Homer and Virgil are disgustingly tame to me, and Milton himself scarcely tolerable.'

Milton's own words may be recalled: 'There are no songs comparable to the songs of Sion; no orations equal to those of the Prophets.'

P. 232. *Swift.*--Compare Cowper in *Hope*:--

> In her own light arrayed,
> See mercy's grand apocalypse displayed!
> The sacred book no longer suffers wrong,
> Bound in the fetters of an unknown tongue;

But speaks with plainness, art could never mend,
What simplest minds can soonest comprehend.

Macaulay described the Bible as 'a book which, if everything else in our language should perish, would alone suffice to show the whole extent of its beauty and power'.

P. 233. *Arnold.*--Wordsworth's opinion was that the prophetic and lyrical parts of the Bible formed 'the great storehouse of enthusiastic and meditative imagination'.

P. 233. *Faber.*--Professor Huxley wrote in the *Contemporary Review*, in his famous article on 'The School Boards':--'Consider the great historical fact that, for three centuries, this book has been woven into the life of all that is best and noblest in English history; that it has become the national epic of Britain, and is familiar to noble and simple, from John-o'-Groat's House to Land's End, as Dante and Tasso were once to the Italians; that it is written in the noblest and purest English, and abounds in exquisite beauties of mere literary form; and, finally, that it forbids the veriest hind who never left his village to be ignorant of the existence of other countries and other civilizations, and of a great past, stretching back to the furthest limits of the oldest nations in the world.'

P. 234. *Eliot.*--Maggie Tulliver, during the home troubles caused by her father's bankruptcy, receives a present of books, among which is the *Imitation of Christ*.

P. 238. *Gaskell.*--The essay by Mrs. Gaskell, first published in *Household Words* in 1854, was suggested by an article by Victor Cousin on Madame de Sablé in the *Revue des Deux Mondes*. Madame was a habitual guest at the Hôtel Rambouillet and friend of the Duchess de Longueville; her crowning accomplishment was the ability *tenir un salon*.

P. 243. *Alcuin.*--Born at York in 735, Alcuin was the adviser of Charlemagne, whose court, under the Englishman's direction became a centre of culture. After fifteen years of court life at Aix-la-Chapelle Alcuin retired to Tours, where he died in 804. His English name is given as Ealwhine.

The catalogue refers to the library of Egbert, Archbishop of York. The translator is D. McNicoll.

P. 243. *King.*--This is an extract from a poem of 1,500 lines preserved in vol. iii of Nichols's *Poems*, where it is said to be probably by Dr. W. King. It first appeared in 1712. See p. 196.

P. 245. *Pope.*--For the fate of the bonfire the reader is referred to the *Dunciad* itself. Pope explains that 'this library is divided into three parts; the first consists of those authors from whom he (the hero, i.e. Colley Cibber) stole, and whose works he mangled; the second, of such as fitted the shelves, or were gilded for show, or adorned with pictures; the third class our author calls solid learning, old Bodies of Divinity, old Commentaries, old English Printers, or old English Translations; all very voluminous, and fit to erect altars to Dulness'. Tibbald, or Theobald, wrote *Shakespear Restored*; Ogilby, poet and printer, is mentioned by Addison on p. 162; the Duchess of Newcastle was responsible for eight folios of poetical and philosophical works; Settle, the hero's brother Laureate 'for the city instead of the court'; Banks, his rival in tragedy; Broome, 'a serving man of Ben Jonson'; De Lyra or Harpsfield, whose five volumes of commentaries in folio were printed in 1472; Philemon Holland, 'the translator general of his age'; Cibber's Birthday Ode as Laureate.

William Caxton (1422-91), of course, printed, at Bruges, the first book printed in English--the *Recuyell of the Historyes of Troye*--in 1474. His printing press in Westminster was set up two years later. Wynkyn de Worde, his servant and successor, started business on his own account in 1491.

P. 246. *Sterne.*--'Sterne has generally concealed the sources of his curious trains of investigation, and uncommon opinions, but in one instance he ventured to break through his restraint by mentioning Bouchet's *Evening Conferences*, among the treasures of Mr. Shandy's library.... I have great reason to believe that it was in the Skelton library some years ago, where I suspect Sterne found most of the authors of this class. I entertain little doubt, that from the perusal of this work, Sterne conceived the first precise idea of his *Tristram*, as far as anything can be called precise, in a desultory book, apparently written with great rapidity.'

This quotation is from Ferriar's *Illustrations of Sterne*, which was published in 1798. He seemed, Sir Walter Scott wrote, 'born to trace and detect the various mazes through which Sterne carried on his depredations upon ancient and dusty authors.' Ferriar wrote the following lines addressed to Sterne:--

> Sterne, for whose sake I plod through miry ways,
>   Of antique wit and quibbling mazes drear,
>   Let not thy shade malignant censure fear,
> Though aught of borrowed mirth my search betrays.
> Long slept that mirth in dust of ancient days,
>   (Erewhile to Guise or wanton Valois dear;)
>   Till waked by thee in Skelton's joyous pile,
> She flung on Tristram her capricious rays;
>   But the quick tear that checks our wondering smile,
> In sudden pause or unexpected story,
>   Owns thy true mastery--and Le Fever's woes,
>   Maria's wanderings, and the Prisoner's throes,
> Fix thee conspicuous on the throne of glory.

P. 247. *Scott.*--The modern poet is Crabbe, and the context will be found on p. 265; Thalaba is the name of Southey's hero.

P. 250. *Montaigne.*--In another essay Montaigne tells us that his library for a country library could pass for a very fair one.

P. 250. *Southey.*--This extract is from Southey's *Sir Thomas More*; a book of colloquies between Southey himself, under the name of Montesinos, and the apparition of Sir T. More: who tells him that 'it is your lot, as it was mine, to live during one of the grand climacterics of the world', and that, 'I come to you, rather than to any other person, because you have been led to meditate upon the corresponding changes whereby your age and mine are distinguished, and because ... there are certain points of sympathy and resemblance which bring us into contact.' The colloquies are upon such subjects as the feudal and manufacturing systems, the Reformation, prospects of Europe, infidelity, trade.

Chartier was the French poet whose 'eternal glory' it was 'to have announced the mission of Jeanne d'Arc'.

'Here are God's conduits,' &c., is from the first of Donne's *Satires*.

P. 253. *Barton.*--The Rev. John Mitford (1781-1859) formed a large library at Benham, where he also devoted himself to gardening.

P. 254. *Bale.*--'I was called to London to wait upon the Duke of Norfolk, who having at my sole request bestowed the Arundelian Library on the Royal Society, sent to me to take charge of the books and remove them.... I procured for our Society, besides printed books, near 100MSS., some in Greek, of great concernment. The printed books being of the oldest impressions are not the less valuable; I esteem them almost equal to MSS. Amongst them are most of the Fathers printed at Basle, before the Jesuits abused them with their expurgatory Indexes; there is a noble MS. of Vitruvius. Many of these books had been presented by Popes, Cardinals, and great persons, to the Earls of Arundel and Dukes of Norfolk; and the late magnificent Earl of Arundel bought a noble library in Germany, which is in this collection. I should not, for the honour I bear the family, have persuaded the Duke to part with these, had I not seen how negligent he was of them, suffering the priests and everybody to carry away and dispose of what they pleased, so that abundance of rare things are irrecoverably gone.'--J. EVELYN (*Diary*, August 29, 1678.)

P. 255. *Whittier.*--Sung at the opening of the library at Haverhill, Mass.

P. 260. *Helps.*--Pope's *Essay on Man*:

> If parts allure thee, think how Bacon shined,
> The wisest, brightest, meanest of mankind.

The other allusions are to Johnson, Byron, Shelley, and Keats.

P. 262. *Crabbe.*--It is explained by Crabbe that while composing 'The Library' he 'was honoured with the notice and assisted by the advice of the Right Honourable Edmund Burke: part of it was written in his presence, and the whole submitted to his judgement; receiving, in its progress, the benefit of his correction'. The poem was published in1781.

P. 260. *Saxe.*--Aristophanes' *The Clouds*, ridiculing Socrates.

P. 278. *Drummond.*--Of Sir Thomas Bodley old Anthony Wood says: 'Though no writer, worth the remembrance, yet hath he been the greatest promoter of learning that hath yet appeared in our nation.'

It may be recalled that R. de Bury had a fine idea, although it did not fructify, to wit:--
'We have for a long time held a rooted purpose in the inmost recesses of our mind, look-ing forward to a favourable time and divine aid, to found, in perpetual alms, and enrich with the necessary gifts, a certain Hall in the revered University of Oxford, the first nurse of all the liberal Arts; and further to enrich the same, when occupied by numerous schol-ars, with deposits of our books, so that the books themselves and every one of them may be made common as to use and study, not only to the scholars of the said Hall, but through them to all the students of the aforesaid University for ever.'

P. 280. *Cowper.*--'This ode,' Cowper states, 'is rendered without rhime, that it might more adequately represent the original, which, as Milton himself informs us, is of no certain measure. It may possibly for this reason disappoint the reader, though it cost the writer more labour than the translation of any other piece in the whole collection.'

P. 282. *Cowley.*--

Who now reads Cowley? if he pleases yet,
His moral pleases, not his pointed wit.
Forgot his epic, nay, Pindaric art!
But still I love the language of his heart.--POPE.

P. 289. *J. M.*--It cannot escape observation that Bodley and his library has been a much more fruitful theme than the University of Cambridge. This is the only poem on the lat-ter subject which I have been able to find; it is quoted in Edwards's *Memoirs of Libraries*. Leigh Hunt has related his experiences in the library of Trinity College 'when the keeper of it was from home'; see p. 218.

P. 289. *Whitelocke.*--The authorship of this fine testimony is attributed to Whitelocke, but I have not traced it, by J. K. Hoyt and Anna L. Ward.

INDEX
(by Title)

INDEX

INDEX

RABELAIS, FRANÇOIS (1483-1553).

www.ingramcontent.com/pod-product-compliance
Lightning Source LLC
Chambersburg PA
CBHW080818020726
47501CB00009B/2330